M000234521

FEMINIST SURVEILLANCE STUDIES

FEMINIST SURVEILLANCE STUDIES

RACHEL E. DUBROFSKY AND

SHOSHANA AMIELLE MAGNET, EDITORS

Duke University Press   Durham and London   2015

© 2015 Duke University Press
All rights reserved
Printed in the United States of America on acid-free paper ♾

Designed by Natalie F. Smith
Typeset in Chaparral Pro by Tseng Information Systems, Inc.

Library of Congress Cataloging-in-Publication Data
Feminist surveillance studies / Rachel E. Dubrofsky and
Shoshana Amielle Magnet, editors.
pages cm
Includes bibliographical references and index.
ISBN 978-0-8223-5920-3 (hardcover : alk. paper)
ISBN 978-0-8223-5892-3 (pbk. : alk. paper)
ISBN 978-0-8223-7546-3 (e-book)
1. Feminism—United States. 2. Feminist theory. 3. Electronic
surveillance—Social aspects—United States. 4. Government
information—United States. 5. Internal security—United
States. I. Dubrofsky, Rachel E. II. Magnet, Shoshana.
HQ1426.F4735 2015
305.420973—dc23   2014045006

Dorothy E. Roberts's chapter, "Race, Gender, and Genetic
Technologies: A New Reproductive Dystopia?," was previously
printed in *Signs* 34, no. 4 (summer 2009): 783–804. Copyright
University of Chicago Press. Reprinted with permission of the
publisher.

Cover art: Design by Natalie F. Smith.

CONTENTS

PART IV. TOWARD A FEMINIST PRAXIS IN SURVEILLANCE STUDIES

FOREWORD

MARK ANDREJEVIC

If in the physical environment the pressing issue of the next several decades (and beyond) is likely to be the dramatic transformation of the global climate, in the social realm (to the extent that it can be distinguished from the physical environment), the main issue will be the shifting surveillance climate. I don't think this is overstating the case: in the areas of politics, economics, commerce, policing, finance, warfare, and beyond, social practices are being transformed by dramatic developments in information collection, storage, and processing, as well as by various techniques of watching, broadly construed. The occasional anecdote about the power of new forms of data monitoring and mining—the retail outlet that learned a young woman was pregnant before she told her family, the ability of mobile phone use to predict whether someone is coming down with the flu, the use of license-plate readers to reconstruct people's whereabouts—are only tiny foretastes of the automated, multidimensional forms of surveillance to come.

We are at a moment in time when we can start to see the surveillant imaginary expand vertiginously, thanks in part to the new avenues for monitoring opened up by technologies that "interact" with us in a growing variety of ways and involve a wide range of senses and sensors, and also to the increasingly sophisticated techniques for putting to use the huge amounts of data these devices, applications, and platforms capture and store. Intimations of a megadata world are starting to multiply: Edward Snowden's revelations about blanket U.S. National Security Agency (NSA) surveillance, media coverage of the huge databases being amassed by companies like Facebook and Google, and the proliferation of data centers across the landscape, including the NSA's giant complex in Utah. It is a moment that requires reflection on what is at stake in the seemingly inevitable slide into a monitored, digitally redoubled life. This volume represents a defining moment in that process of reflection — the cultivation of a critical imagination that keeps pace with the technological developments and their associated practices in reach, scope, and depth, but counters the ahistorical rhetoric of the digital sublime (Mosco 2004) with a deep sensitivity to suppressed historical continuities and antecedents.

This book provides several useful explorations of the meaning of the term *surveillance*, but perhaps the most simple and generic is that it is the coupling of information collection and use with power. We are living in a time when information is becoming an increasingly transformative force, and power is never absent. In other words, the information "revolution" (in the ironically depoliticized sense in which it is so often invoked), viewed through the lens of power, is perhaps better reconceptualized as a surveillance one. If late twentieth-century preoccupations with power were atomic and ballistic, those of the twenty-first century are increasingly informatic. Fantasies of jetpacks and passenger trips to the moon have largely (but not entirely) given way to ones about new forms of informatization, representation, and interaction. The threat of "the bomb" is complemented by that of a "cyber-Pearl Harbor" (Bumiller and Shanker 2012). We are becoming more preoccupied with novel ways of giving wings to our surveillance devices, sensors, probes (and "smart" weapons) than to ourselves. A fascination with the industrial-era power of turbines and rocket ships is supplemented by the information-era fantasy of total information awareness.

It is against this background that surveillance emerges as a pressing topic of study for the foreseeable future. And at this point, it is the research object itself that defines the field — not a methodology, not even a theoretical canon or a developed, shared set of terms and concerns. This collection both confirms such an observation and qualifies it, for it works in the direction of defining a particular set of approaches and issues, specifically bringing to bear methodologies and interests based on intersectional feminist commitments and theories. The study of surveillance is, of necessity, a study of power relations, and while it might be possible to attempt to adopt a disinterested, neutral or "administrative" stance to such an endeavor, the studies presented here suggest the disingenuous or complicit character of any such attempt. As Kevin Walby and Seantel Anais put it in their contribution to this collection, a feminist approach is concerned with getting away from neutral definitions of surveillance and putting critique first in order to continually point out "how ruling relations are enabled by the texts and classifications that make up surveillance" (220). The study of surveillance is also, as this collection points out, a recursive endeavor, at least insofar as research is also a form of monitoring and therefore implicated in the relations of power being examined, as Ummni Khan makes clear in her contribution. As in other instances, what is seen or registered is as important as what is exempted from or obscured by the monitoring gaze.

One of the central themes that emerge from this collection is an engagement with what has been, in one way or another, overlooked or obscured in the emerging formation of surveillance studies. At the most basic level, this includes the wide-ranging scope of what ought to be counted as surveillance, especially those monitoring practices that attempt to exempt themselves from an entanglement with power or to cloak themselves in taken-for-granted imperatives. If technologies like CCTV (closed-circuit television) cameras, drones, and wiretapping lend themselves to an already well-conditioned response to the prospect of state surveillance, the perspectives included in the following pages expand and reconfigure the scope of research to include techniques and technologies that might otherwise fly below the radar of surveillance studies: genetic screening in fertility clinics, photographic evidence of domestic violence, images of babies in the womb, birth certificates, security screening, Twitter practices, and the other seemingly mundane forms of data collection, observation, entertainment, and sorting that increasingly characterize daily life in informated and technologized societies.

This volume explores the ways in which techniques conventionally relegated to the realm of monitoring and documentation—but not surveillance proper—mask and reinforce the gendered, sexed, raced, and classed exercise of power. The ambit of surveillance studies is thereby reconfigured to move beyond the field's more "traditional" focus and its historical ties to sociology's twentieth-century concern with criminology. Rather, it sets out to explore the ways in which a concern with forms of governance and regulation extends into those practices that assume the guise of scientific neutrality, bureaucratic record keeping, or the largely unexamined social imperatives of securitization, efficiency, risk management, productivity, and reproductivity. There is no neutral record keeping—all forms of data collection have imperatives built in—and the power of the work assembled here lies in disembedding and exposing these imperatives, the interests they serve, and the uses they enable.

The initiative represented by this volume is a timely one for the formation of surveillance studies, a formation whose object is increasingly engulfed by what might be described, on the one hand, as the alleged neutrality of the machine (or the algorithm) and, on the other, as the various alibis of security, efficiency, entertainment, and convenience. Consider, for example, Google's protest in response to Microsoft's "Scroogled" campaign, which criticizes the search-engine giant's business model of targeting advertising based on (among other things) the content of users' email messages. Google countered Microsoft's accusations of privacy invasion by noting, "No humans read your email or Google account information in order to show you advertisements or related information" (D. Kerr 2013). It is a telling protest insofar as it frames the issue of monitoring quite specifically: what counts as intrusive is not the uses to which information is being put (a topic Google's response dodges), but the prospect of another human poking his or her nose into one's personal correspondence. By contrast, the algorithm carries with it the promise of automated neutrality, a machinic "disinterest" that simply operates in the service of convenience, customization, and efficiency (as well as a hint of blackmail: "Wouldn't you rather see ads relevant to you than be bombarded by those that aren't?"). We are invited to place ourselves and our faith in the indifferent hands of the algorithm. In the face of such an invitation, one pressing task for surveillance studies (understood as a critical engagement with the relationship between power and information collection) is to excavate the various interests, pressures, prejudices, and agendas obscured by the technocratic alibi of the algorithm and its analogs—that is, those forms of control that operate in the name of security, efficiency, risk management, and so on, while simultaneously obscuring the forms of gendered, raced, classed, and sexualized discrimination they advance in the name of an allegedly general interest.

There may be aspects of novelty in the expanding role of the algorithm, but one of the lessons of this collection is that there is also a deep sense of continuity ranging across those forms of surveillance that take place in the name of information-based rationalization or, perhaps even less extravagantly, those that are portrayed as benign, or as entertaining, or even as activist forms of monitoring. Another lesson that emerges in this volume is the importance of focusing not only on the specter of "abuse" or "misuse" of monitoring technologies and practices, but on their proper use and the implications. The prevailing form of misdirection about the information society mobilized by various pundits, publicists, and flaks is their emphasis on what counts as *abuse* (identity theft, fraud, data breaches, and so on), which works to deflect attention away from concerns about emergent *uses*. Focus on these abuses (as important as they may be) backgrounds the "normal" functioning of data collection and use as taken-for-granted—that is, as non-abusive. The important message that recurs across the essays in this collection is that the sanctioned *uses* of the surveillance technology in question—whether for the express purposes of safety, health, marketing, security, entertainment, or protection—require further investigation and interrogation.

Neutrality is the ruse of the algorithm, which, as some of the contributors here demonstrate, does not emerge full-blown, independent of human intervention, but often incorporates the prejudices of "domain specific" expertise and historical patterns of data collection. Data collection is no more neutral than the algorithm, at least until the (impossible) ideal of a fully recorded life is achieved—and even then, that life must be disaggregated and reassembled if it is to be compared, sorted, and mined. At the same time, the algorithm raises the specter of new and reconfigured forms of discrimination based on the emergent and opaque character of data mining.

Relatively crude forms of red-lining, for example, had the exploitable weakness of being discernible and attributable to established forms of discrimination and prejudice. Data mining offers the prospect of reconfiguring and obscuring these forms of discrimination in ways that are difficult to discern or reverse-engineer. If a particular configuration of variables adds up to a prediction—that someone is a "person of interest," an undesirable employee, a credit risk—that prediction does not necessarily come with any assumed underlying explanation: it passes itself off as free of preconceptions, as simply the numbers speaking for themselves. Thus, the prospect offered up by data mining is that of a reorganized range of categories of discrimination—that is, new proxies for use in sorting and predicting. While it may be illegal to discriminate, for example, on the basis of protected categories for a particular job, the data mine promises new correlations that can serve as opaque alibis, deflecting attempts to demonstrate the links between employment decisions and ethnicity, sex, race, gender, and class. The data can be queried in more specific terms: what is the probability that a particular job candidate will take an extended leave of paid absence, that a prospective student will become a cash donor on graduation, that someone will default on a loan, or that someone will need to be hospitalized? While such questions might be—and have been—amenable to traditional forms of discrimination, data mining promises to generate predictions based on correlations and patterns that cannot be anticipated. This is not to say that ethnicity, class, sex, gender, race, and sexuality will not be implicated, but rather that their roles will be potentially obscured and reconfigured by the range of variables under consideration and the complexity of the correlations on which the algorithm draws. Put in somewhat different terms, the potential threat of data mining lies in the ability to disaggregate discrimination based on more granular sets of attributes. Rather than being broad categories that generalize about employability, insurability, credit risk, security threat, and so on, data-based categories can be more finely sliced and reconfigured to, on the one hand, obscure connections to historical forms of discrimination and, on the other, to reassemble groups that are subject to sorting, targeting, and exclusion.

Dorothy Roberts's essay in this collection notes the way in which, for example, new regimes of targeting and customization underwrite the trend of race-based targeting of pharmaceuticals. As Roberts points out, such developments threaten to resuscitate debunked theories about the biological character of race. At the same time, however, they point in the direction of the disaggregation and reassembly of target groups: not just black patients, but black patients with a heart condition. One might imagine the addition of further variables, some drawn from historical criteria for exploitation, others representing new forms of targeting and specialization (working-class black patients with heart conditions who live in a particular neighborhood, engage in particular types of activities, and so on).

As in the case of other forms of sorting and discrimination, even as data mining promises to become more granular and targeted, it simultaneously subsumes individuals to population-level claims. As one description of data mining in a commercial context put it, "I can't tell you what one shopper is going to do, but I can tell you with 90 percent accuracy what one shopper is going to do if he or she looks exactly like one million other shoppers" (Nolan 2012). The claim of data mining is that these predictions are based purely on statistical correlations and not on underlying preconceptions. In actuality, as Shoshana Amielle Magnet has compellingly illustrated in her work on biometric technologies, biases, preconceptions, and prejudices can be baked into the code, where they continue to operate in opaque ways. Magnet explores how debunked conceptions of race are incorporated into facial recognition technology: "As these scientists label the images according to their understanding of their own biological race and gender identities, preconceptions about gender and race are codified into the biometric scanners from the beginning" (2011, 46). Perhaps one of the giveaways is the difficulty algorithms have in predicting what count as rare and exceptional occurrences—that is to say, historical understandings of what is "to be expected" have a way of working themselves into the algorithm.

A world in which preconceptions, biases, and prejudices are coded into the decision-making infrastructure poses new challenges for attempts to intervene in the network of shared meanings. We might describe this outcome in terms of the autonomization of preconceptions and prejudices: because the symbolic processing power has migrated into the algorithm that effectively shapes the decisions that govern everyday life—who gets hired or approved for a loan, who can cross the border and who cannot, who will be targeted, monitored, included or excluded in a variety of contexts—we are invited to imagine that we have somehow moved beyond the constructed assumptions, prejudices, biases, and "truths" that shape its operation. By the same token, we are invited to adopt an external relationship to the efficacy of such preconceptions: disavowing them in daily life while they continue to do their work behind the screen of the interface.

Consider, for example, the way new technologies promise to "see" for their users. The wearable interface, most recently revived by Google Glass, offers to bring "knowledge" beyond what the viewer already knows to what the viewer sees by, for example, recognizing people for the wearer, accessing information about them and sharing it with the wearer, such that the wearer's gaze is mediated by the information retrieved from the database. The Massachusetts Institute of Technology Media Lab's Sixth-Sense system represents a similar attempt to superimpose wirelessly accessed digital information on the physical world. People can tag particular locations with specific information (reviews for a restaurant or a movie theater and so on), which can then be accessed by others viewing the same location. The technology provides a suggestive metaphor for the fact that our gaze is never unmediated, innocent, or free of preconceptions, background knowledge, and information. Even without the high-tech interface, the physical world is already overlaid with the information the viewer brings to it. Imagine the ways in which such devices might be used by, say, police: forms of background profiling and threat detection might be incorporated into the system so as to categorize each individual as he or she walks by. The result is the automation of shared "knowledge" and preconceptions. That is, a superimposed assessment becomes the result of forms of data processing that take place behind our backs, somewhere in the "cloud" from which the information we are seeing is accessed.

The shared information then comes to serve as a kind of prosthetic collective unconscious—although the process that generates it remains unavailable to viewers, this information nevertheless helps to shape their understanding of the surrounding world. This logic is not dissimilar to that of search engines like Google, which shape the user's experience of the informational world online. When people embark on a search, they see results that are generated by algorithmic logics that remain opaque to them: the results look almost "natural"—the obvious response to a particular search term or query. However, the algorithms that shape the information available to users are developed with a particular set of imperatives in mind, including the goals of attracting and retaining users in an environment conducive to Google's commercial interests.

In some contexts the workings of the algorithm are made partially transparent to users—as in the case of Amazon.com's book recommendations, which allow users to see which past purchases or searches have resulted in a particular book being suggested. For the most part, however, the workings of the algorithm are opaque and are likely to become increasingly so for two reasons. First, the advent of mining "big data"— the unprecedented size of contemporary databases and the emerging techniques for making sense of them (Andrejevic and Gates 2014, 186)—results in algorithms whose results defy explanation or render it superfluous. Someone who buys a particular model of car may be highly likely to be politically conservative, but there is no clear underlying or causal explanation—the pattern is purely correlational. Second, those who control the database and the algorithm have little incentive to make the basis of algorithmic decision making available, not least because this would entail revealing the increasingly powerful forms of monitoring and surveillance on which they are based.

The development of digital monitoring demonstrates the generalization of the logic unpacked in this volume: unacknowledged biases that underwrite dominant power relations work their way into myriad forms of monitoring and documentation. Thus, the direction in which surveillance is headed will require resources that draw on an intersectional exploration of the ways in which forms of exclusion, discrimination, and sorting are built into the taken-for-granted norms that guide the monitoring process. Suppressed or overlooked histories of surveillance practices provide crucial guides for navigating this unfolding surveillance-scape, in which all forms of monitoring are encompassed by the embrace of power. It is the attention to these norms and the suppressed forms of exclusion and coercion they incorporate that provides crucial avenues for debunking the neutrality of the algorithm and the "completeness" of the database. Similarly, the excavation of suppressed histories helps shed light on what has become all too easy to overlook in the contemporary exercise of surveillance.

Additionally, this collection interrogates and undermines the invocation of the notion of an abstract "we" in the face of surveillance technologies that disaggregate, reconfigure, and sort populations according to a growing range of variables. The obliviousness embedded in this invocation finds its expression in the notorious response of Google CEO Eric Schmidt to concerns about the surveillant character of his company's business: "If you have something that you don't want anyone to know, maybe you shouldn't be doing it in the first place" (Metz 2009). The formulation seeks to defuse concerns by conflating random strangers ("anyone") with the real cause of concern: entities both public and private with the power to intervene in ways that affect the life chances of "you," who is likely to be someone other than Schmidt, a fabulously wealthy, straight, white, male, U.S. citizen who can imagine he has the luxury of being blithely unconcerned about the monitoring practices he describes (and benefits from). The charge of "something to hide" transfers the blame for the threat of discrimination, exclusion, and exploitation faced by those differently situated than Schmidt onto the victims: what happens to them is a result of something nefarious they must be hiding. Or, tautologically, if they suffer adverse effects, these must be directly attributable to something about them that is wrong, underhanded, or otherwise deviant. Schmidt's public embrace of willing submission to comprehensive monitoring drives home Rachel Hall's observation in this collection that transparency is effectively the new white.

Google, obviously, is not some diary-invading kid brother or a nosy neighbor, but one of the planet's most powerful private corporations and subject to the subpoena powers of one of its most powerful states— a state which has embarked on widespread monitoring of the population and asserted its right to summarily execute its own citizens in certain circumstances. This is not to say that Schmidt should be concerned himself, but rather that his facile generalization does not take into account the concerns of those differently situated, of those who bear the brunt of the approved uses of surveillance (and not the "abuses" about which Schmidt is certainly as concerned as the next corporate executive). More pointedly, it is to highlight that the temptation to "convince ourselves that vulnerability is equally distributed" (Smith 2010, 8) is limited to those in Schmidt's privileged position. Something similar might be said of the temptation to write in terms of an assumed "we" who are subject to the monitoring gaze, a temptation that itself defines a particular position with regard to emerging surveillance practices. This collection provides a potent reminder of the fact that such a "we" is not to be taken for granted, but rather to be understood as the site of ongoing political struggle.

In developing a feminist set of methodologies and concerns, the pieces in this collection provide a crucial contemporary critical perspective on what counts *for* surveillance and what counts *as* surveillance. It turns out that in both cases the answer is much broader than has been sufficiently addressed by either contemporary debates or academic research. This collection goes a long way toward remedying such omissions and will serve as an important turning point in the critical study of one of the defining practices of the digital age.

ACKNOWLEDGMENTS

We begin by thanking Megan M. Wood: there are no words to convey our gratitude. Simply put, Megan was a lifesaver. She stepped in when we absolutely could not have managed without her. The timely and efficient completion of this volume is due to Megan's hard work and dedication. She was tireless in her devotion to the project, putting up with our endless last-minute rush requests and doing everything with good humor and the kind of efficiency we fear we will not encounter again. Amazingly, she did this because of her belief in the project and her incredible desire to learn, since we were unable to provide any material compensation. Amid all the busywork, Megan was also able to parse through complex theory and see the forest for the trees, helping guide us when we got lost. Her mark is on every page of this work.

We would like to thank Kelly Gates for her wonderful suggestions and insights in a review of an early draft of the manuscript—her input shaped the project. We are also grateful to the anonymous reviewer who provided many invaluable suggestions for the work. Courtney Berger, our editor at Duke, has shepherded us through this process, always supportive, amazingly encouraging and wise, and, of course, patient. To Erin Hanas, the editorial associate at Duke, we are grateful for always keeping on top of things, and particularly, in the final stages, for working tirelessly to make sure this project was completed in a timely fashion. And, of course, we are hugely indebted to our contributors, whose brilliance shapes this volume. They are real troopers for putting up with our repeated requests for revisions (big and small): you are an amazing bunch.

It is with a tremendous debt of gratitude that I (Shoshana) thank my coeditor and friend Rachel. During the last year of our work, I faced a particularly challenging time in my own life. When I turned to Rachel for help, she gave tirelessly of her own time and compassionate energy, taking over tasks when I could not do them, completing them with a generosity of spirit and kindness and with the brilliance for which her scholarship is known. This edited book would not exist without her many and profound interventions. In addition, Rachel is one of the most thoughtful and innovative thinkers that I know—the chance to speak with her about the many ideas in this project has been an incredibly rich intellectual experience. A special thanks also to Simone Browne, who helped greatly with much of the early thinking and ideas for this collection.

As always, I (Shoshana) remain well supported by a generous and generative set of thinkers at my home institution at the University of Ottawa. First and foremost, I would like to thank my colleague and B.F.F. Michael Orsini (and his family: Victoria Gordon Orsini, Emma Orsini, and Lucca Orsini). It actually brings tears to my eyes to think back on the many ways that he has supported me both personally and professionally. He remains one of the most widely read, intellectually stimulating, brilliant people that I know, and it was conversations with him that fueled many of the suggestions that I had early on when Rachel and I were writing the introduction. In addition, with him as chair, the Institute of Feminist and Gender Studies at the University of Ottawa is a truly wonderful place to work. His intersectional feminist analysis and his admirable leadership and comradeship have made coming into work a joy. Just as my pal Michael has changed my life, the same goes for my pals Miranda Brady, Jena McGill, and Cynthia Misener. I simply don't know what I'd do without them. They are rich sources of scholarly inspiration, but they also provided the incredibly depthful friendship I needed to do any work at all. So did Sarah Berry, Meghan Dailey, Jesse Dangerously, Danielle Dinovelli-Lang, Pat Gentille, Sarah Kennell, Jackie Kennelly, Ummni Khan, Evelyn Maeder, Mireille McLaughlin, and my dear "goddessmother" Diana Majury. As always, for Helen Kang and Shanta Varma and my mothers, Sanda Rodgers and Sheila McIntyre, without whom life would simply not exist as I know it. And for my truly wonderful partner Lise Richard, whose scintillating and brilliant presence has completely transformed my life in all the loveliest ways possible. There are no words to convey the absolutely huge depth of my love and appreciation for these five members of my family. I would also like to cite my other generous feminist colleagues and friends, including Corrie Scott, Mythili Rajiva, and Kathryn Trevenen, who have shaped and continue to shape my thinking, including about the ways that we might continue to push intersectional feminist analysis. Finally, I'd especially like to thank my students both past and present, who furnished me with incredible ideas for thinking about surveillance intersectionally: Caitlin Campisi and Dayna Prest (who both still understand more about methodology than I do), Hayley Crooks, JoAnne Gordon, Jami McFarland, Brittany Neron, Celeste Orr, Chaya Porter, Victoria Sands, Jenna Tenn-Yuk, and, of course, Amanda Watson. These are among our finest feminist thinkers, as well as some of the kindest and most generous and generative scholars and activists I know. Although it sounds like a truism, they actually teach me so much more than I teach them.

I (Rachel) am honored to be a part of this project, which was Shoshana's baby—I came along for the ride. Working with Shoshana was the kind of collaborative, productive, and generative experience scholars hope for. She welcomed my input, letting me make an imprint on the work, and eventually encouraging me to take the lead. Her grace and generosity of spirit guided the entire project. Shoshana's work has always been a wonderful inspiration for my own work: I am lucky to share an author line with her.

I (Rachel) am indebted to my professional home, the Department of Communication at the University of South Florida, for the support provided for this project through course releases and research assistants, thanks to my department chairs, Kenneth Cissna and later Carolyn Ellis, who believed in the value of the project. A word of thanks to my friends in Tampa who sustained me with endless laughter and good times, enabling me to get back to the work: Julie Alexander, Warren L. Rose, Chaim Noy, Ruthie Brathwaite, Ambar Basu, Mahuya Pal, and Mariaelena Bartesaghi. Grateful to Kent A. Ono, who inspires and provides wisdom every step of the way, and to Marlene Kadar, the first to insist I begin this academic journey, and who has been there at every turn, beaming her encouragement. Finally, words fail to express my appreciation for my mother Debby Dubrofsky, who is the most loving, vibrant, and lively cheerleader one can hope for, and for my little sister, Seiyan Yang, whose emergence into young adulthood inspires and reminds me why I do what I do: to impress her.

FEMINIST SURVEILLANCE STUDIES

Critical Interventions

RACHEL E. DUBROFSKY AND SHOSHANA AMIELLE MAGNET

At a recent roundtable of academics and privacy advocates discussing surveillance studies and inequality, the conversation variously turned to consumer surveillance, new technologies, and the weakened legislative climate on privacy in both the United States and Canada. While we share the interests of the discussants, we wonder at the place of feminist concerns about surveillance and issues of inequality. For instance, where were the presentations on the use of surveillance technologies by abusers to stalk their intimate partners, the surveillance of disability through the scrutiny of women on sick leave using Twitter and Facebook, the use of surveillance images of women in popular entertainment media, or the importance of penal abolition to surveillance studies given the surveillance and criminalization of women of color (the fastest growing demographic to be included in the prison industrial complex)?

In considering roundtables like these and conversations in surveillance studies generally, we feel the need for a feminist intervention into the burgeoning field of surveillance studies. Our book formally launches the area of feminist surveillance studies. The essays collected here do the groundbreaking work of bringing the insights of critical scholarship and feminist theory to surveillance studies, a field which has yet to fully benefit from major feminist interventions. By the same token, we address a gap in critical feminist scholarship, a field that has not explicitly taken as a focus an examination of the implications of a rapidly expanding surveillance society.

Briefly, implicit in most understandings of surveillance is the idea of real people being watched, often unknowingly, doing real things. The term *surveillance* is generally used to identify a systematic and focused manner of observing, or in the words of David Lyon, "any collection and processing of personal data, whether identifiable or not, for the purposes of influencing or managing those whose data have been garnered" (2001a, 2). Michel Foucault (1995) emphasized the productive potential of surveillance as a technology of statecraft—one by which the state produces the docile bodies essential to its functioning. In particular, he noted that this form of state scrutiny is not only the province of external forms of policing, but also of the internalized systems of discipline by which people come to police themselves. This form of internalized surveillance is often captured by the spatial landscape of the Panopticon, where prisoners are clustered around a guard tower in which they cannot see whether or not they are being watched (the guard may not be looking in their direction, or there may in fact be no guard in the tower). As a result, they learn to behave as if they are always under surveillance, since they can never know whether or not they are being scrutinized. Other useful descriptions of surveillance emphasize its broad aims, defining it as the "collection and analysis of information about populations in order to govern their activities"—a collection of information that is disaggregated and decentralized—a "surveillant assemblage" rather than a singular Big Brother (Haggerty and Ericson 2006, 8).

This collection highlights the contributions that scholarship on surveillance has made (and can make) to the fields of feminist theory, critical race theory, critical cultural studies, communication theory, media studies, critical criminology, and critical legal studies. We also emphasize the long-standing and existing roots these areas of study have in surveillance studies, even though these have not always been labeled and recognized formally as such. Part of the contribution of our project is to show that surveillance should be of wide disciplinary concern for critical scholars, and that it has in fact been an enduring concern in much existing scholarship in terms of gendered, sexualized, raced, and classed representations of bodies, including work committed to ending the institutions that facilitate criminalization. By drawing together disparate fields and placing the burgeoning field of surveillance studies in historical perspective, we find that surveillance is not a new phenomenon. In its most basic structure, the act of surveillance has always existed in some form as the action of observing or the condition of being observed, and has been theorized across disciplines — including ones that do not appear to explicitly engage questions of surveillance.

What are the implications of thinking about concerns related to surveillance specifically as critical feminist concerns using a feminist praxis? What new objects might this theoretical and methodological focus bring into view? The contributions to this volume are by no means exhaustive of the topics a critical feminist approach to surveillance can cover. This collection offers one possible approach to doing this kind of work, and we hope that it serves as a jumping off point for future scholarship. We group the chapters into thematic sections, ones that highlight the porous boundaries that exist in the study of surveillance, as the concerns raised by the authors overlap in so many important and rich ways — whether by theorizing the foundational structures of surveillance to examine specific instances of the scrutiny of individual bodies (Smith and Jiwani, this volume) or whether through an examination of particular bodies that helps to reveal the reliance of surveillance on deep structures of inequality (Dubrofsky and Wood, Moore and Currah, this volume). Nonetheless, the groupings help emphasize key themes in the collection.

Toward a Feminist Praxis in Surveillance Studies

Part of our task is recuperative: to point out that there has been work on surveillance done by feminists for quite some time. As well, we take as our charge to highlight areas where a focus on surveillance requires explicit attention to critical feminist concerns. The "critical" part of our project — which should be understood hereafter as implicit in our use of the term *feminist* — hails from a critical tradition that has at its core an activist and interventionist agenda, and a questioning of the taken-for-granted, of what is often mundane and seamless, with a profound sense that what goes unquestioned can be dangerous, particularly for disenfranchised bodies. Our critical feminist approach involves a feminist praxis that centers intersectionality. We argue that surveillance is inseparable from what feminist theorist Sherene Razack (1998) calls interlocking oppressions, ones that are often integral to the structures that underlie our culture. We understand a feminist praxis to "highlight the interaction between theory and practice that is greater than the sum of those two parts"

(Mahraj 2010, 17). A feminist praxis is not limited to gender issues, but rather sees gender as part and parcel of a number of contingent issues, such as race, sexuality, class, and able- and disabled-bodiedness, insisting that these cannot be viewed in isolation. Each essay in this volume exhibits a feminist praxis in its approach to the study of surveillance.

How we engage questions related to surveillance—and what can be left out in these articulations—is a key concern in this volume. For instance, we've seen scholarly trends toward an analysis of the role newer technologies play in surveillance more broadly (Andrejevic 2007; Gates 2011; I. Kerr et al. 2009), but with much focus on privacy issues. New database technologies, newer forms of information storehouses, as well as newer communication technologies, like cell phones and PDAs (personal digital assistants), have had pernicious implications for individual and group privacy. Privacy is, however, a limited lens for thinking about surveillance, since it is a right not granted equally to all, a fact that needs to be taken into account in such investigations. Of course, "new methods of authentication, verification and surveillance have increasingly allowed persons and things to be digitally or biometrically identified, tagged, tracked, and monitored in real time and in formats that can be captured, archived, and retrieved indefinitely" (Kerr et al. 2009, xxiv), so newer surveillance technologies do have implications for "informational privacy"—defined as "the claim of individuals, groups or institutions to determine for themselves when, how and to what extent information about them is communicated to others" (ibid., xxvii). In light of these developments, we need to ask the larger questions: who is considered to have a right to privacy? Whose privacy is not a concern and why? And importantly, how might a focus on these questions shape the field of surveillance studies? For instance, many communities—including prisoners, those receiving certain forms of welfare from the state, people with disabilities living in institutional care, as well as immigrants and refugees—have historically had, and continue to have, their bodily privacy invaded, but there is almost no public discussion about the infringement of their rights to privacy. As Rachel Hall notes in her contribution to this collection, privacy concerns have not kept vulnerable communities safer in the case of patriarchal violence, which often happens in the "private" space of the home. Hall shows us that part of the project of a feminist approach to surveillance studies is to "shift critical surveillance studies away from matters of privacy, security, and efficiency to a consideration of the ethical problem of combating new forms of discrimination that are practiced in relation to categories of privilege, access, and risk" (147).

This volume makes the case that the ways in which supposedly "neutral" technologies are used requires a feminist analysis to access issues of disenfranchisement. For instance, although whole-body imaging technologies are specifically marketed to emphasize that they do not profile individuals based on the color of their skin, these technologies nevertheless, in directly targeting particular communities (including working-class people, people with disabilities, and Muslim women) in ways that line up with the racist and Islamophobic imperatives of the U.S. state, serve to intensify existing inequalities. For example, backscatter x-rays continue the direct attack on the civil rights of transgender folks, as they can visualize objects including breast prostheses and dildos, and thus "out" trans people to airport screeners, and in doing so, make transgender travelers vulnerable to transphobic screeners. In some cases, particularly in small towns, these newer surveillance technologies result in the outing of transgender folks who pass in their communities, putting at risk their jobs as well as their relationships with their families and friends (Magnet and Rodgers 2012). These technologies also explicitly violate the religious prohibitions of many religious groups, including some Muslim women, and they have a disproportionate impact on people with disabilities, as they visualize urostomy and colostomy bags (ibid.).[1]

One of the components of our feminist praxis is a commitment to self-reflexivity and attentiveness to the ways that feminist thought can be co-opted, for instance, for projects that dovetail with state interests. A few essays in this volume excavate the links that surveillance practices have to the burgeoning prison industrial complex—an important feminist concern since women of color remain the fastest growing demographic of people to be included behind bars (Fraden 2001; M. Alexander 2010)— highlighting how a wide range of practices, from news coverage of crimes by people of color to turning to the police in domestic-violence situations, often results in facilitating the incarceration of vulnerable bodies. Andrea Smith (this volume) demonstrates the ways that relying on police to place perpetrators of violence under surveillance only makes those who are being subjected to aggression also vulnerable to harms caused by the state. In fact, feminist interventions into the law that aimed to involve police have backfired (INCITE! Women of Color Against Violence 2006). For example, mandatory arrest policies, whereby police must file charges in cases of domestic violence, have regularly resulted in the women themselves being charged and ending up in prison (Pollack, Green, and Allspach 2005). Moreover, Smith argues that because we imagine the surveillance apparatus of the state to be a sufficient response to violence, we fail to think of other, more creative solutions. Discussing one woman who lived with a batterer in her apartment building, but feared calling the police, Smith is struck by the fact that "the only potential interveners in this situation seems to be ourselves as individuals or the state. It seems like our only response is either a privatized response to violence or a communal one that is state-driven" (36). The result is not only that we do not "see" other solutions to the problem of violence, but that we also become absolved from having to see the violence in the first place. Smith argues that we need to dismantle penal responses to violence and begin to imagine responses outside this punitive system.

Ummni Khan, in her contribution to this collection, argues that a certain type of feminist response to sex work—one that argues for the criminalization of johns—results in the disproportionate criminalization of vulnerable men. Asserting that there is a strand of feminist thought committed to abolishing prostitution that engages in what she calls "feminist surveillance practices" of male sex-trade clients, Khan shows that these are surveillance practices that continually lead to the disproportionate criminalization of poor men and men of color. Khan demonstrates the collusion between antiprostitution feminist thought and state agencies, which results in what Elizabeth Bernstein terms "carceral feminism" (2010)—a feminist politics that is entwined with criminalization and that fails to address the importance of penal abolition to any feminist movement.[2]

In addition to new theoretical frameworks and ideological commitments, we argue that a feminist approach to surveillance studies also needs new methodological tools. In their contribution to this volume, Kevin Walby and Seantel Anaïs propose that we introduce the pioneering methods of institutional ethnography, developed by feminist sociologist Dorothy Smith, to the practice of examining surveillance documents. An institutional-ethnographic methodological approach to surveillance, Walby and Anaïs illustrate, shows how the categories produced by surveillance documentation are, of course, gendered, racialized, sexualized, and classed.

Surveillance as Foundational Structure

A feminist approach to surveillance studies highlights the ways that surveillance is integral to many of our foundational structural systems, ones that breed disenfranchisement, and that continue to be institutionalized. In an extension of bell hooks's notion of "white supremacist capitalist patriarchy" (hooks 1997), we suggest the (clumsy, but illustrative) term "white supremacist capitalist heteropatriarchal surveillance": the use of surveillance practices and technologies to normalize and maintain whiteness, able-bodiedness, capitalism, and heterosexuality, practices integral to the foundation of the modern state. Smith's contribution to this collection reminds that while the modern bureaucratic state is often the focus of surveillance studies, the surveillance of native peoples is a key foundational strategy of colonialism: technologies of surveillance were integral to settler colonialism. Smith calls for the centering of an anticolonial feminist analysis within the field of surveillance studies, as she recounts how the violence of surveillance through organized settler colonial practices transformed First Peoples into racialized communities, thus facilitating the bureaucratically managed rape of indigenous people, making them "rapeable."

State surveillance practices, which we might simply call state practices (since surveillance is so seamlessly embedded), are processes that are simultaneously about seeing and not-seeing—that is, some bodies are made invisible, while others are made hypervisible (see Smith, Moore, Jiwani, and Hall, this volume). The underlying structures of domination that created the conditions for violence in communities of color—such as the incarceration of indigenous peoples in residential schools or the institutionalized rape that accompanied slavery—are made invisible, while the cycle of violence that residential schools or that slavery created in terms of ongoing violence in communities of color are hypervisibilized, surveilled, and then subject to violent state intervention. As Yasmin Jiwani notes in her essay in this volume, which looks at how the commercial Canadian media covered the Shafia murders (four Afghan women murdered by family members in Canada), when violence happens in communities of color, it is understood as ordinary and expected—people from these communities are configured as always already criminals—whereas violence in white communities is imagined to be exceptional. This racist imagining of violence as key to communities of color justifies new forms of surveillance by the state in ways that facilitate the disproportionate criminalization of communities of color. As Hall notes in her essay on body scanners in airports, whiteness is transparent—a racialization that does not require monitoring—whereas racialized bodies are opaque and therefore suspect. Similarly, Moore's contribution to this volume examines the increasing reliance on a genre of institutional photography—photographs of battered women—by police in cases involving battery, under a system of white supremacy. Moore shows that women of color (particularly dark-skinned women) are not revealed through the mechanism of photography, especially their injuries, in the same way as white women.

Laura Hyun Yi Kang's piece in this volume, about the history of anti-trafficking, highlights how subjecting female bodies to observation has long been a practice in the United States. She examines the surveillance of the "differentially stratified mobilities" of women across borders, noting that the surveillance and scrutiny of women immigrating to the United States bespeaks founding imperialist racialist narratives in the United States. Focusing on trafficking in the League of Nations, Kang asserts that women were simultaneously hailed as objects and subjects of surveillance. The women were, on the one hand, seen as involved in the policing of other women, but on the other hand, at the borders of the nation where they were imagined to be trafficked, they were placed under greater surveillance which resulted in racialized sexist scrutiny.

As Lisa Jean Moore and Paisley Currah (this volume) show in their analysis of the birth certificate, gender and sexuality are inextricably bound to surveillant practices of documentation. Beginning with the binary system of gender imposed on babies born on U.S. soil, each of whom must be categorized and documented as a boy or a girl, living in the modern bureaucratic state is about the policing of gendered identities. Of course, as Moore and Currah demonstrate, the practice of documenting citizens via birth certificates is not a simple recording of bodily identities, but a process of surveillance that produces gendered identities in ways that do both epistemological and ontological violence to bodies that do not fit the male-female binary. In fact, statistics (including tracking and gathering information about gender) is intimately tied to the rise of statehood, as states gain the power to govern in part by collecting knowledge about their citizenry (Bowker and Star 1999, 110). Thus, in the words of the communication theorist Armand Mattelart, "measurement, computing, and recording have been the recurrent traits of the long process of construction of the modern mode of communication, starting with the first manifestations of 'statistical reason'" (1996, xvi). A feminist approach to surveillance studies demonstrates how the production of knowledge, when it comes to vulnerable bodies, is always already bound up with gendered and sexualized ways of seeing. The essays in part 1 make clear that surveillance practices are actually part of the founding mechanisms of many nation-states, as well as of the practices used to keep track of the citizens of these nation-states.

The Visual and Surveillance: Bodies on Display

Part of what we add to ongoing conversations about surveillance is the idea that surveillance practices do not only "dismantle or disaggregate the coherent body bit by bit" (Ericson and Haggerty 2006), but also remake the body, producing new ways of visualizing bodily identities in ways that highlight othered forms of racialized, gendered, classed, abled, and disabled bodies, as well as sexualized identities. Surveillance studies can help to show that many surveillance practices and technologies were initially refined by focusing on the state's most vulnerable communities, bringing into sharp focus how oppression is made functional in a given context. For example, biometric technologies (which are used to identify features specific to an individual's body) were initially tested on prisoners who could not resist their use and were only recently used in a wider range of applications, such as fingerprint scanners on phones for consumer security. In her groundbreaking book *Terrorist Assemblages* (2007), queer theorist Jasbir Puar examines the move within the field of surveillance studies to focus on the "data body" or informational profile. Examining new security practices, including the x-raying of Sikh turbans at airports, Puar reminds that the body is never a cage of pure information, but rather always a racialized, gendered, and sexualized being. Puar asserts that while "surveillance assemblages" tend "toward discounting and dismissing the visual and its capacity to interpellate subjects . . . this discounting is simply not politically viable given the shifts around formations of race and sex that are under way in response to a new visual category, the 'terrorist look-alike' or those who 'look like terrorists'" (2007, 229). A concern in this collection is the interaction between the informational profile (a statistical profile that contains information including age, social security number, and so forth), the surveillance of gender, race, class, and sexuality, and the implications of the visual when it comes to surveillance practices and technologies.

One entry point for discussing visualized displays of the body via surveillance is the rich tradition of feminist scholarship in media studies. This scholarship enables us to focus on the contingencies of the visual and how newer surveillance technologies both produce and are produced by new forms of pleasure in looking. While a camera filming an actor in a scene for a film is not conventionally understood to be an act of surveillance proper, the visual display of bodies inherent to films and other forms of visual media, and to many practices involving surveillance technologies, suggest the need to mine the valuable insights of the rich tradition of critical feminist media studies scholarship for what it has to offer the study of surveillance. Aligning surveillance studies with feminist media studies reminds of the necessity of grounding visualizing practices in a history of systemic discrimination, one helpfully theorized by feminist media scholars. Our aim is to bring this work into the conversation about surveillance and point out that issues key to surveillance studies have been of concern to critical feminist scholars for quite some time.

In a culture that consistently puts women's bodies on visual display, and where this display can have implications particular to their gendering, any analysis of a technology that has the possibility of achieving these ends needs to contend with the complicated intersection of gender and the politics of the visual. From hooks's (1992) analysis of the hypervisibility of black female bodies, to Laura Mulvey's (1975) foundational work on the "male gaze," which examines how the film camera is used to invite the gaze of the audience to scrutinize female bodies, to the ways that bodies are made spectacular in racialized and gendered ways in science and medicine (Treichler, Cartwright, and Penley 1998), feminist scholarship dealing with issues related to surveillance has been around for decades. At the root of Mulvey's work are questions about the politics of looking—about the surveillance of othered bodies—for both the looker and the object being looked at, and the implications of the pleasures derived from this process. Integral to Mulvey's analysis are the gendered implications when the object looked at is a woman, a concern that needs to be carried over to any examination of how the surveillant gaze can make visible gendered bodies. Of course, as hooks (1992) insists, and as the work of Kang (2002) makes clear, racialized female bodies on display in visual media require particular consideration from critical scholars, something to which this volume is attentive.

As Moore, Jiwani, Hall, and Dubrofsky and Wood's essays in this volume make clear, central to much critical feminist media scholarship are questions about the contingencies of the visual display of disenfranchised bodies, a display that also often results from the use of technologies that behave in many ways like surveillance technologies. As Jiwani demonstrates in her contribution, surveillance technologies work to discipline certain bodies in particular ways, making some bodies hypervisible and others invisible, crafting regimes of intelligibility wherein what is rendered invisible is legitimized and taken for granted as an inherent part of the social fabric. Jiwani argues that visibility serves to heighten the focus on particular bodies by foregrounding their difference, and in the case of the coverage of the Shafia murders in the popular Canadian press, this logic of the visual situates Muslim bodies as beyond the purview of what it means to be and to look like a law-abiding Canadian.

While some of the surveillance technologies used to put bodies on visual display may be new, many of the ideas and forms of oppression associated with and reproduced by them are not and can be seen in longer standing forms of media. As Rachel E. Dubrofsky and Megan M. Wood show in their chapter, which examines tabloid coverage of celebrity use of Twitter, Twitter enables the articulation of women as placing *themselves* under surveillance by "voluntarily" posting photographs. Using critical feminist media scholarship, they show how women are framed as empowered and agentic, situating them as complicit in invitations to the male gaze. While new forms of social media are imagined to produce new possibilities for feminist agency online, Dubrofsky and Wood show how age-old sexist and racist tropes persist when self-fashioning in a consumer context is configured as a form of empowerment and active invitation of the male gaze is imagined as a form of agency. Dubrofsky and Wood highlight the racialized implications of such tropes: white women are presented as agentic through the hard work (exercise and diet) they put into making their bodies ready for the male gaze; women of color are always already gaze-worthy in ways that rely on racist sexisms.

We are reminded of how narratives that emphasize the possibilities of the formidable potential of x-ray vision (such as Spiderman and Batman) may serve to shape technological development, as scientists internalize these cultural messages about consumer desires and attempt to actualize them in new technologies, an issue discussed by Hall in this volume, in her essay on whole-body imaging machines that visualize people's bodies naked under their clothes. Surveillance technologies that visualize the body reference long-standing cultural and science fictional preoccupations with x-ray eyes, in which x-ray vision is imagined in media from comic books to news representations to be a form of seeing that is all-powerful and all-revealing, and thus an exciting and powerful technological development. In a culture that sexualizes the visual display of female bodies, this type of technology can have specific implications for female bodies. For instance, attendants of the Transportation Security Administration (TSA) in the United States encourage screeners to pay particular attention when hegemonically attractive women pass through these scanners (Hall, this volume), intensifying existing forms of sexual harassment. In this way, the technologies facilitate x-ray eyes that require security personnel to stare at certain bodies while obscuring the pleasure taken in rendering these bodies visible, as well as mystifying the process by which some bodies are made hypervisible and others invisible. This is a process Magnet has elsewhere termed "surveillant scopophilia" (2011)—that is, when new technologies provide opportunities for pleasure in looking in ways connected to surveillance. How the technologies capture the body can have significant implications, as Moore (this volume) articulates in her discussion of how police photographs of battered women create images in which the battered bodies of women of color do not translate in ways that reproduce the commonsense aesthetics of what a battered woman looks like.

A possible distinction between the use of surveillance technologies and images created by the entertainment industry for mass consumption is that the images and data created by the former are not necessarily or expressly used to construct consumable products for a mass audience, as is the case for the latter. However, in the most popular television genre of the last decade, reality TV, techniques that mimic surveillance practices are used to gather footage that resembles surveillance footage of real people doing real things—that is, not actors performing scripted lines—to create an entertainment product for mass consumption. The reality TV genre puts into relief a poignant concern for our project, one originally raised by feminists looking at the genre of pornography (L. Williams 1989; McClintock 1993), but which permeates media practices nowadays: how does the visual display of "real" bodies doing "real" things add a twist to a critical analysis of representation? What are the implications of saying, "But she really behaved that way. We caught it on film," rather than "She was scripted in this way. The director instructed her to play her role in this manner"? The little existent feminist scholarship on this genre (Hasinoff 2008; Dubrofsky 2011a) is helpful in addressing these concerns, but there is simply not enough, though there is a remarkable burgeoning and thriving field of critical scholarship on racialized bodies in the reality TV genre, all of which can be fruitfully brought into conversation with the work of surveillance scholars.[3]

Newer media suture the subject more personally, more directly, as a producer (not just a consumer) of culture, creating what some now refer to as a "prosumer" (blurring of the lines between the consumer and producer). While newer media can enable the reproduction of historical oppressive power relations existent in "older" media, they also add important new dimensions requiring investigation and understanding. For instance, what happens when we can no longer say about an image (as we might with a representation on a reality TV show) that it was edited and shown out of context? Witness the case of Natalie Blanchard in Quebec, who lost her disability insurance benefits (for depression) because she appeared "too happy" in Facebook photographs that she posted during her sick leave (Sawchuk 2010). Much was made, in particular, of a photograph of Blanchard in a bikini, with online discussions of how good she looked in the bikini and of this somehow attesting to her (sound) mental health. How do questions of empowerment and responsibility become articulated when individuals operate the technologies that functionally surveil them and are used to obstruct their right to the privileges of citizenship, including assistance from the state, as well as to get them fired, to socially ostracize them, and so forth? What are the particular implications of this for female, racialized, queer, and disabled subjects?

Biometric Technologies as Surveillance Assemblages

Biometric technologies are accompanied by a whole host of surveillance practices that specifically focus on the body as we are increasingly locked into what the sociologist Simone Browne calls the "identity-industrial complex," where the body itself is the central target of surveillance practices (2009). As Hall's work in this volume demonstrates, the failure of new technologies to keep people safe intersects with their race, class, gender, sexuality, and disabled- or able-bodied identities. One example of this is the ways that the surveillance of disability is facilitated by new reproductive technologies. For instance, the Newborn Screening Saves Lives Act mandates the collection of DNA information from every baby born on U.S. soil. The genetic information collected from newborn babies is subject to an increasing number of genetic tests—a number that has dramatically expanded alongside new technological advances (Magnet 2012). Of course, this means the state increasingly screens for disabilities in ways that recall eugenics projects, as new technologies are used as a form of mandated surveillance by the state to facilitate the surveillance of disability. As Dorothy E. Roberts shows in her contribution to this volume, the increase in the number of amniocenteses performed is also part of the surveillance of disability, as "it is increasingly routine for pregnant women to get prenatal diagnoses for certain genetic conditions, such as Down syndrome or dwarfism" (176), even in cases where women do not understand what the test is for or its attendant risks.

Of course, new reproductive technologies have different implications for white women and for women of color, and for women in the Global South versus women in the Global North. Roberts reminds us that in 1985 the feminist theorist Gena Corea "predicted that white women would hire surrogates of color in reproductive brothels to be implanted with their eggs and to gestate their babies at low cost" (169), this prediction highlights the differential ways genetic technologies are likely to be accessed. Corea's prediction has come true, as Sayantani DasGupta and Shamita Das Dasgupta show in their contribution to this volume, which looks at the growing surrogacy industry in India. DasGupta and Dasgupta demonstrate that, for the most part, wealthy women from the Global North, as well as some wealthy Indian citizens, pay to have impoverished or financially struggling Indian women implanted with an embryo via in-vitro fertilization. In this piece, we see how the bodies of women of color are literally put into the service of reproducing empire for another country (often North America, Australia, or Europe) by producing offspring for what is often a white couple, and placed under surveillance to make sure they are doing so properly. Like Smith, DasGupta and Dasgupta demonstrate the urgent need for an analysis of colonialism and colonial practices in surveillance studies. They argue that surveillance practices facilitated by the economic necessity of Indian surrogates pave the way for all kinds of gender, class, and imperialist violences.

In examining state attempts—with an orientalist and imperial gaze—to render "terrorist bodies" both pathological and animalistic—Hall illustrates that biotechnologies are deployed to turn these bodies inside out and make them transparent in ways that intensify systemic forms of violence already inflicted on marginalized communities. In her discussion of full-body scanners in U.S. airports, Hall looks at the centering of the notion that white, middle-class, able-bodied, heterosexual passengers should not have their bodily privacy invaded by TSA officials. Race issues are indeed often at the forefront in the marketing of the technologies — for instance, companies aiming to get state institutions to invest in iden- tification technologies claim biometrics will circumvent persistent forms of racial profiling. Biometric technologies render the body in binary code, and industry manufacturers of these technologies claim this code re- veals nothing about race, gender, class, or sexuality, instead representing bodies as anesthetized strands of ones and zeroes. However, it is increas- ingly clear that biometric technologies are in fact a high-tech form of racial and gender profiling that efficiently and quickly sorts people using criteria that often explicitly include race and gender. For example, in order to verify the identity of a particular individual, it would be faster to scan the individual against a smaller group of people with like character- istics, rather than against an entire database. For many biometric tech- nologies, "like characteristics" include race and gender identities. Reify- ing race and gender in this way through their biometric categorization only serves to intensify existing forms of biological racialism and sexism, in which race and gender are imagined as stable biological properties that can be reliably read off the body.

New Perspectives

What does this book tell us that is new? Part of the "new" is the explicit placing of the field of surveillance studies in historical perspective, by taking a transdisciplinary focus and forefronting a feminist praxis. An- other "new" is the overt framing of the concern with widespread sur- veillance as not a new phenomenon, by excavating and highlighting long-standing concerns with surveillance that pre-date the explosion of scholarship on the topic and precede 9/11 (a signal moment for much surveillance scholarship). This collection demonstrates the importance of thinking beyond contemporary developments in new technologies and the intensification of surveillance since the 1980s, tracing the history of surveillance back to organized forms of state control such as slavery, the management of women's reproductive autonomy, the regulation of sexuality, and the institutionalized scrutiny of those living in poverty. Rather than rehashing arguments as to whether or not surveillance keeps the United States safe, we instead take an intersectional critical femi- nist approach to illuminate what constitutes surveillance, who is scruti- nized, why, and at what cost. As we show throughout this introduction and edited collection, surveillance continually impacts people of color, women, queer and trans people, and people with disabilities. From the ways that surveillance has facilitated the state-sponsored rape of indigenous peoples (Smith, this volume) to the ways that surveillance remains central to the policing of the reproduction of women of color (DasGupta and Dasgupta, this volume; Roberts, this volume), in asking what the conditions of possibility for the emergence and intensification of surveillance practices might be, we hope to show the connection of these practices to systemic forms of discrimination.

This collection demonstrates the theoretical significance of surveillance for other fields, from feminist media studies scholarship that looks at how women are put on display in visual forms of media, to critical criminological examinations of how photographic evidence is used in cases involving the battery of women in intimate relationships, to research in sexuality studies that examines the surveillance of transgender folks through new forms of identification and documentation practices. We hope this volume will encourage more cross-disciplinary conversations and alliances. How might we think about how to build coalitions across difference? A feminist approach to surveillance studies also argues for a reimagining of collective responses to the violence of state scrutiny, one that seeks to uproot and defy oppressive structural systems, envisioning collective forms of resistance to violence that do not involve state surveillance of those living either inside or outside its borders, and asks how we might make our communities safer while continuing to refuse surveillance practices. Additionally, we would like to facilitate the generation of new research interests on the topic of surveillance; for instance, to open up avenues for the examination of mediascapes that increasingly blur the lines between what have conventionally been understood as public and private spheres, and the concomitant implications of the use by private citizens of personal technologies to create publicly available and widely circulating images and bits of data. Above all, we contend that the critical implications of surveillance cannot be explored without attentiveness to issues of oppression. We would like this volume to encourage discussions about the implications of surveillance for disenfranchised bodies, conversations that engage long-standing concerns raised by critical scholars looking at the display of gendered, classed, sexualized, racialized, disabled, or able bodies.

Notes

1. There was discussion of removing backscatter x-rays from airports (they were moved to airports in smaller cities in 2012, however), but the Transportation Security Administration awarded the company American Science and Engineering (AS&E) a $245 million contract to purchase its SmartCheck backscatter x-ray detection device for an indefinite period. These scanners remain in use. See "American Science and Engineering, Inc. Awarded $245 million IDIQ Contract for SmartCheck Next Generation Advanced Imaging Technology," press release, 9 October 2012, AS&E website, http://ir.as-e.com/releasedetail.cfm?ReleaseID=712149.

2. Penal abolitionists are part of a mass-based movement committed to ending, rather than rehabilitating, the prison system, arguing that the prison-industrial complex is a fundamentally flawed system that entrenches existing inequalities (Davis and Rodriguez 2000). This movement aims to find alternatives to the prison system as a warehouse for women, poor people, people of color, queer people, and people with disabilities (Davis 2003; Smith 2008).

3. On racialized bodies in reality TV, see Dubrofsky 2011b; Kraszewski 2004; Orbe 2008.

PART I

SURVEILLANCE AS
FOUNDATIONAL STRUCTURE

1

NOT-SEEING

State Surveillance, Settler Colonialism, and Gender Violence

ANDREA SMITH

He [Father Olbés] sent for the husband and he asked him why his wife hadn't borne children. The Indian pointed to the sky . . . to signify that only God knew the cause . . . asked through the interpreter if he slept with his wife, to which the Indian said yes. Then the father had them placed in a room together so that they would perform coitus in his presence. The Indian refused, but they forced him to show him his penis in order to affirm that he had it in good order. The father next brought the wife and had . . . her enter another room in order to examine her reproductive parts.

—David E. Stannard, *American Holocaust*

The focus of surveillance studies has generally been on the modern, bureaucratic state. And yet, as David Stannard's (1992) account of the sexual surveillance of indigenous peoples within the Spanish mission system in the Americas demonstrates, the history of patriarchal and colonialist surveillance in this continent is much longer. The traditional account of surveillance studies tends to occlude the manner in which the settler state is foundationally built on surveillance. Because surveillance studies focuses on the modern, bureaucratic state, it has failed to account for the gendered colonial history of surveillance. Consequently, the strategies for addressing surveillance do not question the state itself, but rather seek to modify the extent to which and the manner in which the state surveils. As Mark Rifkin (2011) and Scott Morgensen (2011) additionally demonstrate, the sexual surveillance of native peoples was a key strategy by which native peoples were rendered manageable populations within the colonial state. One would think that an anticolonial feminist analysis would be central to the field of surveillance studies. Yet, ironically, it is this focus on the modern state that often obfuscates the settler colonialist underpinning of technologies of surveillance. I explore how a feminist surveillance-studies focus on gendered colonial violence reshapes the field by bringing into view that which cannot be seen: the surveillance strategies that have effected indigenous disappearance in order to establish the settler state itself. In particular, a focus on gendered settler colonialism foregrounds how surveillance is not simply about "seeing" but about "not-seeing" the settler state.

Surveillance and the Biopolitical Modern State

David Lyon (2007) defines surveillance as follows.

> For the sake of argument, we may start by saying that it is the focused, systematic and routine attention to personal details for purposes of influence, management, protection or direction. Surveillance directs its attention in the end to individuals (even though aggregate data, such as those available in the public domain, may be used to build up a background picture). It is focused. By systematic, I mean that this attention to personal details is not random, occasional or spontaneous; it is deliberate and depends on certain protocols and techniques. Beyond this, surveillance is routine; it occurs as a "normal" part of everyday life in all societies. (14)

The field of surveillance studies is important, Lyon argues, because of the "rapidly increasing influence of surveillance in our daily lives and in the operation of very large-scale operations" (ibid., 9). The growth in surveillance is often tied to Foucauldian notions of the rise of the disciplinary society and the ascendancy of biopolitics in which peoples become populations to be counted, measured, and regulated in order to promote the life of the normalizing state. Because certain populations are deemed threats to the normalizing state, they must be constantly monitored, and thus are subject to what Ruth Wilson Gilmore (2007) defines as "premature death" in order to preserve the body of the whole. And yet Foucault notes that, ironically, these biopolitical moves were first practiced on the bourgeoisie themselves. Through the disciplining of the bourgeois body, the "normal" body is defined as the measure by which all other bodies are marked as "deviant" (Foucault 1980, 123). Logics of normalization must have some pretense to universality even as these normalizing strategies are not evenly applied. Thus, it is no surprise that these disciplinary techniques come to be used broadly, not just on those populations deemed to be threats.

The Temporality of Settler Colonial Biopolitics

As noted by many critical-race- and ethnic-studies scholars, the manner in which Foucauldian analyses of the state tend to temporally situate biopower during the era of the modern state disappears the biopolitics of settler colonialism and transatlantic slavery.[1] Alexander Weheliye (2014) points out that Foucault's conception of a complicated biopower is juxtaposed against a simpler "ordinary racism" (Foucault 1997, 128). As Foucault asserts, "I am certainly not saying that racism was invented at this time. It had already been in existence for a very long time. But I think it functioned elsewhere" (ibid., 254). Relegated to both a theoretical and geotemporal "elsewhere," Foucault then provides no elaboration on the nature of this "other" racism." As Weheliye (2014) argues, when biopower is rendered as the real racism, whose apex can be found in Nazi Germany, indigenous genocide, slavery, and colonialism disappear into given forms of simple racism that require no account of their logics. Similarly, Achille Mbembe argues that the mechanics of Nazi Germany are not fundamentally different from the "necropolitics" of the colony or the plantation in which "'peace' is more likely to take on the face of a 'war without end'" (2003, 23). Denise Ferreira da Silva's germinal text, *Toward a Global Idea of Race* (2007), also demonstrates that these forms of racism precede the modern state as Western epistemology is itself fundamentally a racial project. A focus on biopolitical racism as it is tied to the modern state thus often occludes analysis of the racial logics of settler colonialism and plantation slavery.

Surveillance studies's focus on the modern state similarly hides an analysis of the settler colonialist and white supremacist logics of surveillance that precede the ascendancy of the modern state. Furthermore, attention to these colonial and white supremacist logics of surveillance require a feminist analysis, since colonialism and white supremacy are structured by heteropatriarchy. For instance, Mark Rifkin's *When Did Indi-*

the combination of male (patriarchal) and heterosexual dominance — describing the severe sex + gender bias among the ruling class.

ans Become Straight? and Scott Morgensen's *Spaces Between Us* call attention to the heteropatriarchal nature of colonial bio/necropolitics. That is, the shift from categorizing native peoples within the U.S. polity according to their membership in distinct nations to lumping them together under the racial category of "Indian" is often understood as a colonial tactic. But what Rifkin and Morgensen demonstrate is that this categorization is dependent on heteronormativity. Since they pose a threat to the colonial order, native nations are broken up into heteronormative individual family units in order to facilitate their absorption into the colonial state. This absorption occurs through a colonialist surveillance strategy by which the sexual and gender identities of native peoples must be constantly marked and policed. Through this surveillance, native peoples become racialized "Indians" who are managed through the politics of biopower (Rifkin 2011). Of course, as racialized subjects, native nations still constitute a threat to the well-being of the colonial state and hence are never properly heteronormative. The United States continues to be obsessed with solving the "Indian problem," whether through boarding schools or land allotments. But Indianization, as it were, allows colonialism to become a population problem rather than a political problem (ibid.). Native nations are seen as sufficiently domesticated to be administered through government policy, rather than seen as a continuing political threat requiring ongoing military intervention.

In addition, as Driskill, Finley, Gilley, and Morgensen (2011) argue, native peoples are fundamentally "queered" under settler colonialism such that conquest is justified by their sexual perversity. Deemed "sodomites," native peoples' presumed sexual perversity justifies their genocide. Indigenous colonization is then achieved through sexual regulation, such as sexual acts of terror (the mass rapes of native peoples in massacres), as well as policies of normalization in which heteropatriarchy is instilled in native communities through allotment, boarding schools, and criminalization, among other contemporary forms of the surveillance and regulation of native peoples. As I have argued elsewhere, sexual violence was a primary colonial strategy by which native peoples were rendered inherently rapeable, and by extension their lands inherently invadeable, and their resources inherently extractable (A. Smith 2005a). Thus, contrary to Lyon's assertion that "the focused, systematic and routine attention to personal details for purposes of influence, management, protection or direction" preceded the rise of the bureaucratic state, these strategies were foundational to the settler state that required the gendered reclassification of the people from various indigenous nations into "Indians."

As Patrick Wolfe (1999) notes, settler colonialism is a structure, not an event; that is, settler colonialism requires the continual disappearance of the indigenous peoples on whose land the settler state is situated (2). Consequently, these colonial heteropatriarchal logics continue. As Jacqui Alexander's critique of the heteropatriarchal postcolonial state demonstrates, on one hand, the postcolonial state (or states that strive to be postcolonial) is imagined to be incapable of self-governance through its previously described presumed sexual perversity. It thus seeks to prove its ability to self-govern by continuing the colonial policing of supposed sexually perverse "nonprocreative noncitizens" within its borders to legitimate its claims to govern. In policing the gender and sexual boundaries of the nation-state by purifying it of imagined racialized and gendered contaminants, Alexander (2005) argues, the postcolonial state succeeds in obfuscating the permeability of its boundaries to multinational capital. This policing, structured under the logics of what Maria Josefina Saldaña-Portillo (2003) terms "aggrieved masculinity," then serves to allay the anxiety of the postcolonial state and postcolonial aspirants in the wake of the postcolonial state's feminization within the heteropatriarchal logics of global capital. While Lyon's analysis points us to the surveillance strategies of the state, an anticolonial feminist analysis demonstrates that the problem is instead the state itself as surveillance strategy. Consequently, it is no surprise that states that have "decolonized" perpetuate the same surveillance strategies, because surveillance is structured into the logic of the state itself. That is, if we relocate the focus of surveillance studies from the bureaucratic state to the settler colonial, white supremacist, and heteropatriarchal state, we may then reformulate our analysis of surveillance.

In particular, I would like to foreground the focus of the field of surveillance studies on "seeing." According to Lyon, "Surveillance studies is about seeing things and, more particularly, about seeing people" (2007, 1). The "watchful gaze," as Lyon labels it, is what gives surveillance its "quintessential characteristic" (2007, 1). A focus on gendered settler colonialism would instead foreground how surveillance is about a simultaneous seeing and not-seeing. That is, the purposeful gaze of the state on some things and peoples serves the purpose of simultaneously making some hypervisible through surveillance while making others invisible. The colonial gaze that surveils native communities to monitor, measure, and account for their "dysfunctional" behaviors conceals from view the settler colonial state that creates these conditions in the first place. A feminist surveillance studies focus on gendered colonial violence highlights that which cannot be seen—indigenous disappearance.

The Settler Surveillance Strategies of Not-Seeing

Settler colonialism fundamentally relies on a logic of not-seeing. In particular, on a not-seeing of the indigenous people's lands in order to allow their colonial takeover. Terra nullius, the legal justification used for the expropriation of indigenous land in Australia and elsewhere—or to use the Zionist justification for Palestinian expulsion, "a land without a people for a people without a land"—is premised on the not-seeing of peoples already there. Within the United States, this expropriation relied on the "doctrine of discovery." As outlined in the case *Johnson v. McIntosh* (1823), "Discovery is the foundation of title, in European nations, and this overlooks all proprietary rights in the natives." "Discovery" necessarily rests on the absence of native peoples, who would otherwise be the actual "discoverers" of their lands. And, as Robert Williams (2005) notes, U.S. jurisprudence has never renounced the doctrine of discovery on which Indian case law is based. Consequently, the colonial project is a somewhat precarious project of disappearing the peoples that it cannot see—a genocide that must disavow itself. As Sarita See argues, "If the history of the American empire is defined by forgetting, its aesthetic is structured by double disavowal. According to the New World aesthetic, it seems possible to erase the erasure of the past" (2009, 66). Thus, the strategies of surveillance are always simultaneously not just about what can be seen, but about disappearing from view that which delegitimizes the state itself. What must not be seen is not only the peoples themselves, but the forms of governance and ways of life that they represent.

Gender violence is a central strategy of settler colonialism and white supremacy. Colonizers did not just kill off indigenous peoples in this land: native massacres were always accompanied by sexual mutilation and rape. The goal of colonialism is not just to kill colonized peoples, but to destroy their sense of being people (A. Smith 2005a). The generally nonpatriarchal and nonhierarchical nature of many native communities posed a threat to European patriarchal societies. Consequently, when colonists first came to this land, they saw the necessity of instilling patriarchy in native communities, for they realized that indigenous peoples would not accept colonial domination if their own indigenous societies were not structured on the basis of social hierarchies. Patriarchy rests on a gender-binary system; hence, it is no coincidence that colonizers also targeted indigenous peoples who did not fit within this binary model. Gender violence thus inscribed patriarchy onto the bodies of native peoples, naturalizing social hierarchies and colonial domination.

The imposition of heteropatriarchy serves not only to secure colonial domination for indigenous peoples, but also to secure patriarchy within the colonizing society against the threats of the alternative governance structures that indigenous societies represent. It is noteworthy that the high status of women and the relatively peaceful nature of many native societies did not escape the notice of white peoples, in particular of white women (A. Smith 2005b).[2] A society based on domination, hierarchy, and violence works only when it seems natural or inevitable. Given an alternative, peoples will generally choose not to live under violent conditions. The demonization of native societies, as well as their resulting destruction, was necessary to securing the "inevitability" of patriarchy within colonial societies. Again, the colonialist surveillance of native bodies served the simultaneous purposes of making them visible to the state while at the same time making invisible the threat to the settler state posed by indigenous governance.

To further remove the threats that indigenous governance systems posed to settler societies, the problem resulting from this colonial disease was relocated from a patriarchal and violent settler state to the "Indian" problem. As Wolfe (1999) notes, the more gender-egalitarian nature of some indigenous societies became anthropologically marked as the sign of their unevolved, premodern status. By adopting patriarchy, colonialists speculated, native peoples might evolve toward "humanity" and "civilization." Native peoples were to be bureaucratically managed through allotment processes, church- and government-run boarding schools, and government-run health programs, among other strategies to facilitate their ascension to humanity. While courts often held that native peoples were potential citizens with the right to vote—unlike African Americans in the antebellum period—such potential could be realized, from the colonialist perspective, only when those peoples mature out of their status as native. In addition, native peoples' were generally assigned the legal status of children, deemed legally incompetent to handle their own affairs and thus legally marked as "nonworkers." Native peoples' pathway to citizenship thus depended on their maturation into adult (i.e., white) workers. Thus, native peoples' acquisition of citizenship and voting rights was framed as a reward for proving their ability to work.

In 1887 the Dawes Allotment Act divided native lands into individual allotments of 80–160 acres. The federal government then expropriated the remaining surplus lands. Native peoples were given fees in trust for twenty-five years, until deemed "competent" by the secretary of the interior. They could then obtain fee patents enabling them to sell their lands. The rationale for this policy was that the practice of communal land ownership among native peoples was discouraging them from working the land. In the 1887 Indian commissioner's report, J. D. C. Atkins explains the need for allotment:

> Take the most prosperous and energetic community in the most enterprising section of our country—New England; give them their lands in common, furnish them annuities of food and clothing, send them teachers to teach their children, preachers to preach the gospel, farmers to till their lands, and physicians to heal their sick, and I predict that in a few years, a generation or two at most, their manhood would be smothered. . . .
>
> This pauperizing policy above outlined was, however, to some extent necessary at the beginning of our efforts to civilize the savage Indian. He was taken a hostile barbarian, his tomahawk red with the blood of the pioneer; he was too wild to know any of the arts of civilization. . . . Hence some such policy had to resort to settle the nomadic Indian and place him under control. This policy was a tentative one. . . . Now, as fast as any tribe becomes sufficiently civilized and can be turned loose and put upon its own footing, it should be done. Agriculture and education will gradually do this work and finally enable the Government to leave the Indian to stand alone. (*Report of the Secretary of the Interior* 1887, n.p.)

The report warns that allotment will not work overnight: "Idleness, improvidence, ignorance, and superstition cannot by law be transformed into industry, thrift, intelligence, and Christianity speedily" (ibid., 4). Consequently, surveillance practices were essential, in order to instill normalizing discipline as a means to forcibly absorb native peoples into the colonial state. This pathway toward civilization required native peoples to adapt to a capitalist work model. The commissioner's report further explained how work could save native peoples from barbarism.

It must be apparent . . . that the system of gathering the Indians in bands or tribes on reservations[,] . . . thus relieving them of the necessity of labor, never will and never can civilize them. Labor is an essential element in producing civilization. . . . The greatest kindness the government can bestow upon the Indian is to teach him to labor for his own support, thus developing his true manhood, and, as a consequence, making him self-relying and self-supporting. (ibid., 6–7)

Thus, through the careful policing and monitoring of native social structures, it would be possible to save native peoples from themselves, as well as to absorb them into colonial whiteness.

Despite these civilizational strategies, native peoples never seemed to attain humanity. Homi Bhabha (1997) and Edward Said (1994) argue that the colonization process involves partially assimilating the colonized in order to establish colonial rule. If the colonized group were to remain completely different from the colonists, it would implicitly challenge the supremacy of colonial rule, by introducing questions around whether the way colonizers live is the only way to live. Hence, in order to preserve the cultural ideals of the colonizers, the colonized had to resemble the colonists—but only partially, for if the colonized were to be completely assimilated, they would be equal to the colonists, and there would be no reason to continue to colonize them. In this way, the promised assimilation was never total or complete, which created a permanent colonial anxiety with respect to the indigenous peoples who were to be absorbed. As Kevin Bruyneel contends, advocacy for bestowing full citizenship on native peoples soon gave way to notions of a more qualified citizenship, as native peoples were deemed to be civilizing too slowly. Because of native peoples' imposed ontological status as children, they were never considered mature enough to earn full independence from their colonial fathers (Bruyneel 2004, 3).

Surveillance and Gender Violence

The surveillance strategies employed to normalize native peoples—from the monitoring of sexual behavior in Indian boarding schools to the surveillance of land ownership through the Dawes Allotment Act—have never come to an end, even though colonial policymakers continually promise they will. The civilizing policies directed against native peoples have never seemed to succeed enough to justify dismantling them. Of course, one indicator used to determine that native peoples are continuing to be a "problem" and are not sufficiently "civilized" is the high rate of gender violence within native communities. As Dian Million (2014) brilliantly notes, the U.S. government's funding of healing programs goes hand-in-hand with the imposition of neoliberal economic regimes on Indian communities. According to this logic, native communities do not deserve the right of self-determination because they are violent. Instead, under the guise of colonial paternalism, the state deems it necessary to carefully monitor and surveil the violence within native communities in order to once again save native peoples from themselves. Of course, in this constant "seeing" of violence within native communities, the state hides from view the fact that most such violence is a direct result of state policy. What must not get seen is the inherent violence of the state itself.

In one example of this dynamic, the Australian government declared a national emergency in the Northern Territory as a result of the publication of the *Little Children Are Sacred* report, which detailed the "problem" of child abuse in aboriginal communities in a manner similar to the way gender violence in native communities is framed in the United States (Povinelli 2011, 59). The government seized control of indigenous lands through military police action, instituted compulsory medical exams for children, and took control of the finances for all indigenous programs. Through this intense surveillance, native peoples could be monitored in terms of school attendance, purchasing choices, and medical practices. While the report itself made an effort not to blame child abuse on aboriginal "culture," it was used by the Australian government to identify aboriginal culture as the problem and thus to justify its surveillance practices. Through these surveillance strategies, the Australian government could "see" and hence surveil the problem of indigenous child abuse, yet it did not see that these abuses were themselves the result of gendered colonial policies, such as the government kidnapping of aboriginal children from their communities in order to place them in violent government schools (Manne 2004)—one example in which state abuse created child abuse as an epidemic problem in native communities. The only solution the state can "see" to ending gender and child abuse is the settler state. What cannot be seen is the fact that such violence is the result of state violence.

Similarly, many native activists who organize around sexual violence in native communities frame their activist work from a decolonization perspective, yet the solutions that emerge from that work usually result in increased federal intervention in native communities, such as the recent Tribal Law and Order Act that was passed in the wake of Amnesty International's report on sexual assault in Indian country, *Maze of Injustice* (K. Robertson 2012). Of course, native activists who engage in such policy work are not ignorant of the risks of advocating for changes in federal policies (Smith 2005b). They are aware of the contradiction of trying to further the long-term project of decolonization while attempting to secure some measure of safety for survivors of violence in the short term. They constantly struggle with the question of whether relying on state surveillance even as a short-term solution to violence diminishes the possibilities of developing alternative strategies which refuse settler colonial logics in the long term.

It is important to note that the apparatus of settler colonial surveillance does not impact only native peoples. The "normalizing" society must necessarily inflict the logics of normalization on all peoples, not just on those who are "oppressed." If it were only the oppressed who were subjected to normalizing logics, the logics would not seem "normal." This is why the intent of genocide is not just to destroy native peoples, but to eliminate alternatives to the settler state for nonnative peoples. If alternatives to the white supremacist, capitalist, heteropatriarchal settler state were to persist, the settler state's status as the prototype for normal would be at risk. Settler logics inform both how violence against native women is addressed, as well as how gender violence in general is addressed. Furthermore, the mainstream antiviolence movement relies on a settler framework for combating violence in ways that make it complicit in the state's surveillance strategies. These strategies then inform how the mainstream movement manages and "sees" gender violence, while simultaneously preventing it from seeing other approaches to ending violence. For example, at an antiviolence conference I attended, the participants supported the war in Afghanistan because they believed it would liberate women from the violence of the Taliban; their reliance on state-driven surveillance strategies for addressing violence through the military and criminal-justice systems prevented them from seeing that militarism itself perpetuates violence against women.

One of the reasons for the antiviolence movement's investment in the state derives from its concerns with the private sphere. As Lyon notes, much of the focus of surveillance studies is on "privacy"—how the state monitors the individual lives of peoples.[3] Of course, as feminist scholars argue, the assumption that the protection of privacy is an unmediated good is problematic, since the private sphere is where women are generally subjected to violence.[4] And, as feminists of color in particular have noted, not all women are equally entitled to privacy. Saidiya Hartman points out that, on the one hand, the abuse and enslavement of African Americans was often marked as taking place in the private sphere and hence beyond the reach of the state to correct. And yet, paradoxically, the private space of black families was seen as an extension of the workplace and hence subject to police power (Hartman 1997, 160, 173). Anannya Bhattacharjee similarly recounts an incident in which a domestic worker complained to her social-justice organization that she was being abused by her white employer.[5] When Bhattacharjee on behalf of the organization contacted the police to report the incident, she was told that "if her organization tried to intervene by rescuing this person, that would be trespassing: In this case, the privacy of these wealthy employers' home was held to be inviolate, while the plight of an immigrant worker being held in a condition of involuntary servitude was not serious enough to merit police action. . . . The supposed privacy and sanctity of the home is a relative concept, whose application is heavily conditioned by racial and economic status" (Bhattacharjee 2000, 29). As Patricia Allard notes, women of color who receive public assistance are not generally deemed worthy of privacy—they are subjected to the constant surveillance of the state. Of course, all women seeking public services can be surveilled, but welfare is generally racialized in the public imaginary through the figure of the "welfare queen." Andrea Ritchie (2006), Anannya Bhattacharjee (2001), and other scholars document how women of color, particularly those who are non-gender conforming, who seek police intervention in cases of domestic violence often find themselves subject to sexual assault, murder, and other forms of police-inflicted brutality.

If the private sphere is not a place of safety and refuge, what then becomes the source of protection from violence in the home? The antiviolence movement has generally relied on the state. As a result, there is often a disconnect between racial-justice and gender-justice groups. Racial-justice groups focus on the state as an agent of violence from which they need protection. Largely white antiviolence groups, and for that matter, many women-of-color groups, have seen the state as the solution to addressing intercommunal gender violence (Richie 1996). As Bhattacharjee (2000) notes, this has put antiviolence groups in the problematic position of marching against police brutality while simultaneously calling on the police to solve the problem of sexual/domestic violence as if it were two different institutions. As one example, I attended a meeting of tribally based antiviolence advocates who were discussing the need to address gender violence from the perspective of tribal sovereignty, and when the time came to develop actual strategies for addressing violence, the response was to call for more FBI agents on the reservation. Gender violence thus stands as the exception to the rule of opposing state surveillance. In this setup, the state becomes the solution to violence, so antiviolence programs must adopt the surveillance strategies of the state when they provide services. For instance, many domestic-violence shelters screen out women who are not documented, who have criminal histories, who are sex workers, or who have substance-abuse issues. One advocate told me that her program did background searches on potential clients and had them arrested if they had any outstanding warrants![6] This, despite the fact that these women have warrants out for their abusers and are trying to escape abusers who have forced them into criminal activity. Moreover, shelters are often run like prisons. As Emi Koyama brilliantly notes, women in shelters are constantly surveilled to make sure they conform to the behavior deemed fitting by the shelter staff. Koyama describes her experience in a shelter.

> I am a survivor of domestic violence. I am someone who has stayed in a shelter, back in 1994. My experience there was horrendous; I constantly felt the policing gaze of shelter workers across the half-open door, and feared "warnings" and punishments that seemed to be issued arbitrarily. No, to describe the practice as "arbitrary" would be inaccurate; it was clearly selective in terms of who gets them most frequently: the poor Black and Latina women with children, especially if they are in "recovery" from alcohol or drug "abuse." Snitching on other residents was actively encouraged: residents were rewarded for reporting rule violations of other residents and their children, even when the allegations were not exactly accurate. I did not know whom to trust. Eventually, the feeling of constant siege by shelter staff and all the "crazymaking" interactions pushed me over the edge, and I cut myself with a knife. Not surprisingly, they put me in a mental hospital, effectively ending my stay at the shelter before I could find a permanent, safer space to live.

Eventually, Koyama became involved in the antiviolence movement, where she worked for a shelter and found herself, against her politics, sometimes engaging in the same policing activities. When a woman who spoke Arabic called the shelter asking for services, Koyama's supervisor told her to tell the survivor that she needed to find another shelter. Koyama complied.

> This episode marked my last day working at the domestic violence shelter, which is more than two years ago now, but I continue to ache from this experience. Of course, this was not the first time that I questioned how shelters were being ran. I questioned everything: its "clean and sober" policy regarding substance use, its policy against allowing women to monitor their own medications, its use of threats and intimidations to control survivors, its labeling of ordinary disagreements or legitimate complaints as "disrespectful communication," its patronizing "life skills" and "parenting" classes, its seemingly random enforcement of rules that somehow always push women of color out of the shelter first. I hated just about everything that went on in a shelter, and I refused to participate in most of these. I never issued formal "warnings" against any of the residents, preferring instead to have dialogs about any problems as casually as possible. I pretended that I did not smell the alcohol in the women's breaths so long as their behaviors did not cause any problems for other residents. I never ever walked a woman to the bathroom and watched her as she peed into a little cup for drug tests, as the shelter policy expected of me to do. I did everything I could to sabotage the system I viewed as abusive: I was *disloyal*. But in many other situations, I failed. To this day, I ask myself why I did not simply ignore my supervisor's order on that day, let the woman come to the shelter and deal with the consequences later. (Koyama 2006, 215)

Essentially, shelter staff take on the role of abusers or prison guards in the lives of survivors.

Women-of-color advocates are in the difficult position of trying to dismantle the structures of settler colonialism and white supremacy in the long term, while securing safety for survivors of violence in the short term. Under these conditions of immediate threat, women of color will often become preoccupied with addressing immediate short-term crises. In addition, these state-driven surveillance strategies for addressing violence force us to see violence in specific ways that foreclose the possibility of seeing violence in other ways. In particular, these strategies frame survivors of violence as themselves the problem: survivors are "sick" and require healing from a professional who will monitor their behavior to ensure that they are healing properly. Those who do not "heal" are no longer deemed worthy of this "antiviolence" project. Thus, by seeing gender violence through the lens of the state, we can only see survivors as clients who need services, rather than as potential organizers who might dismantle social structures of violence.

Indigenous feminism reshapes the manner in which we engage surveillance studies, demonstrating that focus on the surveillance strategies of the state obscure the fact that the state is itself a surveillance strategy. There is not a pure or benign state beyond its strategies of surveillance. Yet, the state, rather than being recognized for its complicity in gender violence, has become the institution promising to protect women from domestic and sexual violence by providing a provisional "sanctuary" of sorts from the now criminally defined "other" that is the perpetrator of gender violence (Richie 2000). As I have argued elsewhere (A. Smith 2005a), the state is largely responsible for introducing gender violence into indigenous communities as part of a colonial strategy that follows a logic of sexual violence. Gender violence becomes the mechanism by which U.S. colonialism is effectively and pervasively exerted on native nations (A. Smith 2005a). The complicity of the state in perpetrating gender violence in other communities of color, through slavery, prisons, and border patrol, is also well documented (Bhattacharjee 2001; Davis 2003, 1981; A. Smith 2005b).

The state actually has no interest in gender or racial justice, since state laws are often, in practice, used against the people they supposedly protect. For instance, the *New York Times* recently reported that the effects of the strengthened anti-domestic violence legislation is that battered women kill their abusive partners less frequently; however, batterers do *not* kill their partners less frequently, and this is more true in black than in white communities (Butterfield 2000). With mandatory arrest laws, police officers frequently arrest those being battered rather than batterers. Thus, laws passed to protect battered women are actually protecting their batterers! Many scholars have analyzed the ineffectiveness of the criminal-justice system in addressing gender violence, particularly against poor women, women of color, sex workers, and queer communities (Richie 1996; A. Smith 2005b; Sokoloff 2005). The mainstream antiviolence movement's reliance on policies embedded in state violence to solve the problem of gender violence depends on what David Kazanjian (2003) refers to as the "colonizing trick": the liberal myth that the United States was founded on democratic principles that have eroded through post-9/11 policies, which obfuscates how the state was built on the pillars of capitalism, colonialism, and white supremacy.

Reliance on state surveillance prevents us from seeing other possibilities for ending violence, such as through communal organization that might be able to address violence more effectively. This is apparent in the mandate of much surveillance studies, which tends to focus on curtailing state surveillance without questioning the state itself. Consequently, this work does not explore possibilities for different forms of governance, ones not based on the logics of patriarchal and colonial surveillance. The work of indigenous activists to develop indigenous nations that are not based on the principles of domination, violence, and control cannot be seen—even by antiviolence activists (A. Smith 2008). An evocative example is an experience I had working with the group Incite! Women of Color Against Violence. I was conducting a workshop on community accountability. We were discussing the following question: if there was violence in your community, is there anything you could do that would not involve primarily working with the police? During this discussion, one woman stated that she lived in an apartment complex in which a man was battering his partner. She did not know what do to do, because she did not trust the police, but she also did not want the abuse to continue. Her comment made me realize how much our reliance on the state has impacted not only survivors of violence but also people who might think to intervene. It did not occur to this woman—nor might it necessarily occur to many of us in a similar situation—to organize in the apartment complex to do something. The only potential interveners in this situation seems to be ourselves as individuals or the state. It seems like our only response is either a privatized response to violence or a communal one that is state-driven. The result is that not only do we not "see" other solutions to the problem of violence, but we also become absolved from having to see the violence in the first place. Essentially, the apparatus of state surveillance, which allows the state to see violence, absolves us from the responsibility of having to see it.

A feminist approach to surveillance studies highlights not only the strategies of the state, but how people have internalized these same strategies, and it asks us to rethink our investment in the state. Without this intervention, the state is presumed to be our protector; we should only modify the manner in which the state protects. For example, during a survey I conducted for the Department of Justice on tribal communities' response to sexual assault, I found that most communities had not developed a response, because they assumed the federal government was taking care of the problem. In fact, as Amnesty International later documented, the federal government very rarely prosecuted sexual assault crimes in Indian country (Amnesty International 2007). Because of an investment in the state, tribal governments had not invested in their own possibilities for addressing violence.

When one asks the question "What can I do?," the answer is likely to call the police or to do nothing. But when one asks the question "What can *we* do?," a whole range of other possibilities arises. In fact, groups around the country have asked that question and have developed a variety of community-accountability models that do not rely primarily on police involvement (Chen et al. 2011).[7] Similarly, many native activists, such as Sarah Deer (2009), are active in organizing tribal communities to develop their own responses to sexual violence. Of course, all of these models have their own challenges. For example, will community-accountability models simply adopt the same strategies used by the state to address violence? How might these models develop without a romanticized notion of "community" that is not sexist, homophobic, or otherwise problematic—or the potentially problematic assumption that a "community" even exists in the first place? How might they address the immediate needs of survivors who may still require state intervention, even as they seek to eventually replace the state? These questions and others continue to inform the development of the community-accountability movement (Chen et al. 2011).

After 9/11, even radical scholars framed George Bush's policies as an attack on the U.S. Constitution. According to Judith Butler, Bush's policies were acts against "existing legal frameworks, civil, military, and international" (2004, 57). Amy Kaplan similarly describes Bush's policies as rendering increasingly more peoples under U.S. jurisdiction as "less deserving of . . . constitutional rights" (2005, 853). Thus, Bush's strategies were deemed a suspension of law. Progressive activists and scholars accused him of eroding U.S. democracy and civil liberties. Under this framework, progressives are called in to uphold the law, defend U.S. democracy, and protect civil liberties against "unconstitutional" actions. Surveillance studies often carries similar presumptions. That is, this field is concerned with the "rapidly increasing influence of surveillance in our daily lives and in the operation of very large-scale operations" (Lyon 2007, 9). It is concerned with what is presumed to be the increasing erosion of civil liberties and the loss of privacy that this surveillance entails. It takes the state for granted, but is concerned that the state not overstep its proper boundaries. And yet, from the perspective of indigenous peoples, the eye of the state has always been genocidal, because the problem is not primarily the surveillance strategies of the state, but the state itself.

If we were to employ a settler colonial analytic, we would see the growth in surveillance strategies less as a threat to the democratic ideals of the United States than as a fulfillment of them. As these surveillance strategies grow, they impact everyone, not just native peoples, because the logic of settler colonialism structures the world for everyone. In particular, surveillance strategies not only allow the state to see certain things, but prevent us from seeing the state as the settler colonial, white supremacist, and heteropatriarchal formation that it is.

Notes

1. See Byrd 2011; Byron 2002; Han 2011; Wynter 1997.

2. See, for instance, Allen 1986; Anderson 1993; Namias 1993; A. Smith 2005a.

3. Lyon does note, "But privacy is both contested, and confined in its scope. Culturally and historically relative, privacy has limited relevance in some contexts" (2007, 19).

4. See, for example, Bhattacharjee 2001b; D. Roberts 1991.

5. Out of respect for person involved and in keeping with organizational confidentiality policies, Bhattacharjee does not give extended details of the incident.

6. Personal conversation, 12 February 2002. The advocate with whom I spoke does not wish to have her program identified.

7. Community-accountability models do not presume that we can expect to engage in "pure" strategies untainted by the current system. The goal is not to tell survivors that they can never call the police or engage the criminal-justice system. The question is not whether a survivor should call the police. The question is why we have given survivors no option but to call the police.

2

SURVEILLANCE AND THE WORK
OF ANTITRAFFICKING

From Compulsory Examination to International Coordination

LAURA HYUN YI KANG

By hailing different configurations of women as objects and subjects of surveillance, the long history of efforts to uncover and combat the "traffic in women" offers an instructive case for feminist surveillance studies at this important moment of field formation. If a feminist critique and modification of an already existing yet discernibly unfeminist surveillance studies through a focused attention on women under surveillance is the task at hand, we might attend to how public outcry against the traffic in women has activated and rationalized state scrutiny and control over female bodies when it comes to disease, sexuality, morality, and labor. The Contagious Disease Acts (1864, 1866, 1869) in England created a "morality police" and authorized officers to subject women suspected of prostitution to compulsory "surgical examination" for venereal disease and forced confinement in a "lock hospital" if they were infected. This example reminds us to bear in mind the historical layers of targeted material-corporeal violence that conditions more contemporary technologically mediated and disembodied modes of surveillance.

The history of antitrafficking compels attention to the transnational and racist dimensions of the surveillance of women. The practices of compulsory examination, treatment, and detention of local women were a crucial component of British colonial administration throughout Asia in the early 1800s. With the spread of imperial settlements and the surge of international labor migrations in the second half of the nineteenth century, borders and transit hubs such as ports and railway stations came to be seen as dangerous vectors in the transmission of disease, especially from the colonies to the metropoles. While the sensationalist discourse of "white slave traffic" engendered sympathetic figurations of female vulnerability, it also fueled and justified suspicious regard of traveling female bodies. Alarm about the high rates of venereal diseases among soldiers in the First World War (1914–1918) galvanized a new round of concerted state actions to monitor and regulate transnational female movement and sexual labor (Gorman 2008, 200).

The early history of antitrafficking includes determined efforts by certain women to contest state tactics of state surveillance as discriminatory and dehumanizing in what we might identify as a determinedly antisurveillance feminism. An oft-repeated account traces the origin of the international movement against the "traffic in women" to the concerted opposition to the Contagious Disease Acts. On the other hand, if we follow the suggestion of Ummni Khan's essay in this volume, where a distinctive form of "feminist surveillance" is the phenomenon under critical scrutiny, we should attend to how the antitrafficking work of women social reformers and feminist activists have aided and abetted state scrutiny and control over both female *and* male bodies. The feminist project of making women and gender visible within and across numerous disciplines and interdisciplinary studies is rendered especially contradictory when articulated in terms of a knowledge field that starts off from the problematization of visibility as a mode of subjection and regulation. Surveillance betrays and degrades the liberatory promise of visibility.

Then too, trafficking frustrates the sweeping reach of surveillance. As one of the most hyperbolized and enduring subjects of journalistic exposés, academic scholarship, government investigations, and international relations, the traffic in women bears an immense and prolific archive of documentation and analysis. However, as activists, policymakers, and academic experts have repeatedly pointed out, the clandestine, coercive, dispersed, and mobile aspects of trafficking resist unequivocal verification and clear representation. The archive of antitrafficking offers up a long, jagged history of both diverse surveillance rationales and tactics, as well as multiple surveillance failures and impossibilities. In this essay I argue that a persistent racist preoccupation with the fate of *white* women demarcates one such fault line. Even as the invocation of a generic "traffic in women and girls" in the early twentieth century expanded the reach of the problem and the corresponding modalities of vigilance, state and civil surveillance of trafficking have always been differentially entrained on different female bodies as vulnerable or dangerous.

The work of antitrafficking in the League of Nations during the interwar period is particularly instructive for examining the multiple contradictions outlined above. The League served as an important historical and institutional pivot between the imperial regimes carried over from the nineteenth century and the post-Second World War emergence of newly decolonized countries and the global governance regime associated with the United Nations. In the aftermath of the First World War, the traffic in women occasioned a compelling rationale and platform for the coming together of nations with divergent interests, shifting borders, and unequal resources. From its inception, the League of Nations was engaged with addressing the traffic as an urgent and indisputably international problem. Article 23c of its covenant thus "entrusted the League with the general supervision over the execution of agreements with regard to the traffic in women and children." Calibrating the surveillance of women's cross-border movements among states and nongovernmental organizations was crucial to the incipient conceptualization and enactment of international cooperation. From 30 June to 1 July 1921, the League convened an International Conference on the Traffic in Women and Children in Geneva. In his opening speech, the Belgian foreign minister Paul Hymans heralded the occasion: "Hitherto treaties of peace have only dealt with questions of frontiers, indemnities and commercial and financial interests. For the first time in the history of humanity other interests are therein included and among them the dignity of human labor and the respect for women and children" (quoted in Metzger 2007, 59). In the spirit of this new internationalism, it was suggested that the phrase "traffic in women and children" replace "white slavery," thereby "making it clear that measures adopted should be applied to all races alike" (League of Nations 1927, 8). Such universalizing platitudes obscured the imperial genealogy, with its persistent racial demarcations and national interests, of the discriminating and targeted surveillance of women's bodies, sexuality, work, and migration. In principle, the framing of the traffic in women as a global human problem necessitating international cooperation and coordination rendered these member states and their varied laws and policies regarding sex work, labor, age of consent, emigration, and immigration the target of a new supranational regime of surveillance, judgment, and proper accreditation. This framing held out the potential of clarifying the uneven sexual economies and topographies, which had been carved out by racism, patriarchy, and competing empires. In practice, however, even after the move to replace "white slave traffic" with the more neutral and inclusive "traffic in women," a distinction and separation continued between "white women" and their racialized others. Persistent racial obsessions and racist blind spots impeded and exposed the limits of the League's attempts to coordinate international policy and action against the traffic in women by implementing what were deemed newly effective modes of undercover surveillance and expert data gathering.

On 15 December 1920, the Assembly of the League of Nations adopted several linked resolutions. In addition to urging those governments who had signed the 1904 agreement and the 1910 Convention for the Suppression of White Slave Traffic to put them into operation "immediately," another resolution called on the League's Council to convene an International Conference of Traffic in Women and Children, which would be charged with the "task of endeavouring to harmonise the opinions of the different Governments in order that common action may be taken" (League of Nations 1921b, 596). Toward that end, the Assembly authorized the Secretariat to issue to all member states a questionnaire that inquired about domestic laws regarding trafficking, the penalties prescribed for specific cases, and statistics for prosecutions and convictions. The 1921 International Conference in Geneva concluded with the recommendation that each member nation submit annual reports on both the traffic in their territories and their domestic antitrafficking efforts. The League of Nations thus took on the role of an international clearinghouse. It also passed a new, more expansive International Convention for the Suppression of the Traffic in Women and Children in September 1921, which increased the age of consent of women engaged in prostitution from twenty to twenty-one. The League also appointed a permanent Advisory Committee on the Traffic of Women and Children, comprising nine national "delegates" and five "assessors," each representing an international voluntary organization. When the League sponsored its own official investigation of the traffic in the 1920s, it proceeded in two stages and resulted in two separate publications. The first, published in 1927 and titled *Report of the Special Body of Experts on Traffic in Women and Children* (hereafter, the 1927 Report), comprised 270 pages. The second report, published in 1932 and titled *Commission of Enquiry into Traffic in Women and Children in the East* (hereafter, the 1932 Report), was much longer, at 556 pages. Paul

Knepper has hailed the two inquiries together as not only "the first world-wide study of human trafficking" but also "the first ever social scientific study of a global social problem" (2011, 96).

The 1927 Report was notable for inaugurating the use of a traveling commission, which comprised specially trained "experts" who visited 112 cities and districts across twenty-eight countries to conduct "on the spot" inquiries. In addition to producing first-person observations of local conditions, these experts interviewed over 6,500 individuals, including government officials, law-enforcement officers, and antitrafficking voluntary associations in these locations. The commission also relied on undercover investigations by specially contracted agents and sometimes met directly with members of the "underworld," including procurers, madams, and prostitutes, in order to uncover "facts" that might be hidden or misrepresented by official statistics and national reports. Thus, the 1927 Report was held up at the time as having "revolutionized League methods in the investigation of social problems" (Boeckel 1929, 234).

Three specific aspects of these two reports compromise the claims to both their international expansiveness and their empirical innovations. First, both reports were blatantly concerned with the fate of *white* women. The 1932 Report is especially striking on this point in its clear demarcation between "Traffic in Occidental Women in Asia" and "Traffic in Asian Women" and in its unabashed concern about the sexual fate of Russian women refugees in China. This provides evidence that the imperialist, racist, and nationalist foundations of early British state regulation of and voluntary vigilance against prostitution from the nineteenth century preconditioned the later antitrafficking work of the League of Nations. Second, there was a specifically American genealogy for the 1927 Report's use of "on the spot" and "undercover" investigations, which had been deployed earlier as part of the "social hygiene" movement in the United States. Third, there were substantive differences in methodology and composition between the two reports, which demonstrate the epistemological blind spots imposed by persistent racialist and racist thinking.

I

The League's racially motivated and demarcated handling of the traffic in women must be framed in relation to a longer history of imperial expansion, labor exploitation, and gendered labor migration in the nineteenth century. Well before the domestic enactment of the Contagious Disease

Acts in England in the 1860s, the practices of medical surveillance, forced treatment, and physical isolation of women were a crucial component of British colonial administration throughout Asia in the early 1800s. A lock hospital was established in the Madras presidency in 1805, and others could be found throughout the British Empire in Asia, including in Penang, in the Malay Peninsula (Burton 1994, 130). In her comprehensive study *Prostitution, Race, and Politics*, Philippa Levine writes, "It is in India, however, that we see the workings of the early system most vividly." Levine continues: "William Burke, inspector general of hospitals for the army in India, outlined his ideal plan in 1827: a register of prostitutes; their compulsory examination fortnightly, with certification for the healthy and hospitalization for the infected; and punitive measures for women failing to appear for examination. These principles would become the core of the empire wide regime enacted three decades later" (2003, 38).[1] Thereafter, Hong Kong's Ordinance No. 12 was passed, in 1857, which mandated brothel registration and regular medical examination. Since "the ultimate goal of regulated prostitution was to provide 'clean native women' for foreign military personnel," the ordinances in Hong Kong were "effectively limited to Asian women servicing foreigners" (Scully 2001, 81–82). British-administered lock hospitals could also be found throughout Asia, including treaty ports in Japan.

In addition to the presence of British colonists and soldiers throughout Asia, several significant migrations in the nineteenth century shaped the peculiar contours of the 1932 Report. A migratory route of women who were "typically already professional sex workers" from Europe and the U.S. to China began with the Opium War (1841–1842) and accelerated after the introduction of steamship travel and the opening of the Suez Canal, in 1869 (Scully 2001, 79). The rapid economic development of port cities like Hong Kong and Singapore was accompanied by the growth of large red-light districts employing mostly Chinese and Japanese women, which were tolerated by colonial authorities as a "necessary evil" to placate the large population of migrant male laborers (Warren 1993, 34). In her account of the "traffic in sexual labor," Eileen Scully (2001) includes Chinese women's immigration to the United States in the 1840s as an early example of the traffic, and she further points to the presence of Chinese and Japanese women in Latin America, Southeast Asia, Australia, and South Africa by the late 1800s. Borders, ports, and other transit zones came to be regarded as especially dangerous and were closely monitored to ward off diseases. The increasingly vociferous discourse of venereal disease as a "racial poison" and a "racial threat" in the 1860s co-incided with an actual decline in infections (Levine 2003, 5). This setup expressed anxieties about racial purity in the face of both increased white female emigration and the immigration of nonwhite others.

The authors of the 1927 Report acknowledge its link to earlier strands of antitrafficking work and its internationalization, which began in England and Western Europe in the nineteenth century. In 1869 Josephine Butler and other reformers founded the Ladies National Association (LNA) for the Repeal of the Contagious Disease Acts. Regarding the compulsory physical examinations as "symbolic rape," the LNA "meticulously kept track of the number of examinations in which no venereal disease was discovered" and considered them to be "the central inequity of the Acts" (Bristow 1977, 82–83). Butler later established the British, Continental, and General Abolitionist Federation, in 1875, which extended the movement to abolish licensed brothels to the continent, since it was believed that the system of state-regulated prostitution in certain continental countries like France encouraged and facilitated the cross-national trafficking of women and girls. The federation convened an International Congress in 1877 and played a crucial role in sponsoring and financially underwriting targeted and on-the-ground investigations of the traffic. The 1927 Report mentions how their efforts led to an official British inquiry into the traffic of women and girls to the continent, which in turn resulted in the 1885 Criminal Law Amendment, as a model precedent for how concerted investigations could lead to effective regulation.

After the repeal of domestic laws in 1889, the continued use of contagious-diseases ordinances in the British colonies and protectorates shifted the focus of antitrafficking measures to these overseas territories. The British, Continental, and General Abolitionist Federation was renamed the British Committee for the Abolition of the State Regulated Vice in India and throughout the British Dominions. In addition to interviewing soldiers returning from abroad, the organization employed both paid agents and voluntary supporters, who conducted investigations in India in 1891 and 1892, and also in Hong Kong, Shanghai, and the Straits Settlements (Levine 2003, 104). The work of antitrafficking enjoined and enabled certain Anglo American women to participate actively in an early form of transnational knowledge production that predated and presaged the League of Nations inquiries. In 1882 Butler personally encouraged the American missionaries Elizabeth Wheeler Andrew and Katharine Bushnell, of the Women's Christian Temperance Union, to undertake an onsite investigation of trafficking and regulated brothels in India, which was later published as *The Queen's Daughters in India* (1899). Andrew and Bushnell reported that "regulation was rampant and that Indian women submitted rather than face expulsion from the cantonments" (Burton 1994, 136). It is significant to note that their vigilant gaze was also trained on the imperial state and its "sanctioning of incorrigible soldierly behavior" (Levine 2003, 104).

In the 1890s there emerged another strand of antitrafficking work in Britain that was affiliated with social-purity reformers, who advocated for the state oversight and regulation of prostitution. The National Vigilance Association (NVA) began to organize an international campaign against "white slave traffic" and garnered the support and endorsement of state officials. It also convened an International Congress on White Slave Traffic in London, in June 1899, which the 1927 Report hailed as "the starting-point of a complete organization for defensive and active measures against the traffic" (League of Nations 1927, 8). The NVA spearheaded a new organization, named the International Bureau (IB) for the Suppression of the Traffic in Women, which fostered "a close and permanent agreement . . . among the philanthropic and charitable societies of different countries to communicate to each other information as to the emigration of women under suspicious circumstances, and to undertake to protect the emigrants on their arrival."[2] The various national committees of the IB became actively engaged in the work of monitoring and managing the transnational movements of European women. In addition to being prominently led by men, the NVA and the IB cultivated and enjoyed a close relationship to the state. They received some financial support from their respective governments and also worked with law enforcement and immigration officials in the exclusion and repatriation of foreign women suspected of being prostitutes (Limoncelli 2006, 51). Such heightened vigilance did not, however, translate into increased protection of women from exploitation. Writing of the period from 1895 to the First World War, Scully points out, "Policing and regulatory responses exacerbated the situation, as migratory prostitutes under siege became more reliant on pimps and more vulnerable to corrupt officials" (Scully 2001, 84).

The IB played a leading role in coordinating the first International Agreement for the Suppression of the White Slave Traffic, which was signed on 18 May 1904, as well as the 1910 International Convention for the Suppression of White Slave Traffic, which the League of Nations later adopted and expanded. Under the auspices of antitrafficking, both the 1904 and 1910 documents asserted the signatory state's responsibility for monitoring the transnational movement of girls and women. According to Article 1 of the 1904 Agreement, the signatory countries would "establish or name some authority charged with the co-ordination of all information relative to the procuring of women or girls for immoral purposes abroad" (League of Nations 1927, 197). Article 2 called for the parties "to have a watch kept, especially in railways stations, ports of embarkation, and *en route*, for persons in charge of women and girls destined for an immoral life" (ibid.). This concerted surveillance over traveling female bodies was later incorporated almost verbatim in the questionnaire that the League of Nations circulated in 1921: "4. Has the government taken any steps to have ports and railway stations watched for the purpose of checking the Traffic in Women and Children? If not undertaking this duty to themselves, have they delegated this responsibility, and if so, to what agency?" (League of Nations 1921a, 230). Articles 3 and 4 of the 1904 Agreement, which addressed the matter of the repatriation of "women and girls of foreign nationality who are prostitutes," were incorporated as question 5: "Has the Government taken steps to ascertain from foreign prostitutes the reasons for which they left their countries? If so, what has been the outcome of this enquiry?" (ibid.). The internationalization of the work of antitrafficking necessitated the move from "white slave traffic" to the more universal rubric of the "traffic in women and children," but much of the discourse and subsequent work of the League of Nations maintained a hierarchical racial distinction. Question 8 in the 1921 questionnaire explicitly focused on protective measures against "White Slave Traffic." Several annual government reports also continued to deploy the term. The persistence of the use of the term *white slave traffic* was not residual but crucial to the fashioning of international consensus in an era marked by both imperialist jockeying and uneven nation formations. In proposing a new International Convention for the Suppression of the Traffic in Women and Children at the second meeting of the Assembly of the League in September 1921, the British delegation framed it as "an unprecedented opportunity for the League to demonstrate political will and determination" (Metzger 2007, 60). The 1921 Convention bore a notable exception in its Article 14: "Any Member or State signing the present Convention may declare that the signature does not include any or all of its colonies, overseas possessions, protectorates or territories under its sovereignty or authority, and may subsequently adhere separately on behalf of any such colony, overseas possession, protectorate or territory so excluded in its declaration." Thus, the very assertion of a new international agreement entailed explicit sanctions of imperial "double standards" imposed onto different women's bodies.

II

The exercise of the League's "political will and determination" was further complicated by the unknowable contours of the purported problem. Trafficking is difficult to espy, document, and control. The two reports and the archives of the *League of Nations Official Journal* repeatedly demonstrate a fissure between convincing demonstrations of diligent surveillance and acknowledgment of the impossibility of a thorough monitoring and documentation of the phenomenon. Since the League, and especially its Social Section which included the Advisory Committee on the Traffic of Women and Children, lacked the financial resources and administrative structure to gather specific details about local and national conditions, it was still largely dependent on official government communiqués and "field reports" submitted by voluntary associations such as the IB. There was the possibility for underreporting the extent and severity of the conditions by state authorities. Pointing to how several of the countries represented on the advisory committee, including France, Italy, and Japan, did not move toward abolition in practice, Jessica Pliley goes so far as to assert "that many governments wanted to appear [to be] actively addressing the problem of trafficking without having to take any meaningful action" (2010, 105–6). Further complicating questions of objectivity and accountability, Great Britain, France, Portugal, Japan, the Netherlands, and the United States submitted replies and reports on behalf of their colonies, overseas possessions, protectorates, or territories.[3] As well, in the first decades of the twentieth century, many nations were in the active and contested process of state-building, making it difficult to attribute such reports to a single, organized bureaucratic agency. In her study of prostitution in Shanghai in the early twentieth century, Gail Hershatter points out that "no systematic statistics were collected" and further questions the record-keeping practices of the state: "Counting, like classifying and regulating, is not a neutral activity. The creation of statistics, in Shanghai as elsewhere, was part of a state-building process, an intrusive aspect of the project of modernity, often resisted by the people it sought to incorporate. Numbers that give the impression of precision were collected by an inconsistent group for changing reasons from a population that had every reason to lie" (1997, 38). There was also some skepticism about the "field reports" of voluntary organizations, a tendency to dismiss them as exaggerated and sensationalistic.

On 21 March 1923, Grace Abbott, an advisory-committee representative from the United States, submitted a memorandum recommending a new international enquiry sponsored by the League. Its scope would be ambitiously broad and multidimensional.

> Geographically the investigation should include, if possible, the principal cities of the world, but, if this is not possible, typical cities should be selected from which there is reason to believe the traffic is or is not being carried on, those in which regulated houses and those in which abolition is the policy, those situated in countries in which prostitutes and all those who live or benefit by prostitution are excluded from admission, and those whose laws regulating immigration make no or inadequate provisions for immoral persons. (League of Nations 1927, 50)

Note how three different kinds of cities were delineated according to state regulations regarding prostitution and immigration restriction, suggesting that an assessment of the efficacy of state regulation itself was at stake. The rubric of "traffic in women" thus enabled a more far-reaching and probing investigation into a broad range of national laws and enforcement mechanisms. Abbott went on to call for the need for an on-the-ground investigation to supplement the limits of the information provided by governments and voluntary associations.

> From official sources, the facts as to the administration of laws designed to eliminate the traffic can be learned. To secure the information as to the traffic itself, it will be necessary to send to the cities included in the survey, agents of high standing with special training and experience to make personal and unofficial investigations. It is recognised that such investigations are difficult, not to say dangerous; but they are absolutely necessary to secure the facts to refute sensational exaggerations or general denials as to the traffic and—what would seem to be for the Committee of supreme importance—an intelligent basis for a sound programme for international co-operation for the suppression of the traffic, if it is found to exist. (Ibid.)

Having earned a master's degree in political science from the University of Chicago and worked with Jane Adams at Hull House, Abbott was a prominent member of a new generation of social workers who "crafted their professional identities and asserted their expertise by embracing scientific practice methods, with an emphasis on investigation, detailed case records, scientific nomenclature, and social diagnosis" (Kennedy 2008, 28). Before serving as the director of the Immigrant's Protective League and being appointed as the first chief of the U.S. Children's Bureau, Abbott had published numerous articles, in such venues as the *American Journal of Sociology*, on a range of issues, including immigrant labor, social welfare, child labor, and juvenile delinquency. Thus, her important role in proposing these investigations demonstrate the early twentieth-century commingling and cooperation of the state, the university, and private philanthropy in the work of surveillance over certain women's bodies.

In addition to Abbott's instigation, the leading position of U.S. actors in overseeing and funding this investigation merits closer scrutiny, especially given that the United States was not a formal member of the League of Nations. As proof and as a model of the efficaciousness of the investigation, Abbott invoked in the memorandum a U.S. Senate inquiry on the "Importation and Harbouring of Women for Immoral Purposes" in 1908–1909, which found that women and girls from Europe and also from Asia were brought to the United States. She stated that "the authorities charged with the enforcement of American law as well as private organisations in the United States interested in the abolition of prostitution will, I am sure, be glad to give all possible assistance" (League of Nations 1927, 50). As appreciatively acknowledged in the introduction to the 1927 Report, both multinational investigations were made possible by donations from the American Bureau of Social Hygiene, which provided $75,000 and then $125,000, respectively, to the two inquiries. The Bureau of Social Hygiene (BSH) was established in 1913 by John D. Rockefeller Jr. and fellow "social purity" reformers as a private philanthropic organization devoted to investigating and combating prostitution. Rockefeller had previously served as the chair of a special grand jury commissioned by the County of New York, in 1910, to investigate the "organized traffic in women for immoral purposes." Subsequently, he envisioned that "this permanent organization, small and operating in relative secrecy, would have some power to effect a solution to the social evil that a more open democratic process would not have" (Gunn 1999, 104). In contrast to the moralism and sensationalism of the earlier purity crusades against the "white slave traffic," the BSH sought to achieve "instrumental reform that was efficient, scientific, elitist" by engaging trained experts to study social problems such as prostitution and venereal disease (Brandt 1987, 39). Before providing financial support for the League's inquiries into the traffic in women, the BSH funded investigations into prostitution in the United States and Europe and published the findings (Kneeland 1913; Flexner 1914; Woolston, 1921). The BSH also financed social programs, such as the Laboratory of Social Hygiene in Bedford Hills: "Women sentenced to this reformatory underwent a battery of physical and psychological tests aimed at isolating factors which contributed to prostitution" (Brandt 1987, 39). Thus, the emerging methods of the social sciences came to supplement and legitimate rather than supplant older private and public modes of discipline and punishment.

The BSH also funded the American Social Hygiene Association (ASHA), which merged two older organizations, the American Federation for Sex Hygiene and the American Vigilance Association, and focused on combating venereal disease through sex education. The ASHA was led by William F. Snow, a professor and public-health expert, and included Jane Addams, a close mentor to Abbott. The ASHA applied what it considered "forward-looking scientific approaches" and private investigators to uncover and document pressing social problems such as prostitution (Knepper 2012, 7). Snow also served as chairman of the League of Nation's Special Body of Experts on the Traffic in Women and Children from 1924 to 1928. He, in turn, was responsible for the appointment of Bascom Johnson, who had served as head of the legal affairs at ASHA and as the director of investigations of the two enquiries. During the First World War, both Snow and Johnson successfully worked with the U.S. Army Commission on Training Camp Activities to control the epidemic of venereal diseases by closing down or moving red-light districts that were near military encampments.[4] Their efforts were related to a nationwide wave of vice commissions in the 1910s, whose investigations led to more repressive laws and policies against women suspected of engaging in prostitution: "Many states established reformatories for women . . . and required medical examinations for venereal diseases prior to marriage" (Lubove 1962, 328). Snow had also served as the vice president of the American Eugenics Society. Eugenicist ideologies of "racial preservation" through forced sterilization and immigration restriction were expressed in the ASHA's *Journal of Social Hygiene*. One article begins, "For any country at any given stage of advancement of its arts, and of exhaustion of its resources, there is an optimum number of inhabitants up to which the country can continue to increase its population without producing an undue pressure upon subsistence. . . . A well-ordered community will strive to reach this adjustment. It may do so by encouraging or discouraging emigration, or by raising or lowering the birth-rate" (R. H. Johnson 1919, 223). Another article, titled "Eugenical Sterilization in the United States," argues that "the relation between the inheritable qualities of our immigrants and the destiny of the American nation is very close. . . . Thus, if the American nation desires to upbuild or even to maintain its standard of natural qualities, it must forbid the addition through immigration to our human breeding-stock of persons of a lower natural hereditary constitution than that which constitutes the desired standard" (Laughlin 1920, 530–31).

The significance of monitoring immigration was prominent in the expanded "Questionnaire issued by the special body of experts on the traffic in women and children" on 3 April 1924, which was printed as annex 2 of the 1927 Report. In addition to requesting government statistics on the "number, age, nationality and length of residence of foreign women who are known to be regularly engaged in prostitution, either in licensed houses or elsewhere," the lengthy, multipart question 5 asks for "any available statistics regarding immigration and emigration for the years 1919–1923," including the "total number of male and female immigrants classified according to nationality," and it specifies "foreign women who have been admitted in the last five years . . . classified according to age-group (under 18, 18–21, 21–30, and over 30), and according to occupations" (League of Nations 1927, 196).

The determining influence of this distinctly U.S. preoccupation with prostitution, immigration, and racial purity in shaping the 1927 enquiry was largely eclipsed by highlighting the incontrovertible rigor of direct observation of "facts" by trained experts. The inclusion of professional women such as Alma Sundquist of Sweden, a physician who served on the three-member traveling commission, further provided an aura of legitimacy. Even as the authors of the 1927 Report ceremoniously acknowledged "the most cordial response" from all the countries that were investigated, "with the result that the representatives of the Body of Experts were given every facility on carrying out their work and received the active help of officials and other persons concerned" (League of Nations 1927, 5), the authenticity and reliability of these independent "expert" observations were repeatedly upheld. Pointing to how Bascom Johnson's "legal training and long experience of social studies proved invaluable," the authors added that the commission was "assisted by a group of highly qualified investigators" (ibid.). The undercover methods used had been refined in the earlier anti-vice campaigns in the United States. Of the mostly U.S. male field operatives Johnson employed, Paul Kinsie, who directed the ASHA's undercover research program, played an especially key role. In his assessment of Kinsie's field reports filed in the ASHA archives, Knepper concludes that "it is clear that he was an excellent ethnographer. . . . Kinsie focused on activities and relationships that comprised the White slave trade, such as tricks for evading surveillance at the border" (2012, 13). In an article relaying a detailed account of how the enquiry came into being, Dame Rachel Crowdy, the head of the Social Section of the League, was particularly laudatory about how the expert commission was "lucky enough to get hold of eight or ten very courageous and very resourceful men and women, and for the last three years those people have been working as part of the underworld" (1927, 157). The League reports conferred both expert confirmation and empirical validation on the traffic in women as a real and actionable international phenomenon.[5]

III

Rather than herald their innovation and scientific rigor, I would argue that the League reports attest to the shared genealogy and porosity among undercover, state-sanctioned, and academic modes of knowledge production, and to how each served to prop up the factual aura of the others' truth claims. Instigated, underwritten, and carried out by particularly interested U.S. agents, the "revolutionary" method of employing undercover agents could not be applied in the second investigation in the Far East. As Knepper notes, "Because the traffic in women in Asia involved Asian women, [Johnson] had 'little use for [a] white investigator'" (2012, 21–22). Instead, the 1932 Report relied on interviews with government officials and testimonies from local voluntary organizations. Thus, the racially discriminating and geopolitically selective origins of antitrafficking in the imperial age were reinscribed in the shift to "international co-operation" built on "expert" and "on-the-spot" investigations.

More significant than the method of information acquisition, the two reports differed in their composition and organization. The 1932 Report imposed a clear racial demarcation between "Occidental women" and "Asiatic women." Indeed, the authors outline two possibilities that had been considered for the report's organization. The first option, of "dividing it into chapters according to the territories visited," would have demonstrated "the problem under enquiry in the light of the social and economic conditions, laws and administrative measures of each territory" (League of Nations 1932, 18). However, with such an approach, "the actual stages of international traffic would appear in fragmentary form with no proper link." In addition, the nation-based organization would produce "a considerable amount of duplication." The commission ultimately elected the second approach, of dividing the report into "chapters treating the problem according to racial groups of victims," because "this arrangement, which, like the international traffic itself, disregards political frontiers, would convey to the readers a more living picture of all causes, methods and consequences of traffic, following it through all stages from place of origin to the place of destination" (ibid.).

The first section of the 1932 Report, "The Findings of the Inquiry," opens with the two racial distinctions clearly denoted in paragraph headings titled "Traffic in Occidental Women in Asia" and, immediately following, "Traffic in Asiatic Women." Although the authors later note that "the bulk of the traffic with which this report is concerned is traffic in Asiatic women from one country of Asia to another," they first point out that "there is a certain movement of occidental prostitutes to the Orient, while hardly any oriental women are known to go for purposes of prostitution to the Occident." The overriding concern with interracial sexual relations, which is categorized as a matter of "international traffic," is expressed and explained in the further subdivision of "occidental women."

> Within the Occidental victims of traffic in Asiatic countries, the most serious problem and one which is fraught with the danger of further development concerns Russian women of the refugee class in Northern China and Manchuria. It is not in the fully accepted sense of the word a traffic between Occident and Orient, as the victims either are residents of China or come from the Asiatic parts of Russian territory. But even when staged entirely within the borders of China, it clearly bears the stamp of international traffic. (League of Nations 1932, 21)

Note the slippage between interracial and international. Even as the rubric of the "international" was marshaled to herald a new, racially neutral concern about the traffic in women and to authorize the League with an unprecedented supranational political will, this passage demonstrates a persistent inability to transcend the racialist and racist worldview of empire. The remarks go on to point out how the demand for Occidental women was decreasing in Asia, adding that, "provided efforts to check traffic [were] maintained, there [would be] no need to fear a revival of the conditions of twenty or thirty years [before], when considerable numbers of Occidental prostitutes, beginning with the countries nearer their homes, went farther and farther afield in the Orient in the various stages of their search for new opportunities to exercise their profession" (ibid.). The assurances against interracial sexual contact is soon reiterated: "Traffic in the East is characterized by the fact that prostitutes going to foreign countries do so exclusively in search of clients among their own countrymen abroad" (ibid., 22). The summary ends with a paragraph subtitled "Less Cynicism than in Occident," which notes that even as the "Asiatic prostitutes" had to contend with more deplorable working conditions, "there was a noticeable absence of vulgar appeal to sensuality, such as is often displayed by occidental prostitutes" (ibid.).

The following substantial section, on "Racial Groups of Victims," is further subdivided into these distinguished groups: "Occidental Women (Excepting Russians of the Far East) as Victims of the Traffic to the Orient"; "Russian Women in the Far East as Victims of International Traffic"; "Chinese Victims of International Traffic"; and "Women of Japanese Nationality as Victims of International Traffic." These sections are followed by shorter sections on "Filipino Women," "Annamite Women" (in reference to women from the Union of Indochina), "Siamese Women," "Women of Malay Race," "Indian Women," "Persian Women," "Arab and Other Women of the Near East," and, finally, "African Victims of International Traffic in Asia." In spite of this vast range of geographical locations and ethnic diversity, the 1932 Report expresses the most urgent concern for the plight of the Russian women refugees as truly "unwilling" victims, forced to engage in prostitution and interracial sexual relations with Chinese men.

Despite the questionable methods, these reports were widely read and endorsed, fueling further enactments against and surveillance of women's cross-border movements. The antitrafficking efforts also fed, with mixed results, into calls for the greater involvement of women in policing and in public patrols. Some women activists publicly objected to how the expanding reach of the protocols and conventions would delimit the mobility of *all* women (Pliley 2010, 101–2). There have been divergent assessments of the prominence of the traffic in women in the League of Nation's activities. Some scholars see it as an achievement and vindication of the hard-fought efforts of women's groups who sent delegates to Geneva to campaign for a range of issues, including an equal-rights treaty. To be sure, the multimodal work of antitrafficking created an opening for a limited number of women professionals and activists in this newly emergent international framework of advocacy and governance. Fröken Forchhammer addressed the topic in the first speech ever given by a woman to the Assembly of the League. The Social Section of the League, which was charged with addressing the traffic in women and children, was the only section headed by a woman, Dame Rachel Crowdy. The permanent Advisory Committee on the Traffic in Women and Children included, in addition to Grace Abbott, Paulina Luisi, a physician from Uruguay, and Princess Bandini of Italy, who also served on the League's eight-member international committee of experts. In 1922 the secretary general took special note of how the Advisory Committee on the Traffic in Women and Children "contained a larger representation of women than any other Committee of the League, since the question with which it dealt required the fullest co-operation of women."[6] Noting the absence of the issue in the first draft of the covenant for the League, from February 1919, Karina Leppanen concludes, "It demonstrates the fact that feminist interests were highly visible in the League and shows how successfully women and feminist organisations lobbied the League from the start" (2007, 527). Stephanie Limoncelli is more measured, and ultimately skeptical. Pointing to the initial resistance from the mostly male leadership, she argues that "officials wanted to ensure coordinated policy for overseeing existing international conventions already signed by member states, including the 1904 and 1910 accords dealing with the white slavery traffic" (2010, 73). Limoncelli concludes, "Bureaucratic logic rather than humanitarian concern seems to have led the League to its anti-trafficking work" (ibid., 73–74). I have proposed a third framing of the League's work of antitrafficking, one that demonstrates how the coordinated surveillance of women's sexuality, labor, and migration made international cooperation thinkable, even as this very effort testified to the intractability of racialist and racist divisions that precluded its effective enactment.

Notes

1. Levine also points out that there was some variation in how infected women were treated, including expulsion from areas near military encampments or cutting off their hair to deter public presence: "In other colonies, the means chosen were less dramatic and ritualized, but still focused on women's mobility: the governing assumption was that knowing women's whereabouts and having the ability to register, detain, or expel them bodily was desirable" (2003, 39).

2. "Minutes of the International Congress on the White Slave Traffic Held at Westminster Palace Hotel on June 21st, 22nd and 23rd 1899," 4IBS/1/1, Box FL192, Archives of the International Bureau for the Suppression of Traffic in Persons, Women's Library, London. Quoted in Thomas Richard Davies, "Project on the Evolution of International Non-Governmental Organizations," http://www.staff.city.ac.uk/tom.davies/IBSTP.html, 8 April 2010.

3. The 1921 questionnaire included a supplementary section on "Colonies and Dependencies," which expressed a persistent worry about interracial sexual relations. A parenthetical note in the section pointed out, "Reports have been received that it is the practice in certain Colonies for immigrant white men to have native women and girls procured for them for immoral purposes, and that these women and girls are provided for them by Chiefs or procurers" (League of Nations 1921a, 231).

4. Johnson had previously served as the director of the Sanitary Corps of the national army, and in 1918 published an essay titled "Eliminating Vice from Camp Cities" in the *Annals of the American Academy of Political and Social Science*.

5. This dynamic has extended into contemporary assessments. Citing Judith Walkowitz's 1980 argument that "'white slavery' and 'child prostitution scandals' in late nineteenth century Britain 'had all the symptoms of a cultural paranoia,'" Barbara Metzger counters the charge with the assertion that "investigations by the League of Nations later confirmed the existence of trafficking as a long-standing phenomenon" (2007, 56).

6. Quoted in Pliley 2010, 96. Pliley further points out that "by 1930 women represented six out of the fourteen governmental delegates and four of the six assessors."

3

LEGALLY SEXED

Birth Certificates and Transgender Citizens

LISA JEAN MOORE AND PAISLEY CURRAH

The story of birth certificate corrections begins, for our purposes, in 1965, when a transsexual woman (a woman born male who transitions to female) asked the City of New York to issue her a new birth certificate identifying her as female. "Anonymous," as described in court documents, did everything she thought was needed to function socially as a woman: her gender identity was affirmed by a medical professional; she passed the "real life" test of living as a woman; she underwent sex reassignment surgery; she began a lifelong course of feminizing hormones (*Anonymous v. Weiner* 1966). But state-issued identity documents still designated Anonymous as male. The "M" gender marker, revealing her history as a transsexual person, opened up the possibility for her identity as a woman to be challenged, undermining her ability to function legally and socially as a woman. The director of the Bureau of Records and Statistics denied her request to have her gender marker changed. The rationale for the denial in the 1965 report—often cited by policymakers and judicial authorities—was a need to protect "the public interest . . . against fraud" (New York Academy of Medicine Committee on Public Health 1966). In 1971 the policy of denying such petitions outright was reformed, to a degree: transsexual men and women born in New York City who could show they had completed full "convertive surgery" were reissued birth certificates that eliminated the box for sex entirely (New York City Health Code 1971), thus still effectively outing an individual as "other" and inviting further opportunities for scrutiny and surveillance.

This story demonstrates the concerns with fraud and the attachment of physical, anatomical appearance to gender stability, indicating the cultural and political urgency to produce a body that matches a "stable" gender identity. Our analysis of the regulatory changes in the birth certificate since 1965 reveals the gendered surveillance apparatuses and administrative systems put in place to ensure that someone *is* who they say they are. Birth certificates link the body to the gendered identity of a sexed individual. In this context, the body is imagined as pristine, biologically coherent, legible, and untainted by culture; the birth certificate, conventional wisdom suggests, simply records the facts, the baby's sex being a permanent and indisputable one. This document, unchanged, is supposed to accompany an individual for life. We suggest that the amended birth certificate to change one's sex and the controversies about this process are indicative of cultural concerns about the truth and permanence of sex and gender (Currah and Moore 2009).

Every day it is apparent how surveillance — the tacit or obvious collection and processing of data about human bodies — has grown in intensity and precision. Electronic monitors of speed recorded through algorithms on the New Jersey Turnpike, targeted marketing through the sidebars on social-media sites, and the ubiquitous security cameras trained on our every move track and aggregate our embodied movements through space and time. As the sociologist David Lyon has written, from modernity onward "the body achieved new prominence as a site of surveillance. Bodies could be rationally ordered through classification in order to socialize them within the emerging nation-state. Bodies were distrusted as sensual, irrational, and thus in need of taming, subject to disciplinary shaping toward new purposes" (2001a, 292). We argue that surveillance is not universally and uniformly applied to all human bodies and, furthermore, that monitoring occurs with different degrees of specificity and intention depending on the presumed coherence of gender and sex (see also Casper and Moore 2009).

Both scholars and transgender-rights advocates have pointed to the many contradictions in state-formulated constructions of gender. Advocates highlight these contradictions to persuade state agencies to adopt more consistent or uniform standards. However, among advocates, there is disagreement about what those gender standards should be. Some argue that self-avowed gender identity should be the only standard in state recognition of gender or sex (International Bill of Gender Rights 1990; The Yogyakarta Principles 2007). Others promote standards in which professionals make the determination based on particular medicalized metrics. Still others argue that since the gender binary reflects hegemonic and increasingly outmoded gendered social and legal structures, rather than any fundamental truths of bodies and identities, gender should not be an element of any official identifying document (Vade 2005). Some scholars, on the other hand, use the contradictions around state recognition of the legal sex of transgender people to demonstrate the radical instability of gender (Butler 1993). Regardless of the contradictions, surveillance apparatuses, such as the birth certificate, are indispensable to our ability to function as sexed and gendered individuals.

It is taken for granted that one needs identity documents in order to move through the world. As Craig Robertson points out, "In our contemporary world, there is a general acceptance that identity can be documented, that someone can be known and recognized through a document" (2010, 250). Robertson's work traces the American passport from its birth and through its hundred-year history, and identifies the ways that connecting an individual human body with a piece of state-sanctioned paper transformed regimes of surveillance. Our work builds on that of Robertson through the examination of the birth certificate. In a departure from much scholarship on identity documents, we argue that gender can never be disentangled from surveillance. In this essay we make a feminist intervention by examining shifts in the legal, medical, and commonsense logics governing the designation of sex on birth certificates issued by the City of New York between 1965 and 2006.[1] We explore the different narratives at work during two moments when transgender-rights advocates, medical authorities, and government officials came together to negotiate legal definitions of sex.

Using participant observation, ethnography, in-depth interviews, and content analysis, we examine the negotiation of gender in the process of trying to obtain state-issued identity documents. Paisley Currah, co-author of this essay, served as an "expert advocate" on the Transgender Law and Policy Institute on the Transgender Advisory Committee (TAC), which met four times between February and April 2012.[2] Data for this essay were collected from Currah's fieldnotes on earlier meetings and the official committee meetings, from official meeting minutes of the TAC, from Currah's autoethnographic account, and from his records on advocacy on this issue in New York City between February 2002 and December 2006. As well, we drew from legal documents, archival research, and interviews with other advocates: Dean Spade, a lawyer with the Sylvia Rivera Law Project; Chris Daley, executive director of the Transgender Law Center; and Mara Keisling, Executive Director of the National Center for Transgender Equality.

Before 9/11, transgender people whose gender identity differed from their legal sex at birth found themselves in a paradoxical situation whereby, for instance, a person's legal sex might change simply by crossing a state line, or one's sex designation on a driver's license might differ from that on file with the Social Security Administration (Currah forthcoming; Greenberg 1999). The modern regulatory project of sex classification has been in crisis for decades, caused by increasing divergence between individual gender definition (or identity) and legal sex designation. Post-9/11 the norms for identity documents have been regulated more stringently. Consequently, mismatching identity documents create significant difficulties for transpeople because systems of surveillance are triggered by mismatching documents. In this era of heightened scrutiny of individuals' bodies and histories, transgender people find themselves under increased surveillance (Currah and Mulqueen 2011). As with other subaltern groups positioned as not members of the imagined normative majority—undocumented workers, immigrants, "aliens" (non-U.S. citizens), and other "suspicious persons"—transgender people are constantly forced to account for themselves by documenting belonging (S. Ahmed 2000) via identity documents and often also via legitimating letters from their physicians (National Center for Transgender Equality 2004).

Birth of a Citizen(ry)

Birth certificates establish the earliest relationship between an individual and the state. The advent of larger, centralized modern state formations puts greater distances between magistrates and citizens, and thus requires standardized systems for identifying and individuating its population (J. C. Scott 1998). Alongside death and marriage certificates, birth certificates are among the "vital statistics" that states use to count, study, and manage their populations (Lunde 1975; Shapiro 1950). These documents are essential for demography—that is, birth rate, mortality rates, fertility, migration—for municipalities and nation-states. Birth certificates aim to make an individual uniquely identifiable, recognizable, and classifiable (Rule et al. 1983; Stevens 1999). In attempting to codify the relationship between an individual and the state, birth certificates constitute one of the technologies of control of modern systems of biopower (Foucault 1976; Foucault 1978).

Birth certificates provide benefits and confer responsibilities. They create recognition for the distribution of rights and resources from the state to individuals, such as voting, social security, Medicaid, and welfare benefits. Birth certificates are inscribed with cultural norms and values exercised through legally certified social relations that are expressed through bureaucratically mandated classifications of the parents' age, marital status, and racial identification. These categories highlight social desires for the organization of human populations based on beliefs about sex, gender, race, and class: binary sexed, biologically driven, heterosexual, racially homogeneous, married families. For example, "legitimacy" is the legal certification of the status of offspring born to parents who are legally married at the time of the infant's birth.[3] Marital status and legitimacy on birth certificates are linked to marriage laws, functioning as disciplinary mechanisms that certify that some births are legitimate while others are not.

Racial and ethnic categories have gone through many permutations on the U.S. Census, on marriage licenses, and on birth certificates. Since the early 2000s, many municipalities used the vital statistics categories recognized by the National Center for Health Statistics. The ten categories for race are White, Black, Indian, Chinese, Japanese, Hawaiian, Filipino, Other Asian or Pacific Islander, Other Entries, and Not Reported. In 1864 politicians coined the term *miscegenation* to refer to the illegal mixing of two or more races as a means to ensure and regulate human reproduction and racial "purity" (Pascoe 2009, 1). As the feminist historian Peggy Pascoe has shown, as late as 1999 antimiscegenation laws included in state constitutions made marriage illegal between a white person and someone with one-eighth or more "negro blood" (ibid., 307). While antimiscegenation laws have been eradicated, racial correlates are used to make arguments about certain types of human births. Case in point: the birth certificate of the president of the United States, Barack Obama, has been dissected and inspected from multiple angles to dispute the legitimacy of his claim to the presidency. Clearly motivated by racist beliefs, the demands of birthers (those who insist on President Obama's alien status) have revealed their incredulity and discomfort with the fact that an African American man resides in the White House. The birther phenomenon clearly illustrates that birth certificates are rife with politics. In a broader epistemological sense, identity documents do not so much confirm identity as produce and authorize it legally.

Breeding Grounds

In the lexicon of vital statistics discourse, the birth certificate is referred to as a "breeder document." That is, it is a primary authenticating identity paper used when applying for other identity documents (New York City Department of Health and Mental Hygiene 2005). Birth certificates contain descriptions of the sex and birth history of the infant, both of which are understood as fixed pieces of data. Unlike aspects of identity that are recognizably mutable — such as one's name, appearance, and ability — sex is assumed to be immutable, like place of birth and biological parentage, and is a fundamental characteristic for identifying citizens. Documenting birth through the birth certificate is an attempt to ground with certainty the material embodiment of the baby's flesh as a gendered legal entity. That is, the state can study, track, educate, tax, and distribute resources to these imagined coherent selves, selves that flow from the entity described in biological terms and affirmed in state documentation. This is also a document that regulates social status, gender roles, and related performances. The dual function of the birth certificate — as documentary record of a historical fact and as a primary identity document — reveals the complex relation between identity documents and shifting identities, and between biological sex and legal gender identity.

The more the science of sex advances, the less unitary and the more troubled the notion of sex as a binary concept becomes (Rosario 2002). For instance, according to Gerard Noriel, in 1829 a French doctor petitioned the state to allow doctors, instead of officials, to determine the sex of infants, because "the municipal officials were unable to determine the sex of a child in doubtful cases" (2001, 53). In an article on the issue of transsexuals and birth certificates, L. O. Schroeder points out, "Legally, a definition of male or female does not exist. The presumption that gender is so well understood as not to need defining does not survive examination" (1973, 239). Gender is shaped by the interplay between a number of distinct and often historically shifting factors — sex chromosomes, gonadal sex, sex hormone pattern, internal nongonadal sex organs, genitalia, secondary sex characteristics, gender of rearing, and gender identity.[4] These characteristics are assumed to align themselves into a simple, unitary, uncontested form, defined as male *or* female. However, even these apparently biological elements are not always in alignment: people with intersexed conditions are born with different constellations of sex characteristics; many transgender individuals make surgical interventions on their bodies or take hormones to alter them. State actors, then, are forced to choose and monitor a particular criterion for defining sex when assigning legal gender identity. Compounding the confusion, in the United States there are state entities with jurisdictional power to define sex. For example, states, territories, and the federal government each issue all sorts of identification documents—from passports to birth certificates to drivers' licenses to pilots' licenses to Social Security cards. Even state entities that do not issue identity documents but do segregate on the basis of gender make their own rules for gender classification—prisons, hospitals, schools, drug rehabilitation centers, youth service providers, social services. To add yet one more layer of complexity, judges have added to the chaos by finding that one's legal gender for one social function may not hold for others (Currah forthcoming).

First Iteration:
Attempts by Transsexuals to "Conceal" Their Sex

The phenomenon of transsexualism was introduced to the U.S. public with the news coverage surrounding Christine Jorgensen's transition in 1951—fourteen years before Anonymous's 1965 petition[5] requesting the New York City Department of Health (DOH) change the gender on her birth certificate. However, the first known "sex change" involving genital surgery had taken place twenty years earlier (Meyerowitz 2002, 19). The historian Joanne Meyerowitz recounts in her comprehensive history of transsexuality in the United States that the DOH had previously granted similar requests for surgery to three others (ibid., 243), but with Anonymous's request, the New York City Commissioner of Health, George James, sought guidance. He formally requested that the New York Academy of Medicine's Committee on Public Health "convene a group, including neurologists, gynecologists, endocrinologists, and psychiatrists" to consider the "enormous psychological, legal, and biological implications" of granting these petitions and to advise the DOH on whether or not it should revise its policy.[6] James noted in his letter that, at the time, nine other birth-registration areas in the United States had accepted requests to change the sex on a birth certificate. After three meetings, some legal research, and the impassioned pleas of the transsexual medical advocate Harry Benjamin, the committee concluded that it was nevertheless "opposed to a change of sex on birth certificates on transsexualism." Their report, which was reprinted in the *Bulletin of the New York Academy of Medicine* and often cited in legal cases in the ensuing years, concludes: "The desire of concealment of a change of sex by the transsexual is outweighed by the public interest for protection against fraud" (New York Academy of Medicine Committee on Public Health 1966, 724).

The official minutes of the meetings illustrate committee members' concerns about fraud: that one would hold oneself out to be a gender one was not. One doctor paraphrased the New York Penal Code at the time — "Nobody is allowed to dress in such a way as to hide his true identity" — and pointed out that a number of "transvestites" had been jailed for this reason. Such statutes were ubiquitous at the time (Hunter, Joslin, and McGowan 2004). The first draft of the committee's report listed as a public interest "the protection of a prospective spouse against fraud."[7] New birth certificates, a federal official informed the committee, could be used to get benefits reserved for one gender or to escape obligations for the other (Council 1965). At the committee's second meeting, the chairperson invited an attorney to brief the committee. While the attorney suggested that a transsexual woman might be able to use an amended birth certificate in a ceremonial marriage (to a non-transsexual man, presumably), he "doubted whether it could be considered a marriage," because she was originally a man. The committee considered adoptions as a method by which to legally recognize the "new sex" of these people — for instance, adding a codicil to the birth certificate stating, "Now known as female." (There was no discussion of the existence of female-to-male transsexuals.) In the end, however, they decided there was no mechanism "not injurious to the public" that would also "make the transsexual happy," so they concluded that "for the protection of the general public, [one's status as a transsexual] should be known." As an illustration of this public interest, one doctor cited the case of "a man who marries one of these persons with the expectation of having a family."[8]

The fear of fraud makes obvious the entrenched belief, held by medical experts, government officials, and the non-transsexual public, that one cannot change one's sex, only its "outward appearance." While the birth sex of infants is almost always assigned based on a visual check of external genitalia, the criterion, according to the committee, should be different for those who change their genitals later in life: while "ostensibly female," "male-to-female transsexuals are still chromosomally males" (New York Academy of Medicine 1966). Of course, it is precisely *because* some transsexual women and men can pass in their new gender, can *become* "the other sex," that authorities believe "the public" must be protected. Indeed, the public was protected by ensuring that the state would "out" transsexual people by listing their birth sex on the birth certificate.

The sociologist Erving Goffman describes the presentation of self to others as having a "promissory character" (1959, 2): "The impressions that the others give tend to be treated as claims and promises they have implicitly made, and claims and promises tend to have a moral character" (249). Humans, in Goffman's estimation, present themselves to one another within a taken-for-granted relationship of trust. We are who we present ourselves to be, with evidence—a biography—to back it up. In this sense, birth certificates function as a sort of promissory document not only about an individual's body, but about the particular history of that body. What is in fact social gender is assumed to guarantee a correspondence between one's present body, its past, and the gender presentation one puts out into the world. The accusation of fraud is made coherent by the belief that the body cannot become the other "sex" physically, and therefore any suggestion or performance of the opposite sex/gender is a lie. The apparently endless articulation of concern about enabling fraud in the committee minutes—producing what one committee member referred to as an "illegal document"—reflects anxiety about transsexuals concealing their "true identity" from the public. The infant's body as described by the medical declaration of sex at birth and represented in the birth certificate stands as a singular, objective, and original truth to be represented throughout the life-course. An amended document is therefore not a correction but a fraudulent document concealing the original truth.

Second Iteration: The No-Gender Alternative

In 1971, six years after the New York Academy of Medicine presented its report to the commissioner of health, the New York City policy was reformed. Instead of denying the petitions of transsexual men and women, the city would issue new birth certificates with *no* sex designation: the box for sex was eliminated. It was, for its time, one of the more liberal policies regarding the sex designation of transsexuals in the United States. To be eligible for this "no gender" certificate, transsexual men and women had to prove they had undergone "convertive" genital surgery, interpreted by the Department of Vital Statistics as phalloplasty or vagino-plasty. Petitioners had to supply a physician's "detailed surgical operative record" detailing a postoperative exam and a psychiatric exam. The re-issued certificates included the statement: "This certificate is filed pur-suant to subsection 5 of subsection (a) of Section 207.05 of the Health Code of the City of New York." The certificates had two markers that re-vealed the individual's status as transsexual: (1) no box for a gender des-ignation, omitting a fundamental vital statistic that reviewers of birth certificates—potential employers, the Social Security Administration, drivers' license bureaus, other government agencies, and social-service providers—might have looked for, especially when confronted with someone who was unable to completely pass in their new gender; (2) if one looked up the particular subsection of the Health Code referred to on the amended certificates, one would learn that "the name of the person has been changed pursuant to a court order and proof satisfactory to the Department has been submitted that such person has undergone conver-tive surgery" (New York City Health Code 1971). While laypeople might not have seen these as markers of a transsexual history, those in the busi-ness of document verification, of *re-cognizing* citizens, would have. Ironi-cally, deleting the gender box made sex more visible through its highly marked absence.

Third Iteration: Mandating Gender Permanence

By 2002, a new social movement of transgender activists and legal advo-cates emerged with activist groups, legal services, and community-based organizations dedicated to trans issues. Annual conferences, newsletters, magazines, and the Internet have done much to create and solidify trans communities in the United States and beyond (Denny 2006). Most gay, lesbian, and bisexual groups had amended their mission statements to include transgender people in their constituency. Media representations of transgender people were beginning to shift from depictions of shock, revulsion, and horror in films such as the *Crying Game* to more sympa-thetic and respectful renderings, such as the films *Boys Don't Cry* or *Trans-america*. The movement was also becoming institutionalized. Medical pro-fessionals specializing in transgender health formed an organization to recommend standards of care. Cases involving transgender issues were beginning to have positive outcomes in the courts. A handful of states and dozens of municipalities banned discrimination against transgender people, including New York City in 2002 (Transgender Law and Policy Institute 2007).

In November 2002 a coalition of fourteen organizations "concerned with the civil rights of transgender New Yorkers" sent a letter to the commissioner of the New York City Department of Health and Mental Hygiene (DOHMH) requesting that the no-sex birth certificate policy be reformed and that the "voices of those individuals and organizations who are most concerned with this issue" be involved with the policy revision process.[9] Allies for this cause in 2002 included the Center for Constitutional Rights, the American Civil Liberties Union, national gay organizations such as Lambda Legal and the National Center for Lesbian Rights, and local gay and transgender organizations. After two years of preliminary meetings, in December 2004 the DOHMH formed the Transgender Advisory Committee, which met four times between February and May 2005. Unlike in the committee in 1965, this committee included members of the transgender community, and all the member medical professionals had experience in treating transgender people—some were strong allies to the transgender community.

While the prevailing view during the 1965 negotiations was that transsexual people were gender frauds per se as one could never change one's essential sex, during the 2002–2006 gender negotiations, discussions centered on developing criteria to distinguish those who were temporarily living in the other gender from those whose transition was "permanent and irreversible" (New York City Department of Health and Mental Hygiene 2005). The crux of the struggle between transgender advocates and public officials turned on which criteria would be appropriate indicia of permanence. Officials initially advocated for particular types of genital surgery—vaginoplasty for transgender women, phalloplasty for transgender men—as testament to the permanence of a transsexual person's gender identity. The requirement for genital surgery would mean most transgender people would not be eligible for an amended birth certificate. As well, requiring surgery to validate gender permanence, thus implying that gender is determined by the body and that surgical body modifications guarantee permanence, belied current models in both transgender health care and in transgender communities' understanding of gender identity; for the advocates, in line with transgender communities' views, gender was determined by one's gender identity—that is, how an individual intrasubjectively and relationally produces their self-concept of gender—rather than through physiological interventions. As expressed in the International Bill of Gender Rights (1990), a foundational document for transgender activism in the U.S. before the first meeting of the Transgender Advisory Committee, transgender community advocates on the committee strategized ideal and realistic outcomes. Their ideal policy was to extend the current (1971) policy—no gender marker—to everyone's birth certificates, as an initial step to get the state out of the business of defining and regulating gender. They decided not to introduce this idea, however, since it could have been read as naïve, radical, or even unintelligible, and risked putting transgender advocates outside the realm of pragmatic policy reform.[10] Moreover, the charge of the committee was to revise the "change of sex" policy, and the advocates understood that gender would remain in use as a biometric identifier. In addition, at the time, New York State courts were hearing challenges to the ban on same-sex marriage. Officials perhaps understood, though they never stated it outright, that the ban on same-sex marriage depended on the state's power to make gender classifications and hence determine who is heterosexual.

From the advocates' perspective, the next best policy would be to allow individuals to change their birth certificates by simply informing the DOHMH that their gender had changed and requesting that the new gender be indicated on their birth certificate. Officials' preoccupation with gender permanence, however, made it unlikely that an individual could change their sex designation without the involvement of specialized experts to "attest" to the permanence of the transition. The most realistic outcome, advocates decided, would be to eliminate the requirement for "convertive" surgery and any requirements for body modification. Advocates understood, but did not emphasize to officials, that many transgender health-care specialists would define, for some individuals, "*appropriate* medical treatment" as not including hormones or surgery. As advocates argued in a memo to the DOHMH during initial negotiations over the policy, "Perhaps the single most erroneous misconception is that sex reassignment consists of a single 'sex-change' operation'" (Sylvia Rivera Law Project 2003). Most people who transition do not undergo either of the genital surgeries required by the 1971 policy. Even for those who would like to have genital surgery, making it a prerequisite for a birth-certificate change imposes a daunting financial burden. Significantly, requiring genital surgery before allowing a legal change in sex on the birth certificate would exclude all but those who wanted and could afford genital surgery, making sex—for transgender people, at least—a privileged category legally mediated by one's class status.

The public officials' anxiety about gender permanence was severe and clearly outweighed other concerns. The narrative that the body's anatomical markers (sexed genitals) define, legitimate, and authorize gender (identity) and make it permanent is crucial to the gender ideological system. In this way of thinking, the "common sense" importance of anatomy is so strongly established that it is immune to arguments that reveal that the criteria are social and structural. Because anatomical changes are expensive and also require the cultural capital to navigate a complicated biomedical-industrial complex, those who can attain this type of physiological change most often rank higher in systems of social stratification. The distinction between those who can afford surgery and those who cannot becomes the arbiter of who can legitimately be a man or a woman: the difference between a transgender woman who has had surgery and one who hasn't is $30,000. Yet the former would have the right "breeder" identity document as a result of being able to purchase anatomical markers.

The idea that the new requirements should ensure that the gender change was permanent dominated preliminary meetings of the official Transgender Advisory Committee. For example, Stephen Schwartz said the commissioner of health wanted assurances of permanence and that there would be "no further changes" to the individual. Schwartz stated he was "concerned about people changing their minds about their transitions" and asked, "How do we make sure it is really permanent?" The DOHMH bureaucrats summed up their concern in the committee's first official meeting: "What is a reasonable minimum standard an individual should have to meet to make a permanent change in one's gender?" A permanent transition, for the officials, was one marked by genital surgery. One urologist pointed out that "on the issue of permanence, it can only be met if the source of the opposite hormone were removed, with an orchidectomy or hysterectomy." Another urologist said that one could only demonstrate their "commitment to their new gender role" with an "anatomical change." Advocates thus began the process of renegotiating the birth-certificate policy with two goals: first, that reissued birth certificates list the reassigned gender; second, that the requirement for "convertive surgery" be eliminated (New York City Department of Health and Mental Hygiene 2005).

The fundamental strategy of advocates, based on our analysis, was to "de-medicalize" the policy, and ironically, rely on the authority of medical experts to do so. They marshaled transgender health care authorities to acknowledge the myriad procedures and varying rates of success for surgical operations. At one point, they submitted a memo from a transgender medical doctor listing 31 surgical procedures to dispel the "one surgery" myth. Transgender health care advocates on the committee argued repeatedly that transgender health care is highly individualized, that there are many routes to transition, and that a requirement for genital surgery was "excessive" since the majority of transgender people do not have it (New York City Department of Health and Mental Hygiene 2005). The lone psychiatrist on the committee, for example, argued that the committee would never be able to agree on "what degree of surgery, hormones, and/or anatomical changes would serve as a standard." He stressed that "gender reassignment is not simply based on anatomical changes, but how that person views him/herself and asserts him or herself publicly."

Advocates invoked medical authorities to show that "permanence" could be attained in social relationships without medical intervention. They pointed to recent trends in nondiscrimination laws to define gender as much broader than anatomical sex. In Boston, for example, women's facilities, such as bathrooms, showers, and locker rooms, are open to anyone whose "gender identity publicly and exclusively expressed" was female, and vice versa for men (Transgender Law and Policy Institute 2007). Schwartz countered that one could not compare standards for access to public restrooms with standards for changes to vital records. "It's a very big deal to change a fact of birth," the DOHMH's counsel added (New York City Department of Health and Mental Hygiene 2005). Advocates also pointed to the New York State policy on changing gender on driver's licenses, which requires a statement from the physician, psychologist, or psychiatrist certifying that "one gender predominates over the other and the licensee in question is either a male or female." Schwartz countered that "predominates [was] not enough," that he wanted something that established once and for all a permanent dominant sex: certification that the change of gender was permanent and irreversible.

With the exception of the two urologists on the committee, whose medical practices included gender-reassignment surgeries, all the other medical people pointed out that "permanence" and "irreversibility" were concepts that didn't make sense medically (ibid.). Most types of body modification can be reversed: individuals can begin a course of feminizing or masculinizing hormones, stop taking them, and perhaps restart taking them later. In very rare cases, individuals can have a second set of gender-reassignment surgeries.

Permanence as Security Measure

The officials' concern with permanence and irreversibility reflected their perception of the government's need for identity fixity. At the first meeting of the Transgender Advisory Committee, Schwartz enunciated his concern that, with regard to transgender individuals' identity document changes, "we won't know who you are." Changing the designation of sex could loosen the link between an individual and the administrative identity document. This bureaucratic fear of "not knowing" a citizen evokes a central problem of modern statehood, exacerbated in a post-9/11 era, but described as early as 1796 by J. G. Fichte in the *Science of Rights*: "The chief principle of a well-regulated police state is this: That each citizen shall be at all times and places . . . recognized as this or that particular person" (cited in Caplan 2001, 50). The concern about making identity fraud easier was explicitly connected to fears about security and to the need to prevent individuals intent on attacking the United States from obtaining identity documents that would mask their true identity.

Short-Lived Victory

Eventually, the medical arguments—that the surgery standard was arbitrary, an unreliable guarantor of permanence, and did not reflect the current state of transgender health care—convinced officials on the committee to change the criteria. In July 2005 the committee recommended that the DOHMH "recognize . . . [that] medical and mental health providers most knowledgeable about an individual's transgender health should determine whether an individual is living fully in the acquired gender." The proposed policy would require affidavits from two medical experts, one from a U.S.-based, state-licensed, board-certified medical doctor and one from a mental-health professional, also licensed in the United States, attesting to the "intended" permanence of the transition. Overall, the policy proposal was viewed as a victory by transgender advocates because it marked a shift from the discursive and legal regime of forty years before, in which transsexual people were cast inescapably as "frauds," to one in which the new gender of individuals could be listed on their birth certificates, even without surgery.

When Schwartz presented this policy proposal to the Board of Health—the appointed body that writes the health code for New York City—in September 2006, members appeared to generally support the measure.

Their questions and comments were innocuous. The chair of the Board of Health, in fact, suggested that the name-change requirement was unnecessary and should be eliminated from the proposal. Schwartz also proposed removing the specific reference to a "change of sex" from the health code on the proposed form. The new form would read "pursuant to section 207.05" only, indicating that the birth certificate had been changed, but not why. A hearing for public comments was scheduled for October 2006, and a vote would be taken at the December meeting of the Board of Health. It was, by all accounts, expected to pass.

Aftermath: Public Reaction to a No-Surgery Standard

Press coverage following the announcement of the proposed policy generated what could fairly be described as a media firestorm. The *New York Times* published a front-page story titled "New York Plans to Make Gender a Personal Choice" (Cave 2006, A1). Numerous wire services covered the policy. An editorial titled "Transgender Folly" railed against dropping the surgery standard (Editorial Board of the Jewish Press 2006). An essay in *Slate*, "New York City Bungles Transgender Equality," by Kenji Yoshino, an oft-quoted New York University law professor who writes on gay rights, described the New York Board of Health as "carried away" by advocates' arguments and invoked national security as one justification for rejecting the proposal (Yoshino 2006).

While the public testimony submitted on the proposal contained predominantly well-reasoned formal arguments from public-interest groups, elected officials, and LGBT institutions in favor of the changes, media coverage generated less formal emails to the Board of Health that were vociferously against it. "Are you people out of your minds????" asked one member of the public. "How enlightened is a person that refuses to accept that there is a biological difference between a man and a woman? If I wish to call myself a dog, I suppose you people would allow that too?" Another wrote, "I am befuddled and wonder if the inmates are now running the asylum. How might it be possible for someone with male genitals to now be listed as being female? Is everyone expected to be blind? I can understand if one had a sex change but simply dressing [in] the clothing of the opposite sex does not qualify a person of that sex. . . . Transgender does not mean transsexual in my book" (New York City Board of Health 2006).

Three months after the policy was formally presented, the DOHMH summarily withdrew most of the changes from consideration. Instead, the only change to the 1971 policy would be to indicate the reassigned gender of the applicants on reissued birth certificates. The requirement for convertive surgery remained. DOHMH officials cited two main concerns: first, the policy's impact on sex-segregated institutions such as schools, workplaces, hospitals, and prisons; second, the impact of post-9/11 federal legislation concerning identity documents. The United States Congress had recognized the importance of birth certificates in the "Intelligence Reform and Terrorism Prevention Act of 2004. . . . We [DOHMH officials] anticipate that automated verification of birth certificate data by federal agencies and state motor vehicle agencies will be a central component of the regulations. . . . Given the anticipated federal regulations and the importance of sex as a key element of identity, it is important to wait for their promulgation" (New York City Department of Health and Mental Hygiene 2006b). Advocates were not privy to the internal DOHMH discussions that led to the withdrawal of the policy. However, both justifications seemed weak. For instance, New York State's drivers' license policy was already significantly looser in that it required a letter from a health-care provider, so under the 1971 (and now current) policy, transgendered New Yorkers born in the City would be likely to have a different gender listed on their birth certificate than on their driver's license.

Legally Sexed

Using the surveillance mechanisms of identity documents, the state implies that it must protect its citizens from would-be imposters. As "sex change" was made possible and acknowledged by the general population as well as policymakers, medical professionals, and bureaucrats, the state wanted to create a metric that ensured that the identity, once changed, would not change again. While cultural representations might allow for the flexibility of gender displays beyond traditional ideological binaries, state actors, often in the service of their constituents, have difficulty accommodating subjects whose gender identity does not "match" their legal sex. Even though, in the most recent period, state officials did acknowledge the possibility of identity changing and the necessity of individuals having identity documents that match, they fought to ensure that this change of sex be one-time, enduring, measurable, and "irreversible." This anxiety about the possible inability of an identity document to maintain a correspondence with an individual throughout their life-span is summed up by a leading bureaucrat on the issue: "But we won't know who you are."

In the end, the barrier put in place in New York City to ensure perma-nence — requiring genital surgery before an M or an F will appear on the reissued document — cannot in fact guarantee the permanence of gender identity or the genitals. While it is unlikely, it is possible for an individual to have gender-reassignment surgery more than once. This policy does not prevent that from occurring, nor does it mandate that individuals born in New York City who *have* undergone genital sex-reassignment sur-gery change their identity documents to match their new body. It does, however, prevent the vast majority of individuals whose gender identity does not match their legal sex from having their gender recognized by the state. At the time of this writing, the Transgender Legal Defense and Edu-cation Fund has filed a lawsuit challenging the birth-certificate policy as "arbitrary" and "capricious." Other groups are working to have city legis-lators pass legislation to mandate criteria for sex reclassification that does not require body modification.

Whether it is the fraud iteration of the 1960s or the current policy, state officials are left upholding a standard that is only possible within a legal framework — that the "essential" nature of identity must be grounded in the body itself. Within the legal framework, the only way to change one's legal sex is to change the body, specifically the genitals. Out-side the legal framework, advocates, gender theorists, and transgender people certainly understand the mutability of sex and gender. While these documents may seem benign, they create pain and suffering at local levels (Cover 1986; J. C. Scott 1998). Gendered surveillance accomplished through birth certificates (and all identity documents that rely on this original paper) means that bodies must reinforce the socially and cultur-ally mandated binary sex characteristics.

Notes

1. When discussing legal designation as male or female, we use the word *sex*. When discussing other classifications, we use *gender*. We understand *sex* to be sub-sumed under *gender*. *Transgender* is used to describe those whose gender identity or gender expression does not conform to social expectations for their birth sex.

2. The New York City Department of Health and Mental Hygiene (DOHMH) con-vened "an expert Transgender Advisory Committee" in January 2005. The com-mittee's task was to "advise the Department and make recommendations on up-dated policies and procedures. The group was composed of DOHMH staff from Vital Records, Vital Statistics, and the General Counsel's office, plus eight outside mem-bers representing transgender expertise in medical, surgical, mental health, legal

and academic fields" (New York City Department of Health and Mental Hygiene 2005).

3. Nonmarital birth rates by race and of Hispanic origin generally changed little between 2007 and 2008. The rate for non-Hispanic white women (33.7 per 1,000) rose 1 percent, and the rate for black women (72.5) was essentially unchanged. The rate for Hispanic women declined 3 percent, to 105.1. The rate for API (Asian or Pacific Islander) women was 28.2 per 1,000. Trends by maternal age since 2002 were similar across population groups (National Vital Statistics Report 2010).

4. See Greenberg 1999; Haraway 1989; Lorber 1993; Lucal 1999; Oudshoorn 1994; West and Zimmerman 1987.

5. This was the fifth petition made to the New York City Department of Health.

6. Letter from George James, Commissioner of Health, the City of New York Department of Health to Dr. Harry Kruse, Executive Secretary, Committee on Public Health, New York Academy of Medicine, April 2, 1965, p. 2.

7. H. D. Kruse, MD, Executive Secretary, Committee on Public Health, New York Academy of Medicine to Subcommittee on Change of Sex on Birth Certificates for Transsexuals.

8. Subcommittee on Birth Certificates, New York Academy of Medicine, minutes of the meeting of June 14, 1965.

9. Letter to Dr. Weisfuse, City of New York Department of Health, November 18, 2002.

10. Paisley Currah's field notes, 2006.

PART II

THE VISUAL AND SURVEILLANCE

Bodies on Display

4

VIOLATING IN/VISIBILITIES

Honor Killings and Interlocking Surveillance(s)

YASMIN JIWANI

In 2009 the bodies of four women were discovered in a submerged vehicle in a section of the Rideau Canal in Kingston, Ontario. Three of the women were daughters of Mohammad Shafia, while the other, Rona Amir, was his first wife. In January 2012 Mohammad Shafia, his second wife, Tooba, and his son, Hamed, were convicted for the murders of the three young women—Zainab, Sahar, and Geeti Shafia (ages nineteen, seventeen, and thirteen, respectively)—as well as of Rona Amir (age fifty-two). Evidence indicated that all four women had been murdered prior to their submersion. The Crown (representing the State) argued that the murders were honor killings, a view buttressed by evidence from Mohammad Shafia, who, in wiretapped conversations with Tooba, had exclaimed that his daughters had "betrayed humankind, they betrayed Islam, they betrayed our religion and creed, they betrayed our tradition, they betrayed everything" (Appleby 2001a, A5), including his honor. The Crown's assertion was countered by the Afghan embassy's statement that honor killings are not a part of Afghan cultural traditions.[1] Despite this denial, the media continually framed the crime as an honor killing, sometimes surrounding the term with quotation marks as if to separate it out from the continuum of gendered violence that prevails in all countries. Media accounts repeatedly mentioned the immigrant origins of the family, their Afghan cultural background, and their migration to several countries before settling in Canada. In contrast to the usual attention devoted to cases of femicide or filicide resulting from intimate partner violence, the media attention to this case signaled it as exemplary of the importation of the backward and barbaric practices of Muslim immigrants.

In this essay I argue that the media works as a surveillance system, identifying which bodies are worthy of attention and, in that process, highlighting cases that mark particular bodies and specific groups as unworthy of belonging to the nation, or as worthy victims who need to be saved from their own communities. In this sense, while surveillance studies as a field has often focused on the construction of risk as embodied by particular groups of men—as, for example, in the case of terrorists and illegal migrants—a feminist analysis suggests that a similar surveilling practice operates when it comes to women within these targeted and stigmatized groups. In the Shafia case, I contend, the extensive media coverage legitimized the surveillance of Muslim women under the pretext of protecting them from the presumed barbaric practices ascribed to Islam and the ultrapatriarchal proclivities of Muslim men, and in placing them under surveillance in these ways, resulted in the intensified policing of Muslim communities. The mediated emphasis on "honor killing" as a particularly exotic variant of femicide contributed to the hypervisibility of the Shafia case against the unstated and muted backdrop of the everyday gendered violence that women experience, or of the prevalent femicide of specific groups of women, including aboriginal women (Jiwani and Young 2006; Jiwani 2009). Rendering the Shafia murders as honor killings became a cipher for all the ideological baggage that is invoked in relation to Islam and Muslims, and it served as an ideological tool to further profile Muslim men as potential abusers and Muslim women as at heightened risk.

Mediating Femicide: Hypervisibility and Surveillance

Surveillance depends on regimes of visibility and invisibility (see Smith, this volume), making visible the potential threats that exist and using cues to profile potential threats. The mass media constitute a primary vehicle for making visible that which is regarded as a potential threat or for using the threat as an exemplar to discipline, regulate, and control those who are perceived as threatening the social, cultural, and political order.

On average, approximately 58 women are killed by their partners per year in Canada (Statistics Canada 2011). This equals approximately one femicide a week. Yet, while some of these murders are covered in local newspapers, they rarely achieve the intensity and extent of coverage devoted to the Shafia murders. In a recent study Dana M. Olwan (2013) reported that her search of the Canadian newsstand database that covers all Canadian media resulted in over 1,300 articles that dealt with the Shafia case. My search of femicide cases, over a six-and-a-half-year period (2005–2012), using the same database and focusing on one of the major Canadian national dailies, the *Globe and Mail*, turned up only 54 stories on femicides. My search terms included "murder and (women or woman) and (domestic violence)." In contrast, a search using the term "Shafia" over the same period of time netted 66 stories, of which 60 were specifically concerned with the trial coverage. Femicides tend to be invisibilized or accorded limited coverage, unless, of course, they involve long, sensational trials that focus on crimes regarded as alien to normative standards. Honor killing, as a category, fits that criterion, as do other aspects of the ten-week-long Shafia trial, which involved 58 witnesses and 162 exhibits.[2] My analysis is based on a close textual examination of the trial coverage as it was reported in the *Globe and Mail*, and is supplemented with insights gained from an examination of other media reports.

Existing studies document the low coverage accorded to accounts of domestic and sexual violence (Benedict 1992; Meyers, 1997), except in instances which involve murder or high-profile personalities. But even in these cases, much depends on the status and race of the victim (Dowler, Fleming, and Muzzatti 2006). As Carol A. Stabile (2006) demonstrates in her historical analysis of raced and gendered crimes, black victims seldom get the kind and extent of coverage that their white counterparts do. This finding is corroborated by Travis L. Dixon and Daniel Linz (2000) in their analysis of race and crime in television news. In the Canadian context, Scott Wortley (2002) notes the under-coverage of black female victims of violence, while Warren Goulding (2001) and Kristen Gilchrist (2010) demonstrate the lack of media attention given to aboriginal victims of gendered violence as compared to white victims of gendered violence. The panoptic power of mainstream media is critical in terms of not only defining what constitutes a crime, but, importantly, identifying victims deserving of societal attention and intervention. With the intensity of attention accorded to the Shafia case, clearly both the victims and perpetrators, though not white, were propelled into the limelight.

Panopticons and Synopticons

Within surveillance studies, Foucault's conceptualization of panopticism remains a central framework of analysis for scholars. While there has been much criticism of the overextension of this "paradigm" (see Haggerty 2006), my use of the concept of panopticism concerns the "circuits of communication" (Foucault 1995, 217) and their cumulative knowledge, which serves as a benchmark for how one "knows" the world and others within it. According to Foucault, panopticism is, "a functional mechanism that must improve the exercise of power by making it lighter, more rapid, more effective, a design of subtle coercion for a society to come" (ibid., 209). This power is evident in contemporary society with its pervasive mechanisms of surveillance ranging from identity cards and passports at borders to the security and traffic cameras populating urban landscapes (see Lyon 2006). It was these kinds of surveillance mechanisms that allowed the authorities to apprehend and arrest the Shafias and to decipher how the victims were murdered. Soon after the family reported that the women were missing, the police installed devices in the Shafia's vehicle, which allowed them to wiretap the private conversations between Mohammad and Tooba Yahya; cell-phone towers were used to locate Hamed Shafia's whereabouts on the night of the murders; and his laptop was examined for incriminating evidence. Similarly, forensic technology established that the women had been drowned, but it was unclear how or where. But it was the panoptic power of the mass media—especially the mainstream and commercial media that captured the murders—that marked the murders as an exceptional case signifying an impending Muslim threat.

The sheer amount of coverage of the Shafia trial through numerous media platforms ensured that it became instantaneously available to all. Individuals loaded videos of the murder scene, courthouse, and commentaries on honor killings onto social-media platforms such as YouTube. These sites constitute what Thomas Mathiesen (2011) has called synopticons—allowing the many to see the few. In other words, the synopticon inverts the relation of the gaze inherent to the panopticon, resulting in what Mathiesen calls a "viewer society," wherein the acts of seeing and being seen, surveilling and being surveilled are coupled. Through the mass media, viewers are able to perceive actors across the social spectrum. In this case, the media coverage allowed Canadian audiences to view the Shafia trial, hear and read the witness testimonies, see the perpetrators, and know the victims. As one columnist opined, "We've come to know such intimate and tender things about these girls and women, their belly button studs, their purple nail polish, the lushly romantic texts their forbidden boyfriends sent. . . . So-called honor killings are a crime against nature, against humanity, against family love and, above all else, against females" (Timson 2011, L3).

The continual focus on the Shafia case—both in print and electronic media—suggests that it operated within a field of visibility that promoted an actuarial gaze. Allen Feldman defines the actuarial gaze as the "visual organization and institutionalization of threat perception and prophylaxis, which cross cuts politics, public health, safety, policing, urban planning and media practice" (2005, 214). He contends that through the scopic regimes of the media, the carceral lattice enmeshing different subject populations is recrafted and visualized in a manner that "screens, repeats, and screens off shock and trauma" (ibid., 212–13). According to Feldman, issues of visibility and invisibility are structured into the actuarial gaze.

> As much as it exposes and classifies, [the actuarial gaze] also creates zones of visual editing, structural invisibility, and *cordon sanitaire*, resulting in the decreasing capacity of surveilled, stigmatized and vulnerable groups, classified as risk-bearers, to make visible their social suffering, shrinking life-chances and human rights claims in the global public sphere. To the very degree that the traumatic realism of the state and media monopolizes truth-claiming about hazard, threat and violence over and against the everyday life experience of populations and spaces objectified as affected and infected by risk, human rights violations are rendered invisible or marginal. (Ibid., 213)

While Feldman describes the actuarial gaze in reference to the repeated and continuous circulation of images from the collapsing Twin Towers on September 11 to the widespread propagation of the tortured victims at Abu Ghraib, his analysis is also applicable to the gendering of surveillance. Using "shock and awe" tactics, the actuarial gaze makes visible violations of the moral order, acts of criminality, and other transgressions, but it erases from the public eye everyday violations of human rights, human suffering, and structured inequalities. In the Shafia case, the young women and Rona Amir (Mohammad Shafia's first wife) had, on numerous occasions, sought help. The young women had called on the authorities at school, and one of them had even sought refuge in a shelter for a time so as to escape the abuse. Similarly, Rona Amir had continuously asked for help from a woman she knew in the United States, but nothing came of it (Appleby 2011b, A10). These instances of violence were rendered invisible in terms of media attention at the time they occurred. They didn't surface until the court trial, at which point they became fodder feeding into the stereotypical construction of the Muslim patriarch as an angry, oppressive tyrant.

Thresholds of In/Visibility: The Somatechnics of Difference

In the post-9/11 context the Muslim body became signified as the bearer of risk, carrying within it the threat of destruction—either through stealth weapons technologies, through the infiltration of Shariah laws, or through the presumed fecundity of Muslim women whose offspring threaten to invade the Western nation-state (Grewal 2003; Werbner 2007). Indeed, the furor and moral panic over the issue of Muslim women wearing the hijab and niqab in Europe, the United States, Canada, and Australia signify the condensed anxieties and fears about the possible invasion of Islam in the West, its incursion into and infiltration of the body politic, as well as its potential to engulf Western culture(s) (Razack 2008; J. W. Scott 2007; Zine 2009). Jasmin Zine (2009) effectively demonstrates how the tropes of "disciplining culture," "death by culture," and "death of culture" play into the coverage that Muslims, and especially Muslim women, receive in the dominant Western press. Each of these tropes relies on the disciplinary and surveilling power of the state, which identifies the specific cultures that are to be disciplined (through technologies of racial profiling for instance). The "death by culture" trope focuses on Muslim women's apparent vulnerability to the perceived violence of their cultures. Honor killings become a signifier of that particularity of violence seen as endemic to Islam. This again, through media coverage, provides a rationale for disciplining particular cultural groups. Finally, the trope of "death by culture" summons forth fears of invasion, of a nation being engulfed by recalcitrant minorities with deviant cultural and religious practices. All of this rests on the corporeality of the body—that which signals its difference.

In the Shafia trial coverage, these tropes were evident in the manner in which the press reports described both the victims and the perpetrators of the murders. For instance, the young women victims were consistently described as normal teenagers caught in a culture conflict with their ultrapatriarchal father and their Afghan Muslim upbringing. Their aspirations to conform to dominant norms through the wearing of Western clothes and through heterosexual relations outside the familial context were consistently highlighted (Jiwani 2014). Thus, they were portrayed as victims of "death by culture"—implying that it was the cultural tradition of honor, as invested in them, that caused their death. The repeated circulation of these young women's photographs and "selfies" (self-photographs) in various poses, mostly in Western dress, made them seem more "like us" and hence elicited considerable sympathy from the audience.

At the same time, the reporting, through the panopticism of the media, served as a disciplining tool; it communicated to Afghan Canadian communities, as well as to other Muslims, that their communities were under surveillance and that femicides were not permitted in Canada. However, rather than this being a general condemnation of all kinds of femicides within any and all communities, it was the specificity of honor killings as associated with Muslim culture and Afghan traditions that were castigated as "un-Canadian" and therefore uncivilized. As the Ontario Superior Court judge Robert Maranger stated in his judgment, which was widely reported in the press: "It is difficult to conceive of a more despicable, more heinous crime. . . . [T]he apparent reason behind these cold-blooded, shameful murders was that the four completely innocent victims offended your completely twisted concept of honor . . . that has absolutely no place in any civilized society" (Bascaramurty and Freeze 2012, A1). The lead prosecutor, Gerard Laarhuis, in his statement to the media declared, "This verdict sends a very clear message about our Canadian values and the core principles in a free and democratic society that all Canadians enjoy and even visitors to Canada enjoy" (Appleby 2012, A6). The civilizational discourse is apparent in these quotes, as is the binary of Canada as progressive, egalitarian, and free of gender-based violence, in contrast to Afghanistan or other Muslim majority countries, which are cast as "uncivilized" and gender oppressive. But here again, femicide was not regarded as the root issue; the media instead constructed the Shafia murders as another sign of the importation of Islam with its presumed barbaric practices, a sign that represented a threat to an imagined community of white Canadian bodies.

We continually see commercial media and state attempts to distinguish between different kinds of violence against women through the representation of the Shafia murders as "honor killings." As the feminist theorist Sherene Razack aptly notes,

A crime of honor is a crime originating in culture/race, whereas a crime of passion originates in gender (abstracted from all other considerations). A crime of honor thus involves body, emerging as it does as a cultural tradition, and a crime of gender is mind, a distinctly individualized practice born of deviancy and criminality. The honor/passion distinction not only obscures the cultural and community approval so many crimes against women have in majority culture, but it reifies Muslims as stuck in premodernity while Westerners have progressed as fully rational subjects with the capacity to choose moral actions, even if the choice is a bad one. (2008, 128)

Razack's insightful analysis demonstrates how cultural differences are freighted with the burden of gendered violence, absenting the responsibility for such violence and failing to note the prevalence of patriarchy in all societies. What makes the elision possible is the strategic use of cultural signifiers to demarcate and stigmatize particular groups or communities.

Signifiers attached to the bodies of those who are considered different are often used to mark cultural deviance. Joseph Pugliese refers to such culturally coded signifiers as somatechnics, which he defines as "the indissociable way in which the body of a subject is always already technologised and mediated by cultural inscriptions. In the West, this somatechnologisation of unassimilable culturalist difference can be seen to be operative across the broad spectrum of cultural artefacts inscribed by the sign 'Islam,' including the black beard, the hijab, the headscarf and the niqab" (2009, 13). The notion of somatechnics as techne related to the body returns our analytical focus back to the corporeal body "in which the body, the social-economic-political conditions of embodied subjectivity, and the relationship between the body and the body politic are taken as important sites of political struggles" (Salter 2006, 178). Here, corporeality is the site where relations of power are played out. Bodies that are absented from political considerations—from the field of power, as it were—are bodies whose corporeal presence is denuded of significance. These are the bodies that don't count in Judith Butler's (2004) terms, precarious bodies, bodies that are ungrievable. Precarious lives are often relegated to the zone of structured invisibility within the actuarial gaze. They only enter the realm of the panopticon or the synopticon when their visibility becomes corporeally coupled with threat; surveillance then becomes the technology by which such bodies are made visible, with that visibility intimately tied to ways that these bodies are made vulnerable to state violence. Razack captures this connection elegantly when she writes, "The eviction of groups of people from political community begins with their difference, coded as an incomplete modernity that poses a threat to the nation" (2008, 84). That "incomplete modernity" comes through the surveillance of particular racialized and gendered communities. For example, this phenomenon occurs in the disproportionate media surveillance of Afghan communities in Canada—followed by allegations in press reports of Afghans as tribalistic, primitive, and atavistic. In the aftermath of the tragic events of September 11, the popular columnist Margaret Wente, for instance, described Afghans in the following way: "Those who are responsible are most likely men from remote desert lands. Men from ancient tribal cultures built on blood and revenge. Men whose unshakable beliefs and implacable hatreds go back many centuries farther than the United States and its young ideas of democracy, pluralism, and freedom" (2001, A1). Here, orientalism becomes the lens motivating the placement of these bodies under surveillance as well as the theory rendering them intelligible through the mass media. Edward Said (1978) identifies four dogmas of orientalism, of which the fourth one is particularly relevant in this context: "that the Orient is at bottom something either to be feared (the Yellow Peril, the Mongol hordes, the brown dominions) or to be controlled (by pacification, research and development, outright occupation whenever possible)" (1978, 300–301). Orientalism has legitimized, and continues to legitimize, violent surveillance technologies and practices aimed particularly at Muslims and others from the Middle East (Jiwani 2011; Magnet 2012; Razack 2008). In the trial reporting examined, the Muslim affiliation of the perpetrators was clearly identified through references to prayers, Afghanistan, and polygamy, whereas the victims were consistently portrayed as rebelling against this imposed identity and social requirements.

The trial press accounts also clearly identify the somatechnics of the perpetrators in ways that discursively demarcated them as different from the norm. Tooba Yahya Mohammad, for instance, was described in one account as "slight and pale, wearing a modest black tunic top over matching pants, cuffed at the wrist and ankle, her small chin quivered now and then, but she held it together—she is an Afghan, after all, tough and proud—until, as part of a court procedure, the prosecutor read aloud the names of her four surviving children" (Blatchford 2009, A2). As evident in this quote, the somatechnology that Pugliese describes in terms of identifiable cultural artifacts, such as a hijab, were conspicuously absent. Instead, the somatechne used to demarcate difference is stereotypical attributes of Afghan culture—Afghans as "tough and proud," reminding the reader of a famous orientalist poem by Kipling, "The Young British Soldier."[3] Nonetheless, there were photographs displayed in court that showed the young Shafia women wearing hijabs, demonstrating that somatechnes worked to position these young victims as simultaneously at risk of patriarchal Islam while remaining emblematic signifiers of the oppressiveness of Islam.

Pugliese further posits that the somatechnics of difference, where difference is signified as being unassimilable and as culturally foreign, result in a "prostheticized citizen subject" (2009, 21). The nonwhite body can never enjoy full or authentic citizenship; rather, it remains an other—conditionally tolerated, but never part of the body politic. Prosthetic citizenship can be taken away or withheld. It is never permanent. Whiteness as a racialized technology of power determines who can be granted citizenship and, with it, the security of belonging to the nation-state and of having rights that are recognized as rights and upheld within that body politic. The criteria by which specific bodies are seen as legitimate citizens as opposed to others who are denied such recognition rests on the race line (to use a term from Dubois about the ways in which U.S. culture is organized around a color line—that is, that white supremacy structures the U.S. polity according to race [1965/1999]).

Mohammad Shafia, his second wife, Tooba Yahya, and his son, Hamed, remain prosthetic citizens. One way in which the media ensured this status was through the constant reference to their immigrant status and origins. Indeed, a key point held against Mohammad Shafia was that he had immigrated into the country on the basis of his capital and investment in property. He had "bought his residency in Canada under the federal investor-immigrant program" (Appleby 2012, A6). As prostheticized citizens, then, their murders are located outside the realm of the normative—this, despite the reality that in the year preceding this quadruple murder, forty-five women were killed in Canada as a result of domestic violence (Statistics Canada 2011). Seen as others, the murderers' "fit" within Canada as a sovereign state is questioned. They mark the border between "us" and "them." Shades of Afghanistan, with its "primitive, tribal culture," are invoked in this coverage, clearly demarcating the boundaries between nations, cultures, and religions. It is, as Pugliese (2009) would suggest, a case of *compulsory visibility*.

The Aftermath

Rachel L. Finn's (2011) study of surveillant staring (being stared at) experienced by South Asian women in the United States emphasizes the corporeal aspects of being subjected to the daily "citizen-to-citizen surveillance" that has resulted from the heightened focus on security issues post-9/11. Drawing from Sara Ahmed, Finn argues that the signifiers of cultural differences and their embodiment in "strangers"—discursively defined as inassimilable others—serve to demarcate racialized boundaries and homogenize differences within those regarded as strangers. She notes, "Surveillance is an *active social process* that reinforces the differential structural positioning of its targets" (2011, 424). In a sense, this kind of surveillance demonstrates the synoptic influence of the mass media. Convinced about what terrorists "look like" based on images and messages from the media, citizens then take it on themselves, with permission and encouragement from state authorities, to spy on others. Yet it is Finn's argument about how the bodies of others become defined as racialized boundaries that is of interest here, for if bodies signify borders, then the threat of difference as an invasive force becomes that much more potent. Conversely, if bodies are seen as borders to be invaded, rather than as a threat, then these bodies signify borders that can be overcome, transcended with the might of state power.

In the Shafia case, both during the trial and after the verdict had been announced, the Canadian government granted $2.8 million to antiviolence organizations to help them sensitize service providers to signs of potential honor killings (Olwan 2013). In Montreal the Shield of Athena, an organization that provides multilingual services to victims of domestic violence was granted a hefty $350,000 to aid victims of honor crimes (Radio Canada 2012). Cultural sensitization becomes one way in which the state, through nonprofit organizations, carries out its surveillance of particular bodies. In contrast, as Olwan (2013) contends, organizations such as the aboriginal women's organization Sisters of Spirit, along with many other aboriginal groups, were deprived of much-needed funding. These then represent the bodies that can be invaded or overcome and bodies that are precarious—that is, bodies that simply don't count.

The notion of different bodies as constitutive of a boundary separating "us" from "them"—the watchers from the watched—offers a way to reconceptualize security and surveillance. In the first sense, it brings home the notion of the marked body as a threat where the threat is no longer abstract but corporealized, where surveillance becomes, as Finn remarks, "democratized," making it a duty for all good citizens to maintain heightened vigilance to signs of deviant differences. Recasting the body as border makes apparent the spatial relations of power; thus, the visibility of the marked body operates against the invisibility of the unmarked body, which is the body in dominance (e.g., whiteness against blackness). Here, as Rachel Hall also argues in her contribution to this volume, the white body is normalized and acts as the standard against which the racialized body is compared, and against which its differences are accentuated and signified within particular frames of meaning. John Gabriel (1998) refers to this as the power of exnomination, where the nominated body is the profiled body, or as Hall suggests (this volume), the profiled body is opaque, impenetrable, and therefore always suspect. The nominated body thus represents the borders of the social order, and interactions with such a body come to represent transgressions which may be seen as impure and dangerous. Hence, the Muslim bodies that committed the "honor killing" come to be framed in the same manner— as polluting agents who threaten to destabilize the social order by engaging in a heinous crime. That crime, through nomination, is defined as "honor killing" and thereby abstracted from the more widespread and prevalent pattern of femicides.

Women, as Floya Anthias and Nira Yuval-Davis (1992) have underscored, are boundary markers in most ethnic groups. As women are reproducers of the nation, their role in upholding the moral order is a necessary foundation for the continuity of patriarchal power. However, where such patriarchal power has been defined as illegitimate and unacceptable (as in the case of Muslim men who are perceived as ultrapatriarchal), the potential exercise of such power is immediately put under surveillance. Witness, for instance, the state-mandated publications and workshops geared toward immigrant Muslim families in Europe. The stated aim of these is to inculcate in Muslim immigrants and refugees the proper norms regarding gender relations and sexual rights. The assumption that citizens at large customarily practice such egalitarian relations and equitable rights is simply taken for granted and rarely interrogated (Olwan 2013; Razack 2004). Shoshana Amielle Magnet (2011) discusses how the border becomes outsourced, inscribed on bodies that are different and that reside elsewhere. Surveillance thus occurs outside the nation in order to preempt any threat from entering the nation. She argues that this strategy of outsourcing relies on racialized, gendered, and hetero-normative logics. This is one form of "outsourcing the border," as Magnet (2012) would describe it. The state-imposed criteria as to who can enter the borders of the nation state are installed in source countries to deter those who cannot or will not "fit" into the country of destination. The out-sourcing of surveillance then works in conjunction with the in-sourcing of surveillance — through the provision of services and the sensitization of service providers who work with victims of honor killing. This, I would suggest, is surveillance with a small "s," in contrast to Surveillance, which deploys state technologies to actively and overtly spy, contain, and disci-pline others (e.g., passport control).

Conclusion

Compared to the long-standing invisibility of gendered violence com-mitted on the bodies of sex workers, transsexuals, and indigenous women, the violence of the Shafia murders hit the screen, shocking and awing audiences into a heightened awareness of the phenomena of honor kill-ings. This particularly exotic variant of femicide assumed media currency for several identifiable reasons: it involved an Afghan family (with all the connotations of tribal and atavistic Afghan culture); those involved were Muslims (the current of Islamophobia being an inherent part of the ori-entalist lens of the mass media); and it violated middle-class norms of morality (as is the case with all crime stories). Shaima Ishaq (2010) has pointed out that, prior to 2001, there were two cases of familial homi-cides that resembled the Shafia case, but neither one was described as an honor killing. The salience of honor killings as a particular form of femi-cide is clearly a post-9/11 phenomenon in the West. Through the panoptic capacity of the mainstream media and the synopticons of social media, honor killings have become the cipher signaling Muslims and their cul-tures as a threat, thereby legitimizing the surveillance and profiling of Muslim women, men, and their communities.

Gender plays a crucial role in this context. The body of the Muslim woman is imbued with significations that define her as a threat but also as a *victim par excellence*. When women are cast as victims who need to be saved from "death by culture," their bodies and the associated vulnerability they face rationalize state-mediated interventions and the surveillance of Muslim men. Compulsory visibility thus informs us, as a viewer society, that the threat "they" represent needs to be kept at bay. "We," as the citizen audience, are in turn tasked with surveillance of these others. In the meantime, the state outsources its surveillance to the countries where Muslim immigrants come from in order to manage and mold them to fit—albeit conditionally, as prostheticized citizens—into the Canadian body politic. Once, in the country, they are subjected to a democratized surveillance (surveillance with a small "s," the surveillance of everyday life).

In the final analysis, it can be argued that race (with all its signifiers of difference) is the threshold calibrating visibility and invisibility, and by corollary, absence or presence in the actuarial gaze. However, power is implicit in structuring the relations whereby different groups of women and men become the objects of the actuarial gaze or are located outside of its glare.

Notes

1. "Hamed Shafia Begins Appeal of Murder Conviction," *Globe and Mail*, 1 February 2012, A3. There is a debate among Muslim scholars about whether, in fact, honor killings are sanctioned by Islam. There is no mention of honor killings in the Qur'an, and the words that reference violence against women are ambiguous and open to interpretation (compare Ammar 2007; King 2009; R. M. Scott 2009).

2. The *Globe and Mail*, it should be noted, publishes sixteen newspapers across the country and is owned by the Thomson family (also owners of Thomson-Reuters) in partnership with Bell Media, a major media conglomerate. Hence, its stories are reproduced and often act as a catalyst for additional coverage on other media platforms.

3. Kipling's poem was printed in the *Globe and Mail* in the immediate aftermath of September 11. The published extract privileges the following lines:

> When you're wounded and left
> On Afghanistan's plains,
> And the women come out
> To cut up what remains,
> Just roll to your rifle
> And Blow out your brains
> An' go to your Gawd
> Like a soldier. (Barbar 2001, F4)

5

GENDER, RACE, AND AUTHENTICITY

Celebrity Women Tweeting for the Gaze

RACHEL E. DUBROFSKY AND MEGAN M. WOOD

While women's bodies have long been objectified in popular media, social media raise new questions key to feminism about women's agency and responsibility, since social-media platforms ostensibly empower women to operate the technologies that objectify and surveil them. Visual-media technologies—including surveillance technologies embedded in so- cial media—are always already part of an objectifying process that has particular implications for gendered bodies. We look at popular tabloid coverage of women celebrities that feature their use of Twitter, specifi- cally stories about celebrities posting pictures of themselves. What are the implications when women are presented as having agency (taking charge of how they are displayed), and therefore expressly complicit in the creation of the images that display their bodies? How might a criti- cal feminist perspective, with a focus on surveillance, make sense of the gendered and racialized dimensions of visual social-media practices of self-representation?

Celebrities are a particularly salient focus since the celebrity body, as Imogen Tyler posits, "has become a central means through which con- temporary social values are distributed and, through consumption, iden- tification, and mimicry, become hardwired into everyday practices of subjectivity" (2011, 24). Discussions of female celebrity bodies are nothing new in the popular press, but the rise in the use of social media and the increase in data-valance (the tracking of people through data, especially digital data) add a new twist, with potentially new implications for critical scholars interested in surveillance technologies when it comes to questions of race and gender.

Discussion of the Twitter activity of celebrities in tabloid articles enables the framing of women as agentic, empowered, and authentic in their sexualized bodily displays: they control the means of objectification and willingly self-objectify. This dangerously elides the misogynist context that hails them to perform in particular ways. A close examination of discussions of Miley Cyrus, a young white female singer, and Kim Kardashian, a reality-TV star who is often framed as a woman of color in popular media, shows that while white women are presented as actively fashioning their bodies for public display (through exercise and diet), the few bodies of celebrities presented as women of color, such as Kardashian, are positioned as always already gaze-worthy, reducing their agency.

Our work contributes to scholarly discussions about digital culture.[1] While many academic studies on Twitter focus on mining data from tweets to demonstrate trends in public opinion and behavior (Ahmad 2010; Dumenco 2011; Farhi 2009; Greer and Clark 2011; Lowery 2009), this chapter is situated within a small, growing body of critical work on digital media and surveillance. Some of this work looks critically at Facebook, addressing its implications for gender identity and interaction (Cohen and Shade 2010) and how digital environments like Facebook and MySpace are organized around and shaped by race and class (boyd 2012). Such work has explored the general relationship of race and the Internet (Nakamura 2002; Everett 2009) and of race and software (Chun 2006); the connection of the raced technology "gap" with other social and economic "gaps" (Mack 2001); the use of technology by youth of color (Watkins 2009); online hate groups (Daniels 2009); transnational identities and collaborative ownership in digital-media technologies (Ghosh 2005); simulation gaming and racial identity (Galloway 2006); the racialization of biotechnologies (Chow-White 2012; Duster 2012; Nelson and Hwang 2012); and the critical intersections of race and digital media (Nakamura and Chow 2012; Chopra and Gajjala 2011). We bring to the ongoing conversation scholarship on surveillance practices on television (Andrejevic 2004; Andrejevic 2006; Corner 2002; Couldry 2002; Dubrofsky 2011; Gillespie 2000; McGrath 2004; Palmer 2002; Pecora 2002). Implicit in this essay is a call for feminist media scholars to update theorizing about the gaze and for scholars doing work on technology, digital media, and surveillance to take a transdisciplinary approach to account for the current cultural landscape and critical implications for gendered and racialized bodies and identities when it comes to practices of surveillance.

Method

Our focus is on Twitter because of its tremendous popularity (Papacharissi 2010; Parmelee and Bichard 2013) and because celebrity activities on Twitter are often mentioned in gossip columns, with frequent discussions of celebrities posting photos.[2] As of January 2014, Twitter had amassed over 645 million users (Statistic Brain 2014), including 21 percent of the U.S. adult population (Lunden 2013). Twitter is the most popular microblog tool and is featured extensively in popular media. It is used daily by political campaigns and news organizations, and it is also used for public outreach by nonprofits and celebrities (Zhao and Rosson 2009, 245). Since our interest is in the visual display of women's bodies, we focus on celebrity gossip magazine stories that discuss celebrities posting photographs of themselves on Twitter. We look at how the tabloids use celebrity activity on Twitter to authenticate celebrity behavior. We take as a premise that the Twitter activity of celebrities is likely mediated by public-relations (PR) workers. However, our focus is not on the actual activities of celebrities — or their PR teams — but rather on how tabloids, in their stories, use the Twitter activities of celebrities to make statements about the celebrities, particularly in ascribing agency and authenticity to their actions.

Between March 2012 and October 2012, we collected articles from a variety of online celebrity news blogs, mainstream tabloid websites, and the website versions of mainstream celebrity gossip magazines. We did this in two ways: first, we identified the top ten celebrity entertainment magazine publications in the United States using the ShareRanks.com database, which generates ranks for popular publications by genre based on ratings collected by the website's visitors. For the sake of practicality, we eliminated publications that did not have a searchable archive or didn't focus on celebrity gossip. Our list included *Us Weekly*, Radar Online (the online version of *Star* magazine), *In Touch Weekly*, and *OK!* magazine, which together yielded between one thousand and three thousand articles. Second, to find the most popular sources for celebrity gossip based on number of hits using the Google search engine, we searched for Twitter-related keywords such as "Twitter," "tweet," "twitpic," "hashtag," and "trending" in conjunction with the terms "celebrity" and "star," which yielded articles from various gossip blogs and gossip sites. Searching Google, we generated more hits using the terms "celebrity + Twitter" than by looking only at mainstream publications. We eliminated from both sets of articles—online gossip blogs and celebrity entertainment magazines—those that contained the keywords but did not relate to celebrity Twitter use. Many of the websites have a "related stories" column adjacent to the articles which identifies stories similar to the ones searched. In some cases, our search was expanded by finding relevant articles in these columns. The process produced a set of about one hundred articles. We analyzed the articles for how women celebrities were discussed in terms of bodily displays in photographs they posted of themselves on Twitter. We also looked at the few articles we found on male celebrities and Twitter: only fourteen out of one hundred articles were explicitly about male celebrities. We examined these as a way of accessing the particular ways in which the stories about women celebrities were gendered.

We see gender and race as culturally and contextually situated social constructs, not as essential or biologically determined. We consider how ideas about race and gender are constituted within the parameters of the text—how race and gender are constructed through "digital bodies" (boyd 2007) and how these are presented in popular gossip magazines. By "digital bodies," we mean the ways we "write ourselves into being" (Sundén 2003) online. Digital bodies convey information about physical bodies, which includes visible markers that play a part in constructing a person's race or gender in a profile picture or twitpic.

The Gaze, Authenticity, and Empowerment

As discussed in the introduction to this volume, the rich body of feminist scholarship on practices of looking has been concerned for quite some time with the implications of surveillance practices for gendered and racialized bodies, though the term *surveillance* is not explicitly used. Building on Laura Mulvey's influential work on the gaze (1975), John Berger's *Ways of Seeing* (1972), Marita Sturken and Lisa Cartwright's *Practices of Looking* (2001), and Shoshana Amielle Magnet's (2007) work, the framing of Twitter activities of celebrity women by tabloid magazines can be usefully theorized using Mulvey's notion of the male gaze in film. The male gaze regulates and structures its object within a social-historical system of gendered domination, tying "woman down to her place as bearer of meaning, not maker of meaning" (Mulvey 1975, 6). Anne Kaplan notes that even though one does not literally or necessarily have to be "male" to own and activate the gaze, the male gaze functions as "masculine" (1983, 30): it occupies a masculine subject position—one that objectifies the image gazed upon.

We pick up Magnet's (2007) work examining the activities of users on the website suicidegirls.com, which looks at what happens when the "objects" of the gaze are also the producers of the gaze, also what we look at when examining the ways in which the activities of women celebrities on Twitter are framed in the tabloids. The celebrity Twitter user is a "prosumer" (blurring between the roles of consumer and producer: a consumer who is also a producer of the product being consumed) (Tapscott and Williams 2007), and because what celebrities tweet is presented as under their control—not an image produced by a filmmaker, for instance—one cannot assert that they are being wrongfully objectified by others. This instantiates claims to authenticity and agency, since the celebrity creates her own image. Unlike in conventional notions of the gaze, where the object of the gaze is not part of the production process, the women posting photographs of themselves on Twitter are framed by the tabloids as active participants in the process of producing the images (even if, in fact, their accounts may be managed by a PR team). This is similar to what Magnet (2007) observes with respect to suicidegirls.com. What does it mean that these women are presented as the subjects and objects of their own desiring: "owning" the gaze and explicitly aiding in reproducing it?

Mulvey situates the image produced on the film screen as part of a "hermetically sealed world . . . indifferent to the presence of the audience, producing for them a sense of separation and playing on their voyeuristic phantasy" (1975, 9). On Twitter, this is not the setup: users bring others—in real time—into their private (ostensibly "real") worlds. As well, the position of viewer and of the person gazed at can change (a gazed at person becomes a viewer when he or she looks at a photograph another person posts on Twitter, for instance). However, because we are looking at how tabloids, in their stories about celebrities, discuss photographs posted by celebrities, the dynamic outlined by Mulvey remains: readers gaze upon the photographs reproduced in the tabloids, producing a setup akin to a "hermetically sealed world" with a separation between the image and the audience. But unlike in the scenario outlined by Mulvey, the people being looked at are real people—not actors performing a role in a film. As well, while Mulvey notes that in scripted films the spectator is given "an illusion of looking in on a private world" (ibid.), on Twitter and in the tabloid stories about celebrity use of Twitter this illusion is reconfigured, since the private world looked at is populated by real people doing real things (rather than actors performing a role). The setup may be contrived and orchestrated by the celebrity and a team of PR workers, but similar to reality TV, there is what Dubrofsky (2011a) has elsewhere termed a "call to the real." The call to the real pinpoints the idea that despite the constructed context of surveillance on reality TV shows, and the fact of editing and labor by TV workers to shape the final product, the element of real people filmed doing real things animates a sense that underneath it all there is something "real": "real, authentic, surveilled selves are constructed" (ibid., 22) at the same time as the genre denies this claim by declaring that reality TV can access the real. Megan M. Wood (2013) coins the term "call to authenticity" to describe, with particular emphasis on notions of authenticity, how Twitter animates the same paradox: the more one is seen as disclosing via surveillance technologies like Twitter, the more one is constructed as being "real." People who are authentic despite surveillance are presented as most authentic. For instance, when a tweeting celebrity gets "in trouble" because of what she tweets, she is seen as more authentic because, despite the context of surveillance, she was completely herself and behaved as if she were not under surveillance; or she is presented as overcome by real, strong emotion—feelings so real that she expressed them despite the context of surveillance (and possible negative consequences). The call to authenticity pinpoints the correlating relationship between the extent of personal disclosure (including "slip-ups") and perceived authenticity: the more one is seen as disclosing in ways that belie the structure of surveillance of Twitter, the more one is presented as being "real" (authentic).

Another noteworthy difference between Mulvey's theorizing about the gaze in film and how celebrities are configured in tabloid stories about their Twitter activities is in how the feminine is framed. Mulvey positions the feminine onscreen as passive, though inviting of the gaze, but in tabloid articles women celebrities are constructed as *specifically* active and agentic in putting their images on display via Twitter and in their invitation of the gaze (they post pictures themselves—they are not unknowingly captured in a paparazzi shot or passively filmed by a film camera).

In her essay on body scanners, Rachel Hall explains that willfully submitting to airport security "is coded as 'hip' in the postfeminist spirit of agency and empowerment via preparation of the body in anticipation of the male gaze" (this volume, oo). Similarly, celebrities displaying their bodies on Twitter are presented as willing and self-aware participants in creating images to put on display and as actively fashioning the body for consumption (through exercise). We bring into the conversation feminist scholarship on postfeminism to highlight the ways Twitter is used in the tabloid articles to forefront hypersexualized femininity as a form of agentic empowerment through the call to authenticity.[3] Briefly, postfeminism is a discourse as well as a popular cultural context where gender inequality is no longer an issue (McRobbie 2008), leaving a space for intensified and troubling stereotypes of femininity to thrive (Ringrose and Barajas 2011). The current cultural context of postfeminism implies that women self-representing online is empowering, giving them agency over their identity making.[4] The call to authenticity in this context animates the idea that one "practices" female celebrity successfully by disclosing on Twitter (Marwick and boyd 2011), enabling representations of women who willingly subject themselves to the gaze as a form of agency. In so doing, women are both lauded (empowerment in self-representation) and responsible for the consequences of this display.

Working for the Gaze: White Women on Display

Emphasizing notions of agency and empowerment, tabloid articles discussing the activities of white women celebrities on Twitter frame the women as working hard (through diet and exercise) to fashion desirable bodies ready for display. Notably, this trope is not present in tabloid discussions of the Twitter activities of celebrities framed as women of color. This is a racialized idea. The number of articles discussing women of color was also much lower than those discussing white women. White women attest to their postfeminist desire to be agents in their own objectification by working hard to shape bodies ready for display, and then use surveillance technologies (Twitter) to show off these bodies. Women of color, while presented as willingly inviting the gaze (through the posting of photographs), are passive in their sexualization since their bodies are articulated as always already gaze-worthy, regardless of their actions.

Cyrus is a popular focus in the articles we examined. Cyrus is framed as enthusiastically objectifying herself, aware that followers desire her, and actively enticing them to gaze upon her body in a sexual manner. For instance, *Us Weekly* writes, "Miley Cyrus may be a taken woman, but she's wooing her Twitter followers with what they're missing! . . . The 19-year-old newly engaged star posted a new Twitter profile photo of herself wearing a tight crimson bustier top. The sexy ensemble pushes up her cleavage and flaunts her tiny waist" (Eggenberger 2012a). Notably, none of the stories state something neutral like "Cyrus posted a photograph of her toned abs," or "Cyrus is wearing shorts in this photograph," instead opting for terms that make her agentic": "proudly" presenting her body, "showing off," "wooing" her followers, or "flaunting" her body. Her participation suggests consent and engagement with modes of objectification, as well as empowerment through her agency: the act of posting a photograph on Twitter verifies that Cyrus eagerly embodies and invites the male gaze, and her own actions (posting of twitpics) attest to her authentic desire to objectify herself.

Stories regularly mention Cyrus's diet and workout routine, positioning the act of posting photographs on Twitter as her way of proudly displaying the results of her hard work: *Us Weekly* writes, "Miley Cyrus showed off her long and lean stems — sculpted by her daily Pilate's sessions — on Twitter Monday" (Finlayson 2012a). Another story details that "the singer has been proudly showing off the results of her frequent workout sessions — and controversial gluten-free diet — by flaunting her abs in midriff-baring tops and her legs in short rompers" (ibid.). In yet another story, Cyrus is said to be "flaunting . . . her diminishing weight" (Ornstein 2012), and in one more, she "showed off her new look" (Radar Staff 2012a). Radar Online labels Cyrus's actions as "'Look at me!'" moves in a story titled "Flesh-Flaunting Miley Cyrus Is Sending 'A Terribly Sick Message,' to Young Women," about her posting of a Twitter photograph (Goodhand 2012). Not only does Cyrus seemingly enthusiastically post photographs of herself, but embedded in the stories about these activities are references to the hard work she does on her body to warrant the attention of the male gaze, attesting to Cyrus's (ostensible) desire to attract the male gaze. Importantly, the stories salaciously frame Cyrus's body in terms of the labor she does on her body.

What we outline isn't particular to Cyrus, though she was the focus of a significant portion of the articles we gathered. A few notable examples of other white women celebrities portrayed in a similar fashion are Fergie, of the music group Black Eyed Peas; Britney Spears, a popular female singer; and Heidi Klum, a celebrity model and reality-TV star. Fergie, we are told, "showed off her bangin' bikini body via Twitter in Cancun, . . . flaunted major cleavage and proudly displayed her rock hard abs in a printed two-piece" (Z. Johnson 2012). Klum, "*Project Runway's* sexy host, 39, shared a few photos of her skimpy bikini bod—and massive cleavage—with her Twitter followers . . . [and] revealed her taut tummy and sexy cleavage" (Corneau 2012d). Spears has "got a bangin' bikini bod! . . . [T]he pop superstar—flanked by her sons in swim trunks—showed off her toned bikini bod in a purple swimsuit in a photo posted to her Twitter page" (Corneau 2012a). Like the stories about Cyrus, the work the women put into shaping their bodies is consistently referenced, presented as part of what makes them proud to show their bodies: they worked hard to arrive at this point, and their reward is to display their bodies for all to see. Hall refers to this body fashioning as "a gendered model of reflexive governance" (this volume, 136)—that is, women self-reflexively participate in and regulate the display of their bodies.

Discussion of the photographs in the tabloids relies on a call to authenticity, since the photographs are presented as unmediated (though the photographs might be the result of much work on the part of PR teams), invoking a postfeminist logic where women are empowered and agentic through self-generated authentic sexualized displays. The work to fashion the body fits with notions of ideal U.S. citizenship, coupled with a postfeminist ethos: those who succeed are those who work hard. Efforts women put into their appearance work hand-in-hand with the invitation to gaze upon their carefully fashioned bodies: they labored to produce this body and their reward is for us to gaze with desire. The more effort the white women put into crafting their bodies for consumption, the stronger the invitation to gaze upon their bodies. The male gaze is a reward for white women willing to put in the necessary hard work.

Always Already Gaze-Worthy: A Woman of Color

Kim Kardashian is one of the most discussed celebrities in the articles collected during the time frame we examined. In terms of race, Kardashian's mother, Kris Jenner, is of English, Dutch, and Scottish ancestry, and her deceased father, Robert Kardashian, was an Armenian American.[5] Kim Kardashian is, as far as conventional notions of race go, Caucasian. However, if one googles "Kim Kardashian" and "race," it is apparent that there are ongoing conversations about Kardashian's racialization. Scholars note that Kardashian's relationship to race is complicated at best. Kardashian has markers that can signify her as a woman of color, making her not quite white (see Haltiwanger 2010; Peterson 2010): her dark complexion and curvy body are used to racialize her in the popular press (Natisse 2010), as are her relationships with black men. The manner in which the tabloid articles we examine discuss Kardashian's Twitter activity reflects Kardashian's complicated relationship to whiteness and racialization, poignantly illustrating how racialization is situated and contextual, not essential.

Stories about Kardashian posting pictures on Twitter consistently articulate her in even more sexual terms than white celebrities, her body framed as innately sexual, rather than as gaze-worthy because of the hard work she puts into it (even if, in fact, Kardashian may labor on her body), with an excessive sexualized focus on her curves, especially her derriere. This is a presentation usually reserved for women of color, especially Latina and black women, and is how Rihanna, a female celebrity of color (black Caribbean) is discussed in the tabloids during the time period we studied.[6] Kardashian is repeatedly framed as irrepressibly sexual, possessing a limitless ability to arouse: "Kim heated things up by sharing beyond racy photos of herself," writes Radar Online, followed by "less than a day later, Kim daringly posted a sexy snap of herself down on all fours and flaunting her bombshell booty in what appears to be a black thong, thigh-high boots and a cropped and fringed leather jacket" (Radar Staff 2012c).

Kardashian's sexuality is characterized as surreal, exceptional, and unnatural. For instance, her body's sexual appeal seems to defy even the English language: new words are created to describe her assets. Detailing a twitpic, Radar Online writes, "The *boobiful* reality star shows off her assets in a red bikini top and coverlet, soaking wet with the caption 'Wet & wild'" (Radar Staff 2012c, emphasis added). Later that year, Radar Online again found itself at a loss for words in the English language: "Kim Kardashian loves showing off her bikini body—even without any touch-ups! The *bootyful* reality star posted a pic of her crazy curves poured into a skimpy swimsuit, boasting it was 'Photoshop-free'" (Ornstein 2012, emphasis added). Kardashian's body is not only inherently superhumanly sexy, but exceeds the confines of the feminine human form, wild, animalistic, and out of bounds; it cannot be tamed by a bikini or a thong, instead arousingly spilling out all over the place because of her "crazy curves" and "beyond racy" physique. Kardashian's body is discussed as if it has a will of its own, divorced from any actions she might take. At the same time, her attributes are essentialized, ascribed to a body that no amount of dieting or exercise could fashion. Her spectacular form occurs naturally, without express effort on her part.

The absence of the trope of diet and exercise in stories about Kardashian puts into relief the implications of framing white women as actively cultivating male desire through the work they do on their bodies: Kardashian's body, articulated as that of a woman of color, is always already an object of male desire, regardless of her actions—always already gaze-worthy, naturally awe-inspiring without the need for touch-ups (Photoshop-free). Significantly, her body unwittingly drives the public into a sexual frenzy, suggesting Kardashian has an inherent, irrepressible, animalistic sexuality that is beyond her power. Pointedly, Kardashian's sexuality is not, as it is with Cyrus, under her control. Hypersexualizing Kardashian and discussing her body as if it has a will of its own works to position Kardashian as *not* human, as a sexual animal that cannot be contained or controlled, that arouses everyone around her regardless of her intentions. Key in this setup is that Kardashian's agency is removed in her sexuality: she is denied even the postfeminist hint of empowerment through self-fashioning ascribed to white celebrities.

The racialization of Kardashian gains salience within a larger historical context. Patricia Hill Collins (1990) argues that the subjection of black women's bodies on the auction block during the nineteenth century—a founding surveillance technology of the white supremacist U.S. state, as Katherine McKittrick (2006) reminds us—haunts current depictions of black bodies. Under this type of surveillance, black bodies were put on display in a central space for potential buyers to gaze upon, chattel for sale, and thus denied human status and agency. As is the case with the white women celebrities, Kardashian is presented as complicit in her own objectification by readily posting photographs of herself on Twitter. This willing objectification has particular racialized implications, since Kardashian's sexuality, unlike that of white women, is presented as instinctive and beyond her control, and her ability to sexually arouse is naturalized. In this setup, Kardashian is at once configured as eagerly serving a white supremacist imperative through the act of posting revealing photographs of herself and positioned as unable to control her own sexuality, which is presented as driving others into a sexual frenzy. Kardashian may be an active and keen participant, but she has no control over what happens once she agrees to participate.

Closing Thoughts: Gendered Narratives

Twitter enables writers of tabloid articles to imbue white female celebrities with a particular kind of strategic postfeminist agency whereby they willingly put themselves on display and in so doing can be positioned as authentically desirous of the gaze through the work they do to cultivate this gaze. Kardashian, on the other hand, framed as a woman of color, is not afforded the same agency, her body articulated as naturally inviting the gaze regardless of her actions or desires. Nevertheless, in discussing photographs posted on Twitter by women celebrities, tabloid articles consistently reference the agency of each woman in inviting the gaze: they choose to post the photographs, they do so willingly. This rhetoric is not unlike "rape myth" discourse, in which a woman who previously consented to sex or a woman who dresses provocatively "asked for it" (Tazlitz 1999; Torrey 1991). In this case, the act of posting pictures of oneself on Twitter naturalizes white supremacist heterosexist patriarchy. The images are always already part of a misogynist culture, making it difficult to pinpoint the ways in which the visual display of women's bodies is consistently problematic in a culture where women are disenfranchised. This enables a logic whereby women celebrities are agents in the stories produced about them, dislocating them from a cultural context in which women's bodies are fetishized and obfuscates the demands to perform female celebrity in particular ways—authentic-seeming sexualized displays—facilitated by the use of social media. Underlying this presentation is the idea that feminism is obsolete for white women, since they have full control over the means of objectification: they are not being objectified by patriarchy (or the press); they are freely opting to fashion the images they put on display. For women of color, the picture is bleaker: they do not fully participate in their own objectification, but rather are always already there to be gazed upon with desire, regardless of their actions.

Though tabloids might present white women as having some degree of agency, this agency is limited, which becomes particularly salient when examined alongside articles about male celebrities on Twitter. The first and most striking thing is the quantity of stories about female celebrities that discuss their Twitter activity versus the scarcity of stories about male celebrities and their Twitter activities, even though some of the most famous Twitter celebrities are male (e.g., Ashton Kutcher, Charlie Sheen, Justin Bieber—all white—and Kanye West, who is black).[7] As stated earlier, only fourteen out of one hundred of the articles we collected are explicitly about male celebrities; twenty-four additional ones mention male celebrities, but focus on celebrity women.

The Twitter activity of male stars featured in the tabloids, in contrast to stories about the Twitter activities of their female counterparts, are *not* articulated through a focus on their sexuality and a desire to put themselves on visual display. We found only one article that discussed a picture of a shirtless male torso, which was tweeted by Pauly D (an Italian American participant on the reality show *Jersey Shore*). His posting was discussed as a reaction to an unflattering photo leaked to the Internet earlier: he posted the picture to "prove the unflattering photo . . . was not how he normally looks" (Eggenberger 2012c). In other words, he was not "exposing," "flaunting," or "showing himself off" in a way that reveals his desire for sexual attention (which is how similar actions by women are characterized); rather, he posted the photo to "prove" (read: control) representations of his appearance.

Though not the focus of this essay, tabloid discussions of women celebrities' Twitter activity often mention their mental and emotional states in order to evaluate their character. We note this because it is striking that in the tabloid stories about the activities of male celebrities on Twitter, where the emotional state of the men might seem just as likely a focus as it usually is for the women, it was not. At worst, the men are seen to have momentary lapses in judgment, and at best, their tweets are considered intentional performances. The disclosures of the men are treated as a reaction to a specific set of circumstances. For instance, when Charlie Sheen, who made headlines for much of 2011 for drug and alcohol abuse and marital problems, deleted his Twitter account, the website TMZ reported that he had done so "because he just didn't feel like he was getting anything out of the Social Network anymore" (TMZ Staff 2012a). When he reactivated the account, tabloid speculation did not focus on why he had quit to begin with or whether he was mentally stable (as it usually does with women in these situations), but emphasized his "upcoming episode of 'Anger Management'" (his new TV show) and how he intended to keep his tweeting "professional."[8]

Men are given license to "rant and rave" (Corneau 2012b), to "apologize," "joke," "misfire" (Dobuzinskis 2011), and to be "misconstrued" (Corneau 2012c), with tabloid discussions centering on their actions as professional extensions of their celebrity careers. In contrast, the majority of Twitter activity by celebrity women is presented in tabloid articles as indicative of deep-seated personality flaws, emotional and mental instability, or a strong desire to attract the male gaze. Most strikingly, tabloid stories about women celebrities use Twitter activity to verify and authenticate them as willing sexual objects, while in stories about male celebrities, Twitter activity serves as no more than a professional tool.

Notes

1. Earlier works focusing on online gaming culture and similar digital social environments highlight the fluidity of online identity and the ways individuals can disrupt the usual constraints of gender, race, and sexual identity performance online (Bruckman 1992; Burris and Hoplight 1996; Dickel 1995; Poster 1995; Turkle 1995). Other scholars examine the ethics of studying user interaction online (Acland 2009; Hookway 2008; Jacobson 1999), as well as issues of privacy and how users manage personal information (boyd 2008; Lenhart and Madden 2007; O'Neil 2001; Tyma 2007). Recent qualitative studies on social media have centered on the popular social-networking site Facebook, exploring its use by students (Stern and Taylor 2007; Walther et al. 2008), its geography and structure (Dubrofsky 2011b; Papacharissi 2009), its role in interpersonal relationships (Tong et al. 2008), and its use in education (Mazer, Murphy, and Simonds 2007).

2. Users can tweet photos to their followers ("twitpics"), which stream on profiles as regular tweets, showing either the picture or providing a link to the picture in a different webpage, depending on the devices used to upload data and view Twitter.

3. See Dow 1996; Projansky 2001; Walters 1995.

4. See Attwood 2011; Banet-Weiser 2012; Ringrose 2011.

5. Historians and activists note that the categorization of Armenians as Caucasian is complicated given the racial genocide of Armenians in the early twentieth century (Akçam 2012; Shirinian 2012).

6. There were not enough stories about Rihanna for a focus on her.

7. A list of the top 100 most followed Twitter accounts, which is refreshed daily, can be found at Twitter Counter, http://twittercounter.com/pages/100/.

8. See Corneau 2012c; TMZ Staff 2012a; TMZ Staff 2012b.

6

HELD IN THE LIGHT

Reading Images of Rihanna's Domestic Abuse

KELLI D. MOORE

Denise Ferreira da Silva's (2001) notion of the "analytics of raciality" and Sally Engle Merry's (2001; 2002) concept of the "regime of domestic violence governmentality" prompt my analysis of how black women's bodies have been written, through photography, into the culture of white domesticity in the United States and the institution of law. I am inspired by Ferreira da Silva's argument that to account for how race operates as a "strategy of power in modernity," we must "address the very conditions of production of the symbolic mechanisms deployed in the constitution of people of color as modern subaltern subjects" (2001, 427). In this essay I consider the nineteenth-century criminal mug shot and Mammy portrait as photographic genres that established visual codes of whiteness and femininity. Ancestors to police images of battered women, the mug shot and Mammy image fix the body before an aesthetic-scientific gaze crucial to the production of the legal reasoning that undergirds slave and criminal law.

As a way of accessing the issues at stake in my argument, I attend to the use of the camera flash in police photographs of the battered face of the popular U.S. singer Rihanna Fenty, who is black and originally from Barbados. My analysis of the images shows how women are situated as scientific objects, placed in an antagonistic relationship to camera lighting: the flash regulates skin color to produce the subject of domestic abuse. Ferreira da Silva's and Merry's theories clarify the function of Rihanna's image as facilitating what Christine Shearer-Cremean and Carol L. Winkelmann (2004) note are contradictory, temporal, and contingent trauma narratives of battered women.[1]

I also examine Sham Ibrahim's multimedia artwork of Rihanna titled *Disturbia* (2009) and Rihanna's television appearance on ABC's *20/20* in November 2009. Ferreira da Silva's analysis of raciality is helpful in situating these as significant moments in which the black female subject of domestic violence gets written into law and public culture. I add to this an analysis of what I call Rihanna's "coming into voice" on *20/20* about her abuse, which follows Lisa Cartwright's (2008) articulation of the "coming into voice" of subjects with communication disorders who learn to speak through human and technological facilitators. For Cartwright, facilitated communication opens a space of empathic identification or moral spectatorship that is constitutive of the extralegal space in which Ibrahim and Rihanna respond to police photography of domestic violence. Ibrahim's multimedia artwork and Rihanna's appearance on *20/20* critique the scenes of visual evidence gathered by police, which transmogrified these into signifying visual codes of whiteness and femininity. The use of light and color across different media and materials — digital media, skin, fabric, and cosmetics — serve as nonverbal forms of communication that facilitate "coming into voice" and the production of subjectivity in the prosecution of domestic abuse.

Photography and the Analytics of Raciality: From the Nineteenth Century to the Twenty-First

In the late 1990s the legal historian Jennifer Mnookin remarked, "Despite more than 125 years of photography's sustained legal use, the history of photographic evidence remains almost entirely untold" (1998, 7). Police photographs of battered women, like the police image of Rihanna's battered face, have no official label that mark their unique history and rhetorical functions as legal institutional photography, as coveted objects of criminal procedure, and as prime movers in the aesthetic practices of the criminal courtroom in the United States. Accumulating in police databases since the 1980s, images of battered women are treated by law professionals and the public as visual evidence. Their untold, unmarked relation to the scientific apparatus of racism obstructs the view of the gendered and racialized conditions under which this body of photography proliferates. Images of battered women are key artifacts of the regime of evidence-based domestic violence, the emergence of which in the late twentieth century is largely overlooked.

Merry uses the term "regime of domestic violence governmentality" to refer to Anglo-American legal procedures that regulate intimate affective relationships in the twentieth century (2001; 2002). Her analysis attends to how the state authorizes the containment of domestic abuse and the regulation of communication between intimate partners. Protection orders, mandatory arrest, no-drop prosecution, and intervention programs are meant to effect changes in the subjectivities of batterers and battered women.[2] No-drop procedural action requires police to pursue charges, provided there is evidence of probable cause, with or without the victim's consent, while mandatory arrest demands that police responding to domestic disturbance calls arrest abusive partners. Strategies of evidence-based prosecution remove police discretion, which previously fueled inaction on domestic-abuse investigations. State policies produce particular forms of gendered subjectivities where male batterers are typically disciplined and punished for abusive behavior, and female victims are overwhelmingly protected by state orders which designate geographical and physical spaces of safety and security. Police photographs of domestic-violence injuries, providing visual evidence of domestic assault, as in the case of Rihanna, are an important component of the paperwork generated when police initiate a domestic-violence investigation.

In *Toward a Global Idea of Race* (2007), Ferreira da Silva accounts for the centrality of human difference in the production of juridical universality—the law of reason—in post-Enlightenment thought. The idea of race precedes Enlightenment rationality. Racism is more than an exclusionary practice documented by the sciences. The biological and social sciences manufacture evidence of human difference, ultimately forming an apparatus of knowledge, which I propose *produces the legal subject of domestic abuse*. Ferreira da Silva's analysis of raciality argues that "blackness and whiteness indicate distinct kinds of modern subjects [including] how the white body and the social (geographic, economic and symbolic) spaces associated with *whiteness* have been produced to signify the principles of universal equality and freedom informing our conceptions of the Just, the Legal and the Good" (2001, 423, emphasis in original). The scene in which the subject becomes caught up, absorbed, overwhelmed within techniques of normalization is described in terms of engulfment—a key aspect of the analytics of raciality that tracks the intricate circumstances and positioning of Rihanna on camera. Both the "analytics of raciality" and the "regime of domestic violence governmentality" take their cue from Foucault's concept of biopower—the techniques of power mobilized by nation-states in the normalization and management of populations. Ferreira da Silva's and Merry's respective analyses add nuance to the work and affects of biopower. Their work encourages the discernment of the somatization of biopolitical technique, which is produced as experiences of global space and interiority, and as I demonstrate, is the function of whiteness in Rihanna's engulfment in the racialized regime of domestic-violence governmentality.

The "analytics of raciality" describes an aesthetic arsenal that "consistently rewrites post-Enlightenment European consciousness and social configurations in transparency" (Ferreira da Silva 2007, 20). As aesthetico-scientific texts that lay open the body, photographs are endowed with the ability to rewrite the body of the racial other into new photographic genres. The nineteenth-century and post-Reconstruction eras designate key moments in which the racial other was produced through scenes of representation whose violence are rearticulated in the police image of Rihanna's battered face. For example, Jonathan Finn (2009) observes that human racial difference structured nineteenth-century experimentation with photographic technology, ultimately shaping legal institutional practices of how criminality was visualized.[3] Experiments with photographic technology during the nineteenth and early twentieth centuries were part of the discourse of scientific racism and established disciplinary power relations between the photographer and the photographed. From Louis Agassiz's coerced portraits of slaves born in Africa, to Francis Galton's experiments with composite portraiture documenting "successful" and "unsuccessful" human breeding, to Alphonse Bertillon's system of anthropometric measurement of the criminal, the first half-century of photographic technology documented experimental practices of looking, measuring, and categorizing the human body according to a transcendental hierarchy of higher and lower orders of humanity. Photographs of the criminal and the asylum inmate, and the slave daguerreotype emerged concurrently and displaced the prison as the quintessential model of legal panopticism. These institutional gazes developed as sciences; their power to categorize and identify continues to find diverse state and private applications in human fingerprinting, DNA analysis, and facial-recognition technology (Finn 2009; Gates 2011; Magnet 2011).

Laura Wexler's (2000) analysis of the photos of black nursemaids frequently referred to as "mammies," moves away from the site of the criminal mug shot and slave daguerreotype to illustrate the production of human difference and femininity. Wexler's discussion of Mammy photos adds a crucial photographic link to the management of domestic relationships that Merry describes. Mammy portraits regulated post-slavery domestic relations in the United States. The images functioned as important tokens of sentimental feeling for white masters of black women held in bondage. Post-Reconstruction, white keepers of black female labor engaged in photography practices that displayed "few or no visible debilitating marks of slavery" through sartorial details and gestural comportment (Wexler 2000, 74).[4] The images are distinctive for the clean, dignified, ladylike poses in which black nursemaids were photographed, often holding their tiny white charges while wearing stylish and morally tasteful dresses. Wexler's concept of the "innocent eye" explains the representational practices in which middle-class white women were portrayed "as if looking out from within, without seeing, the race and class dynamics of the household" (ibid., 6). The "innocent eye" is a sentimental photographic gaze that imagines the black nursemaid according to visual codes of white femininity. These images wrought a "tender violence" that reordered white consciousness through a sentimental and innocent photographic gaze by exploiting the black nursemaid's apparent "absence of wounding" from slavery (ibid., 74). The "absence of wounding" displayed in Mammy portraiture and the *presence* of wounding in the Rihanna image derive from the same aesthetic arsenal. By analyzing the crucial role of photography in rationalizing the postslavery domestic sphere in the United States, Wexler aesthetically situates the black nursemaid's fragmentary ascendance into whiteness via sentimental appearance. The particular aesthetic practices embedded in the image of Rihanna's abuse offer a window into the role of photography in domestic-violence adjudication.

The technical recording of Rihanna's injuries involved a complex negotiation between skin color and skin trauma mediated by camera lighting and physical comportment. The close-up image features the singer with her eyes closed. Her lips and nose appear swollen. There are abrasions and bruises on both sides of her forehead and cheeks. She has what looks like the beginning of two black eyes. Her short, jet-black hair disappears into the black background of the image. Awash in light, the performer's complexion appears whitened by the camera flash. If, as Ferreira da Silva

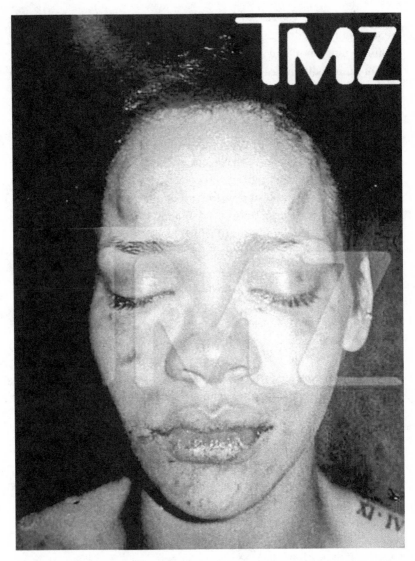

6.1 Los Angeles Police Department photograph of Rihanna's injuries, 2009.

(2007) argues, the very concept of post-Enlightenment rationality is informed by the idea of race, the flash photography that dissipates Rihanna's skin color and throws her wounds into relief produces the black female body as a limit of legal reason. Legal photography institutes a mode of representation that focuses on the body's exterior, or phenotypic qualities. In domestic-violence cases the state is interested in overseeing over time the development of bruises, punctures, scrapes, and so forth to provide evidence of abuse for criminal-trial juries. The police image simplifies into a "look" (Mulvey 1975) the complex affective and cultural relationships animating the violence between the black U.S. recording artist Chris Brown and Rihanna. The photograph voyeuristically focuses public attention on the presence of physical wounds that are legally actionable. Held by the camera flash, the singer's appearance displays visual codes of whiteness and femininity reminiscent of the graceful and dignified poses of black nursemaids. Similar to the proper dresses and groomed hairstyles that ostensibly incorporated the black nursemaid into white domesticity postslavery, Rihanna's whitened skin provides her access to "the Just, the Legal and the Good," which Ferreira da Silva (2001) associates with post-Enlightenment rationality. The image of Rihanna's abuse writes her black female body into the "regime of domestic violence governmentality" through visual codes of whiteness.

Richard Dyer (1997) observes how whiteness as signification emerges in the modern era in part through the technocultural production of movie-lighting techniques.[5] Whiteness demands technological projection where the preferred subject of the camera gaze appears "whiter than white" (Dyer 1997, 122). Dyer identifies the theater stage and television studio as quintessential technical realms where the production of whiteness and femininity is supplemented through cosmetics and lighting techniques. Visual whiteness is privileged in part through photographic regimes that control the hue and brightness of skin color. For the black subject, then, the scene of photography can operate as a "scene of regulation" in which the black body is normalized by the whitening camera flash (ibid., 4). Seated still before the police camera, Rihanna's pose is that of a scientific specimen, passive, immobile. Placed in an antagonistic relation to light, her image renders the structural antagonism between the black female body and the techniques of juridical universality. Pivoting from what he sees as a preoccupation with ideas of movement and passage in academic work on slavery, Harvey Young (2010) argues that stillness is an overlooked performance that negotiates the representation of the black body in visual media. The law's institutional documentation of domestic violence demands a performance of stillness which Young identifies in the coerced daguerreotype images of slaves born in Africa. The close-up shot of Rihanna's head, cut off from the rest of her body, centers her closed eyes and bruised skin, recalling the intimate gaze of the genre of Victorian memento mori, sentimental postmortem photography. Rihanna's deathly stillness is a performance of submission that coordinates with the camera flash that bombards her skin with light, isolating and throwing into relief the trauma to her skin that is already in the process of disappearing from the gaze of juridical universality.

In a sense, battered women are literally "to be looked at" (Mulvey 1975) by the state in a strategy of engulfment exemplified by Charles Goodwin's (1994) concept of "professional vision." Professional vision refers to the discursive practices—such as highlighting, coding schemes, and production of graphic representations—used by professionals to see and record. In his discussion of how law professionals deconstructed the video shot by George Holliday in 1991 of Rodney King being brutalized by police, Goodwin asserts "central to the social and cognitive organization of a profession is its ability to shape events in the domain of its scrutiny into the phenomenal objects around which the discourse of the profession is organized" (1994, 29). The use of light in flash photography to disassociate skin color from skin trauma is constitutive of police professional vision and seeks to regulate claims about domestic abuse. Forensic-evidence photography guides confirm the role of professional vision in the governance regimes Merry examines. Evidence photography guides and reports recommend a variety of procedures for documenting abuse. For example, point-and-shoot single-lens reflex cameras over 35 mm do not have a focusing distance that fill the (camera) frame (Pex 2000). High-resolution digital images have supplanted Polaroid technology in domestic-violence cases (Etengoff 2002; Kershaw 2002). Digital cameras are thought best for documenting bite marks, scratches, scars, and cuts, but not for bruises unless blood accumulation is close to the skin surface. The best time to photograph is between two and five days after injuries are sustained. The priority of capturing the disappearing injury is also evinced by police instructions about the manipulation of light for optimum exposure (Pex 2000). As one police protocol recommends, "Visible light penetrates into the skin deeper than UV light and is sufficient to document most bruises. Addition of special wavelength sources and filters can improve the visualization of [a battered woman's] injuries by enhancing the blue color and improving the contrast against the normal skin tones" (Pex 2000, 1). The use of the penetration metaphor is not inconsequential here, nor is the police photographer's reference to "normal" skin tones. Photography guides imply that the photographer needs to pass through the epidermal boundary into the "inner life" of the dark-skinned subject. As police-photography instructions attempt to manage skin color through lighting practices, something like Goodwin's idea of professional vision performs its "sovereign role as a regulating power" (Ferreira da Silva 2007, xvi).

Rihanna's whitened appearance models an institutional disciplinary practice of entering the black female body into the domain of universal justice under the cover of whiteness and femininity. Whitened out by the camera flash, Rihanna's image recalls the controversial 1994 *Time* cover featuring O. J. Simpson, whose face had been darkened to make for a more threatening mug shot of an accused killer of a white woman. Darkness and masculinity associate Simpson with the highest form of criminal behavior, while, in contrast, visual whiteness and femininity render Rihanna an empathetic witness. Both images presume a transparent body, which aligns with Rachel Hall's arguments about how the "aesthetics of transparency" (this volume) function in privileging white bodies at airports.

Reading Photography of Rihanna's Abuse

The police photography of Rihanna's domestic abuse facilitated critical responses to the visual epistemologies of law enforcement and Rihanna's own experience of "coming into voice" about the violence she endured. The online tabloid TMZ published the police image documenting the singer's injuries days after the assault. Kevin Glynn coins the term "investigative tabloidism" to describe the "morally motivated and self-consciously adversarial stance" (2000, 124) that leads tabloid media into melodrama, which I argue, has created an extralegal space to work through issues of victimization and grievance in Rihanna's assault case. In *Moral Spectatorship* (2008), Cartwright uses the concept of "working through" to examine the role of technology in facilitating disordered communication in the genre of deaf women's film. Cartwright pivots away from Freud's idea of working through as it relates to the talking cure to suggest that "we might also look to nonverbal vocalization, gesture, gaze, and touch—all present in the field of play—as important means through which acting out and working through are carried forward between analysand and analyst" (2008, 57). TMZ's investigation of the Rihanna case led to extralegal critical responses that took up the transparent aesthetics constitutive of the knowledge-making practices of the police. The responses from Ibrahim and Rihanna came in the form of nonverbal communication, by which color, textiles, images from popular culture, and light were mobilized to "talk back" to the regime of knowledge in which the experience of domestic abuse was reduced to a coveted photographic "look." The transparent aesthetics practiced by law enforcement operate through an association between objectivity and whiteness. The visual disclosure of domestic abuse that would bring battered women into the domain of universal justice occurs by reference to the cultural codes of white femininity, a coding forefronted in Rihanna's interview on ABC's 20/20 and in Ibrahim's art.

Disturbia

The new-media artwork by Ibrahim, *Disturbia* (2009), critiques how images of battered women—objects of police surveillance—are transformed into images for public consumption. Ibrahim created a form of appropriation art by modeling the police image of Rihanna after Andy Warhol's 1962 silkscreen *Marilyn Diptych*. The reworked image of Rihanna's abused face, published on Ibrahim's personal website, was digitally altered from a copy published by TMZ. In his rendition, Ibrahim replicates the garish color palette used in the comic strips Warhol used to reframe a screen shot of Marilyn Monroe from the film noir *Niagara*.[6]

The still image of Monroe used in *Marilyn Diptych* was captured for a publicity shot for the film. Created a few weeks after the movie star's death, *Marilyn Diptych* rehearsed the industrial mode of production with the massive manufacture of identical, interchangeable factory goods. Warhol's use of color in the piece juxtaposed twenty-five color images of Monroe with twenty-five black-and-white images of the star. Art historians suggest that the movement between the vitality of the color images and the dull, smudged ink of the black and white images signify the life and death of Monroe.[7] Warhol's *Marilyn Diptych* preempts Rihanna's police image, specifically its citation of the memento mori genre of photography. Warhol's work may have also sought to mark the production of the film in Technicolor—a rarity for film noir at that time.[8]

Disturbia is suggestive of Dyer's argument that the white face operates as a form of media control (1997, 94). Rihanna's battered face is re-

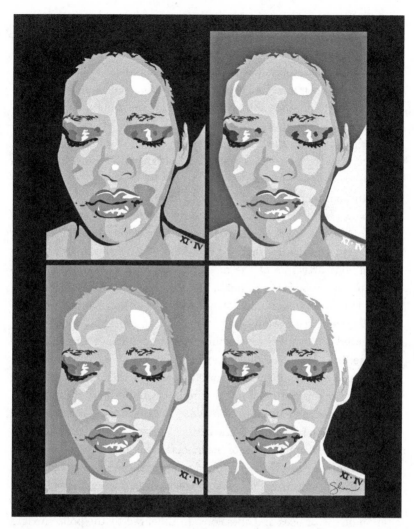

6.2 *Disturbia* (mixed-media artwork). ©2009 Sham Ibrahim.

peated in a series, rewriting Warhol's original repetition of the face of Monroe. In *Marilyn Diptych*, Warhol keyed into the process of mechanized production, aligning an iconic vision of white femininity with the serialized outputs of assembly-line production. The serialized repetition of the white female face is an example of how the "primary effect of the power of race has been to produce universality itself" (Ferreira da Silva 2007, 427). In *Disturbia* Ibrahim draws Rihanna into the domain of universal justice by substituting copies of Rihanna's face for Monroe's. Rihanna and the marks of violence on her face are linked to Marilyn Monroe's iconic performances of white femininity.

Ibrahim's interpretation of Rihanna's image is a gesture acknowledging new modes of production enabled by fiber-optic networks, in particular publicity images. Understood in terms of unrestricted movement, publicity is a commodity that wants to be free. By reworking one of the most famous artworks of the master of appropriation, Ibrahim comments on the imposition of publicity into everyday life. Media scholar Wendy Hui Kyong Chun understands publicity as stemming: "from the breach between seeing and being seen, between representing and being represented. Publicity is an enabling violence—but not all publicity is the same. The key is to rethink time and space—and language—in order to intervene in this public and to understand how this public intervenes . . . in order to understand how the Internet both perpetuates and alters publicity" (2006, 126). Ibrahim's *Disturbia* considers time, space, and the language of *color*, refashioning the battered Rihanna as Warhol's *Marilyn Diptych*, which is arguably one of the most famous publicity-art images of the twentieth century. The background colors of the images that comprise Ibrahim's work shift from black to orange to white to blue. The individual portraits use muted pastels that also shift from panel to panel, a possible citation of the bruises and abrasions documented by the police images of Rihanna. *Disturbia*'s shifts in color suggest the passage of time during which Rihanna's physical injuries gradually fade away. Ibrahim makes color speak, whereas in the police photograph of Rihanna, color can only remain silent, muted.

The changing colors of Ibrahim's series evoke the movement of information, facilitated by digital technology, from the space of law into the public domain. In 2002 the *New York Times* reported the introduction of digital cameras that would replace the Polaroid technology previously used by law enforcement to investigate domestic-violence crimes.[9] The report, like Ibrahim's *Disturbia*, marvels at the affordances of digital media.

Ibrahim's vibrant use of color disrupts the status of the police as arbiters of transparency. The perception of skin trauma is not the central point of information in Ibrahim's image; the use of color only suggests the wounds rendered by the police image. The viewer must also see the original police image to decode law enforcement's encoding of the "look" of domestic violence (see S. Hall 1980). Rihanna's death mask in Ibrahim's image returns us to her commodified identity, her celebrity status as a performer, the organizing concept of the image. In the absence of any text or caption, the viewer must read the use of color to decode the information in the image. Ibrahim's appropriation of both Rihanna's image and Warhol's *Marilyn Diptych* attunes the viewer to the promiscuity of Rihanna's image, oscillating between legal photography and entertainment.

20/20 Visions: Rihanna Speaks Out

In November 2009, nine months after Rihanna was assaulted, Diane Sawyer interviewed her for *20/20*. Rihanna's appearance on the program is suggestive of how the visual evidence of domestic abuse continued to produce multiple narratives about justice across social-media platforms. The *20/20* interview begins by interspersing moving images of the beaches of Barbados with childhood portraits of Rihanna. The singer is shown performing as Diane Sawyer's voiceover introduces the interview. At one point, Sawyer asks Rihanna to consider the infamously leaked image of her face.

> *Sawyer*: The picture taken that night, have you looked at it?
> *Rihanna*: I get very . . . embarrassed. I feel humiliated. I get angry all over again every time I see it. The whole thing plays back in my head, so I don't like to see it.
> *Sawyer*: Why be ashamed? Why would you be ashamed?
> *Rihanna*: I fell in love with that person. That's embarrassing. That's embarrassing that that's the type of person that I fell in love with. So far in love, so unconditional that I went back. It's humiliating to see your face like that. It's humiliating to say that this-this-this happened, to accept that. (Zak 2009)

As an internationally famous performer, Rihanna makes her fortune through timely, highly manicured, and choreographed rebrandings of her stage persona, of which this interview is one part. The police photograph of Rihanna's battered face also contributes to this branding, even if the creation and circulation of this image is not under her (or her PR team's) control. Police photographs of battered women's injured faces and bodies participate in what surveillance-studies scholar Roger Clarke (1994) calls the "digital persona," where electronically collected and stored data appears as a model of the individual's identity and behavior. Rihanna's responses to Sawyer's questions disclose how the circulation of the image led to a humiliating exposure of her digital persona, inseparable from Rihanna's unique experience of controlling her artistic stage persona. Significantly, Rihanna notes how the mere sight of the police image induces a nightmarish "playback" of the violent encounter with her former lover. Her appearance on 20/20 attempts to deterritorialize from memory the image of her abuse.

Cartwright suggests we read "more closely the relational practices of empathy through a system that allows us to track the qualities and directions of its movement across texts, subjects and social contexts" (2008, 239). In Rihanna's case, the assault complaint, labeled the *People of the State of California v. Christopher Brown* (BA353571), did not result in a felony trial. Rihanna's appearance on 20/20 thus became an extralegal space in which to adjudicate and redress the violence she experienced (and experiences again when she encounters the police image). Her appearance on the program is informed by the "regime of domestic violence governmentality" and the "analytics of raciality" that regulate feelings around violence and represent what violence is, or looks like.[10] Working through the shame and humiliation commonly experienced by battered women, the performer engages the aesthetics of transparency (R. Hall, this volume) when she offers her story of domestic abuse to the public.

Throughout the 20/20 interview, Rihanna remains seated, wearing a white turtleneck dress with fur epaulets, nude lipstick, and nude nail polish. Her hair is stripped of pigment. The ombre coiffure fades from dark to light and seems an updated version of hairstyles worn by Marilyn Monroe and Mae West. Sawyer and Rihanna are seated in a darkened studio, the walls lit blue and hung with red drapes. While Rihanna's seated figure provides the white in the "Red, White, and Blue" scene, Sawyer's body disappears into the darkened background. Through color, lighting, framing, and dress, the scene suggests that the United States has incorporated the performer's story of abuse into the national discourse of intimate-partner violence.

The makeup and clothing worn by Rihanna on 20/20 are examples of the aesthetics of transparency (Hall, this volume), which privilege white-

6.3 Screen capture of Rihanna's interview with Diane Sawyer on 20/20. "Exclusive: Rihanna Speaks Out," 9 November 2009, ABC News website.

ness. The lighting and the singer's performance of stillness contribute to the public process of working through her assault and to the online circulation of documentation of the violence. During the interview, Sawyer shows Rihanna video footage published online after TMZ's publication of the police image. A young black man and two young white women are featured in separate video testimonials, each wondering what Rihanna did to provoke Brown. In a nonverbal response to these questions, the singer engages the aesthetics of transparency and stillness (Young 2010). Young's concept of "phenomenal blackness" captures the resistant visibility Rihanna achieves on 20/20 in the face of disbelief by the public about her claims of abuse. In Young's analysis, black athletes and artists at the turn of the century deployed gestural practices of resistance based on their experiences of racial violence and on a sense of anticipated violence (a violence to come). Fixed before the 20/20 camera, faced with the public's assumption that she provoked Brown, Rihanna preempts the "violence to come." The singer's radiant stillness strains against the inanimate postmortem image rendered by the police. Rihanna mimics, through white clothing and nude cosmetics, the flash photography police use to document domestic abuse and the limitations of dark skin for this documentation. Her 20/20 appearance and her static position before the gaze of the law are brought into conceptual alignment as scenes and strategies of racial engulfment: Rihanna's still body, physically subjected to the bio-political regime of domestic-abuse adjudication, becomes the visual site of somatic resistance. In *Babylon Girls: Black Women Performers and the Shaping of the Modern* (2008), Jayna Brown observes how black women artists who perform negotiate their commodified bodies within racist entertainment contexts and urban geography. Brown notes that black women performers express "a deeper awareness of how expressive art-istry brings into view the staged nature of racialization and the performed nature of defiant responses to racial [and sexist] discursive claims" (2008, 283). On the 20/20 television broadcast, Rihanna appears "at home every-where and nowhere . . . [as if her] survival required spontaneity, agility, and awareness of the political conflicts and currents around [her]" (ibid., 242). On the *Fashion Bomb Daily* blog, Claire Sulmers (2009) wrote about Rihanna's use of color and sartorial choices as well as the complementary television lighting, noting that Rihanna's fashion choices emphasize her strength: "I, like many other Rihanna fans sat riveted watching her inter-view with Diane Sawyer on 20/20. Though the incident was quite trau-matic for her, she seemed strong, resolute, and fierce. What better way to flaunt her renewed spirit than in Fendi's $2,200 Fur-Trim Turtleneck Sweater Dress?" Rihanna's engagement of whitening techniques recalls the racial and gendered valence of categories of goodness, purity, and innocence traditionally held by white women and accessed through black women's sentimental appearances. The police image of Rihanna's battered face is fed back to the public on 20/20 through Rihanna's and the camera's rendering of soft, white, feminine elegance.

Conclusion

Through my reading of the police photograph of Rihanna's physical abuse and its circulation, I propose we see a moment in which the black female body is written into, but stands outside juridical universality. Ferreira da Silva's analysis of raciality would suggest that photography is a scientific tool that manufactures knowledge of human racial difference. Whitened by the camera flash, Rihanna's appearance exposed more than the prob-lem of lighting in photography. Taken literally, Rihanna's entry into the arena of justice demanded the technical evacuation of her skin color. In cases of domestic violence, law enforcement's use of flash photography recalls the practice of "not-seeing" discussed by Andrea Smith (this volume). Not-seeing is a technique that foregrounds the logic of the white supremacist heteropatriarchal state and informs subsequent encounters with racial others. In Smith's example, the denial of preexisting native peoples, and of their ways of being, enabled the colonization of lands and resources that established the United States. The performance of not-seeing that the camera flash enacts on skin color creates a visual code that organizes the regime of domestic-violence governmentality, centering a normalized female body that is white. Rihanna, as racial other, is held by the light, cordoned by the flash, existing at the edge of juridical universality.

It is no irony that the practice of not-seeing is constitutive of a looking practice that involves conquest. In this chapter I pursued a critique of the rationale of law-enforcement photography by theorizing ways in which Ibrahim's *Disturbia* and Rihanna's television appearance on 20/20 "talked back" to the regime of domestic-violence governmentality. With its use of color and repetition, *Disturbia* suggests that iconicity is manufactured through reason and feeling. Rihanna's appearance on 20/20 performed an affective citation of the codes of whiteness and femininity, producing her as an empathetic witness. Engulfed within the visual codes of whiteness and femininity, Rihanna embodied Ferreira da Silva's concerns with "matters that take place on the other side of universality" (2001, 421). The idea of race is more than a political-philosophical thesis of the Enlightenment; it is a powerful technological strategy of en-lighten-ment, producing the space, both real and virtual, that negotiates which bodies may enter the domain of justice.

Notes

I would like to thank Rachel E. Dubrofsky for her kind editorial recommendations, Sherene Razack, and Christina Spiesel for generously reading and commenting on early iterations of this essay. I would also like to thank the participants of the 2013 Law and Society Conference panel "We Are Not Post-Racial, Or, the 'and' in Law and Society to Come" for their encouraging engagement with ideas crucial to the development of this essay.

1. See especially Shearer-Cremean and Winkelmann 2004, chap. 7. For studies of how photography of abused women in medicolegal settings influences trauma narratives, see also Garcia and Suess Kennedy 2003; White and Du Mont 2009.

2. For an analysis of the effects of evidence-based policies, see Guzik 2009.

3. See also Ewen and Ewen 2006; Fusco and Wallis 2003; Tagg 1993.

4. Wexler (2000) analyzes at length an image called *Nursemaid and Her Charge*, produced between 1865 and 1868 by George Cook of Virginia. For an analysis of nursemaid clothing, see Severa 1995.

5. See also Wilderson 2010.

6. In the film, Monroe plays Rose Loomis, the adulterous wife of George Loomis, a military veteran played by the actor Joseph Cotten. Monroe's character and her lover, Patrick, played by Richard Allen, plan to murder George. The aftermath of George's recent stay at an army mental hospital for "battle fatigue" is a notable prefiguration of posttraumatic stress disorder and its connection to war culture. George's disarray animates the onscreen violence between him and Rose and the murder plot conceived by Rose and Patrick. See Hathaway 1953.

7. Gardner and Kleiner 2010; Wilson and Tate Gallery 1991.

8. For an analysis of the Technicolor motion-picture color process, see Brian Winston's *Technologies of Seeing*. Winston offers a critique of the Technicolor process as a racist technology.

9. The *New York Times* reports, "Photographs of bruises or broken furniture, if taken at all, are usually shot with Polaroid cameras. Those snapshots, which are often blurry and fail to make the injuries visible, can take days or even weeks to reach the courts. But with digital photography, evidence that has been practically impossible to gather quickly or gather at all—clear and detailed images of injuries like swollen eyes, bruised cheeks and handprints around the neck—can be transmitted by computer to prosecutors and judges at the earliest stages of a case" (Kershaw 2002).

10. On the "regime of domestic violence governmentality," see Merry 2001; Merry 2002. On the "analytics of raciality," see Ferreira da Silva 2001; Ferreira da Silva 2007.

PART III

BIOMETRIC TECHNOLOGIES
AS SURVEILLANCE ASSEMBLAGES

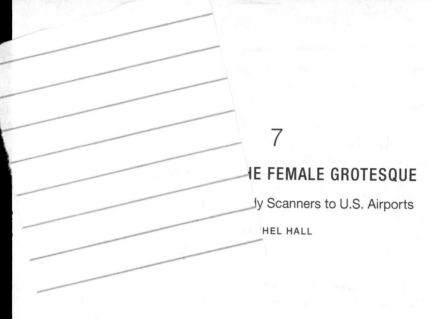

7

IE FEMALE GROTESQUE

ly Scanners to U.S. Airports

HEL HALL

In response to the threat of international terrorism, the United States has swiftly and uncritically embraced what I call the aesthetics of transparency in the post-9/11 era.[1] Broadly, the aesthetics of transparency is motivated by the desire to turn the world (and the body) inside out such that there would no longer be secrets or interiors, human or geographical, in which terrorists or terrorist threats might find refuge. The military and security state's objection to interiority is both physical and psychological, referring as much to the desire to rid the warring world of pockets, caves, spider holes, and veils as it is concerned with ferreting out all secrets, stopping at nothing in its effort to produce actionable intelligence from detainees. The aesthetics of transparency can thus be defined as an attempt by the security state to force a correspondence between interiority and exteriority on the objects of the preventative gaze or, better yet, to flatten the object of surveillance, thereby doing away with the problem of correspondence altogether. Circulating within the broader framework of the aesthetics of transparency, opacity effects visualize a body, geography, building, or institution as possessing an interior, a realm beyond what is visible. Opacity effects raise suspicion by the mere fact that they dare to present something that is not entirely visually accessible to the viewer or monitor.

The U.S. security state's desire to flatten the object of surveillance has influenced the development and implementation of new surveillance technologies in the post-9/11 era. In the United States and other Western nations, where the political leadership feels besieged by the threat of international terrorism, periodic media spectacles of deadly terrorist threats remind publics what is at stake if "we" do not adopt and uniformly submit to new surveillance technologies. In this manner, spectacles and specters of the terrorist threat nourish a political culture of compulsory transparency or unquestioning support for technological solutions to the threat of international terrorism. Media coverage of enemies of the United States in the war on terror and terrorist attacks or near misses in the "homeland" create a supportive context for the reception of new surveillance technologies. In this environment, the enemies of the United States in the war on terror (both iconic and ordinary) serve as the "opaque" bodies or "bad" examples from which the "transparent" traveler is encouraged to distinguish her body in domestic visual cultures of terrorism prevention. I do not understand these spectacles of opacity as intentional efforts on the part of media corporations to serve as agents of propaganda for the U.S. military or security state. Rather, I suggest that some military, government, and media professionals share an aesthetic orientation, which implies a global politics of mobility.

In the post-9/11 era, colonial binarism is subtly recast. Instead of "the West and the Rest," domestic-security cultures of terrorism prevention invest tremendous energy and resources into producing docile global citizen-suspects who willingly become "transparent" or turn themselves inside out, such that they are readily and visibly distinct from the "opaque" enemies of the United States in the theaters of the war on terror. As Yasmin Jiwani observes (this volume), when bodies are recast as borders, the invisibility of unmarked or "transparent" bodies operate in relation to the hypervisibility of nominated or profiled bodies. According to the aesthetics of transparency animating these distant yet interdependent security cultures, it is the production of particular bodies as stubbornly opaque which justifies violent practices of torture and interrogation, and abandons them to the necropolitics of indefinite detention (Mdembe 2003). By contrast, the docile citizen-suspect's presumed ability to participate in the project of biopolitics by affirming life in line with the conventions set by the U.S. security state makes physical violence against his or her body both unnecessary and unacceptable. Docile citizen-suspects are presumed capable of practicing what Nikolas Rose (1999) and Mitchell Dean (2009), among others, call "reflexive governance." The term refers to the ways in which neoliberal strategies of governance "offload" risk management and homeland defense onto citizens (Andrejevic 2006b). In post-9/11 cultures of terrorism prevention, reflexive governance refers to the citizen's "voluntary" transparency or her demonstration of readiness-for-inspection. I place *voluntary* in quotes to signal the coercive aspects of a performance demanded by the security state for the passenger to be permitted to board his or her flight.

Animal Opacity

Elsewhere I argue that two Western media images from the war on terror offer a particularly poignant example of how photography may be used to produce opacity effects: a photograph of Saddam Hussein's spider hole (a very small subterranean hideout), taken from above, looking down into the darkness; and the image of his medical examination, featuring the dark cavity of his mouth being pried open by a U.S. military inspector (R. Hall 2007). Analysis of the latter image establishes how Hussein and other spectacular models of "stubborn" opacity hail docile citizen-suspects to "voluntarily" perform transparency within the domestic-security cultures of terrorism prevention. In the visual cultures of the war on terror, opacity effects are racialized via photographic depictions of skin tone, hair, and head coverings. As Kellie D. Moore argues (this volume), any skin tone other than the whitest of white threatens to obscure the truth sought via the surveillant gaze.

For the privileged Western spectators of the war on terror, wartime surveillance provides discipline *and* entertainment, or better yet, discipline-as-entertainment. Consider CNN's online special report "Saddam Hussein: Captured." The site offers an interactive reenactment of Hussein's capture.[2] Hussein is figured as the stubborn, misbehaving outlaw who must be physically and forcibly subdued. The scene of capture is akin to a scene from an early reality-TV program like *Cops* or some other true-crime show. The "money shot" of this genre features cops violently subduing animalized suspects. Such programs rehearse the drama of a predictable power dynamic between individuals coded as inferior based on their race, class, and lack of education, and the rational cops, who know how to "handle" them.

While we don't get to see Saddam Hussein taken down, the images and video of his medical exam accomplish a similar spectacle of dominance and submission. In the image of his medical inspection, U.S. soldiers confirm the identity and reality of his body by demonstrating its depth and

7.1 Captured former Iraqi leader Saddam Hussein undergoes medical examinations in Baghdad in this 14 December 2003 file photo (image from television). Associated Press file photo/U.S. Military via APTN.

penetrating the surface. "We" get to see the dark cavity of his mouth and extreme close-ups of his teeth. The medicalization of this encounter signifies Hussein's physical submission to U.S. authority, connotes his animality, and—to the Eurocentric viewer—may suggest a benign version of U.S. imperialism, which has science, medicine, and the Enlightenment on its side. This painstakingly documented and widely circulated medical exam rehearses what Robert Stam and Ella Shohat have called the "animalizing trope" of empire or "the discursive figure by which the colonizing imaginary rendered the colonized beastlike and animalic" (1994, 19). This medical scene is reminiscent of the spectacular examination of slaves on the auction block. In drawing this comparison, I am not trying to be provocative, but rather insisting that the animalizing trope of empire is a racist strategy of dehumanization.

In the context of post-9/11 security cultures like those in U.S. airports, screening a passenger using high-tech surveillance technologies is one of the ways in which her difference from the animalized suspects in the war on terror in the United States is symbolically performed and reinforced.

Ironically, surveillance technologies first tested on incarcerated populations are now also capable of producing distinction from incarcerated populations when used to securitize the privileged mobility of air passengers. Shoshana Amielle Magnet (2011) has demonstrated how surveillance technologies play a role in managing incarcerated populations. The unstated presumption of the United States that technology is on "our" side (of those waging war on terror) subtly exerts pressure on suspects in the security cultures of terrorism prevention to submit to screening by these technologies, and to do so in a manner demonstrating that they are also on the side of the technology and of those waging war on terror. As Jasbir Puar has argued, "Pivotal here is the notion of capacity, in other words the ability to thrive within and propagate the biopolitics of life by projecting potential as futurity, one indication of which is *performed* through the very submission to these technologies of surveillance that generate these data" (2007, 200). Passengers perform transparency as willing submission to the scanner machines or else they suffer the indignities of a publicly staged physical inspection of their bodies by another human being. It is these charged distinctions, between machine and human, vision and touch, which enable the citizens of the United States and other Western nations to recognize themselves as fundamentally different from and somehow more innocent than the ordinary Iraqis, Afghanis, and other non-Westerners subjected to detention, torture, and abuse (in many cases without probable cause) in the name of the war on terror.

By contrast to the spectacular and ordinary enemies of the United States in the war on terror, the docile passenger-suspects moving through domestic-security cultures are presumed to be self-subduing. The air passenger need only wait to be told what to do, proceed calmly toward the machine, wait her turn, step on the footprints, raise her hands above her head, and freeze until she is told she is free to go. The passenger's "voluntary" participation in the biopolitical project of terrorism prevention is also, then, a more or less convincing performance of whiteness, where whiteness is conceptualized not in an essentialized biological sense but as a "racialized technology of power," as Jiwani (this volume) puts it. Other feminists have forcefully articulated the racial dimension of biopolitics. Citing Rey Chow's assertion that biopolitics is implicitly about the ascendancy of whiteness, Puar writes, "The terms of whiteness cannot remain solely in the realm of racial identification or phenotype but extend out to the capacity for capacity: that is, the capacity to give life, sustain life, promote life—the registers of fertility, health, environmental sustainability, and the capacity to risk" (2007, 200). In the context of post-9/11 security cultures of terrorism prevention, the capacity to risk and to have one's risky ventures securitized is a marker of whiteness in this broader sense. I name this racialized, securitized capacity to risk "transparency chic." An index of the First World traveler's "privileged paranoia," or her desire to reap the rewards of mobility while avoiding the risks, transparency chic takes the form of a willingness to open the live body, its accoutrements and possessions, as well as its digital double, to routine inspection and analysis.[3]

Transparency chic also works the other way: the passenger's performance of voluntary transparency lends the surveillance technologies in question an air of transparency. The passenger's public performance of submitting to these machines supports the notion that airport security screening is an innocent, impersonal, and objective process. Security officials borrow the myths of nonintervention and total transparency used to support no-touch security solutions from the visual culture of medicine. José Van Dijk identifies the assumptions underlying these rationales: "The myth of total transparency generally rests on two underlying assumptions: the idea that seeing is curing and the idea that peering into the body is an innocent activity, which has no consequences" (2005, 7–8). Despite insistence by the U.S. Transportation Security Administration (TSA) that visual technologies for scanning the body render human contact between TSA screeners and passengers unnecessary, these technologies serve a hybrid method of surveillance, which combines vision with touch. As Lisa Parks first observed, technological mediation serves as a precursor to and justification for human contact in the case of haptic vision: "What distinguishes close sensing from other forms of surveillance is the authority the state has granted to supplement vision with touch" (2007, 190). Parks notes that TSA guidelines stipulate that human screeners must scan any body or belonging by machine before they handle it (ibid.). Touch is thus defined as human-to-human contact and does not include human-to-machine contact. The threat of physical search rationalizes each new technological solution and energizes passenger performances of voluntary transparency staged as encounters between humans and machines.

Transparency Chic

The pressure to perform voluntary transparency via submission to screening by the new surveillance technologies demands, in turn, what Robert McRuer (2006) named "compulsory able-bodiedness." McRuer demonstrates the interrelation between what Adrienne Rich called "compulsory heterosexuality" and compulsory able-bodiedness. His analysis of various popular-culture texts also demonstrates how the cultural ideals of heterosexuality and able-bodiedness are further inflected by normative ideals regarding body types, beauty, and health. In post-9/11 security cultures, approximating the state's idea of what passes for normal becomes a matter of national security. In this context, if you fear humiliation and judgment at the checkpoint because your body does not approximate the cultural ideal, that has nothing to do with the technology's prying eyes, rather, it is your fault: your failure to master the body project leaves you at risk of humiliation.

Full-body scanners, which were rapidly installed in airports across the United States and beyond in response to Umar Farouk Abdulmutallab's failed attempt to down Northwest Flight 253 from Amsterdam to Detroit on 25 December 2009, examine the rough outlines of the passenger's anatomical form in order to identify "objects against bodies" or "forms that aren't traditionally part of the human physique" (Sachs 2010). Of note here is the telling use of the term *traditional* to describe "the human physique" (in the singular). Like whiteness or heterosexuality, transparency claims the ground of neutrality, while in fact the transparent body desired by the security state is not neutral but, more accurately, normate, the term Rosmarie Garland Thompson (1996) has used to refer to what is understood as the generalizable human being or the body type thought to be normal. In the context of post-9/11 security cultures, the appearance of normalcy takes on the characteristics of transparency, defined as that which we do not see or notice, as opposed to those signs of bodily difference from the norm, which register visually in the form of stigmata. Magnet (2011) makes a similar argument regarding how the outsourcing of the U.S. border externalizes the threat of terrorism and inscribes it on othered bodies and bodies that reside outside the nation. The white body is normalized and serves as a standard against which others will be judged (Jiwani, this volume). And as Moore's analysis of Ibrahim's appropriation art and Rihanna's appearance on ABC's 20/20 demonstrates, "the transparent aesthetics practiced by law enforcement operate through an association between objectivity and whiteness" (this volume, 116). Built into the aesthetics of transparency as it is currently mobilized by the U.S. security state is the desire for a generalizable body type which can be easily recognized as innocent or nonthreatening and thus efficiently be "cleared" for takeoff.

Consider a graphic entitled "Technology that Might Have Helped,"

Published: December 27, 2009

Technology That Might Have Helped

The Transportation Security Administration has techniques that might have detected the explosives taken on board a trans-Atlantic flight Thursday, but they are in limited use in the United States and around the world. Related Article »

X-ray backscatter
Reveals concealed items through high-resolution X-ray imagery. The T.S.A. has purchased 150 backscatter units that will be installed next year. The image resembles a chalk etching.

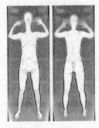

Millimeter wave screening
Reveals concealed items without exposure to ionizing radiation. There are currently 40 of these units in use at 19 airports in the United States. The image resembles a fuzzy photo negative.

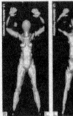

7.2 *New York Times* graphic depicting body images produced by x-ray backscatter and millimeter wave screening technologies. *New York Times*, "Technology That Might Have Helped," 27 December 2009 (www.nytimes.com/interactive/2009/12/27/us/terror-graphic.html).

published by the *New York Times* two days after Abdulmutallab's failed bombing of Flight 253.[4] The graphic pictures the images produced by x-ray backscatter and millimeter-wave screening machines, respectively. In addition to showing readers the difference between the images produced by the two types of technology, the *New York Times* describes the differences in terms of visual technologies with which the reader is already familiar. The image produced by backscatter machines "resembles a chalk etching," whereas the image produced by the millimeter-wave machines "resembles a fuzzy photo negative."

It could also be said that the elongated head and spindly fingers on the backscatter image resemble a humanoid alien from a midcentury science-fiction film, while the sleek metallic perfection of the figure in the millimeter-wave image is reminiscent of the star robot in Fritz Lang's *Metropolis*. Note that both of the sample body images on display appear hollow, flat, futuristic, slender, fit, relatively young, and able-bodied— not to mention the fact that the images picture all bodies, regardless of skin tone, as fuzzy white or metallic silver outlines.

Media discourses about full-body scanners domesticate them by reference to the norms of U.S. popular and consumer cultures, which celebrate Euro-American standards of beauty, health, and fitness. Consequently, the transparent traveler is defined via her ability to discipline the grotesquely opaque body, whose abjection communicates the perpetual threat that the docile passenger-suspect's body will somehow fail to perform transparency up to code. Consider a cheeky, flirtatious piece of gonzo journalism entitled "Reporter Faces the Naked Truth about Full-Body Airport Scanners" (2010), for which Andrea Sachs of the *Washington Post* underwent a full-body scan by a millimeter-wave machine so she might "experience the technology's prying eyes first hand." Rather than report information regarding what firms would profit from the technology's adoption or raise questions regarding its use, the reporter modeled for the reader how to make the adjustment to a new layer of security. The article's tone oscillates between sexual teasing and self-punishing narcissism. Sachs stresses the threat of being found unattractive in the images produced by the new machines. The experience of having one's clothes virtually peeled away by the new scanner is articulated in terms of vanity and sexual attractiveness or (gasp) repulsion, rather than as a process that renders each body suspect. There is no tucking or lifting or sucking in of guts that the TSA cannot see through with the new machines.

Even as Sachs worries about what she considers to be her major corporeal flaw (a belly button placed too high on her torso), she mock scolds herself to put vanity aside for the sake of homeland security: "Get over yourself, honey: The full-body scanning machines at airport security checkpoints weren't created to point out corporeal flaws but to detect suspicious objects lurking beneath airline passengers' clothing." Sachs's "get over yourself," comment is meant to reassure passengers that when scanned, the body becomes nothing more than a medium or environment, but it also presumes the passenger's feminine vanity and irrelevance. What the feminist philosopher Mary Russo conceptualizes as the "female grotesque"—that cavernous figure associated "in the most gross metaphorical sense" with the female anatomical body—circulates here as a comic foil to the opaque terrorist. As Russo has written, the word "grotesque evokes the cave—the grotto-esque. Low, hidden, earthly, dark, material, immanent, visceral. As bodily metaphor, the grotesque cave tends to look like (and in the most gross metaphorical sense be identified with) the cavernous anatomical female body" (1994, 1–2). While the enemy's stubborn opacity rationalizes physical penetration and punishment of his body in the theaters of the war on terror, the mock vanity of the female grotesque reduces serious critique of the full-body scanners to a self-deprecating joke. In the end, Sachs tells the reader that the security expert conducting her scan eventually erased the image, but it stuck with her. She ends the article by expressing her support for the new technology, given the very real threats to America's safety posed by terrorism. "In the end," Sachs (2010) writes, "I found it comforting to know that the body scanner would uncover items missed by older equipment and that we travelers have one more layer of protection against those exceedingly crafty terrorists."

There is a politics to feeling afraid of another "crafty" terrorist attack and comforted by the installation of full-body scanners at U.S. airports. In the context of airport security, performing voluntary transparency is coded as "hip" in the postfeminist spirit of agency and empowerment via preparation of the body in anticipation of the male gaze. Because the new norms of airport security culture borrow from the norms of U.S. consumer culture, they presume a passenger who sees "her" body as a project. In their essay on how celebrity white women tweet and how those tweets are read on gossip sites, Dubrofsky and Wood (this volume) update Mulvey's theory of the male gaze for the postfeminist digital era, arguing that the recipient of the gaze is a participant in creating the image on display and actively fashions the body for consumption. They point out that it is only white women celebrities who are granted agency in the form of producing their bodies for the male gaze. Famous women of color are regularly discussed, critiqued, and celebrated on gossip sites, but their bodies are consistently treated as "natural" and therefore beyond their control. The bodies of famous white women, however, are depicted as ongoing projects or life works, of which those white celebrities can be proud because of the effort they have put into producing their bodies as attractive by the standards of the male gaze. Building on these keen insights, I argue that in the context of airport security the "good" passenger-suspect operates according to a gendered model of reflexive governance, which defines itself in opposition to the female grotesque. In short, the "good" passenger acts like a vain white woman from the United States who is always ready for sex. Indirectly, then, the "good" passenger's take on the new surveillance technologies constructs the terrorist threat by reference to the figure of the female grotesque, the woman who fails to prepare her body for the male gaze, or the woman who refuses male sexual advances.

Ultimately, Sachs models feminine heterosexual acquiescence to the new surveillance technologies. This framing of the new surveillance technologies resonates with a romantic view of the security state as the terrified passenger's knight in shining armor and finds its precursor in American comic books and films featuring a lusty, muscle-bound superhero with x-ray vision. Consider the following iconic scene from the 1973 film adaptation of *Superman*: on a balmy night in Metropolis, Lois Lane interviews Superman on her terrace. She wears a billowy, flowing white gown and cape (you know what he's got on). As Lois questions Superman about his special powers, she learns that he has x-ray vision but cannot see through lead. "What color underwear am I wearing?," the inquisitive reporter asks frankly. A lead planter stands between them. His response is delayed, so Lois moves on to other probing questions. It is not until later, when she steps out from behind the planter, that he answers her. "Pink," he says flatly, chastely. "What?," she asks, looking confused. "They're pink, Lois." She turns to him for clarification and finds him staring at her crotch. "Oh," she nods in understanding and blushes slightly. A few minutes later, as they are flying over the city together, Lois continues her interview with Superman in her head, posing additional questions in a whispery, child-like voice full of wonder: "Can you read my mind?"

In this romantic sequence from *Superman* (1973), acts of seeing and showing-through double as sex acts for the human-superhero couple, expressing the romantic longing for a super man capable of recognizing and potentially fulfilling feminine desires. Superman's ability to literally see through Lois's evening gown extends, metaphorically to his magical capacity to read her mind. In the terms of 1970s popular psychology, his x-ray vision is not only a superpower but also a metaphor for true love or what it means to be "in sync" with another person. The superhero's x-ray vision produces pleasure for the intrepid reporter who secretly wears pink underwear. The experience of being "seen through" feminizes Lois, temporarily softening the tough-as-nails city reporter. At the end of the flight scene, Superman drops Lois off on her terrace, leaving her in what appears to be a blissful, postcoital trance so he can return to the thank-less work of fighting crime.

Lest you think I am making too much of one silly article, Sachs's modeling of feminine heterosexual acquiescence to the new surveillance technologies is representative of many more stories, photographs, and political cartoons that also rely on gendered and sexualized scripts of encounters between passenger-suspects, on the one hand, and surveillance technologies or representatives of the security state, on the other. One can see this media narrative neatly encapsulated in the 6 December 2010 cover image of the *New Yorker*, which upends the romantic formula of *Superman* by reversing gender roles to comic effect.

In so doing, influential U.S. media outlets like the *Washington Post* and the *New Yorker* participate in and promote what Magnet has called "sur-

7.3 "Feeling the Love,"
by Barry Blitt. Cover art
for the *New Yorker*,
6 December 2010.

veillant scopophilia," which refers to the ways in which new surveillance technologies produce "new forms of pleasure [for some] in looking at the human body disassembled into its component parts while simultaneously working to assuage individual anxieties about safety and security through the promise of surveillance" (2011, 17). This selective treatment aligns the new technologies with U.S. consumer and popular cultures of surveillance, where sex and sex appeal (or the tragic lack thereof) are the only story being told. The "sexy" or comically asexual exposed body is uniformly white. In this manner, the sexualization of the new surveillance technologies in U.S. discourse domesticates the machines while obscuring the global racial norm used to determine which bodies are presumed capable of reflexive governance via high-tech screening and which bodies are presumed incapable or unwilling to practice reflexive governance and must therefore be forcibly subdued.

Female Grotesque

The coding of "voluntary" transparency as hip in a postfeminist sense is based, in turn, on a gendered and sexualized construction of the terrorist threat addressed by the new surveillance technologies. In its coverage of Umar Farouk Abdulmutallab's nearly successful attack on Northwest Flight 253 from Amsterdam to Detroit on 25 December 2009, ABC News depicted the would-be terrorist as a grossly undisciplined woman. The news organization posted government photographs of the accused bomber's underwear (Esposito and Ross 2009). In the photos, the suspect's briefs have been turned inside out to reveal a packet of explosive powder sewn into the crotch. The garment figures the terrorist's opacity in the visual and linguistic registers of failed feminine hygiene.

When I first saw the underwear photos, I wondered whether Al Qaeda wasn't intentionally crafting a brilliant, interactive durational performance art piece spoofing the deepest, darkest recesses of the American psyche. The article refers to the suspect's "underpants"—a garment worn by women and children in the United States. As a woman, it is difficult not to see a resemblance between Abdulmutallab's underwear kitted out with a secret, explosive compartment and a pair of women's underwear outfitted with a maxi pad or panty liner. The tattered, torn, and stained underwear connotes the shame of soiling oneself and arouses in the viewer the fear of losing physical control over the body and the nightmare of being publicly exposed in a compromised state. The photos call to mind the old parental admonishment to "make sure you have on clean underwear in case you're in an accident." The public shaming was reprised in the fall of 2012 when Lee Ferran of ABC News reported that the bomb failed to detonate because Abdulmutallab's underwear was dirty. Abdulmutallab's race is not marked explicitly, and his body remains out of frame, but it is the articulation of orientalism and the female grotesque, in this case, which implicitly demands and condones his public emasculation.

In addition to depicting Abdulmutallab within the visual codes of failed female hygiene, the "underpants" exhibit also queers the terrorist. As Puar has observed, "The depictions of masculinity most rapidly disseminated and globalized at this historical juncture are terrorist masculinities: failed and perverse, these emasculated bodies always have femininity as their reference point of malfunction, and are metonymically tied to all sorts of pathologies of the mind and body—homosexuality, incest, pedophilia, madness, and disease" (2007, xxiii). We can recognize this pattern of visual representation in the underwear exhibit. The not-so-subtle final shot in the series displays only the explosive packet. The article explains, "Tragedy was averted only because the detonator, acid in a syringe, did not work" (Esposito and Ross 2009). The photo displays the packet lengthwise next to the tape measure, with the explanation that "all photos include a ruler to provide scale" (ibid.). Earlier in the article

The bomb packet is a six-inch long container of the high-explosive chemical PETN, less than a half cup in volume, weighing about 80 grams.

In the second photo (right), the packet of explosive powder has been removed from the underpants and displayed separately.

A government test with 50 grams of PETN blew a hole in the side of an airliner. That was the amount in the bomb carried by the so-called shoe bomber Richard Reid over Christmas 2001.

UNDERWEAR WITH EXPLOSIVE PACKET

The underpants bomb would have been one and a half times as powerful.

Acid in Syringe Was Detonator

The packet of PETN explosive powder is shown separately here.

Tragedy was averted only because the detonator, acid in a syringe, did not work.

"It's very clear it came very, very close," said Rep. Pete Hoekstra, R.-Mich., ranking minority member of the House Intelligence Committee. "The explosive device went off, but it became an incendiary device instead of an explosive device, which is probably what saved that airplane."

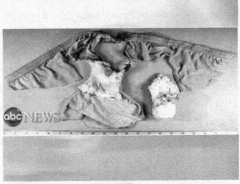

UNDERWEAR AND EXPLOSIVE PACKET

The acid in the melted plastic syringe, pictured below, caused a fire but did not make proper contact with the PETN.

Abdulmutallab told FBI agents he received the bomb from and was trained by al Qaeda in Yemen over the last few months.

PETN PACKAGE

7.4 Forensic government photos of Farouk Abdulmutallab's underwear with explosive powder packet. In Richard Esposito and Brian Ross, "Exclusive: Photos of the Northwest Airlines Flight 253 Bomb," 28 December 2009, ABC News website.

the authors reported, "The bomb packet is a six-inch long container" of the highly explosive chemical, "less than a half cup in volume, weighing about 80 grams" (ibid.). The final shot queers the aspiring terrorist by indirectly referencing his willingness to tuck his penis between his legs in order to make room for a substitute phallus.

One cannot help but be struck by the sober tone of the underwear exhibit, which documents a deliberate process in which select government officials displayed, lit, and shot the underwear and the explosive packet, first together, then separately. The forensic authority visually communicated by the exhibit connotes the would-be terrorist's abject degradation in the face of that authority. In the photographs, the underwear appears to have been ripped or cut off of Abdulmutallab's body, and in the second photo, the explosive packet has been removed, exposing a hole burned through the crotch of the underwear. Ostensibly, the hole communicates the irrational extremism of a person who would strap a bomb to his body, but it may also signify the threat of penetration—a threat that extends beyond Abdulmutallab's individual body to the bodies of all suspects of the United States in the war on terror. As Jeremy Packer first observed, "Citizens become bombs, not simply by choice or through cell propaganda and training, but by Homeland Security itself" (2006, 381). Abdulmutallab's failed attempt to become a bomb extends outward to all air passengers, who are treated as potentially explosive until they voluntarily submit to be scanned by surveillance technologies and/or patted down by security officials.

The underwear exhibit offers an over-the-top example of the moralizing function of opacity effects. The implicit comparisons invited by the exhibition hail the U.S. media consumer to perform "good" global citizenship, which is imagined, in comparison to the terrorist grotesque, as less voluminous, "dank," and "dirty." The underwear exhibit presumes the media consumer's difference from and moral superiority to the "opaque" body on display. By portraying the would-be terrorist according to the conventions of the female grotesque, the underwear exhibit implicitly invites U.S. and other Western media consumers to distinguish themselves from this contemptuous figure by rendering their own bodies less grottoesque. Russo (1994) argues that modern discourses of risk rely on the conceptualization of women in spatial terms via two figures: the aerial sublime and the female grotesque. The aerial sublime symbolizes transcendence, technological progress, and futuristic aspiration, but her symbolic work relies on the female grotesque, who embodies the outer (as inner) limits of the project of modernity and the risk of its catastrophic failure. Indeed, the full-body scanners proposed as a solution to the threat of plastic explosives like the underwear bomb promise to "clear" passengers of suspicion by rendering transparent images of their bodies, which appear as flat, hollow, unadorned, or otherwise unmodified outlines.

Another *New Yorker* cartoon, from the 18 January 2010 issue, explores the threat of humiliation posed by whole-body scanners. In the cartoon the passenger suffers not only the humiliation of bodily exposure but also the embarrassment of having a comforting travel companion revealed. The passenger, a grown man, has a teddy bear hidden beneath his clothing and strapped to his waist. Instead of TSA agents viewing his body image in a closed, offsite location, as they do in actual practice, the cartoon agency projects life-size full-body images of the passenger onto the wall of the airport just to the side of the checkpoint, where passengers waiting to be screened laugh and point at the unlikely revelation. While the passenger's live body is drawn straight and narrow, with the slim hips of a man, his security image is drawn in the pear shape that is fatphobically associated with the female grotesque in U.S. popular culture. The security image functions like a funhouse mirror. The question is whether the distortion is supposed to read as a projection of the passenger's body dysmorphic disorder or as a critique of the security state's filters, which threaten to feminize and infantilize the passenger, according to this cartoon.

In practice, full-body scanners may unnecessarily expose a medical condition such as a disability or a colostomy bag, rather than a teddy bear. As feminist scholars Magnet and Tara Rodgers argue, the body scanners may create terror and dread for passengers, "especially if these technologies 'out' individuals in their communities, violate their religious beliefs, or single them out for public humiliation, stress, and harassment" (2012, 13). The authors make a compelling case that these new surveillance technologies disproportionately affect "Othered bodies, including the intersections of transgendered, disabled, fat, religious, female and racialized bodies" (ibid., 14). The *New Yorker* cartoon alludes to the threat of public humiliation but domesticates that threat via the figure of the ordinary white male traveler who fails to be hip or sexy while proceeding through the checkpoint. He becomes the sympathetic, comic foil to the ideal of transparency chic, someone with whom ordinary readers are encouraged to identify, rather than with those othered bodies for whom the stakes of exposure via full-body scans run much higher.

Transparency chic presumes a healthy, able-bodied passenger-suspect.

7.5 Artwork in the *New Yorker*, 18 January 2010, p. 47. © Michael Crawford/The New Yorker Collection/The Cartoon Bank.

Physical ailments, disabilities, limitations, or chronic medical conditions may prevent a particular suspect from being adequately self-subduing via the performance of submission to scanning by machine. This state of affairs requires the TSA officers to substitute or supplement technological mediation with a physical search. For example, a passenger who relies on a mobility device cannot assume the proper position required for screening by the full-body scanners: standing with arms above head. This person fails to perform transparency insofar as she is unable to assume the required position and produce the correct gestures in a performance that would culminate in the production of a particular type of security image of her body. Likewise, cyborg passengers with implanted defibrillators cannot pass through metal detectors because their devices set off the detector and therefore defeat the purpose of this method of scanning the passenger for contraband. Paradoxically, the medical cyborg is at once too vulnerable and too advanced for the metal detector. The TSA refers to his condition in visual terms that cast further suspicion on the passenger with a "hidden disability."

Where metal detectors and body scanners prove insufficient, TSA workers must substitute or supplement technological mediation with physical contact. Transparent mediation by close-sensing technologies becomes a semi-public, intimate physical encounter with a TSA official. Physical pat-downs and searches performed on such passengers typically happen in a designated area just to the side of the queues for the metal detectors and x-ray machines. Interestingly, these areas are frequently cordoned off by a series of glass or plastic partitions. This creates a situation in which passengers proceeding through the regular screening process can watch as TSA officials handle passengers pulled for additional screening. The function of the transparent partitions communicates voluntary transparency on the part of the TSA, even as it heightens the theatrical aspects of the encounter, now enticingly framed by a glass box.

Sometimes these inspections go horribly wrong, as in the case of Thomas Sawyer, a sixty-one-year-old man and cancer survivor, who said a TSA pat-down inspection broke his urine bag. Anne E. Kornblut and Perry Bacon Jr. (2010) of the *Washington Post* reported that Sawyer suffered the further indignity of having to board his flight covered in urine without the benefit of an apology from the TSA officer involved in the incident. Sawyer's experience (and that of countless others who have been subjected to a physical search because of a medical condition or disability) raises the question of whether or not physical pat-downs constitute a violation of the Health Insurance Portability and Accountability

Act of 1996 (HIPAA) or the Americans with Disabilities Act of 1990. The Department of Health and Human Services lists law-enforcement agencies among those organizations *not* required to follow HIPAA's privacy and security rules.[5] During a national or public-health emergency, the secretary of Health and Human Services may waive certain provisions of HIPAA even for those organizations usually required to follow its privacy and security rules. Thus, it seems that public physical inspection of passengers with medical conditions does not constitute a violation of HIPAA.

Whether or not public pat-downs of passengers with medical conditions and disabilities constitutes a violation of the Americans with Disabilities Act is more difficult to determine. The act "prohibits discrimination on the basis of disability in employment, State and local government, public accommodations, commercial facilities, transportation, and telecommunications."[6] The TSA proclaims that its commitment to customer service extends to all passengers, "regardless of their personal situations and needs." In an effort to meet the needs of passengers with medical conditions and disabilities, the agency established a coalition of over seventy disability-related groups and organizations "to help us understand the concerns of persons with disabilities and medical conditions."[7] This research has informed the TSA's approach to passengers with "all categories of disabilities (mobility, hearing, visual, and hidden)."[8] Coverage by the program indicates that TSA screeners have been briefed on the range of conditions they may encounter. Coverage also means specialized travel tips for passengers with medical conditions or disabilities and their traveling companions. The general theme of these disability-specific tips is that passengers with medical conditions or disabilities and their traveling companions are responsible for initiating communication about their condition with TSA officers.

In some cases, the travel tips offered attempt to head off charges of privacy violation and discrimination in one fell swoop. For example, those who dislike the exposure of a pat-down inspection at the checkpoint are advised to "request a private area for your pat-down inspection if you feel uncomfortable with having a medical device being displayed while inspected by the Security Officer."[9] In the case of passengers with medical conditions or disabilities, offsite inspection is offered as an option less stigmatizing than undergoing physical inspection at the checkpoint before an audience of one's peers. By contrast, the prospect of being transferred from the public checkpoint to an offsite location for further inspection and interrogation implies the threat of physical harm and arrest to those suspected of terrorism. That is not to say that passengers with medical conditions or disabilities are presumed innocent. In what is perhaps the most harrowing section of advice for passengers with medical conditions and disabilities, the TSA addresses the visual problem of dressed wounds.

- Whenever there is a metal detector alarm in the area of a dressing, the Security Officers will conduct a gentle limited pat-down of the dressing area over top of your clothing.
- Clothing will not be required to be removed, lifted, or lowered during the pat-down inspection.
- The Security Officer will not ask you to, nor will he or she, remove a dressing during the screening process.
- In the event a Security Officer is not able to determine that a dressing is free of prohibited items via a pat-down, you will be denied access to the sterile area.

Particularly striking is the use of the term *sterile* in reference to the securitized area just beyond the checkpoint in the context of a discussion of how to treat passengers with dressed wounds. The final bullet point pits the "sterility" of the securitized zone against the "sterility" of the passenger's dressed wound. One form of sterility demands exposure, while the other requires a protective covering. In its treatment of the range of medical conditions and disabilities TSA officers may encounter, the agency's tone is alternately insistent and tender as it communicates its unwavering commitment to expose what might otherwise be hidden by the pretense of a medical condition or disability.

Given the hypersexualized media narratives surrounding the rapid installation of full-body scanners in U.S. airports beginning in early 2010, it is perhaps not all that surprising that the main objection given voice by major U.S. media outlets concerned the protection of passengers' sexual privacy. This was true despite the fact that the new technologies also raised concerns about radiation exposure from the backscatter machines (see J. Marshall 2010).[10] In response to the charge that the new machines violated sexual privacy, the TSA stressed that the security images produced could not be saved or stored. In order for the next passenger to be scanned, the previous image had to be deleted. James Ott (2010) of *Aviation Daily* reported that the TSA chief John Pistole assured the public that no mobile phones or cameras were permitted in the remote viewing rooms where agents inspected the full-body images. In other words, the TSA understands the privacy violation in terms of the politics of information rather than the politics of performing submission to comprehensive surveillance, or understands it in terms of the live experience of being produced as one of the security state's many suspects.

The TSA stresses the measures it takes to de-eroticize the body images it makes. The organization notes that faces are blurred or blocked out, no hair is visible, and human monitors are of the same sex as the passengers being screened (the TSA appeals to this same heteronormative logic when it describes and defends its organizational procedures for conducting physical pat-downs). In the TSA's arguments for why these images are not pornographic, we learn by negation what is sexualized: faces, hair, and heterosexuality. And in early 2011 Ashley Halsey III, of the *Washington Post*, reported that the TSA had debuted a software patch on millimeter-wave machines at Las Vegas Airport. The full-body scanner machines using radio waves now produce a gray "cookie-cutter" outline of the human body. The generic quality of the figure is designed to alleviate privacy concerns because every body image generated by the machine looks exactly the same. The lack of graphic detail serves as a control on the potential eroticism of full-body images. This is a body image designed to do nothing for the spectator—nothing, that is, other than sanitize the technology and, by extension, the security state's relationship to passengers' bodies.

The automatic detection software highlights suspicious regions with a yellow box on that part of the generic body. This cues the TSA officer to physically inspect only that region of the passenger's body. Significantly, the generic body image appears on a screen attached to the scanning booth so that both the TSA officer stationed beside the machine and the passenger are able to look at the image together and wait for the green light or "OK," at which point the TSA officer waves the passenger on her way. In January 2013 the TSA announced it would be removing all backscatter machines from U.S. airports, not due to health concerns but because the machines' manufacturer, Rapsican, had failed to develop a software patch to translate detailed images of passengers' bodies into a generic outline of the human form.[11] The aesthetic produced by the privacy software patch is of a generic outline, defended on the grounds that it does not offend privacy. However, the image is revealing in that it pictures precisely what these technologies produce: a new normate body.

Conclusion

My critique of the full-body scanners contributes to the larger, collaborative project initiated by feminist scholars of surveillance: to shift critical surveillance studies away from matters of privacy, security, and efficiency to a consideration of the ethical problem of combating new forms of discrimination that are practiced in relation to categories of privilege, access, and risk.[12] U.S. public discourse has domesticated the new surveillance technology via gendered and sexualizing scripts of being seen-through as a form of romantic love, attraction, and repulsion. These discourses have thereby framed the new technologies and the airport security checkpoint as yet another opportunity to succeed or fail at attractively imaging one's body for the male gaze and according to Euro-American standards of beauty, health, and fitness. In this manner, U.S. public discourse about the scanners has ignored the fact that the differential application of high- and low-tech surveillance methods is organized according to a racial norm, where race is understood not in the narrow terms of phenotype but in the broader terms of who is presumed capable of participating in the biopolitical project of terrorism prevention and who is written off as stubbornly opaque.

Using sex to obscure race and ethnicity in U.S. public discourse about post-9/11 security culture is not a minor oversight. Rather, it is a tragically superficial distraction that supports the unthinking adoption of a differentially applied preemptive legal framework at home and abroad. A narrow view of new surveillance technologies through the lens of sexual privacy misses the fact that the racial norm is what has facilitated the rollout of preemptive laws in the war on terror and made the domestic culture of terrorism prevention palatable to citizens of governments who feel besieged by the threat of terrorism. The difference between how suspected terrorists in the war on terror and passenger-suspects in U.S. airports are treated renders the indefinite extension of surveillance on both fronts palatable to a majority of U.S. citizens, demonstrated through a critique of the aesthetics of transparency operative in new surveillance technologies and of the discourses surrounding their adoption.

Notes

1. I first articulated some of these ideas in 2007. For an extended analysis of the aesthetics and politics of transparency, see my book *The Transparent Traveler: The Performance and Culture of Airport Security* (Duke University Press, 2015).

2. The online special report is no longer available, but the initial story is (CNN .com 2003).

3. Marita Sturken reads the work of some of the artists included in the show

Safe: Design Takes on Risk (2005) at the Museum of Modern Art as critical commentaries on risk culture as a form of "privileged paranoia" (2005, 82). See also Antonelli 2005.

4. See "Technology That Might Have Helped," *New York Times*, 27 December 2009, http://www.nytimes.com/interactive/2009/12/27/us/terror-graphic.html.

5. See "Health Information Privacy," U.S. Department of Health and Human Services website, http://www.hhs.gov/ocr/privacy.

6. "A Guide to Disability Rights Laws," U.S. Department of Justice, Civil Rights Division, July 2009, http://www.ada.gov/cguide.htm.

7. See "Travelers with Disabilities and Medical Conditions," Transportation Security Administration website, http://www.tsa.gov/traveler-information/travelers -disabilities-and-medical-conditions.

8. See "Travelers with Disabilities and Medical Conditions," Transportation Security Administration website, http://www.tsa.gov/traveler-information/travelers -disabilities-and-medical-conditions.

9. See "Mobility Impairments," Transportation Security Administration website, http://www.tsa.gov/traveler-information/mobility-impairments.

10. Electronic Privacy Information Center (EPIC) filed a Freedom of Information Act request and obtained documents from the Department of Homeland Security (DHS), which provided evidence that the government failed to conduct proper safety tests on the x-ray scanners before installing them in airports and dismissed TSA employees' concerns about excessive exposure to radiation. EPIC argues that the documents indicate that the DHS mischaracterized safety findings by the National Institute of Standards and Technology (NIST). A NIST official stated in an email that the agency had not tested the scanners for safety over time. The TSA has yet to respond to requests by TSA union representatives at Boston Logan Airport for the TSA to allow its screeners to wear radiation-monitoring devices or dosimeters. See Romero 2011.

11. With 250 backscatter machines already installed in airports and warehouses, the TSA canceled its contract with the security company, which, at the company's expense, had to remove the machines by 31 May 2013. The TSA continues to use millimeter-wave body scanners. See Halsey 2013.

12. Exemplary in this regard are Kelly Gates (2011) and Shoshana Amielle Magnet (2011). The feminist critique of privacy insists that defending the privacy rights of individuals is an insufficient and problematic goal of surveillance studies as a field, given that welfare recipients, people living in poverty, and queers have never been entitled to privacy, as well the fact that privacy has not always kept women safer (i.e., violence against women and children often occurs in the home). For a critique of the use of biometric technologies on welfare recipients, see Magnet 2011. For a critique of the privacy debate from the perspective of low-income mothers, see Gilliom 2001. For a critique of the heterosexism of the privacy critique of surveillance, see McGrath 2004.

8

THE PUBLIC FETUS AND
THE VEILED WOMAN

Transnational Surrogacy Blogs as Surveillant Assemblage

SAYANTANI DASGUPTA AND SHAMITA DAS DASGUPTA

"Our bump!"

Below these words is a striking image: a brown-skinned pregnant woman, swathed in a sparkling silver and pink sari, her protruding abdomen the focus of the photograph, her face conspicuously absent. Fecund, colorful, exotic, this online photograph is but one of many such "headless" belly images on blogs with names like *Million Rupee Baby*, *Chai Baby*, *Our Adventures in Indian Surrogacy*, *Masala Baby*, and *Baby Masala*. The pregnant bodies captured on the sites are not those of the bloggers. This is a new version of the parenting blog: written by U.S., European, Australian couples who have contracted Indian women to be their gestational surrogates.

The image of the sari-clad headless surrogate has become something of a symbol for Western rhetoric around transnational surrogacy. In the U.S. women's fashion magazine *Marie Claire* ran an article which catapulted transnational surrogacy into mainstream consciousness in United States, with the sensationalist title "Surrogate Mothers: Wombs Rent."[1] One prominent caption read, "The number of Indian women willing to carry an American child is growing fast" (Haworth 2007). That *Marie Claire* article was accompanied by a full-page color photograph featuring the bodies of three sari-clad pregnant Indian women. The brown-skinned women's protuberant bellies were swathed in saris in rice-paddy green, vermilion orange, and eggplant purple. Yet, in contrast to the women's bodies, the women's heads and faces were strikingly absent. Even when the Indian surrogate's head was visible, her face was usually swathed with a veil or a surgical mask (Chu 2006; Haimowitz and Sinha 2008). Ostensibly, the heads and faces of Indian surrogates are left out to protect them from community and family censure; in cultural contexts where surrogacy may be stigmatized, it might be assumed surrogates have had sexual intercourse to get pregnant. Yet, images of headless (or veiled) Indian surrogates clearly serve other rhetorical agendas regarding gender, race, class, sexuality, embodiment, reproduction, technology, and nationhood.

Visual cultural studies and gender studies have long theorized the relationship between women's bodies and the public gaze. The portrayal of women's bodies and body parts as passive recipients of a masculine heteronormative gaze has been discussed by many, from feminist film theorists (Mulvey 1975) to social activists writing on gender and advertising (Kilbourne 2000). Indeed, we have elsewhere suggested that the *Marie Claire* image of the headless Indian surrogate is one that encourages in the viewer "a gaze pregnant with Orientalist possibilities, in which the faceless body of the surrogate is very literally unable to look back" (Das-Gupta and Dasgupta 2010).[2] This image can also be understood in light of Michel Foucault's (1995) construction of the docile body frozen in time and space, removed of subjectivity. In the words of Marina DelVecchio (2011), writing on violence against women in advertising, "If a woman is looked upon as an object, without feelings, life, soul, or thoughts, then it is easy to ingest images of her that defy her humanity. . . . She is merely a body, a vacant, empty, vessel intended to contain the needs of others . . . and her body, which is the most desired aspect of her existence . . . is open for interpretation and domination."

Commercial transnational gestational surrogacy, or "transnational surrogacy," in India is a practice marked by foreign (often North American, Australian, and European) infertile couples (intended parents, or IPs) hiring the services of Indian surrogates, who are implanted with fertilized ova of the IPs' choice and carry "their" fetuses to term.[3] As gestational surrogates only, these Indian women have no genetic relationship to the fetus they are carrying. After delivery, the surrogates hand over the babies to the intended parents in exchange for money. The process is mediated by agencies and fertility clinics engaged in transnational reproductive commerce. Similarly, popular-culture narratives about transnational surrogacy are authored almost uniformly by reporters or by Western IP bloggers, not by the surrogates themselves.

In this chapter we examine the blogging practices of Western IPs vis-à-vis Indian surrogates, suggesting that such blogs serve as locations of surveillance. In particular, we interrogate two cultural practices of Western IP bloggers: the posting of online 3-D and 4-D ultrasound images of "their" fetuses gestating in the wombs of Indian surrogates; and the posting of "belly shots" or "bump shots" of the surrogates, which are the headless or veiled images of the mid-sections of (brown-skinned, sari-clad) surrogates.

Using both scholarship in surveillance studies and about reproductive technologies, we make the case that transnational surrogacy can be understood as not only about gender, race, and visuality, but also about power and technoscience, citizenship, reproduction, production, and consumption. In addition, transnational surrogacy in India cannot be understood outside of its historic and political contexts—particularly as a phenomenon that exists within a post-9/11 globalized marketplace, where the impetus for economic "outsourcing" (for cheaper goods, services, and labor) comes into direct conflict with the xenophobic nationalist anxieties of Western nations about breached borders and veiled bodies. As such, we locate our discussion of transnational surrogacy in India within the emerging discipline of feminist surveillance studies, borrowing specifically from Deborah Wilson Lowry's (2004) assertion that reproductive technologies can be understood as "surveillant assembl...

viduals identifying as women, both Western surrogates and Western intended mothers (IMs). We did not know the ethnicity of most message-boarders, except when we recognized a name from the Indian surrogacy blogosphere or when the message-boarder posted a profile picture.[5]

In previous work (DasGupta and Dasgupta 2011), we examined blogs and message boards as locations of auto/biography, understanding blogs as forms of digital diary writing. In the words of Laurie McNeil, "In their immediacy and accessibility, in their seemingly unmediated state, Web diaries blur the distinction between online and offline lives, 'virtual reality' and 'real life,' 'public' and 'private,' and most intriguingly . . . between the life and the text" (McNeil 2003, 25). The lens of feminist surveillance studies serves to deepen our understanding of these digital diaries.

In their foundational work in surveillance studies, Kevin D. Haggerty and Richard V. Ericson (2000) suggest that the notion of a "surveillant assemblage" is a way to understand surveillance beyond the Orwellian Big Brother or the Foucauldian panopticon. Drawing from the work of Gilles Deleuze and Félix Guattari (1987), Haggerty and Ericson are concerned not with one form of technology, but rather with how fluid systems of technologies and practices work together to analyze and break down bodies into their component parts, gathering and organizing this information, and operating in ways that are not "top down" (a panoptic gaze looking down from above) but increasingly horizontal in nature, where, in their words, there is a "rhizomatic crisscrossing of the gaze such that no major population groups stand irrefutably above or outside of the surveillant assemblage" (2000, 618). In addition, they assert, "A great deal of surveillance is directed toward the human body. The observed body is . . . broken down by being abstracted from its territorial setting. It is then reassembled in different settings through a series of data flows. The result is a decorpo-realized body, a 'data double' of pure virtuality" (ibid., 611).

Lowry builds on these understandings to assert that reproductive technologies and services form "an assemblage that monitors and distributes information about pregnant women" (2004, 364). She points to gestational ultrasonography's abstraction of the fetus from the maternal body as an example of how the surveillance assemblage of reproductive technologies breaks down, abstracts, and reassembles female bodies. In addition to Lowry's understanding of reproductive technologies as surveillant assemblages, Hall's (2007; this volume) formulation of the aesthetics of transparency influences our discussion. Hall locates her analysis at national rather than reproductive borderlands, where Ziplock bags revealing the body's hygiene products represent the state's investment in policing bodies and bodily interiors. Such policing becomes framed as a way to "root out terror," that is, perceived threats to a particular formulated notion of national (and racial) integrity. In Hall's words, "The aesthetics of transparency is motivated by the desire to turn the world (the body) inside-out such that there would no longer be any secrets or interiors, human or geographical, in which our enemies (or the enemy within) might find refuge. . . . [It] establishes a binary opposition between interiority and exteriority and privileges the external or visible surface over the suspect's word" (2007, 321). Fetal images are consistent with Lowry's discussions of reproductive-imaging technologies, such as ultrasound, which fetishize the fetus as something separate from the mother. And yet, images of pregnant surrogates, even "veiled" or headless surrogates, seemingly contradict this impulse, bringing the fetal context (the gestating maternal body) firmly into view. These two gestures appear to bring into conflict Hall's assertion that an aesthetics of transparency relies on a "binary opposition between interiority and exteriority." We investigate the tension between the kind of reproductive surveillance undertaken in clinic rooms and the sort of national borderland surveillance conducted in airports. While the former visualizes reproductive interiority in the form of the fetus, the latter brings into focus the exteriority of the gendered and racialized "foreign" subject—desired for the products of her labor, yet simultaneously distanced and suspect. We examine how transnational IP blogs, which routinely post both sorts of images, exemplify a new, globalized world order of surveillance not operated from "above" but horizontally, as part of a digital "rhizometric crisscrossing of gaze[s]." The ultrasonographic and photographic images posted on the blogs of ͗fertile couples from the Global North become part of the information ͗ ͗ and "centers of calculation" (Haggerty and Ericsson 2000, 603) ͗ʼnal surveillant assemblage, playing out on the bodies of ͗al South.

͗ʼrspective on questions of surveillance high-
͗ʼnsnational surrogacy and the tenuous
͗ʼlitics, as well as gendered, racial-
͗ied borderlands are policed
͗ʼrogacy, gamete dona-
ʼssentially playing catch-
.reproductive technologies
ʼtage. We suggest that trans-

national surrogacy brings to the fore in surveillance studies scholarship the critical importance of not only gender, race, and embodiment, but also colonialism.

Background: Global Surrogacy and Its Informational Networks

Since becoming legal in 2002, the Indian surrogacy industry has been booming. U.S. media headlines consistently compare Indian surrogacy to other forms of Indian "tech support" (World Vision 2009), although this conflation is decidedly vexed.[6] Every major city in India has joined in the surrogacy trade and offers gestational surrogacy services to all who can afford the fees, including foreign (mostly Western) clients and wealthy Indians.

Explanations for this growth industry are many. In a country with an overwhelming number of economically desperate citizens, where English is spoken commonly among the professional classes, and world-class medical services and technologies are available at drastically cheaper rates, Indian transnational surrogacy is a lucrative market. Consider that in India the cost of gestational surrogacy might be $22,000 or less, while in the United States it might run to $100,000 (Fontanella-Khan 2010).[7] Indian surrogates reportedly receive $2,000–$5,000 (Wade 2009a), money often used for family expenses, which might include a child's surgery, a new dwelling, or a spouse's business. Despite its clear benefits to Indian women in terms of economic gain, surrogacy in India is marked by a drastic lack of regulation, practice guidelines, and transparency, allowing for exploitation of the surrogates.[8] Indeed, Amrita Pande (2009a) found that Indian surrogates did not discuss surrogacy as a "choice," but rather as an economic "compulsion." Yet even as the Assisted Reproductive Technologies (Regulation) Bill–2010 proposed by India's Ministry of Health and Family Welfare is awaiting legislative approval, the industry keeps growing in response to the demands in the West (Government of India 2010; Pande 2009b).

The digital "information networks" of transnational surrogacy include online brokers such as Planet Hospital (www.planethospital.com) and Surrogacy India (www.surrogacyindia.com), who make the connections between Western IPs and Indian fertility clinics. While surrogates are usually recruited by local, "on the ground" women engaged by Indian fertility clinics, various online modes of communication, such as email and Skype, facilitate negotiations between Western IPs and Indian physicians, allow IPs to view ultrasounds and other screening tests, and mediate the IPs' relationship with both the surrogates and the fetuses they bear.[9] Online communications include blogs and message boards that help Western IPs connect with others like themselves.

Although the rhetoric of transnational surrogacy in India, like the rhetoric about surrogacy in the West, is marked by assertions about "gift exchange" and "sisterhood," these ideas serve to obfuscate the commercial and exploitative aspects of the industry (DasGupta and Dasgupta 2010). Indeed, we found that despite evoking a rhetoric of sisterhood vis-à-vis their Indian surrogates, IPs tend to focus in their blogs on connections between IPs rather than on connections to surrogates. We have elsewhere argued that IP blogs constitute a sort of cross-border "cybernation" (here labeled "digital nation") marked by bonds between Western IP bloggers, regardless of North American, European, or Australian citizenship, united through various practices, including the "othering" of both Indian surrogates and India itself, as well as the espousing of colonial and capitalist worldviews (DasGupta and Dasgupta 2011). Surveillance is, of course a key part of nation building, and the digital nation of IP bloggers has characteristics of what David Lyon (1994) would call a "surveillance society." This surveillance society is involved in a colonialist project that particularly manifests itself in gendered, racialized, and otherwise embodied ways. The surveillance statecraft of the Western IP "nation" breaks down the brown woman's body into its component parts, creating what Haggerty and Ericson call "a series of discrete signifying flows" (2000, 612), while simultaneously protecting its digital-national borders from the brown woman's disruptive presence. Like Hall's (2007) airport-security ziplock bags, the surrogate's interiority is made transparent, but, simultaneously, her exteriority is either veiled or decapitated — effectively "disappeared."

Offline Surveillance Practices:
Regulating Surrogate Consumption

Bringing a needy woman from the village to the clinic is a small first step in the whole process of "manufacturing" what Pande (2010) calls "the perfect mother-worker." This mother-worker is produced through a disciplinary project that deploys the power of language along with a meticulous control over the body of the surrogate. While the practice is not consistent across clinics, many Indian surrogates spend their pregnancy at the clinic's attached dormitory, where the surrogates' nutrition, health, and activities are controlled by the clinic's staff (Haworth 2007; Oprah .com 2007). Although some surrogates at other clinics "hide out" in rented apartments for the duration of their pregnancy to escape the censure of their local communities, the practice of "housing" surrogates in dormitories is growing in popularity.

Pande notes that "The perfect surrogate—cheap, docile, selfless, and nurturing—is produced in the fertility clinics and surrogacy hostels" (2010, 970). The physical manifestations of this production are a strictly regulated schedule involving the surveillance of bodily activities, including eating, medication, and rest, as well as stringent control over mobility, access to other children, and family. The rhetorical manifestations of this production process include assertions by the clinic staff about the interchangeability and disposability of the surrogate body (which is repetitively framed as a "vessel" or "rental house"), and the differentiation between "good" (selfless, giving, nurturant) and "bad" (greedy, demanding, assertive) mother-workers (Pande 2010). The growing phenomenon of the Indian surrogate dormitory (or "hostel") can be understood as one manifestation of offline surveillance—consistent with Foucault's "disciplinary project" (1995). Haggerty and Ericson distinguish the surveillant assemblage as different from the Foucauldian disciplinary project, they see it as something which does not "approach the body . . . [rather] it is . . . to be molded, punished, or controlled" (2000, 612). The body is something that must first be "known." If we look at the surrogate dormitory not solely as a disciplinary space, but also as a space that allows Western IP bloggers and message-boarders to "know" the bodies of "their" surrogates, the surveillant possibilities of the surrogate dormitory become clear.

Through a surveillance of consumption, the interiority of surrogate women, or at least an aspect of this interiority (what they put into their bodies), becomes readily apparent to Western IPs. On blogs and message boards, dormitories are usually lauded as ways to "understand" surrogate (read: fetal) nutrition. On a now defunct discussion forum called Surrogacy India Online Support Group, Western women discussed the need for surrogates to have vitamin supplements and debate the qualities of a "typical Indian diet." The conversations here are very much in the vein of increasing "knowledge" about caloric intake, typical Indian meals, and other aspects of surrogate nutritional health. One forum participant,

Myleen, writes, "I just want to make sure that the surrogate has all that she needs to create a healthy environment for the baby. It is YOUR baby. Nothing wrong with asking." Another participant, Mandy, adds, "We all want our surrogates to eat healthy, that's why i [sic] chose Dr. Patel because they are in a surrogate house and can be assisted with access to nutritious food" (Surrogacy India Online Support Group 2009). Sarah, a forty-year-old from Berkeley who runs a catering company with her husband and teaches Jewish ethics lessons to children, says, "When I was told by my doctor they could get someone in Stockton [California], I don't know what they're eating, what they're doing. Their physical environment would have been a concern for me." Sarah continues: "The way they have things set up . . . [in India] is that the surrogate's sole purpose is to carry a healthy baby for someone" (Carney 2010). Additionally, Nayna Patel, of the Akanksha Infertility Clinic, promotes Indian surrogacy by tapping into a narrative of a morally pure mystic East, suggesting that Indian surrogates are "free of [read: Western] vices, like alcohol, smoking, and drugs" (Gentleman 2008). Echoing this sentiment, another Western IP suggests, "One of the nicest things about [India] is that the women don't drink or smoke." Although most U.S. surrogacy contracts forbid such activities, the Western IP asserts, "I take people in India more for their word than probably I would in the United States" (Carney 2010).

The Public Fetus: Fetal Citizenship on Intended Parent Blogs

Many scholars of reproductive technology, including Rosalind Petchesky, Emily Martin, Carol Stabile, and Janelle S. Taylor, have long argued that obstetric ultrasound technology has created a "cult of the public fetus," whose task involves "revealing and unmasking what has been hidden and obscured, inevitably draw[ing] us into a politics of vision" (Taylor 2004, 189).[10] The fetus becomes a fetishized figure, both "already a baby," representing the "patient" as separate from the mother, and a sort of "'baby man,' an autonomous, atomized mini-spacehero" (Petchesky 1987). Established as a separate visual identity outside the mother, the fetus becomes a public persona in the U.S. cultural imagination, used for agendas that range from selling Volvos to promoting anti-abortion campaigns.[11] In the words of Paul P. Brodwin, "Laparoscopy and fetal photography . . . furnish ever more invasive and naturalized depictions of the fetus, which performs the crucial ideological work (in the context of new Right politics in the United States) of visually separating mother and fetus, asserting fetal autonomy, and reducing women to passive reproducing machines" (2000, 4).

A central practice of "ultrasound culture" is cherishing fetal ultrasound images, which take positions of honor on mantelpieces, in photo albums, in wallets, on refrigerators, and, importantly, online. No longer relegated to medical, private, or real-life locations, blogs, Facebook photos, and Flickr and Twitter accounts are rife with images of fetal ultrasounds. The practice is so common that media outlets, from online maternity blogs (Koch 2010) to the venerable *Wall Street Journal* (Wong 2009), have debated whether posting ultrasounds is appropriate sharing in the age of digital communities or simply "TMI" (too much information). Following suit, not unlike similar (nonsurrogacy) sites in the "mommy blogosphere," transnational surrogacy IP blogs often post ultrasound images of "their" embryos/fetuses. From very early images of three implanted embryos or "three little nuggets" (prior to scheduled selective termination) at *Our Dream to Have a Baby through India Surrogacy* to 4-D images of thirty-two-week fetuses with recognizable facial features at *Chai Baby*, ultrasound blog posts are a common feature of transnational surrogacy sites.[12] Indian ART clinics recognize 3-D and 4-D fetal ultrasound images as an important product that allows transnational clients to feel connected to "their" pregnancies. In 2007, when this technology was still relatively new, the Akanksha Infertility Clinic proudly advertised the availability of 4-D ultrasounds on their website, saying, "Parents can . . . appreciate the fetal parts like face, spine, limbs, fingers and every single organ as if they are actually looking at the fetus. 4-D ultrasound enables us to see real time images of fetal movements like yawning, thumb sucking, swallowing, etc." (Kohl 2007). The surveillance of embodied interiority also becomes a way to police surrogate mobility. In the surrogate dormitory, ultrasounds are used as markers of "good surrogate behavior." In the words of one of Pande's interviewees, Varsha, "I am being extra careful now because Doctor Madam has said if everything looks all right in the ultrasound I can go visit my children. I don't want to do anything that will make Madam change her mind about letting me go home for a day or two" (2010, 982).

The cultural work of online ultrasound posts by IPs is ultimately different than that of nonsurrogacy sites, in that they serve to reduce the distance between the body of the intended parent and the fetus, making invisible the body of the gestating surrogate. As opposed to a gestating woman's multiply mediated relationship with her fetus (through a technologist, a screen, and so on), the surrogate's fetal images are exponentially mediated—first by a physician who performs an ultrasound in India, then via emails of the images to the IP, and then through the IP blogger who subsequently posts these online. The posted ultrasound images effectively obscure any perceived differences between an intended mother through surrogacy and a gestating mother: bloggers who are pregnant and IP bloggers are able to post ultrasound images of "their" fetuses, granting an internal vision in a (digital)space where material bodies—whether pregnant or not—are effectively dis-appeared.[13]

Baby Bumps and Belly Shots:
The Veiled or Headless Surrogate

Although it garnered significant negative reactions at the time, the August 1991 cover of the U.S. fashion magazine *Vanity Fair*—which featured a decidedly pregnant Demi Moore, a Hollywood actor, clad only in diamonds—marked a Western cultural shift in the ways pregnant bellies are publicly viewed (Stabile 1998). The celebrity "belly bump" has become a great cultural fascination and is fetishized. Similar to fetal ultrasound images, photographs of pregnant women's midsections are now de rigeur on social-networking sites and blogs. Similarly, IP bloggers frequently post images of belly bumps—the fundamental difference being, of course, that the bellies in question do not belong to them. Such images—of brown skinned, sari-swathed surrogate bellies—have the potential to erase the embodied surrogate. If posting ultrasound images on blogs effectively "abstracts" a fetus from its "territorial setting" (Haggerty and Ericson 2000, 611), then posting a surrogate belly bump potentially resituates the fetus in the maternal body. Yet, this embodied presence is not without its own complexities. While some blogs include photographs of the pregnant surrogate's body and face, most "belly shots" are so called because they are limited to the surrogates' midsection. For instance, the IP bloggers "Amani and Bob" posted the image described at the opening of this chapter (protruding abdomen of a brown-skinned pregnant woman wrapped in a sparkling silver and pink sari, her face absent) along with the following text, highlighting the complex connections between visual consumption and economic consumption or gift giving.

Introducing . . . our front bump!

Our bump! Don't look side on as I did, and think "what a lovely slim pregnant lady" the pic is taken from front on, so belly is poking out the front. Our SMR [surrogate mother] was very shy and squirmy and ran away from the camera. Bless her. A bump is a bump, I see a bump and I am loving that bump! I have a gift for SMR that I have had tucked away for ages. Dr Shivani doesn't encourage gift-giving until after baby is born. I am busting to send it and to write SMR a card and tell her how wonderful I think she is, and what an amazing job she is doing. But we have to wait (Thursday, 1 April 2010).[14]

The blogger's comments reinforce an orientalist gaze, suggesting a paradoxical relationship to the surrogate: ascribing agency to the surrogate posing for the image (she runs from the camera, for instance), at the same time as the blogger makes clear the belly and fetus belong to the blogger. This comes through in the comments as well. For example, commenter George, a single father of two babies by Indian surrogacy, remarks on the above: "beautiful! can i rub her belly for good luck? looks like she dressed in all her finest for the pic, and she said she is shy? lol." George emphasizes the surrogate as agentic (she dressed up for the occasion), at the same time as he frames her as a kind of good-luck charm, an object one "rubs" for good luck. As well, the various commenters use the pronoun *your* instead of *her* when referring to the "bump," as does the blogger herself ("Our front bump!"), cementing the idea that the headless belly "belongs" to the blogger IM, not the surrogate, or suggesting, even more disturbingly, that the surrogate herself "belongs" to the IM ("Our SMR"), and therefore so does the surrogate's pregnant uterus. The cultural capital of the belly shot—almost as ubiquitous on the blogs as the ultrasound images—is always prominent. For instance, Johnny and Darren, a gay Australian couple who had their babies by Indian surrogacy, remark on Amani and Bob's pregnancy-bump photo: "Great picture, you both must be happy to have this. I know when we received ours it took pride of place on the fridge door."[15]

The request to "see the bump" is heard consistently in other transnational surrogacy narratives. This is illustrated in the documentary *Our Family, Made in India* (Heinemann 2011), featuring Rhonda and Gerry from Mesa, Arizona, as they Skype with their Indian surrogate, Jaya. During the phone call, Gerry asks, "Is your belly growing? Let's see!" When the surrogate, who is carrying twins, obligingly stands (after the request is translated by her interpreter), he responds, "There's our babies!" An almost identical Skype call is filmed in the documentary *Can We See the Baby Bump Please?* (Surabhi 2012) but from the Indian side. After being asked, through a translator, to show her bump, the Indian surrogate stands. The translator angles the computer with its built-in camera toward her midsection, instructing the surrogate to smooth her clothing over her belly so the overseas IPs can better see her bump through the magic of the online video connection.

The problematic nature of the belly shot is articulated by bloggers themselves. The blogger at *Chai Baby* notes,

> Today we received some beautiful photos of our surrogate. We didn't ask for them and as it turns out it is something that SCI [the Indian surrogacy agency] are trying to do more of, so we can see the progress of our surrogacy. . . . Before i received our photos, i felt that the "belly shot" was a bit exploitative and felt generally uncomfortable about it all. It seemed to reduce our surrogate to the bits that carried our babies. Now i have these wonderful shots of our smiling surrogate, with a tentative wave to the camera and it's different. She is smiling and looks content and clearly pregnant, with our babies.[16]

Although the blogger notes that the surrogate is smiling, the image she posts is consistent with the surveillant assemblage's practice of separating bodies into component parts: a classic side belly shot without a head. The agency of the surrogate implied by the mention of smiling and waving is undermined by the fact that the image represents something the surrogacy agencies, not the surrogates themselves, orchestrate to please their precious overseas clients and provide a desired image, one that assists in deciphering for the IPs the otherwise "shy," invisible, and incomprehensible surrogate.

Conclusion: Interiority and Exteriority, the Fetus and the Veil

How are we to understand the seemingly contradictory gestures of posting fetal images and images of headless or veiled surrogates' bellies? These images enact a tension between the gestating mother, the IP, and the fetus, between exteriority and interiority, between material embodiment and the reconstitution of "data double" bodies in digital space. By locating the fetal image in the space of the blogosphere, the blogger reinscribes fetal autonomy, while at the same time implanting the fetus in the IP digital nation. Simultaneously, the headless gestating belly provides a nod to the presence of the surrogate, while disallowing any real agency, any literal or figurative "face."

Feminist surveillance scholars Shoshana Amielle Magnet and Tara Rodgers (2012) have discussed how post-9/11 Transportation Security Administration surveillance practices, including backscatter x-rays (which visualize the body naked underneath its clothes), effectively "out" transgender, disability, and other marginalized identities. Using Hall's (2007) "aesthetics of transparency," they suggest that this "outing" occurs as well with Muslim—or presumed Muslim—individuals with the state's desires to "see beneath the veil" of women wearing the burqua or niquab. In their words, "Claims about the importance of visualizing veiled bodies reference stereotypes about the inscrutability of racialized subjects (Said, 1978 as quoted by Magnet and Rodgers). More specifically . . . they reference a feminized Orient, one whose secret interiors must be "unveiled" and "exposed to the light of Western knowledge" (Gabeba Baderoon, 2003 as quoted by Magnet and Rodgers). Similarly, in his analysis of early twentieth-century postcards of veiled Algerian women, Mallek Alloula (1986) posits,

> The first thing the foreign eye catches about Algerian women is that they are concealed from sight. . . . [T]he eye cannot catch hold of her. . . . The opaque veil . . . discourages the scopic desire (the voyeurism) of the photographer. . . . These veiled women are not only an embarrassing enigma to the photographer but an outright attack upon him. It must be believed that the feminine gaze that filters through the veil is a gaze of a particular kind: concentrated by the tiny orifice for the eye, this womanly gaze is like that of the camera. . . . [T]hrust in the presence of a veiled woman, the photographer feels photographed. . . . [H]e is dispossessed of his own gaze. (1986, 521–22, 524)

Although Alloula's work is not often considered in the context of surveillance studies, his insights regarding the veiled, gendered subject, the colonial project, and visual desire deepen our understandings of both the surveillant assemblage and the aesthetics of transparency. Indeed, the impetus to "unveil" the hitherto "veiled" has been prevalent in recent U.S. narratives justifying the wars in Afghanistan and Iraq, in which public acceptance of war becomes tied to investments in the "unveiling" of Muslim women—a concern that can be understood as not so much about the freedom of women as about the inhibition of the misogynist and colonial proprietary gaze (Abu-Lughod 2002; Ahmed 1992; Viner 2002), as well as the visual neutralization of (brown-skinned, Islamic) "terrorist" threats.[17]

What we suggest is that the Western IP's gaze vis-à-vis the Indian surrogate is one which, like the backscatter x-ray, claims the ultimate in interiority through its "unveiling" of the boundaries of the surrogate's reproductive body. The fetal ultrasound becomes a mechanism by which the surrogate's "secret interiors" are "'unveiled' and exposed to the light of Western knowledge" (Magnet and Rogers 2012). Yet, the surrogate herself remains veiled, incomprehensible, and faceless. Indeed, the image of the headless or veiled surrogate may be symbolic of the anxiety of the Western IPs regarding their distant surrogates, whom they cannot readily "gaze upon" or "catch hold of." In the words of the IP Lisa Switzer,

> There's somebody else that I don't see and I don't know, and I have no contact with, that's carrying a child for me. I worry about her, because I look at what the standard of living is around here. I know that these women who are doing this surrogacy . . . they're getting paid quite a bit of money by their standards. The living conditions here . . . these are not Western living conditions. These are very very poor conditions. And my heart goes out to the people who live this way, but they don't know any better. (Haimowitz and Sinha 2008)

We see here the tension between transparent interiors and inscrutable exteriors, paralleling the same tensions in the type of surveillance done at national borderlands to "root out terror." In the words of Hall, "The aesthetics of transparency can thus be defined as an attempt by the security state to force a correspondence between interiority and exteriority on the objects of the preventative gaze" (this volume, 127). The distant, impoverished surrogate represents a reproductive, if not traditional, national security threat. Her poverty, her foreignness, her racial otherness all represent sources of potential "terror" to the IP digital nation. In turn, the IP digital nation attempts to neutralize this threat by "knowing" the surrogate's nutritional and vitamin status and visualizing her uterine interiors in the form of the fetal ultrasound. Ubiquitous requests to see her baby bump via Skype and emailed photos may represent what Hall calls an attempt to "flatten the object of surveillance" (this volume, 128), yet the surrogate's ultimate distance and inscrutability remain.

In the Levinasian formulation of mutuality, it is the "face" of the other that is brought into the light of recognition by the self who heeds the other's "primordial call" (Irvine 2005). As such, the headless belly-bump shot signals an undermining of this sort of recognition: it is a "re-veiling" of the surrogate such that not only is she unable to "be recognized" or to gaze back, but her reproductive body alone is present and not her subjecthood. For the Western IP digital nation, it is ultimately the fetal "face" which is unveiled through biotechnology, and it is this fetal image which replaces the surrogate's own literal and figurative face in the Western IP gaze. In the words of Barbara Katz Rothman, "Babies, at least healthy white babies, are very precious products these days. Mothers, rather like South African diamond miners, are cheap, expendable, not-too-trustworthy labour necessary to produce the precious product" (2004, 19).

In Margaret Atwood's postapocalyptic novel *The Handmaid's Tale* (1985), Earth's few remaining fertile women are forced to be "handmaids"—bearing children for the (infertile) ruling class. In the Red Center, their restrictive dormitory, they are taught that no other parts of their bodies other than their uteruses matter; their hands and feet, for instance, are subject to torture and abuse. So, too, are the handmaids' heads and most of their faces covered by a "stiff white veil," which they must wear or risk punishment of death. There are no mirrors in their world; they are not meant to see or be seen, but exist solely for the reproductive potential they offer "the Commander" and his wife. Faces disappear from the memory of one handmaid, even as she herself becomes "de-faced" by her surroundings.

> I try to congure [*sic*], to raise my own spirits, from wherever they are. I need to remember what they look like. I try to hold them still behind my eyes, their faces, like pictures in an album. But they won't stay still for me, they move, there's a smile and it's gone, their features curl and bend as if the paper's burning, blackness eats them. A glimpse, a pale shimmer on the air; a glow, aurora, dance of electrons, then a face again, faces. But they fade, though I stretch out my arms towards them, they slip away from me, ghosts at daybreak. Back to wherever they are. Stay with me, I want to say. But they won't.
>
> It's my fault. I am forgetting too much. (Atwood 1985, 193)

Where, in all this, is the voice of the Indian surrogate? Like her veiled or headless image, she is by and large voiceless—made invisible and mute—on IP blogs and discussion sites, unable to participate in Haggerty and Ericson's (2000) "rhizometric criss-crossing of the gaze." She is looked upon, but does not look and cannot implicate others in her looking. These conversations remain haunted by her faceless image, as is this essay itself. In our critique, our desire to contextualize the sighting of her (internal and external) body and its broader sociopolitical implications, we seek to conjure her face and spirit. We do not "speak for" but "speak with" her, listening hard for her reply.[18]

Notes

1. This article was preceded on 1 January 2006 by an episode of the *Oprah Winfrey Show*, "Wombs for Rent," which featured a special report by reporter Lisa Ling on the Akanksha Fertility Clinic. Many have attributed the widespread U.S. awareness of and fascination with Indian transnational surrogacy to this television program and to Oprah's famous assertions that Indian transnational surrogacy was "beautiful" and that it represented a situation of "women helping women."

2. Here we are using the concept of orientalism, as discussed by Edward Said (1978), as a process by which the "the Orient" is constructed as a cultural, political, and social entity.

3. Most frequently, the fertilized egg carries genetic material of both the intended parents. However, it might include ova donation from someone other than the intended mother, sperm donation from someone other than the intended father, or both.

4. For the blogs of heterosexual couples, see *Amani and Bob's Indian Surrogacy* (http://amaniandbobsurrogacy.blogspot.com/), *Made in India* (http://152am.blogspot.com/), *Million Rupee Baby* (http://millionrupeebaby.blogspot.com/), *The Switzers* (http://switzertwins.wordpress.com/), *Baby Masala* (http://babymasala.blogspot.com/), *Cocoa Masala* (http://cocoamasala.blogspot.com/), *+1 (Make that 2) Will Make Us a Family* (http://plus1makesusafamily.blogspot.com/), *Our Dream to Have a Family through India Surrogacy* (http://jonngem.blogspot.com/), and *Chai Baby* (http://havingababyinindia.blogspot.com/). For the blogs of same-sex male couples, see *Spawn of Mike and Mike* (http://spawnofmikeandmike.blogspot.com/), *Two Afro Dads* (http://2afrodads.blogspot.com/), *Orea Zoi* (http://orea-zoi.blogspot.com/), and *From India with Love* (http://johnnyanddarren.blogspot.com/). The message boards we consulted were SurrogateMothersOnline and the now defunct board run by Surrogacy India (http://www.surrogacyindia.com/).

5. Most message-boarders include with their comments a "tag" that has personal information such as "Mother to [names and ages of their children, often with the tag 'by surrogacy']." Gestational surrogates were identifiable by tags such as "GSx3" or "GS seeking IPs." Information about stillbirths and miscarriages was also included through comments like "GS to 1 Angel Baby."

6. Media reports describing gestational surrogacy as the "outsourcing of pregnancy" are too numerous to name here (two examples: Kung 2010; Subramanian

2007). Surrogacy may well be more akin to sex work, which does not require technical skill, but only the mere corporeality of the female body. As opposed to sex work, however, surrogacy is not solely a service industry; rather, it creates a "product"—a baby, who, when viewed through a Marxist lens, is irrevocably separated from the worker who produced her. Ultimately, surrogates, often poor, are motivated by desperate economic necessity.

7. Amrita Pande (2009b) reports slightly lower numbers, such as $50,000 to $80,000 in the United States and Canada, and between $5,000 and $12,000 in Akanksha clinic in Anand, Gujarat.

8. DasGupta and Dasgupta 2010; Haimowitz and Sinha 2008; Pande 2009a. Unadulterated condemnations of surrogacy are not without complexity. The belief that poor women in the Global South are not "free" to make choices due to the compulsion of their poverty denies their agency and reduces them to uncomplicated "victims" who deserve our pity and protection. In contrast, the same latitude is not necessarily offered to surrogates of the Global North, who are assumed to exert their "free will" and to "choose" to earn money by surrogacy, and thus are perhaps less deserving of social protection. While it might be true that some surrogates in the Global South are forced into the work (Pande 2009a; DasGupta and Dasgupta 2010), this is not the case for all (Pande 2009b; Zakaria 2010). Not unlike their counterparts in the Global North, the majority of the women in the Global South use their bodies for the economic advancement of their families and themselves (Conan 2010; DasGupta and Dasgupta 2010; Pande 2009a; Pande 2009b).

9. Indeed, recommendations about various modes of online communication between surrogates and IPs has become a mini self-help industry in and of itself. For instance, a blog called *The Next Family* (http://thenextfamily.com/) suggests Skype, iChat, FaceTime, blogging, emailing, and texting as ways for surrogates and IPs to stay connected.

10. See Martin 1992; Petchesky 1987; Stabile 1998; Taylor 2000; Taylor 2004; Taylor 2008.

11. In *The Public Life of the Fetal Sonogram* Janelle Taylor discusses a 1991 Volvo ad that ran in *Harper's*, in which there was a recognizable sonogram of a fetus with the tag "Is something inside telling you to buy a Volvo?"

12. See *Our Dream to Have a Baby through India Surrogacy* (September 2010), http://jonngem.blogspot.com/2010/09/ultrasound-results.html.

13. It is important to frame this discussion by noting that the public fetus does not operate the same way in all global contexts. Fetal ultrasonography is a decidedly vexed practice in India, where ultrasounds have often been used for sex-selective abortion, whereby female fetuses are selectively terminated due to overwhelming cultural son preference. An estimated ten million female fetuses were aborted in the two decades from 1980 (Boseley 2006; Dhariwal 2006), lowering the sex ratio from 972 females to 1,000 boys at the beginning of the twentieth century to 933:1,000 by 2001 (Balakrishnan 1994; Patel 2006). In certain parts of the country, mainly the northwest, the sex ratio dwindled at an even more alarming rate, from

882:1,000 in 1991 to 874;1,000 by 2001 (*Times of India* 2009). Legislation—which prohibits clinicians from revealing fetal sex via ultrasound—has curbed but not halted this practice.

14. Amani and Bob's Indian Surrogacy (Thursday April 1, 2010), http://amani andbobsurrogacy.blogspot.com/2010/04/introducing-our-front-bump.html.

15. See Amani 2010.

16. See Charliecat and John 2010.

17. The conversation about Muslim women's agency, or lack of, vis-à-vis hijab and burqua wearing, as well as the Western impetus to unveil, is rich and can be approached through the work of Lila Abu-Lughod, Leila Ahmed, and others. These scholars suggest that Western justifications for wars in Afghanistan and Iraq have been tied to an impetus to unveil (and thereby "save") Muslim women. The implication is that the concern with veiling is not so much about freedom for women as it is about the inhibition of the misogynist and colonial proprietary gaze. This is similar to Frantz Fanon's (1965) argument that the French were concerned with the unveiling of Algerian women not because they cared about women's freedom, but because it inhibited their proprietal gaze.

18. For more on the complexities of "speaking for" vs. "speaking with" subaltern subjects, see Spivak 2007.

9

RACE, GENDER, AND GENETIC TECHNOLOGIES

A New Reproductive Dystopia?

DOROTHY E. ROBERTS

In the 1980s Margaret Atwood, Gena Corea, and other feminists imagined dystopias in which white women's reproduction was valued and privileged and the reproduction of women of color was devalued and exploited. In *The Handmaid's Tale*, published in 1985, Atwood envisioned the repressive Republic of Gilead, where handmaids were forced to serve as breeders for elite men and their infertile wives in order to perpetuate the white race, while blacks, as well as handmaids who failed to bear children, were exiled to toxic colonies. That same year, in *The Mother Machine*, Corea predicted that white women would hire surrogates of color in reproductive brothels to be implanted with their eggs and to gestate their babies at low cost.

Three decades later, feminist scholars have continued to critique the hierarchy that the anthropologist Rayna Rapp aptly calls "stratified reproduction" by contrasting the opposing relationships of white women and women of color to reproduction-assisting technologies (1999, 310). At the turn of the twenty-first century, even more advanced reproductive technologies that combine assisted conception with genetic selection, or reprogenetics, threaten to intensify this opposition (Parens and Knowles 2007; Roberts 2005). With preimplantation genetic diagnosis (PGD), clinicians can biopsy a single cell from early embryos, diagnose it for the chance of having hundreds of genetic conditions, and select for implantation only those embryos at low risk of having these conditions (J. A. Robertson 2003; Singer 2007; Spar 2006). As Reprogenetics, a New Jersey genetics laboratory that specializes in PGD, puts it, this technique allows for the "replacement to the patient of those embryos classified by genetic diagnosis as normal."[1]

At a time when wealthy white women have access to technologies that assist them in having children who not only are genetically related to them or their partners but have also been genetically screened, various laws and policies discourage women of color from having children at all (Roberts 1998; A. M. Smith 2007). As Rapp stated at a Radcliffe Institute conference, "Reproductive Health in the Twenty-first Century," in October 2004, "Some women struggle for basic reproductive technologies, like a clinic where sterile conditions might be available to perform C-sections, while others turn to cutting-edge genetic techniques" (quoted in Drexler 2005). The African American studies scholar Marsha Darling similarly writes, "This stunning array of biotechnology is being directed at developing eugenical population control strategies especially for low-income and poor women of color globally," while "reproduction enhancement options under the rubric of 'choice'" are reserved "for economically and racially privileged women in the global North" (2004).

While welfare-reform laws aim to deter women receiving public assistance from having even one additional healthy baby, largely unregulated fertility clinics regularly implant privileged women with multiple embryos, despite knowing the high-risk multiple births pose for premature delivery and low birth weight.[2] The public begrudges poor mothers a meager increase in benefits for one more child, but it celebrates the birth of high-tech septuplets that require a fortune in publicly supported hospital care (Andrews 1999, 55–61). The multibillion-dollar apparatus devoted to technologically facilitating affluent couples' procreative decisions stands in glaring contrast to the high rate of infant death among black people, which remains more than twice the rate for whites (Mathews and MacDorman 2007). Indeed, the infant mortality rate is climbing in Mississippi and other Southern states (Eckholm 2007).

My prior writing on this reproductive caste system also contrasted policies that penalize poor black women's childbearing with the high-tech fertility industry that promotes childbearing by more affluent white women (Roberts 1998, 246–93). I recently reconsidered the positioning of white women and women of color in the reproductive hierarchy, however (Roberts 2005). Rather than place these women in opposition, I tied them together in relation to the neoliberal trend toward privatization and punitive governance. Both population-control programs and genetic-selection technologies reinforce biological explanations for social problems and place reproductive responsibility on women, thus privatizing remedies for illness and social inequity.

Population-control ideology attributes social inequities to childbearing by poor women of color, thereby legitimizing punitive regulation of these women's reproductive decisions (Roberts 1998). Stereotypes of black female sexual and reproductive irresponsibility support welfare-reform and law-enforcement policies that severely regulate poor black women's sexual and childbearing decisions (Neubeck 2001). By identifying procreation as the cause of deplorable social conditions, reproductive punishments divert attention away from state responsibility and the need for social change. Black mothers' crack use, for example, became a primary explanation for high rates of black infant mortality, although this disparity long predated the crack epidemic.[3]

Like punishments for poor women's childbearing, reprogenetics also shifts responsibility for promoting well-being from the government to the individual by making women responsible for ensuring the genetic fitness of their children. The individual woman becomes the site of governance through self-regulation of genetic risk (Mykitiuk 2000). The medical model of disability that promotes eugenic elimination of genetic risk instead of ending discrimination against disabled people supports state reliance on individuals to secure their own well-being through the use of genetic technologies. This diversion of attention away from social causes and solutions reinforces privatization, the hallmark of a neoliberal state that seeks to reduce social-welfare programs while promoting the free-market conditions conducive to capital accumulation. Thus, reproductive-health policies involving women at opposite ends of the reproductive hierarchy play an important role in the neoliberal state's transfer of services from the welfare state to the private realm of family and market.

In the last several years, while working on a book project exploring the growth of biotechnologies that incorporate race as a genetic category, I have come to reconsider once again the opposition of white women and women of color in the reproductive caste system in relation to reproductive technologies. The position I just described, like the 1980s reproductive dystopias, still casts white women as the only consumers of reproductive technologies and women of color only as victims of population-control policies. It assumes that white women are the only ones with access to these technologies and those women of color play no part in the politics of reprogenetics, except by their exclusion or exploitation.

The recent expansion of both reproductive genetic screening and race-based biomedicine, however, signals a dramatic change in the racial politics of reproductive technologies. First, the important role of genetic screening, which makes individual citizens responsible for ensuring good health by reducing genetic risk, may support the wider incorporation of reprogenetic technologies into the neoliberal health-care system. Second, companies that market race-based biotechnologies now promise to extend the benefits of genetic research to people of color (Bloche 2004; Kahn 2007). Media promoting genetic technologies prominently feature people of color in images representing the new genetic age, in contrast to prior portrayals that emphasized whiteness as the exclusive standard of genetic fitness.[4] Moreover, some clinics that offer high-tech reproductive services, including PGD, explicitly appeal to clients of color.[5] Women of color are now part of the market and cultural imaginary of the new reprogenetics. We need a new reproductive dystopia that accounts for the changing racial politics of genetics and reproduction.

In this essay I critically explore the role of race and racism in the emergence of reproductive technologies that incorporate advances in genetic science. What are the implications of including women of color in the market for reprogenetic technologies, particularly when this is done with the expectation that women will use these technologies to manage genetic risk? In investigating this question, I hope to shed light on the critical relationship between racism, neoliberalism, and reproduction.

Expanding the Market for Reproductive Technologies

In *Killing the Black Body*, I discussed the role of race in images promoting the fertility industry (Roberts 1998, 251). I pointed out that pictures showing the success of reproduction-assisting technologies were always of white babies, usually with blond hair and blue eyes, as if to highlight their racial purity. When the *New York Times* launched a prominent four-article series called "The Fertility Market" in January 1996, for example, the front page displayed a photograph of the director of a fertility clinic surrounded by seven white children conceived there (T. Gabriel 1996, A1). The continuing page contained a picture of a set of beaming in vitro fertilization (IVF) triplets, also white (ibid., A18).

In the 1990s the only time black babies figured in media coverage of these technologies was in stories intended to evoke revulsion precisely because of their race. One instance was a highly publicized lawsuit brought by a white woman against a fertility clinic she claimed had mistakenly inseminated her with a black man's sperm, resulting in the birth of a mixed-race child (Schatz 1990; Sullivan 1990). Two reporters covering the story speculated, "If the suit goes to trial, a jury could be faced with the difficult task of deciding damages involved in raising an interracial child" (Kantrowitz and Kaplan 1990). The perceived harm to the mother of receiving the wrong sperm was intensified by the clinic's failure to deliver a white baby.

Other notorious news stories from the 1990s included the case of twin boys born to a white Dutch couple who discovered when the babies were two months old that one was white and one was black (Elliot and Endt 1995). The fertility clinic had fertilized the mother's eggs with sperm from both her white husband and a black man. A landmark California dispute from 1993, *Johnson v. Calvert*, involved a black gestational "surrogate," Anna Johnson, who was denied any rights to the child she bore for the genetic parents, a white man and his Filipina wife, Mark and Crispina Calvert.[6] The press paid far more attention to Anna Johnson's race than to that of Crispina Calvert. It also portrayed the baby as white. By relying on the Calverts' genetic tie to the child to determine legal parenthood, the California courts ensured that a black woman would not be considered the natural mother of a white child (Roberts 1998, 280–81). While the stories involving whites portrayed the positive potential of new reproductive technologies, the stories involving women and children of color revealed their potential horror.

Today, however, the high-tech fertility business, including genetic-screening services, no longer appeals to an exclusively white clientele. Although fertility clinics perform sex selection for a range of clients, the controversy surrounding this service has centered on Chinese and Indian women (Bumgarner 2007; Darnovsky 2004). Images on fertility clinic websites routinely show people of color alongside claims advertising clinic services and their benefits. To be sure, pictures of white babies continue to dominate some websites. The home page of the Rinehart Center for Reproductive Medicine, in Illinois, displays the head of a blond-haired baby emerging like the sun from billowing white clouds to illustrate its promise of "turning your dreams of starting a family into reality."[7] Sher Institutes for Reproductive Medicine, with nationwide locations, streams photo strips of its "success stories," showing dozens of children, all of whom appear to be white.[8] Similarly, a full-page advertisement for the Virginia-based Genetics and IVF Institute, which recently appeared in the *New York Times Magazine*, features a giant photo (covering about a half page) of a white baby with blond hair, blue eyes, and rosy cheeks.[9] The headline asks, "Over 40 and Thinking of Having a Baby?" followed by the solution: "DONOR EGG Immediate Availability." In the text below, the company boasts of offering "Doctoral Donors with advanced degrees and numerous other donors with special accomplishments and talents." The assumption that whiteness, intelligence, and talent are connected and hereditary remains robust in the reprogenetic marketplace.

Nevertheless, the images associated with reproductive technologies have dramatically diversified in recent years. Reproductive Health Specialists, in Illinois, displays a photograph of a large group of white couples holding white babies, captioned "Baby Picnic."[10] But its website also contains a photograph of a smiling black man and woman and a drawing of a pregnant black woman attended to by a black male partner and female physician. Likewise, Houston IVF's website shows a beaming black couple holding a black baby.[11] The Illinois-based Karande and Associates takes a very multicultural approach, displaying a photo of a pregnant East Asian woman on the page for scheduling an appointment, a black woman and child for its link to donor egg information, and a South Asian man and child for the insurance information link.[12] There are numerous advertisements on Craigslist.org explicitly soliciting egg donors of color. Similarly, Pacific Fertility Center boasts that it "maintains a diverse egg donor database including Jewish egg donors, Asian egg donors, and a variety of backgrounds and ethnicities."[13]

Some fertility clinic websites not only market their reprogenetic services to people of color, but they also perform race-based genetic testing as part of those services. Pacific Fertility Center's website includes the statement "Genetic screening is also recommended, based on ethnic background."[14] Reproductive Genetics Institute, in Chicago, similarly includes race in the factors it takes into account in its genetic testing: "Screening Results and Accuracy: By combining the results of the ultrasound and blood test along with the age, race and weight of the mother, a number can be generated by computer which represents the risk of the pregnancy being affected by Down syndrome or another chromosome problem. Experience has shown that, together, the ultrasound and blood screen will identify approximately 90% of babies with chromosome abnormalities."[15]

Fertility clinics' use of race in genetic selection procedures may help to reinforce the erroneous belief that race is a biological classification that can be determined genetically or that genetic traits occur in human beings according to their race. Social scientists' demonstration that race is an invented social grouping was confirmed by genomic studies of human variation, including the Human Genome Project, showing high levels of genetic similarity among people of all races (Cooper, Kaufman, and Ward 2003; Graves 2001). At the onset of the Human Genome Project, some scholars believed that the science of human genetic diversity would replace race as the preeminent means of grouping people for scientific purposes (Lewontin 1995; Reardon 2005). Yet the use of race as a biological category in genetic research and biotechnology is intensifying.[16]

The marketing of high-tech reproductive services to women of color is part of a broader inclusion of minority groups in the testing and production of cutting-edge biotechnologies. In June 2005 the Food and Drug Administration (FDA) approved the first race-based pharmaceutical, BiDil, to treat heart failure specifically in African American patients (Saul 2005). BiDil is the combination of two generic drugs that doctors were already prescribing regardless of race. Yet the FDA permitted its maker, Nitro-Med, to market BiDil as a drug for black people. Making BiDil race specific also allowed NitroMed to extend its patent to the year 2020, giving the company market exclusivity and the potential to reap huge profits on drug sales (Kahn 2004). The manufacturer's unproven theory supporting the need for a race-specific therapy is that the reason for higher mortality rates among black heart patients lies in genetic differences among "races," either in the reason for getting heart disease or in the reason for responding differently to the medications used to treat heart disease (Kahn 2004; Sankar and Kahn 2005).

BiDil is only one example of the growing trend toward "the strategic use of race as a genetic category to obtain patent protection and drug approval" (Kahn 2006, 1349). In his survey of gene-related patent applications, the legal scholar Jonathan Kahn (2006) discovered that the use of race has increased fivefold in the past twenty years. Claims about justice in scientific research have shifted away from protecting socially disadvantaged subjects from unethical practices and toward promoting access to clinical trials and biotech products (Epstein 2007). There is strong support for racial therapeutics among some black advocates, researchers, and physicians precisely to redress past discrimination and fulfill long-standing demands for science to attend to the health needs of African Americans (Puckrein 2006; see also Roberts 2008). This increased commercial and popular demand for race-specific pharmaceuticals threatens to reinforce a false belief in the biological origin of race.

Advanced reproductive technologies similarly constitute a form of race-based medicine. Rather than serve an exclusively white clientele, fertility clinics are marketing genetic technologies to women of color on the basis of race and ethnicity, and incorporating race in genetic-screening procedures. Contemporary reproductive dystopias, then, should not categorically exclude women of color from their imagined users of genetic selection technologies. The expansion of race-based biotechnology, including genetic selection, fits within the neoliberal trend toward privatization and punitive governance, and requires adjusting feminist reproductive dystopias.

Neoliberalism and Reproductive Dystopia

The marketing of reprogenetics to women of color is taking place in the context of neoliberal shifts in governance that may encourage the expansion of genetic-screening technologies to a broader clientele. Widespread prenatal testing has already generated greater surveillance of pregnant women and assigned them primary responsibility for making the "right" genetic decisions. It is increasingly routine for pregnant women to get prenatal diagnoses for certain genetic conditions, such as Down syndrome or dwarfism (Powell 2007; Saxton 2007). It is also often expected that they will opt for abortion to select against any disabling traits identified by genetic testing. Many obstetricians provide these tests without much explanation or deliberation because they consider such screenings to be a normal part of treating their pregnant patients. The director of reproductive genetics at a large Detroit hospital reported that at least half of the women referred there with an abnormal amniocentesis result were "uncertain about why they even had the test" (Consumers Union 1990, 486). Moreover, current tort case law creates incentives in favor of genetic testing by imposing legal duties on obstetricians to offer it (Ossorio 2007, 330; Weil 2006, 52). While there are virtually no legal consequences for doctors who encourage genetic tests, doctors who fail to use them may be liable for damages in "wrongful birth" lawsuits.[17]

Although genetic counseling should be nondirective, many counselors show disapproval when patients decide against selective abortion. A genetic counselor asked a woman who decided to bear a child with Down syndrome, "What are you going to say to people when they ask you how you could bring a child like this into the world?" (quoted in Helm, Miranda, and Chedd 1998, 59). Brian Skotko's (2005) survey of 985 mothers who received postnatal diagnoses of Down syndrome for their children similarly discovered that many of the mothers were chastised by health-care professionals for not undergoing prenatal testing: "Right after [my child] was born, the doctor flat out told my husband that this could have been prevented or discontinued at an earlier stage of the pregnancy," wrote one mother who had a child with Down syndrome in 2000. A mother who had a child in 1993 recalled, "I had a resident in the recovery room when I learned that my daughter had DS [Down syndrome]. When I started to cry, I overheard him say, 'What did she expect? She refused prenatal testing.'" Another mother reported, from her experience in 1997, "The attending neonatologist, rather than extending some form of compassion, lambasted us for our ignorance in not doing prior testing and for bringing this burden to society—noting the economical, educational, and social hardships he [the child] would bring." Regarding a postnatal visit, a mother who had a child in 1992 wrote, "[My doctor] stressed 'next time' the need for amniocentesis so that I could 'choose to terminate'" (Skotko 2005, 70–71). As a result of such pressure, many pregnant women now view genetic testing as a requirement of responsible mothering (Harmon 2007).

Poor women, especially women of color, currently face financial and other barriers to receiving high-tech infertility services (Elster 2005). Because genetic screening is now considered an essential part of preventive medicine, however, these technologies are becoming integrated into social-welfare systems and private-insurance schemes and are likely to become increasingly available to poor and low-income women (K. Bumiller 2009; van den Daele 2006).[18] Unlike IVF, whose primary purpose is to increase fertility, PGD functions to help women avoid starting a pregnancy that entails disfavored genetic traits (Franklin and Roberts 2006, xx, 97).[19] The aim of IVF is to produce the birth of a live baby; the aim of PGD and fetal diagnosis is to prevent the birth of certain children. While government welfare systems have disdained facilitating childbearing by poor women of color by declining to fund fertility treatments, they may therefore treat genetic testing differently.

The current ban on federal funding of abortion places a significant limit on state genetic selection programs (Powell 2007, 49–50). In states that do not provide Medicaid funding for abortion, poor women can receive state-sponsored genetic testing but have to pay for the cost of selective abortions themselves. Yet it is not hard to foresee future federal and state legislation that exempts "therapeutic" abortions based on genetic testing from the ban on abortion funding. Prior to the 1973 Supreme Court decision *Roe v. Wade*, which upheld the constitutional right to abortion, many states permitted therapeutic abortions recommended by physicians while criminalizing elective abortions sought by women with unwanted pregnancies (Schoen 2005, 153–86).

Indeed, some clients of reprogenetics have claimed moral superiority over women who have had abortions for nonselective reasons. In an op-ed piece in the *New York* Times, Barbara Ehrenreich (2004) calls on women who have aborted fetuses based on prenatal diagnosis to support the general right to abortion. She notes that these women sometimes distinguish themselves from women who have "ordinary" abortions. One woman who aborted a fetus with Down syndrome states, "I don't look at it as though I had an abortion, even though that is technically what it is. There's a difference. I wanted this baby" (quoted in Ehrenreich 2004, A21). On a website for a support group called "A Heart Breaking Choice" a mother who went to an abortion clinic complains, "I resented the fact that I had to be there with all these girls that did not want their babies" (quoted in ibid.). The incorporation of eugenic values in arguments for women's reproductive freedom neglects the history of abortion regulation, which limited women's reproductive freedom by distinguishing between approved therapeutic and disapproved elective abortions. An attempt to solicit supporters of selective abortion to join the cause of abortion rights misunderstands the nature of reproductive politics in the neoliberal age.

The expansion of genetic research and technologies has helped to create a new biological citizenship that enlists patients to take unprecedented authority over their health at the molecular level (Rose 2007). According to the British sociologist Nikolas Rose, "Our very biological life itself has entered the domain of decision and choice" (2007, 40). Some scholars have highlighted the enhancement of human agency, as "patients are increasingly urged to become active and responsible consumers of medical services and products ranging from pharmaceuticals to reproductive technologies and genetic tests" (ibid., 4) and to form alliances with physicians, scientists, and clinicians to advocate for their interests (Franklin and Roberts 2006, xvii).

Biological citizenship also reflects the shift of responsibility for public welfare from the state to the private realms of market and family. As Rose observes, responsibility for the management of health and reproduction has devolved from the "formal apparatus of the government" to "quasi-autonomous regulatory bodies" such as bioethics commissions, professional groups, and private corporations (2007, 3). Selling genetic testing products directly to consumers is big business for private fertility clinics and biotechnology companies. Biomedical research and technology have correspondingly become major sources of capital accumulation, aided by federal patents on genetic information, FDA approval of pharmaceuticals, and public funding of lucrative private research ventures, such as California's stem-cell research initiative.

In this neoliberal context, genetic testing serves as a form of privatization that makes the individual the site of governance through the self-regulation of genetic risk (Mykitiuk 2000). Reproductive genetic technologies, in particular, introduce a new gendered division of labor and surveillance as women bear the brunt of reprogenetics' contribution to the neoliberal restructuring of health care (ibid.). The Canadian legal scholar Roxanne Mykitiuk (2000) points out that, contrary to the deregulation that typically occurs in the service of big business, the new duties imposed on women constitute a reregulation that supports capital investment in market-based approaches to health care and other social needs while state investment in public resources shrinks.

In addition, reprogenetics incorporates a seemingly benign form of eugenic thinking in its reliance on reproductive strategies to eliminate genetic risk rather than on social strategies to eliminate systemic inequities. Some disability-rights advocates oppose prenatal genetic diagnosis that leads to discarding embryos and fetuses predicted to have disabilities because these procedures devalue people who have disabilities, sending the message that they should never have been born.[20] They argue that although disabilities cause various degrees of impairment, the main difficulty in having a disability stems from pervasive discrimination. "Rather than improving the medical or social situation of today's and tomorrow's disabled citizens," write the bioethicists Erik Parens and Adrienne Asch, "prenatal diagnosis reinforces the medical model that disability itself, not societal discrimination against people with disabilities, is the problem to be solved" (2007, 13).

The reasons why some parents do not want a disabled child are varied. While some women may use genetic selection in an upwardly mobile quest for the "perfect child," others want to prevent their children from suffering the pain, illness, and physical limitations that accompany disabilities or worry that they are not capable of dealing with disability's social consequences.[21] Yet given medical professionals' implicit directive favoring genetic selection and powerful stereotypes that negatively depict disabled people, many women are left with a false impression of the nature of parenting a disabled child and the quality of disabled people's lives (which genetic testing cannot predict [K. Bumiller 2009]). Pregnant women are rarely able to make truly informed decisions about what to do with test results because they, obstetricians, and counselors typically have little information about the lives of disabled people and their families (Parens and Asch 2007, 33–37; Wendell 1996, 81–84).[22]

Moreover, some of the undesirable events likely to happen to a child with a serious disability that parents may reasonably wish to prevent, such as limited educational and employment opportunities are caused by social as much as physical impediments (Steinbock 2007, 119). Unable to count on societal acceptance or support, many women feel compelled to turn to genetic testing to ensure their children's welfare (Kittay 2007, 181; Lippman 1991, 39). Without judging the morality of individual women's decisions, we must critically evaluate the social, political, and legal incentives for genetic testing as well as consequences of genetic testing for people with disabilities. Building on the disability critique, we must also question the role that the eugenic approach to disability plays in neoliberal governance.

Rose, the British sociologist, rejects critical intellectuals' use of eugenics rhetoric to contest PGD and other aspects of contemporary biological politics (2007, 54–68). He argues that the eugenics practiced in the first half of the twentieth century was a particular biopolitical strategy that sought to improve the population as a whole through deliberate state action. This effort "to control the biological makeup of the population" as a whole, he claims, distinguishes eugenics from the new biopolitics' concern with the genetic health of individuals (ibid., 56). "What we have here, then, is not eugenics but is shaped by forms of self-government imposed by obligations of choice, the desire for self-fulfillment, and the wish of parents for the best lives for their children" (ibid., 69). Rose dismisses the relevance of eugenics to contemporary biopolitics too categorically. He downplays critical aspects of the past eugenics regime that characterize both contemporary population-control policies and genetic-screening technologies such as PGD. By eugenic thinking or values, I refer to the belief that reproductive strategies can improve society by reducing the births of socially marginalized people. The eugenic approach to social problems locates them in reproduction rather than in social structure and therefore seeks to solve them by eliminating disfavored people instead of social inequities. Its chief epistemological device is to make the social order seem natural by casting its features as biological facts. As Donald A. MacKenzie observes, eugenic theory is "a way of reading the structure of social classes onto nature" (1981, 18). Programs based on such a belief set up standards for reproduction that subsume childbearing under prevailing hierarchies of power.

Eugenics did not function only "in the service of a biological struggle between nation-states" (Rose 2007, 66); it functioned to maintain the racial, gender, and class order within the nation. (Moreover, alliances between American and Nazi eugenicists in the 1930s show a willingness to cross national boundaries in the interest of white supremacy.)[23] Thus, contemporary proposals to solve social problems by curbing black reproduction—such as the *Philadelphia Inquirer's* suggestion to distribute the long-acting contraceptive Norplant as a remedy for black poverty (Kimelman 1990)—are similar to past eugenic policies in that they make racial inequality appear to be the product of nature rather than power. By identifying procreation as the cause of black people's condition, they divert attention away from the political, social, and economic forces that maintain the U.S. racial order. I therefore believe it is accurate and helpful to identify the ways in which contemporary reproductive-health policies incorporate essential features of eugenic ideology, despite the important differences that Rose highlights.

Futhermore, the distinction between past state-imposed and current voluntary programs is not as clear-cut as Rose suggests. On the one hand, Rose ignores the system of punitive governance that accompanies the neoliberal shift to individual self-governance. Welfare is no longer a system of aid, but rather a system of behavior modification that attempts to regulate the sexual, marital, and childbearing decisions of poor unmarried mothers by placing conditions on the receipt of state assistance (Mink 2002; Roberts 1998; A. M. Smith 2007). Meanwhile, federal and state governments aggressively intervene in marginalized communities to manage their social deprivation with especially punitive measures. The U.S. prison population has grown to proportions unprecedented in the history of Western democracies, as an astounding number of young black men are locked up (Garland 2001; Sentencing Project 2005). The racial disparity in the foster-care population mirrors that of the prison system, as child-protection authorities remove grossly disproportionate numbers of black children from their homes (Roberts 2002). Population-control policies that attribute social inequities to the childbearing of poor minority women are a critical component of this punitive trend away from state support for families and communities (Roberts 1998; A. M. Smith 2007). Rose's reference to "the enabling state, the facilitating state, the state as animator" (2007, 63) does not apply to policies designed to penalize child-bearing by poor women and women of color.

On the other hand, Rose's focus on state direction of twentieth-century eugenic programs obscures the crucial role of private enterprises in dis-seminating and implementing eugenics. Just as influential as the manda-tory sterilization laws passed in most states were the campaigns waged by private groups such as the American Eugenics Society, the Human Better-ment Association, and the American Genetics Association to educate the American public about the benefits of eugenics, as well as the American Birth Control League's programs to distribute birth control to the unfit (Kevles 1985). As Rose acknowledges, "Eugenics was not disreputable or marginal: it defined one dimension of mainstream thinking about the re-sponsibilities of politicians, professionals, scientists, and individuals in the modern world" (2007, 59).

Some feminists who use eugenics rhetoric to critique modern genetic-selection technologies explicitly acknowledge the distinction between state-imposed programs and private decisions made by individuals. For example, the U.S. sociologist Barbara Katz Rothman (2001) calls the mar-keting of prenatal diagnostic technologies a form of microeugenics, fo-cused on the individual, in contrast to macroeugenics, focused on popu-lations. I also explicitly distinguish between population-control policies and those that promote reprogenetics while drawing attention to their common support of neoliberal approaches to social inequities (Roberts 2005). This distinction, however, should not eclipse the coercive nature and social function of contemporary reprogenetics (Ward 2002; Wendell 1996, 156). Genetic-selection procedures are increasingly treated as social responsibilities reinforced not only by cultural expectations but also by legal penalties and incentives. Does the state-supported reproductive-genetics industry exist only to give individual citizens more reproduc-tive choices, or, as Laura Hershey asks, is it "primarily for the benefit of a society unwilling to support disability-related needs?" (1994, 31; see also Wendell 1996, 154).

Rose's analysis of contemporary biopolitics helps to illuminate the radical change from state management of the population's health to indi-vidual management of genetic risk, aided by new genetic technologies.

These technologies facilitate the shift from state responsibility for ensuring health and welfare to private responsibility, all within the context of persistent race, gender, and class inequities; devastating reductions in social programs; and intense state surveillance of marginalized communities. Genetic screening is increasingly recommended not only to avoid having children with serious early onset disabilities or diseases with a high likelihood of occurring, but also to eliminate the risk of developing certain diseases as an adult (Obasogie 2006). A recent article in the *Journal of the American Medical Association*, for example, encouraged families affected by hereditary cancer syndromes, including breast, ovarian, and colon cancer, to use PGD to screen out embryos genetically predisposed to develop cancer (Offit, Sagi, and Hurley 2006). In the neoliberal future, the state may rely on the expectation that all pregnant women will undergo genetic testing to legitimize not only its refusal to support the care of disabled children but also its denial of broader claims for public provision of health care.

Extending Choice to Women of Color

The role reprogenetics plays in neoliberalism's integrated system of privatization and punitive governance is obscured by liberal notions of reproductive choice. Despite the potential for reprogenetics to diminish public health care and intensify regulation of women's reproductive decisions, its sponsors often defend the industry's immunity from state regulation in the name of women's reproductive freedom (Rothman 1989, 116; Darling 2004). Extending the availability of genetic-selection technologies to women of color does not correct the role played by reprogenetics in advancing a neoliberal agenda. The depletion of public resources for general health care and for supporting people with disabilities would exacerbate economic inequities along racial lines, hitting poor minority communities the hardest. In addition, the expectation of genetic self-regulation may fall especially harshly on black and Latina women, who are stereotypically defined as lacking the capacity for self-control. The use of high-tech, expensive technologies by a privileged slice of women of color suggests that those who do not use them for financial, social, or ethical reasons may be blamed for the social consequences.

There may always be certain reproductive technologies that are reserved for the wealthiest people and are outside the reach of most women of color. The market will privilege a tiny elite among people of color who can afford high-tech reproductive innovations while relegating the vast majority to the state's most intense reproductive surveillance. Indeed, the neoliberal reification of market logic is likely to expand the hiring of poor and low-income women of color for their reproductive services. The incidence of payments to these women to gestate fetuses or to produce eggs for genetic research could intensify (Haworth 2007) even as they are encouraged to use genetic technologies to screen their own children.

In addition, marketing race-based biotechnologies to consumers of color can reinforce the biological meaning of race. By incorporating invented racial categories into genetic research, scientists and entrepreneurs are producing biotechnologies that validate people's belief that race is a natural classification. A renewed trust in inherent racial differences provides an alternative explanation for persistent gross inequities in blacks' health and welfare despite the end of de jure discrimination. These technologies promote the view that deepening racial inequities that result from neoliberal policies are actually caused by genetic differences between whites and other racialized groups. The biological explanation for racial disparities provides a ready logic for the staggering disenfranchisement of people of color through mass incarceration and other punitive policies, as well as the perfect complement to color-blind policies implementing the claim that racism has ceased to be the cause of their predicament. Including women of color in the market for reprogenetic technologies does not eradicate the racial caste system underlying reproductive stratification.

A reproductive dystopia for the twenty-first century could no longer exclude women of color from the market for high-tech reprogenetics. Rather, it would take place in a society in which racial and economic divisions are reinforced by the genetic testing extended to them. In this new dystopia, the biological definition of race is stronger than ever, validated by genetic science and cemented in popular culture by race-based biotechnologies. The state has disclaimed all responsibility for supporting its citizens, placing the duty of ensuring public welfare in all women's self-regulation of genetic risk. The medical model of disability is embedded in a neoliberal health policy that relies on widespread use of genetic technologies to disqualify citizens from claiming public support and to avoid the need for social change. The new biologization of race may seem to unite blacks, and other nonwhite "races," by confirming the genetic uniformity of people belonging to the same race and their genetic difference from others. In the new dystopia, however, genetic-selection technologies that incorporate race as a biological category reinforce class divisions between elite people of color who can afford the full array of high-tech procedures and the masses who suffer most from neoliberal policies bolstered by these very biological explanations of racial inequities. But I can also imagine a new utopia arising from feminists' radical resistance to enlisting women as genetic screeners in service of a neoliberal agenda, a resistance that is emboldened by new alliances—joining reproductive-justice with anti-racist, disability-rights, and economic-justice movements that recognize their common interest in contesting a race-based reprogenetic future.

Notes

Dorothy E. Roberts's chapter, "Race, Gender, and Genetic Technologies: A New Reproductive Dystopia?," was previously printed in *Signs* 34, no. 4 (summer 2009): 783–804. Copyright University of Chicago Press. Reprinted with permission of the publisher.

1. See the Reprogenetics website, http://www.reprogenetics.com.

2. On welfare-reform laws, see Mink 2002; A. M. Smith 2007. On unregulated fertility clinics, see Arons 2007, 1; Parens and Knowles 2007. On implanting privileged women with multiple embryos despite knowing the risks, see Helmerhorst et al. 2004; Mundy 2007; Reddy et al. 2007.

3. See McCaughey 2005; Roberts 1998, 154–59; Zerai and Banks 2002.

4. See the websites of DNA Tribes (http://www.dnatribes.com), GeneTree (http://www.genetree.com), and National Geographic's Genographic Project (https://genographic.nationalgeographic.com).

5. See the Pacific Fertility Center's appeal to prospective donors at the Egg Donor Agency website (http://www.pfcdonoragency.com/egg-donor/egg-donor-agency) and information about egg donation at http://www.pacificfertilitycenter.com/treat/agency_donation.php.

6. Johnson v. Calvert, 5 Cal. 4th 84, 19 Cal. Rptr. 494 (1993), cert. denied, 114 S. Ct. 206 (1993).

7. See the Rinehart Center for Reproductive Medicine website, http://www.reproductivemedicineinstitute.com/.

8. See the Sher Institutes for Reproductive Medicine website, http://haveababy.com/.

9. See Genetics and IVF Institute, advertisement, *New York Times Magazine*, 29 July 2007, 21.

10. See images of the "baby picnic" at http://ivfplus.net/baby_party.htm.

11. See the Houston IVF website, http://www.houstonivf.net/Home.aspx?keyword=houston%20ivf&gclid=CNCdpL6F5MACFQypaQodhKwANw.

12. For images from the Karande and Associates website, see http://www.inviafertility.com/.

13. See the Pacific Fertility Center's appeal to prospective donors at http://www
.donateyoureggs.com.

14. See the Pacific Fertility Center website, http://www.pacificfertilitycenter
.com/Treat/agency_donation.php.

15. See the Reproductive Genetics Institute's webpage on first-trimester screening, http://www.reproductivegenetics.com/.

16. See Bonham, Warshauer-Baker, and Collins 2005; Burchard et al. 2003;
Duster 2005.

17. For example, the Supreme Court of Ohio recently held that parents of an un-
healthy child born following negligent failure to diagnose a fetal defect or disease
may bring suit under traditional medical malpractice principles for the costs arising
from the pregnancy and birth of the child. See Schirmer v. Mt. Auburn Obstetrics
and Gynecologic Associates, Inc., 108 Ohio St. 3d 494, 2006-Ohio-942 (Ohio S. Ct.
2006). For an argument in favor of using tort law to compensate for "procreative
injury" caused by reproduction assisting technologies, see Kleinfeld 2005.

18. For an extensive review of insurance coverage of infertility treatments, see
Arons 2007, 8–13: "Fourteen states currently require some types of health insurance plans to include coverage of certain infertility services or to make such coverage available" (8).

19. PGD also serves to increase fertility when it is undertaken to improve IVF
success rates (Franklin and Roberts 2006, 97).

20. See Parens and Asch 2007; Saxton 2007; Wendell 1996, 151–56.

21. See Franklin and Roberts 2006, 132–62; Wendell 1996, 82–83.

22. A recent survey of research on the experience of disability in families concluded, "There is an increasingly dominant body of research that finds aggregate
patterns of overall adjustment and well-being to be similar across groups of families with and without children with disabilities" (Ferguson, Gartner, and Lipsky
2007, 85).

23. When the leading American eugenicist, Harry Laughlin, received an honor-
ary degree from the University of Heidelberg, in 1936, he wrote to German officials
that the award represented "evidence of a common understanding of German and
American scientists of the nature of eugenics" (quoted in Kevles 1985, 118).

PART IV

TOWARD A FEMINIST PRAXIS IN SURVEILLANCE STUDIES

10

ANTIPROSTITUTION FEMINISM AND THE SURVEILLANCE OF SEX INDUSTRY CLIENTS

UMMNI KHAN

For far too long, the social control, surveillance, and criminalization of sex work has focused on the figure of the "prostitute" as the deviant, the femme fatale, or the immoral transgressor.[1] The participation of sex-industry clients was often excused based on gendered narratives that cast them as helpless to their libidos or to the seductive wiles of sex workers. In the last few decades, however, increased attention has been paid to clients as subjects of research and objects of criminalization (Lowman and Atchison 2006). Though such research and criminalization are still not as prevalent as the study and arrest of sex workers, clients in the Global North are emerging as a category of social deviance to be surveyed, analyzed, and disciplined.

On a state level, this surveillance and discipline manifests in criminal justice and police initiatives that target suspected clients, including street sweeps, publication of names, vehicle seizure, and rehabilitative "john schools" that endeavor to deter men from buying sexual services. Client targeting, however, is not only happening at the state level. One sector of the feminist movement is also actively involved in the surveillance and construction of clients as deviants: antiprostitution advocates who couch all sex work within the terms of "violence against women." I (and many other sex-worker-rights advocates) refer to this sector as prohibitionist feminism because of its reliance on criminal prohibition as a key strategy to eradicate the sex industry (van der Meulen, Durisin, and Love 2013, 14). While prohibitionist feminism rests on a solid bed of essentialism, its adherents have also generated social science "evidence" to empirically substantiate their anti-prostitution claims.

In this essay I focus on one prohibitionist group, Prostitution Research and Education (PRE), to analyze how its empirical reports participate in surveillant logics, reify clients as deviants, and legitimate intensified state surveillance and criminalization. Founded in 1995, PRE is a U.S. nonprofit organization committed to establishing the harmfulness of prostitution and advocating for state solutions, including alternatives to prostitution for the workers and punitive responses for the clients. I focus on PRE's U.S. document, *Comparing Sex Buyers with Men Who Don't Buy Sex* (Farley et al. 2011), but also refer to three other publications produced in collaboration with PRE: *Challenging Men's Demand for Prostitution in Scotland* (Macleod, Farley, Anderson, and Golding 2008); *Men Who Buy Sex: Who They Buy and What They Know* (Farley, Bindel, and Golding 2009), which focuses on men in England; and *A Thorn in the Heart: Cambodian Men Who Buy Sex* (Farley, Freed, Phal, and Golding 2012).[2] Despite regional differences, all four texts draw on interview data with male clients and construct the men as distinctly misogynist, deviant, dangerous, and sexually violent. PRE closes each report with a call to strengthen criminalization, surveillance, and stigmatization of sex clients.

My analysis of PRE's reports first situates social-science discourse—specifically surveys, interviewing, statistics, and the narrativization of data—within the ambit of surveillance. Second, I problematize the methodology and interpretation, delineating how PRE's client reports are deeply flawed and patently distortive, even on their own positivist terms. This refutation of PRE's empiricism demonstrates the faulty foundation of its prohibitionist ideology, which is important given that PRE's executive director, Melissa Farley, is a key spokesperson for antiprostitution, and her testimony is frequently used to "prove" the harms of prostitution in legal and policy arenas.[3] Third, I examine how prohibitionist feminist social-science discourse can be understood as a surveillant practice in alliance with state surveillance and as exhibiting a carceral mentality. In particular, I consider how PRE's recommendations bolster the policing of the sex industry, endorse surveillant biometric strategies, disproportionately impact racialized and working-class men, and justify prison sentences as a means to discipline clients.

I posit that part of the project of feminist surveillance studies is to take a critical look at how surveillance is being used in the name of feminism. In particular, I invite the reader to consider how feminist prohibitionist discourse participates in the "surveillance of sexuality," which constitutes the deviance it purports to merely record (Walby and Smith 2012, 54). While the feminist prohibitionists at PRE may intend to name, confront, and eradicate violence against women in the sex industry, their method rests, in part, on constructing the desire to purchase sexual services as fundamentally deviant. This deviantized desire is gendered masculine for two reasons: the majority of people who purchase sexual services are men, and the small female demographic is almost completely ignored in the scholarly literature, particularly in the feminist prohibitionist literature (Weitzer 2005b, 225). This gendered construction of masculine deviance relies on a social-science approach to surveillance and on empirically unsound data which dehumanizes clients and supports the punitive state. Elizabeth Bernstein has named this approach to equality "carceral feminism," involving "a sexual politics that is intricately intertwined with broader agendas of criminalization and incarceration" (2010, 51). As with many criminalization agendas, those with the least social capital disproportionately suffer from this form of sexual politics. Nonetheless, all male clients, including privileged men, are vulnerable to surveillance, shaming, and criminalization (see, for example, Zennie 2013). I suggest that feminist attention to gendered oppression and issues of surveillance should include consideration of the surveillance and criminalization of nonnormative male desires.

The Study of Prohibitionist Feminist Surveillance

Kevin Haggerty defines surveillance as a dynamic that involves "monitoring people or things typically as the basis for some form of social intervention" (2009, ix). Surveillance studies usually focuses on state or corporate actors, and considers aspects of architectural design, technological systems, digital interface, impersonal observation, panoptic effects, and consumer analysis or media communications. Much critical scholarship is dedicated to exposing how new technologically advanced surveillance strategies touted as objective are deeply ideological apparatuses that disenfranchise those who are most marginalized. This is urgent work. At the same time, the glitz of high-tech surveillance should not prevent us from also paying critical attention to surveys as a traditional form of (and etymologically connected to) surveillance. Using surveys of people as a technique of social control has occurred since at least as far back as the nineteenth century (Converse 2009, 13). Survey research that involves human subjects, by definition, reduces and objectifies complex subjectivities into data. Whether quantitative or qualitative analysis, research exposes its subjects to the violence of interpretation, which includes the questions that are asked of them, the words that are reproduced or omitted, the numerical translation of the answers, and, of course, the rhetorical framing of the final report. In this way, as Haggerty states, "Surveys and statistical analyses that measure, quantify and numerically characterize populations are epistemological modes linked to the rise of a surveillance society" (2002, 12).

I build on Haggerty's interlinking of surveys and surveillance. Of course, there are differences to note between low-tech surveys and high-tech surveillance. The surveys and statistics I examine represent discrete periods of data collection undertaken by an NGO, as opposed to systematic surveillance procedures implemented by governmental or corporate actors. To generate truth claims, survey-generated surveillance does not require state-of-the-art instruments; the observation and recording of data during interviews happens on an interpersonal level without the need for technological devices. Nonetheless, old and new surveillance strategies can share many problematic features. Both frequently rest on a positivist ideology that constructs numerical representation as "hard facts" and perpetuates the notion that scientific empiricism will deliver reliable truths. Both often begin with particular assumptions about risk, opportunity, and behavior. Both elicit only some kinds of information based on the theoretical premise and political commitments of the surveyors. Both can work as a form of social sorting that "obtains personal and group data in order to classify people . . . according to varying criteria, to determine who should be targeted for special treatment, suspicion, eligibility, inclusion, access, and so on" (Lyon 2003, 20). Given these overlapping characteristics and functions, new techniques of surveillance can be understood as an extension, elaboration, and sophistication of the traditional survey.

From this broader perspective, PRE's surveys thus participate in the project of surveillance, generating data that constructs clients as posing specific risks to women and thereby justifying special (criminal) treatment. To advance their prohibitionist truth claims, the client reports draw on quantitative and qualitative methodologies, using question-naires, as well as structured and semi-structured interviews. I outline some of the most blatant examples of bias and distortion from both a qualitative and quantitative perspective. In doing so, I understand that social-scientific representation of "truth" can never be ideologically neu-tral. However, given that PRE is working within the epistemic framework of positivist truth, and that these reports are used to affect legal and policy outcomes, it is important to look beneath their surface, to expose and consider deeply problematic elements that undermine their persua-sive value.

The scope of this essay does not allow for a comprehensive critique of every qualitative or statistical claim. Rather, I seek to highlight some of the most obvious weaknesses in PRE's methodology, approach, interpre-tation, and conclusions, to set the stage for my final critique of the inva-sive and punitive criminal sanctions PRE recommends for clients. My cri-tique is guided by Ronald Weitzer's incisive articles "Flawed Theory and Method in Studies of Prostitution" (2005a) and "Rehashing Tired Claims about Prostitution" (2005c). Joel Best's helpful books *Stat-Spotting* (2008) and *Damned Lies and Statistics* (2012) provide further tools to recognize distortive empirical practices. I also turn to feminist-methodology texts to understand the extent to which PRE has failed to learn from the critical insights feminists have brought to the production of knowledge through quantitative and qualitative interviews and questionnaires. Most helpful in this regard are Sharlene Nagy Hesse-Biber's extensive anthology *Hand-book of Feminist Research* (2012) and Caroline Ramazanoglu and Janet Holland's *Feminist Methodology* (2002).

Methodological Flaws and Distortions in the PRE Reports

All four reports were generated by PRE in conjunction with local non-governmental organizations (NGOs) and volunteers who share a nega-tive view of prostitution. As stated, PRE is a nonprofit organization dedi-cated to disseminating antiprostitution truth claims in public debates. As Weitzer (2005a) argues, its founder, Farley, produces writings and presen-tations that perpetuate a totalizing view of prostitution as exploitative, as violent, and as an expression of male domination. This is exemplified on PRE's webpage entitled "Prostitution and Trafficking—Quick Facts," where prostitution is defined by the following (Farley and Butler 2012):

A) sexual harassment
B) rape
C) battering
D) verbal abuse
E) domestic violence
F) a racist practice
G) a violation of human rights
H) childhood sexual abuse
I) a consequence of male domination of women
J) a means of maintaining male domination of women
K) all of the above

PRE conflates a multitude of issues, origins, and causes in its grab-bag attempt to establish prostitution as inherently heinous. The webpage also cites dozens of other antiprostitution advocates, including some big names in radical feminism, such as Andrea Dworkin ("Male dominance means that the society creates a pool of prostitutes by any means necessary so that men have what men need to stay on top, to feel big, literally, metaphorically, in every way" [1997, 2]) and Sheila Jeffries ("The sex industry markets precisely the violence, the practices of subordination that feminists seek to eliminate from the streets, workplaces, and bedrooms" [1997, 267–68]). In the acknowledgments section of *Comparing Sex Buyers with Men Who Don't Buy Sex* (hereafter *Comparing Sex Buyers*), the reader gets more information about the political commitments of those involved in the research. The report is funded by the Demand Abolition Project, which "focuses on eliminating men's assumption of the right to prostitution which would thereby eliminate the institution of prostitution" (Farley et al. 2011, 5). Based on this political goal, it is clear that the funders have a literal investment in the production of social-science knowledge that would justify their antiprostitution stance.

Best refers to such projects as "advocacy research" because they are implemented by activist groups who already have a committed opinion of the topic under study and whose primary purpose is to produce data to convince others to adopt their opinion (2001, 47). Accordingly, there is a strong indication that PRE's research will be vested in producing evidence that supports the construction of prostitution as a violent institution. Of course, from a feminist and critical-theory perspective, there is no such thing as a completely objective approach. As Ramazanoglu and Holland say, "The notion that political commitment is an inextricable part of the process of social investigation, and is compatible with knowledge of social realities, even if this knowledge is partial, is central to feminist methodology: 'detachment is not a condition of science'" (2002, 54, citing D. E. Smith 1988, 177). Knowledge is thus always shaped by the researcher's experiences, belief systems, background, community, and identity, and is interpreted within a sociohistorical context. The fact that PRE has taken a stand on the issue of prostitution and is an advocate for its abolition, in part through the criminalization of clients and third parties, does not mean the knowledge it produces is without value, but it does mean that an evaluation of its reports should look for the ways in which this perspective may color the methodological choices and knowledge claims.

When evaluating the reliability of a survey-based research project, one of the first issues to consider is the sampling group. For each of its reports, PRE interviewed 101–133 men the NGO identified as "sex buyers." For *Comparing Sex Buyers*, PRE also interviewed 100 men who claimed they did not buy sex, in order to generate data on the differences between the two groups of men. From these small samples, PRE generalized about the characteristics, behaviors, and attitudes of all male sex buyers, and from the additional interviews of non-sex buyers, they sought to differentiate clients from the general male population.

For three of the surveys—*Challenging Men's Demand for Prostitution in Scotland, Comparing Sex Buyers*, and *Men Who Buy Sex*—the majority of the men were recruited using newspaper advertisements. For *A Thorn in the Heart*, the men were recruited via a snowballing technique that began with interviewers asking their neighbors and acquaintances to participate in the study. These methods are called "convenience samples" by social scientists doing fieldwork and are nongeneralizable because the group is not a random selection of sex buyers (or non-sex buyers) (Weitzer 2005a, 938). Such samples can be skewed for a number of reasons. For example, regarding the newspaper-recruited male subjects, the advertisement reached only readers of that particular periodical. Furthermore, the kinds of people who would answer an advertisement and wish to discuss their sexual practices and attitudes may not be representative of all sex buyers or non-sex buyers. With regard to the snowballing technique, the resulting sample group was by definition narrow, since interviewers had begun with people with whom they were already acquainted. Since PRE is an advocacy group that aligns prostitution with violence, how this belief might have influenced who was selected for the study must be taken into account. It should be noted, too, that it is impossible to conduct a random sample of sex buyers. Given the taboo, criminalized, and secretive nature of the trade, access to the sex-buying population is always challenging. PRE's reports, however, do not qualify or nuance their knowledge claims based on the limitations of the samples; rather, they generalize and recommend serious criminal sanctions based on a nonrandom sample of men. Out of the four reports, the only one to recognize the limitations of the research was *Comparing Sex Buyers*. Toward the end of that report, the authors acknowledge that men who respond to such advertisements "may differ in unknown ways from the general population of men, including sex buyers" (Farley et al. 2011, 41). Nonetheless, this section concludes that sex buyers are likely much worse (in terms of undesirable criminal behavior) than the report indicates, because subjects in self-report studies tend to respond in ways that they perceive to be socially desirable: "We assume with some confidence that the numbers reported in this study are conservative and are likely underestimates of many of the attitudes and behaviors we were assessing" (Farley et al. 2011, 41). This assumption plays on what criminologists refer to as the "dark figure," the proportion of crime that goes unreported (Best 2012, 33). As Best argues, "Activists usually believe that the problem they seek to bring to public attention is both large and largely unrecognized, [so] there is a substantial dark figure of hidden cases" (ibid., 50). PRE ends its section on the limitations of the research not only by using the power of the unverifiable "dark figure" to suggest that the numbers are reliable as an indicator of male sex buyers' unsavory and criminal characteristics, but also by implying that such men are probably even worse in this regard than the study can verify. There is no mention of the crucial fact that data from the small nonrandom sample are not generalizable.

Another area of interest in considering the reliability of the PRE studies are the questions used to gather data. As Best argues of advocacy research, "Advocates word questions so as to encourage people to respond in the desired way" (2012, 47). The PRE reports are based on self-administered questionnaires and interviews. While the reports describe the topics covered by the questions, none of the actual questions are included, despite the fact that the reports are posted on the PRE website and thus presumably not subject to space constraints. This lack of transparency is problematic. Weitzer has noted this methodological flaw in studies authored by Farley and ones by Jody Raphael and Deborah L. Shapiro, researchers who frame prostitution as violence (Weitzer 2005a,

939). In response to this criticism, Raphael and Shapiro contend that Weitzer should have asked to view the survey before making assumptions about its potential bias (2005, 967). As I agree that it is incumbent on the researcher to provide the wording of key questions without compelling the reader to chase after them (Weitzer 2005c, 972), I decided to be proactive. I emailed PRE on 2 October 2012 to request a copy of the questions used to generate the reports. Farley responded within a few hours, stating she would "consider" my request, and asked about my view on the issues. She also inquired whether I had published in the subject area. I responded that I was interested in evaluating whether the questions in the PRE reports may have shaped the kind of data produced, and I attached three articles I wrote that touched on the issue of sex work (email correspondence, 4 October 2012). Farley ultimately did not share the questions. In an email dated 24 October 2012, she explained that PRE has shared the questionnaires with psychologists, but suggested that nonpsychologists have had difficulties with the interpretation, analysis, and comparison with norms. Farley thus sidestepped the issue of research transparency by drawing on disciplinary distinctions. Furthermore, there are no indications that the questions used involved complex psychological theories or concepts. In any event, Farley does not elaborate on her justification for concealing the questions.

Whatever Farley's intentions, by withholding the questions from the reports, PRE prevents the reader from analyzing how ideological beliefs may have influenced the wording or encouraged particular kinds of answers. It also prevents replication of the study, which would allow other researchers to test or extend the results. This methodological subterfuge is troubling enough, but the fact that Farley inquired about my own perspectives on the issue while considering my request further adds to concerns about PRE's research methods. Since her reason for not sharing the questions—my status as a nonpsychologist—came only after I shared my views on sex work, it seems likely that the real reason she denied my request was because of the perspective expressed in my publications, which calls into question the academic integrity of the reports. From a feminist perspective, this refusal signals a troubling reluctance to recognize and dialogue across difference (Reay 2012, 627). Ultimately, without the actual questions being available for analysis, the knowledge generated in the reports is highly suspect.

Another misleading practice used in the reports was the selective but decontextualized inclusion of quotes. For example, PRE peppers the report *Comparing Sex Buyers* with little snippets from their interviews of "Sex Buyers" and "Non-Sex Buyers." While there is some diversity in each group, the sex buyers' quotes are often more crude in tone than are those of the non-sex buyers, and the non-sex buyers often sound like committed radical feminist men. Take, for example, two quotes from sex buyers: "Just stick your dick in"; "Being with a prostitute is like having a cup of coffee — when you're done, you throw it out" (Farley et al. 2011, 3). Then take two quotes from non-sex buyers: "I am a sexual being, but it's not a turn-on for me, knowing that the other person needs to be coerced"; "I would say you are better off masturbating. Prostitution is a degrading thing for both parties" (ibid.). The quotes are taken out of context, so the reader cannot assess how statements that may have come before or after might frame the quotes in a particular way. While this weakness in methodology is not unique to PRE, the decontextualization is heightened since none of the quotes are assigned to a particular subject — pseudonyms are not used. In table 1 for example, eleven quotes are attributed to "Sex Buyers" and eight quotes to "Non-Sex Buyers," but none of the quotes in each category are further differentiated. Because of this, potentially, all eleven of the sex buyer quotes indicating a crude attitude toward sex workers could be from a single interviewee, and all eight of the non-sex buyer quotes indicating an understanding of prostitution as exploitation could likewise be from a single source. Yet, the way the quotes are presented leads the reader to believe each quote is from a different person — which it might be, but the reader has no way to confirm this one way or another. Compare this choice with the way Teela Sanders cites the interviewees in her study of fifty clients, *Paying for Pleasure* (2008). After each quote, Sanders provides a pseudonym, and in an appendix she lists all the men by their pseudonyms along with biographical data such as the subject's age, occupation, and marital status. Not only does this practice allow the reader to differentiate quotes from different men, but the pseudonyms and biographical information humanizes the men, allowing the reader to imagine the subjects as individual people without compromising their privacy. PRE's practice of unidentified quotes has the opposite effect: the decontextualized quotes make the subjects appear one-dimensional and homogenous. This reductionist approach allows PRE to more easily stereotype sex buyers as a deviant category of men deserving condemnation and, more important, criminal sanctions.

Due to the problems outlined above — the committed antiprostitution stance which drives PRE's research; generalizations based on convenience samples; inattention to the limitations of such research; exploitation of the "dark figure" to suggest sex buyers are worse than they will admit; withholding the survey and interview questions used to create the reports; Farley's seeming unwillingness to share the questions with scholars who oppose her essentialist antiprostitution perspective; and the lack of differentiation between excerpted quotes—serious doubts emerge about the reliability of the qualitative and quantitative data.

Comparing Sex Buyers also distorts statistical data to create a pejorative picture of sex buyers. Advocacy research often takes recourse to this kind of data, as it holds much traction in sociopolitical debates. As Haggerty argues, "Rhetorical uses of statistics can do more than provide support, they can also perform a type of social magic by giving political claims a degree of urgency and aura of scientific truth that they might otherwise lack" (2002, 8). I expose the methodological and semantic tricks behind PRE's "social magic." To do so is important because PRE justifies its recommendations for expanding and strengthening the criminalization of clients, in part, through the persuasive power of statistical data. While combing through each statistic is beyond the scope of this chapter, I point out a few blatant manipulations of numerical data that demonstrate the weakness, if not the downright deceptiveness, of PRE's statistical claims.

At the beginning of the document, PRE provides a "Summary of Findings and Recommendations," where it professes that "sex buyers engaged in significantly more criminal activity than non-sex buyers" (Farley et al. 2011, 4). This statement is not qualified, and the tabulation of criminal activities is based on self-reporting, so there is no way to know if any of the men have accurately reported their activities. As PRE itself notes, interviewees may consciously or unconsciously hide facts to present in socially desirable ways. PRE discusses this concern in relation only to "sex buyers." Yet one might reasonably consider that the men who were willing to admit to "buying sex" might have been more forthcoming about their illicit activities than were the other men interviewed. In comparison, the men who claimed they did not purchase sexual services may have been particularly vested in coming across as upstanding citizens and might not have been willing to share information regarding any criminal activity in which they may have been involved. Furthermore, a close examination of the information contained in table 16, "Crimes Committed by Sex Buyers and Non-Sex Buyers," shows the extent to which the differentiation between the two groups is contrived. For instance, PRE inflates the association of criminality with sex buyers by including bizarre—even comical—

"crimes." Under "property crimes," for example, PRE lists "selling balloons without a permit" as an offence committed by one sex buyer. The inclusion of such a minor infraction in PRE's evidence of the deviant nature of clients suggests an attempt to stretch the numbers.

This number stretching also occurs in PRE's categorization of crimes, which illustrates its efforts to create an indelible link between sex clients and violence against women. In the section "Summary of Findings and Recommendations," PRE states, "All of the crimes known to be associated with violence against women were reported by sex buyers; none were reported by non-sex buyers" (Farley et al. 2011, 4). Taken at face value, this statement suggests a stark and significant difference between the two groups of men. But, if the reader looks at the fine print in table 16, which lists the crimes, the difference between the two groups appears disingenuous and forced. The types of offences PRE categorizes as "Violence Against Women or Typically Associated w/VAWA" are "impersonating a police officer; violating a restraining order; indecent exposure—public urinating; intimidating witnesses; lewd and lascivious behavior; destruction of property" (Farley et al. 2011, 35). None of these offences necessarily signal violence against women, and no explanation is offered as to why such offences are "typically associated with" violence against women. While there *may* be an association between these offences and violence against women—for example, violating a restraining order might be related to stalking—without more details with regard to the specifics of each crime, the connection remains open to interpretation. In any given instance, public urination could be more directly related to the criminalization of poverty, as homeless people risk arrest when they engage in basic survival activities (D. M. Smith 1994, 492). Conversely, from such a broad perspective, other offences that PRE lists under separate categories might also have been classified as being "associated with violence against women." For example, "carrying a concealed weapon" was included in the "weapons" category, and "assault but charges were dropped" was included in the "assault" category, yet both could easily have been included in the "Violence Against Women" category, at least according to the vague terms of the report. Significantly, however, these offences happened to have been committed by non-sex buyers. Categorization here carries out important ideological work: if these offenses were included in the category of offences "associated with violence against women," PRE would not have been able to make the claim that non-sex buyers had not engaged in criminal activities associated with violence against women.

PRE's categorization of offences under separate headings in table 16 is problematic in other ways as well. For example, not only does PRE define, without explanation, the crime "destruction of property" as typically associated with violence against women, but it chooses not to include that particular offence in the category "Property Crimes," which would arguably be its proper classification. Similarly, urinating in public might better be categorized under the subheading "Crimes Against Authority— Disorderly Conduct," which appears on the next page and includes activities like "disturbing the peace" and "drinking in public." PRE offers no explanation for how it organized categories, but it is hard not to suspect ideological motives to skew the report in particular ways. By placing select activities that might *potentially* relate to violence against women under a heading that defines the activities as *unequivocally* related to violence against women, PRE constructs and then inflates the statistical connection between "sex buyers" and violence against women (despite the fact that the activities are nowhere in the document proven to specifically indicate violence against women).

PRE's rhetorical strategy is clearly to present its data in a dramatic fashion via the category "Violence Against Women or Typically Associated with VAWA." The careful reader, when looking at the fine print under this heading, will note that with regard to the 100 sex buyers interviewed, only six associated "criminal" incidents are noted—and they correspond exactly to the six offence types PRE chose to list under this category. In addition, because PRE does not differentiate between sex buyers, it is possible that a single person committed all six of the crimes that PRE listed as associated with violence against women. But even if, for the sake of argument, we assume each criminal incident was committed by a different sex buyer, this suggests that, at most, a mere 6% of sex buyers self-reported activities that PRE associates with violence against women. Yet, PRE's summary converts this statistic into a dramatic narrative: "All of the crimes known to be associated with violence against women were reported by sex buyers; none were reported by non-sex buyers" (Farley et al. 2011, 4). PRE chooses not to present their own data in percentages or numerical terms, instead using the terms *all* and *none* to present a certain story about the implications of the statistic. Best refers to such narrative translation as the packaging of a statistic in the most impressive format: "Quantities can be expressed in different ways, and we ought to be alert for packaging choices that inflate the importance of figures" (2008, 65–66). It is obviously more impressive to state that "*all* of the activities known to be associated with violence against women were committed by sex buyers" than to state, somewhat anticlimactically, that six out of 100 sex buyers engaged in acts that PRE associates (for unknown reasons) with violence against women. PRE thus manipulates not only the qualitative but also the quantitative data to bolster an essentialist view of prostitution as violence and sex buyers as deviant, and to deliver the empirical goods to its funder, the Demand Abolition Project.

Deterrents and Policy Considerations: Surveys as Carceral Projects

Unfortunately, not only does PRE frame the data ideologically to reinforce its antiprostitution stance, the organization's primary goal is to advance a carceral agenda through state apparatuses. The carceral, as defined by Michel Foucault (1995) and taken up by Bernstein (2010) in her theorization of carceral feminism, denotes not just the use of incarceration as the privileged means of social control, but also the proliferation of carceral mechanisms that survey and discipline outside of prison walls. Under the sections "Deterrents to Prostitution" and "Policy Considerations" in *Comparing Sex Buyers*, PRE advocates a multilayered carceral strategy to punish, survey, stigmatize, and deter clients. PRE encourages neoliberal, right-wing approaches to crime control which construct deviant populations and use public resources to expand the prison industrial complex and the powers of criminal justice.

Several of PRE's suggested strategies specifically advocate for panoptic and synoptic surveillance. In addition to jail time and increased fines, suggested punishments include placement on sex-offender registry lists, public shaming in newspapers or billboards, and DNA collection. Constructing clients as sex offenders who must be put on registries not only further reifies and expands this demonized category, but also individualizes and decontextualizes sexual violence while deflecting attention from the systemic causes of violence against women. Furthermore, as Erica Meiners argues, "The expansion of SOR [sex offender registries] contributes to the criminalization of public space and participates in producing public feelings (disgust, fear) that work to legitimate surveillance and incarceration technologies at the core of the PIC [prison industrial complex]" (2009, 51). Officially denouncing clients by publishing their names in newspapers and billboards calls on the community to participate in public-shaming rituals, a strategy that relies on what Mathiesen (1997) calls the "synoptic" community gaze, whereby the many watch the few (1997, 218). Through this "synoptic" dynamic, sex clients become the object of penal voyeurism, which is gratified by disgracing the stigmatized men.

While the advocacy and support of sex-offender registries and public-shaming strategies evidences PRE's carceral feminism, *Comparing Sex Buyers* concentrates primarily on persuading the reader of the need to forcibly extract DNA samples from arrested sex buyers. An entire section of the report is dedicated to advancing these arguments: "Given the criminal history of sex buyers documented in this research, one would anticipate that other criminal activity including sexual violence might occur in the future. Obtaining DNA samples from arrested johns may be useful to consider matches with evidence obtained in past and future crimes. DNA samples would be predicted to serve as a deterrent to buying sex since most people who commit crimes do not want their DNA taken" (Farley et al. 2011, 42). Again, PRE performs a rhetorical sleight of hand. Setting aside the report's various methodological and statistical problems, even PRE's own data does not support the generalization that sex buyers are likely to have a "criminal history," since only a minority of the sex buyers they surveyed had been convicted of crimes, and none of the crimes listed had any documented relation to sexual violence or violence against women. PRE's study provides no empirical reason to anticipate that sex clients, whether they have a criminal record or not, will engage in sexual violence. In addition, PRE apparently has no interest in due process, bodily autonomy, or the rights of the accused. Obtaining DNA samples of arrested—not convicted—clients for the purpose of deterring potential clients either presumes that all arrested men are guilty or, even more troubling, that whether such men are in fact guilty is irrelevant. Furthermore, as Melissa G. Grant argues in her critique of DNA collection of arrested clients, "By threatening people with the possibility of being marked for life in a government database, these well-funded campaigners—with allies in law enforcement, including the Department of Justice—are using a questionably legal policing practice, a combination of 'scared-straight' strategies that became a signature of the war on drugs and the extension of the surveillance state propelled by the war on terror" (2012, para. 1).

Table 20 in *Comparing Sex Buyers* evidences PRE's carceral feminist alliance with the punitive state, which lists fourteen people who support PRE's arguments for DNA testing of arrested sex buyers. The supporters include not just people working for NGOs, but people associated with law enforcement and prosecutorial offices, three of whom are also quoted elaborating on the benefits of DNA testing. The FBI special agent Roger Young justifies collecting DNA samples by making extreme claims about the harms posed by johns: "If it were known that DNA samples were obtained from all arrested johns then it would assist in the prevention of prostitution and the very harmful effects prostitution causes with every aspect of society, morally, socially, economically—and our national security" (Farley et al. 2011, 43). This statement signals a classic moral panic, whereby those associated with an unpopular activity—in this case, buying sex—are objectified as a dangerous class of persons, as "folk devils," in Stanley Cohen's words (2011, 2). Agent Young's characterization of the pervasive threat that sex clients pose to society recalls the construction of gays and lesbians in the 1950s, which also deemed "deviant" sexuality a threat to national security (Kinsman and Gentile 2010). In both cases, sexuality outside of a heteronormative relational context is categorically demonized and the "moral entrepreneurs" who attempt to regulate sexual activity are not required to provide any evidence of wrongdoing.

The supporting quote provided by Alice Vachss, a prosecuting attorney, further reveals the deeply conservative commitment to social justice through penal policy that is embraced by PRE and its allies. After concurring with PRE's advocacy for DNA databases for clients, Vachss states, "But one warning: the testing backlog is already so severe that any legislative addition to the DNA sampling list must provide for funding the testing process or else it compromises the existing system" (Farley et al. 2011, 43). This reveals how the push to criminalize and survey clients is inextricably linked to increasing financial support for neoliberal carceral strategies of social control. Significantly, *Comparing Sex Buyers* never considers how funneling money into invasive biotechnologies and the prison industrial complex may divert public funds from social welfare, employment training, housing, and health care for those most at risk of engaging in survival sex work. As Bernstein argues, such instances of antiprostitution feminism are based on casting "carceral politics as gender justice" (2010, 65).

Furthermore, the racism of this carceral politics is made evident when PRE attempts to inflate the number of people who would agree with their DNA collecting strategy while disregarding the concerns of those fighting racialized oppression in the criminal-justice system. The report states,

Several people who are involved in work against violence against women did not agree to be put on this list—not because they object in principle to taking DNA samples from arrested johns. They understand that the criminal justice system is racist and is currently so biased against men of color that they fear this practice would disproportionately and unjustly harm men of color. Sadly, we understand this reasoning. Since we have no evidence that men of color buy sex any more or less frequently than white European-American men, the proportion of all men who are arrested for buying sex (and thus whose DNA we propose would be sampled) should be in proportion to their numbers in the population at large, and should not exceed—or be less than—the population percentage of those men. (Farley et al. 2011, 43)

PRE pays lip service to concern that men of color will be disproportionately harmed by such policies, but nonetheless persists in its call to action. While PRE is correct in stating that there is no evidence that men of color buy sex more frequently than do white men, there is ample evidence that men of color are disproportionately criminalized (M. Alexander 2012), including disproportionately criminalized for buying sex (Brewer, Muth, and Potterat 2008; Wortley, Fischer, and Webster 2002). Despite their performance of understanding issues of disenfranchisement, PRE does not retract their advocacy of carceral biotechnologies.

PRE's disregard for the specificity of racialized state violence is dramatized in the concluding paragraph of *Comparing Sex Buyers*. In describing the goals of the prostitution "abolitionist" movement, PRE analogizes African American resistance to slavery and white supremacy to "prostituted women's enduring resistance" to subjugation. In listing support for this analogy, PRE cites a blog entry from *AfroSpear*, which describes itself as "A Think Tank for People of African Descent." There is nothing in the cited blog entry that addresses sex work, yet PRE capitalizes on the rhetorical power of antislavery struggles to advance its antiprostitution stance. Not only does this appropriation decontextualize the blog entry, it elides the specific violence of white supremacy and institutional slavery. Further, PRE exploits this analogy, despite the fact that the report's recommendations seek to strengthen the carceral state, which effectively furthers a legacy of slavery that continues to disproportionately dehumanize African American people, particularly in the United States (Wacquant 2002).

Conclusion

I have explored how PRE's survey research operates as a form of surveillance, how its data are distorted to reify clients as deviants, and how its prohibitionist stance on sex work is in alliance with the carceral state. As we engage in critical surveillance analysis, it is important to consider not just how the government, corporations, employers, or individual stalkers engage techniques of monitoring, categorizing, and spying in ways that dehumanize and target vulnerable bodies, but also how social-science research techniques can be complicit in these reifying processes. In the case of PRE's client reports, this reifying process legitimates and intensifies the dehumanization and oppression of those most targeted for criminalization and police surveillance. In particular, the construction of clients as deviants bolsters and legitimates the criminal-justice system, where the usual suspects—racialized and working-class men—are disproportionately rounded up and criminalized in the service of the prison industrial complex. Moreover, this criminalization further strengthens the hegemonic association of such men with sexual danger and perversity.

In addition, it is not just male clients who suffer when buying sex becomes criminalized. Female sex workers are victimized by prohibitionist sociolegal discourses. When prostitution is defined as an antisocial and criminal activity, sex workers continue to be stigmatized. As Lowman argues, "The prohibition and stigmatization of prostitution are the main obstacles to creating safer working conditions for prostitutes" (2000, 1007). In Sweden, where the buying but not the selling of sex is criminalized, sex workers continue to be victimized (van der Meulen 2011). Police sweeps of clients still displace sex workers, forcing them to seek out clients in remote and isolated areas, where they are more vulnerable to violence. This dislocation also makes it harder for sex workers to access health and social services. Moreover, in a legal scheme where buying sexual services is criminalized, some clients will seek sexual services in indoor settings. For street sex workers, fewer clients means increased competition, and the resulting pressures to agree to less safe sexual practices, including not using condoms or servicing men who are intoxicated.

Singling out sex clients as a deviant class and celebrating those who do not buy sex as good sexual citizens contributes to veiling the violence that happens to women in private, sanctified settings. After decades of feminist research that has sought to expose the ways marital sexual relations sometimes occur within a context of economic exploitation or violence, the vilification of clients can work against feminist challenges to the idealization of marriage and monogamy. Indeed, the entire goal of *Comparing Sex Buyers* is the production of difference between sex buyers and non-sex buyers, as is evidenced by the report's subtitle: "'You Can Have a Good Time with the Servitude' vs. 'You're Supporting a System of Degradation.'" The juxtaposition of the two quotes—the first from a sex buyer who appears to enjoy the sex worker's supposed servitude, the second from a non-sex buyer who understands prostitution as a "system of degradation"—idealizes men who condemn prostitution within prohibitionist ideology. Yet, as feminists have pointed out for decades, often the man who poses the most sexual threat to a woman is a husband, boyfriend, or family member. By applauding men who prefer sexuality within a long-term relational context, PRE obscures the violence that frequently occurs between intimate partners.

Prohibitionist feminism is fundamentally antifeminist. It is up to intersectional feminist scholars—who recognize the links between sexual normativity, neoliberalism, surveillance practices, and penal responses to social injustice—to expose the flawed methodology and problematic theory behind reports like those authored by PRE, and to challenge the carceral strategies that they explicitly foster. In this way, we can demonstrate how men, as well as women, can be subject to gender injustice, especially when they exist at the intersection of multiple forms of marginalization.

Notes

1. See Jeffrey and MacDonald 2006; Pheterson 1990; Pheterson 1993.

2. See, respectively, Farley et al. 2011; Macleod, Farley, Anderson, and Golding 2008; Farley, Bindel, and Golding 2009; and Farley, Freed, Phal, and Golding 2012, all available at the Prostitution Research and Education website, http://prostitutionresearch.com/.

3. For example, Farley was an expert witness for the Canadian government in the *R. v. Bedford* case, to support the criminalization of prostitution. See "Affidavit of Dr. Melissa Farley," http://myweb.dal.ca/mgoodyea/Documents/Canada/Farley%20affidavit%20April%2008.pdf.

11

RESEARCH METHODS, INSTITUTIONAL ETHNOGRAPHY, AND FEMINIST SURVEILLANCE STUDIES

KEVIN WALBY AND SEANTEL ANAÏS

Scholarly examination of the relationship between feminism and surveillance studies is important precisely because surveillance studies scholars have not, for the most part, placed difference, gender, and sexuality at the forefront of their enquiries. Feminist analyses are generally critical of how power operates through classifications and categories. The joining of feminist critiques with surveillance studies fosters a research agenda focused on how assumptions about sex and gender are embedded in the classifications and categories on which surveillance relies. Numerous feminist scholars have shown how the categories that surveillance depends on are gendered, sexualized, and racialized.[1] As Shoshana Amielle Magnet and Tara Rodgers (2012) note, feminist inquiries can also examine how gendered and sexualized surveillance intersects with racism, ableism, and transphobia (see Ball 2005; Monahan 2009).

Yet it is important to reflect on what scholars mean by "feminism" and "surveillance studies," as a number of combinations of these approaches are possible. First, there are many schools of feminist thought. As Kathy E. Ferguson long ago argued, "The feminist movement is divided internally" (1984, 4). Second, there are many schools of thought within the subfield of surveillance studies. Some of these are rooted in the social sciences, while others stem from the humanities — for instance, the intersection between critical media studies and feminist surveillance studies (see Dubrofsky 2011a; Dubrofsky 2011b).

While surveillance studies generally and feminist surveillance studies specifically are exciting new areas of research, some scholars have raised questions about the conceptual and methodological clarity of the subfield of surveillance studies.[2] Gary Marx (2007) and Christian Fuchs (2013) refer to surveillance studies as a subfield because it is a meeting place of multiple disciplinary perspectives (e.g., sociology, political science, law, communications studies). Multidisciplinarity is significant because it opens up a larger conceptual and methodological tool kit for enriching empirical research. It is tricky, too, because multidisciplinary sites sometimes result in a lack of conceptual and methodological focus, which is what Marx (2007) has argued is happening to surveillance studies. This becomes all the more apparent when surveillance studies in the social sciences is compared to policing studies, security studies, and intelligence studies, three other subfields with which surveillance studies overlaps. These three other subfields are interdisciplinary and already offer research agendas that examine surveillance. We interpret this to mean that more can be done to devise innovative research methods for a social-science-oriented surveillance studies. In response to the call by Fuchs (2011) and Marx (2007) for conceptual and methodological clarity in surveillance studies, we argue that social scientists must generate a set of conceptual and methodological positions that do justice to the critical merger of feminist theory with surveillance studies.

To address the need to foster a social-science-oriented method in surveillance studies generally and feminist surveillance studies specifically, we draw from feminist contributions focused on organizations, notably the work of the Canadian feminist sociologist Dorothy E. Smith. Smith's research on how texts coordinate everyday experiences and translate and transfer information from local sites to extralocal organizations has much to offer surveillance studies. Smith develops a feminist method of inquiry called "institutional ethnography," which can be used to investigate the key role of texts in surveillance practices. Institutional ethnography provides one way of adding conceptual and methodological clarity to surveillance studies generally and enhancing a social-science-oriented feminist surveillance studies in particular.

We proceed in three parts. We begin by raising critical questions about surveillance studies in relation to policing studies, security studies, and intelligence studies to argue that clear and distinct conceptual and methodological positions are needed in surveillance studies. In so doing, we provide a rationale for drawing from the work of Smith on institutional ethnography, which we argue can enhance social-science-oriented feminist surveillance studies. Next, we discuss feminist contributions to understandings of surveillance, categories and classifications, and bureaucratic organizations. We then turn to Smith's work to illustrate one particular way of doing feminist surveillance studies that offers methodological guidance for social scientists who study how power relations become embedded in the classification and categorization practices that surveillance entails.

What Does Surveillance Studies Do?

First we offer a reflection on what several scholars refer to as a research methods gap in social-science-oriented surveillance studies. Marx (2007) and Kevin Walby (2005b) argue that surveillance studies is in need of a methodological program that will inform empirical research. There should be a set of methodological positions and strategies that are unique to surveillance studies if it is to be a distinct subfield. Similarly, Fuchs (2011) posits that the core concepts of surveillance studies require refinement. He contends that the limitation of surveillance studies in the social sciences arises from an inconsistency of definitions. There is a conflation of neutral (surveillance is any kind of watching) and negative (surveillance involves coercion) definitions of surveillance, just as there is conflation of information gathering (looking around on social media) and surveillance (which Fuchs suggests always involves state or capitalist organizations monitoring and attempting to control or manage different populations). According to Fuchs, not all examples of watching or monitoring are examples of surveillance. Conceptual conflation has significant consequences. For instance, if surveillance is defined as "any form of systematic information gathering, then surveillance studies is the same as information society studies and the surveillance society as a term is synonymous for the category of the information society" (Fuchs 2011, 126). If the methodological and conceptual distinctiveness of surveillance studies cannot be located, "there are no grounds for claiming that surveillance studies is a distinct discipline or transdiscipline" (Fuchs 2010, 14). Marx similarly claims, "A field needs greater agreement (or well-articulated disagreements) on what the central questions and basic concepts are, on what it is that we know empirically and what needs to be known, and on how the empirically documented or documentable can be ordered and explained. . . . Reaching these objectives should be the next steps for the field" (2007, 126). Writing about the research-methods gap in surveillance studies, Marx more bluntly states, "There is too much talk [a.k.a. meta-theory] and not enough research" (ibid.).

The trouble with methods Marx (2007) points to and the difficulty with theory Fuchs (2011) outlines, give rise to the following question: what is the distinctive methodological and conceptual position of surveillance studies in the social sciences? David Lyon (2003) describes surveillance as the collection of information and then the administration of a population based on that collected information. Kevin D. Haggerty similarly defines surveillance as "the collection and analysis of information about populations in order to govern their activities" (2009b, 160). These definitions have their own limitations because "surveillance" is made up of other processes often explored on their own outside of the overarching analytical category of surveillance. For example, policy, practices, law, texts, organizations, privacy, and power are all readily connected to surveillance, but they just as often serve as distinct substantive concerns on their own. Surveillance is like the weather: we talk about it every day, but it is an amalgamation of processes and practices grouped together which could be studied for their particularities. It is not clear how we might go about studying such a multifaceted process as surveillance. It is difficult to know what surveillance studies does because there has been little self-reflexivity about what surveillance scholars do. This reflexivity is important in social sciences (Bourdieu 2004) if surveillance studies scholars want to enhance the conceptual and methodological approaches that inform our work.

The methodological and conceptual distinctiveness of surveillance studies becomes even more elusive when surveillance studies is compared to three other long-standing subfields: policing studies, security studies, and intelligence studies. Policing studies has focused on domestic, municipal, and provincial police agencies — not only on the police, but also on private agencies involved in the maintenance of order. Collecting information about social groups and acting on this information is the fundamental task of policing agents. Much research has been published in policing studies focusing on the collection and analysis of information by policing agents, public and private, such that some scholars, including Marx (1979), claim that the study of information gathering and the analysis of information belongs to the domain of policing studies.[3]

Policing studies not only takes surveillance as its central object of analysis, but also extends this claim by suggesting that surveillance is the key axis through which social control is organized. In other words, policing studies makes a claim about the importance of surveillance at both the methodological and the conceptual level. What does surveillance studies do beyond what policing studies has been doing for decades? Perhaps policing studies focuses more narrowly on public and private policing agencies in a domestic context, while surveillance studies focuses on a wide array of agencies. While this may be the case—surveillance studies does focus on a wider array of agencies that collect information about a population group and then administer that group based on the information collected—a look at security studies and intelligence studies raises additional questions about the methodological and conceptual distinctiveness of surveillance studies.

The second subfield we consider is security studies, which has long focused on the collection of information and administration of populations in national and international contexts.[4] The central focus of security studies is on regulation that happens at different scales: the national, federal, international, and global, concentrating on agencies that collect information and administer populations across borders. Certainly this is the form that security studies takes when it is conjoined with international relations theory. Like policing studies, security studies examines surveillance and further claims that surveillance is the organizing axis of states, borders, and government actions. There is considerable overlap between surveillance studies and security studies, too, which again reveals that more can be done to enhance distinct research methods in surveillance studies.

Intelligence studies represents a narrower niche field of political science.[5] It focuses on the same array of agencies as security studies, which includes national and federal as well as international and global agencies. Yet the information on which intelligence studies scholars focus is distinct, in that intelligence is information that is not a matter of the public record, and it is a kind of information subject to different collection and analysis strategies than information gathered by police or security agencies. Intelligence studies focuses explicitly on the consequences of surveillance. In other words, intelligence studies already claims a focus on surveillance as its defining feature.

In sum, these subfields claim surveillance as an object of analysis, and did so prior to the development of surveillance studies, which in the social sciences can be traced back to Lyon's book *The Electronic Eye* (1994). This brief overview of surveillance studies suggests that there is work to be done to create innovative conceptual and methodological positions in surveillance studies: surveillance studies in the social sciences lacks methodological distinctiveness when compared to policing studies, security studies, and intelligence studies. Smith's (1987) material focus on texts in organizations as an approach to empirical research can help address this issue, with particular utility for a feminist take on surveillance studies in the social sciences.

What Kind of Feminism for Surveillance Studies?

Feminist theory comprises numerous political and analytical positions, ranging from gender essentialism to radical constructivism, a kind of "big tent" of feminism.[6] The big tent has grown because feminist scholarship has moved toward intersectional analysis to initiate a critique of essentialist arguments.

The school of feminist thought we draw from highlights the significance of how gender inequalities and power relations are reproduced in organizations. The focus here is less on identity per se and instead on how organizations categorize, classify, and label people. This approach is Marxist materialist—that is, it places emphasis on organizations and social relations. As an important example of this approach, Kathy Ferguson's (1984) book on the feminist case against bureaucracy critiques how knowledge practices within organizations can be male-streamed—reflective only of the experiences of men. Ferguson focuses on how knowledge practices that operate through categories and classifications restrict life chances for women and other people who are subjugated within these organizations. She analyzes organizational hierarchies and how administrators within these organizations maintain these hierarchies through surveillance of office staff. In Ferguson's account, "supervision from above" and "a complex system of written record-keeping" (1984, 7) lead to a control-oriented work environment. Ferguson provides a fascinating assessment of how women are subjugated within organizations through practices of monitoring and oversight that are implicitly configured according to gendered categories. As Ferguson notes, all the counting, checking, measuring, and recording that occurs in organizations reifies conventional understandings of gender roles.

Smith's work (1987; 1999) on conceptual practices of power and textual

relations within organizations has likewise demonstrated how accounting and monitoring practices in organizations exclude the voices and
perspectives of women as well as other marginalized communities. Like
Ferguson, Smith focuses on how organizations are implicitly configured
according to gendered categories. Importantly, Smith develops a methodological program. While Smith's work is not explicitly geared toward
understanding surveillance—she has never identified as a surveillance-
studies scholar—her writings (materialist in the Marxist sense of materi-
alism) focus on knowledge practices and organizations in ways that lend
themselves to studying and critiquing how surveillance practices, management, and accounting reproduce power relations within organizations and in other social spheres that those organizations regulate. What
Smith's work allows researchers to do is empirically investigate how surveillance processes are put together through work with texts in organizations. Smith's work and specifically her method of inquiry—institutional
ethnography—can be extended to productively enrich feminist surveillance studies.

Institutional Ethnography and Feminist Surveillance Studies

Researchers studying surveillance can benefit from engaging with Smith's
(1987) feminist method of institutional ethnography (IE) because that
approach is unique in its ability to explicate how texts coordinate surveillance practices in organizations. Smith's focus on how managerial and
professional forms of governance (hereafter referred to as "ruling relations") lift women specifically and people generally out of their embodied
and local ways of knowing, is an insight that has fostered many feminist
and critical interventions across the social sciences. The affinity between
Smith's definition of ruling as "discursive, managerial, and professional"
(1999, 49) and the material world of surveillance processes made up of
texts, writing, inscribing, reading, and interpreting can be a key focus of
feminist surveillance studies.

IE is a method of inquiry that problematizes social relations at the
local site of lived experience. Broadly, it examines how sequences of texts
coordinate consciousness, actions, and ruling. Smith's approach emerged
out of feminist debates in the late 1960s. IE's material focus on texts (e.g.,
applications forms, occurrence reports) is what allows it to investigate beyond the locally observable into the extralocal relations that regulate the
local through managerial practices and surveillance. This is because the

institutional ethnographer follows surveillance texts to see what kinds of assumptions about sex and gender are embedded in these. For instance, an institutional ethnographer would follow the path of an application form, observe how it is worked with in an organization or in any agency it is sent to, see what categories and classifications it deploys, and examine how surveillance translates the rich experiences of everyday life to a series of words, numbers, and classifications. Part of learning IE is adopting Smith's approach to social inquiry, since IE is not a tool one can use without adopting a Marxist feminist materialist perspective. Theory and method are intertwined in IE.

Alison I. Griffith's (1995) research provides an example of how IE is done. Her inquiry started when, as a single mother, she encountered discourses in the education system that cast single parents as defective families. Griffith began to explore how office administrators at the Board of Education and teachers, social workers, and psychologists at schools used the idea of "single-parent families," and how this was codified in texts and assessments to measure the performance of children in schools (and, by extension, their families at home). She found that single-parent families fell under more scrutiny by these organizations. This research was extended into an interview-based exploration of how women with children in elementary school negotiate the notion of normal families and the various texts, evaluations, and assessments that apply this understanding of family (Griffith and Smith 2005). Griffith and Smith show that the standpoint and experiences of mothers disappear into these texts, evaluations, and assessments, and that the work of mothers and teachers becomes coordinated through this discourse about normal families and the related texts and assessments. The focus on texts is important because as James Rule (1973) has shown, texts extend the surveillance capacity of organizations. Rule argues that the surveillance capacity of organizations is shaped by the number of files, the degree of centralization of files, the speed with which the texts flow between locales in the network, and the number of contact points between the organization and the subject population (1973, 37–40).

Since IE uses interviews and observations to follow around surveillance texts and observe how these texts are used, IE can help address the research-methods gap in surveillance studies (recall Marx 2007). IE should be of special importance to surveillance researchers because it allows researchers to empirically investigate how surveillance processes are put together in organizations through work practices involving texts.

Surveillance involves first and foremost the collection of information regarding a subject population. Information is collected, sorted, sent, and received by people in organizations. However, Smith notes that "information" is not something that we can study alone since "the term *information* is itself deceptive. It hides the production and reading of texts that have a specifically standardized form enabling them to be treated as equivalent to one another and to be read using procedures that *read through* . . . the words and/or numbers to an imputed actuality beyond them" (2006, 72). An IE approach to feminist surveillance studies explores the production and reading of texts that are part of surveillance, exposing how surveillance reduces everyday life to numbers, categories, and classifications. It is this final step in IE that can assist a feminist project, since the purpose is to show how classifications become gendered and sexed.

Using IE as a method can help feminist-surveillance-studies scholars break surveillance down into its constituent parts (texts, work, organizations) and make the process amenable to detailed ethnographic study. As a method of feminist inquiry, IE focuses on the reading and writing of texts in organizations and how this work with texts contributes to ruling practices. Texts refer to words, images, or sounds that are set into a material form that are read, seen, heard, or watched. Texts are actual material things, written and read in the same place and time as the writer or reader engages with them, and then sent to other readers or writers who work with the information. An example would be an occurrence report completed by a police officer after monitoring a suspect, or a threat assessment completed by an intelligence officer after spying on a social-movement group. The occurrence report might be sent to an attorney within police services or to police officers in another jurisdiction, while the threat assessment might be shared with other security intelligence agencies in the same country or in other countries. A text in IE could also be a video such as CCTV footage or a freeze-frame picture from the same material that is interpreted by someone watching the camera and translating what they see into a set of notes, which are then used in an investigation or prosecution (see Walby 2005a). Texts are sent and received between work sites. The flow of information that IE explores always emerges in actual and multiple locations—termed "processing interchanges" (Pence 2001)—where information is produced in the form of a text, form, file, or dossier. When these texts facilitate the monitoring of people in their everyday lives and the governance of those lives based on the conveyance of the texts between organizations, we call this the "material relations of surveillance." These relations are grounded in textual practices that can be analyzed using IE's feminist methodological lens. The material relations of surveillance are the sending and receiving of texts that allow for surveillance to happen. To be sure, IE is set up for social scientists and sociological investigations of organizations (but is still appropriate for use in allied scholarly fields). IE requires ethnographic research in organizations where surveillance practices are happening. The institutional ethnographer can enter the sites in the surveillance network where texts are created, translated, and interpreted, to explore how surveillance processes connect down with the local and connect up with organizations.

Participants in the material relations of surveillance are connected through texts and the organizational features that shape work processes. Texts transport the observations and discriminations of surveillance practices from one setting to another, at the same time as the particularities of our everyday lives disappear into these data flows. Surveillance texts must be treated as active in coordinating work across organizations. However, it is only at the local site that researchers can begin to inquire into surveillance practices. For example, consider the police officer writing out the occurrence report or the intelligence officer writing out the threat assessment. They compile these documents based on a reading of other texts, such as their own notes, or other occurrence reports or threat assessments from different officers, or video surveillance footage. It is the site of reading and writing of the surveillance texts themselves that the institutional ethnographer wants to find and observe. This is why detailed empirical investigations using interviews and observations are key in IE. Interviews and observations must be used to try and understand the ways in which surveillance happens and to investigate all the work people do to make surveillance happen in organizations. When the text is sent from site to site, it coordinates action by multiple workers in many organizations. This coordination function is what institutional ethnographers refer to as the active text. That the text is active also necessitates its reading or activation by a person who is doing some kind of monitoring or who is trying to make some sense of the information. Institutional ethnographers refer to this reading and interpretation as activation of information within the text. Activation of a text involves the interpretive processes of reading (D. E. Smith 1990, 121). Of course, texts are activated in different ways at different times and places. Discrimination and interpretation are constant features of surveillance, as numerous surveillance-studies scholars have indicated (see Haggerty 2009b; Monahan 2009). The point is that without an ethnographic focus on people who do the work of reading, interpreting, and inscribing texts, researchers are left with only general and abstract claims about information instead of exploring the production and reading of texts on which actual surveillance practices are based. The ethnographic component is crucial in light of the research-methods gap in surveillance studies (also see Marx 2007).

In IE the purpose is to explore how diverse individuals and groups with real experiences are reduced to categories and numbers in the data flows and organizational processes of surveillance. To get at these processes, IE relies on interview transcripts, observations, and secondary documents as data. Asking respondents how they work with texts or how they are the subjects of surveillance can explicate the ways that surveillance reaches down into people's lives and connects up with extralocal organizations. When interviewing, it is crucial to listen for mention of and ask about texts (Devault and McCoy 2002, 765), as they are the key element of the material relations of surveillance. The institutional ethnographer should conduct interviews outside of the initial work location, and ideally interview those who are monitored, those doing the monitoring, those working with the texts and conveying information, and any other people involved in these material relations of surveillance. Interrogating these practices at processing interchanges where people work with texts exposes both the subjective aspects of reading and writing involved in text production as well as the other organizations that the text connects into the surveillance network. After interviewing those working in organizations who are part of the material relations of surveillance, one should analyze their talk (in the form of an interview transcript) to figure out how the work of doing surveillance and categorizing people in texts is conducted. After interviewing those who are being monitored, one should analyze their talk to locate how their lives and experiences are governed through surveillance practices. A commitment to IE in the context of feminist surveillance studies, then, is a commitment to qualitative research and ethnographic investigation of surveillance practices.

Once the institutional ethnographer has conducted interviews with those who are being monitored, those doing the monitoring, and those working with the texts, it is possible to construct a map of what texts are involved, where these texts go in the surveillance network, and how they connect back to the governance of everyday life. The maps depict the material relations of surveillance between organizations as well as the work that goes on within each unit in the organizations involved. For instance, Walby (2005a) mapped out how video surveillance footage can lead to a process that involves many more texts (e.g., occurrence reports, legal documents) and agents (e.g., Crown prosecution, defense lawyers), and where the experiences and realities of the person caught on tape get reduced to institutional jargon and categories. Institutional ethnographers produce maps of these interconnections as a way of visualizing them, and to show interviewees where in the organizational process their experiences disappear from view. Interviewing is crucial for understanding how people work with texts, while mapping is key for demonstrating the scope of the surveillance network and the places where texts are worked.

A good example of an IE is Janet Rankin and Marie Campbell's (2009) research on how hospital reform has led to the creation of new texts and work regimes that involve the surveillance of nurses and a reduction of the lives of patients to a series of standard numbers and classifications. Rankin and Campbell report on interviews with nurses who are monitored, but also with administrators who create the categories and classifications used to influence monitoring practices and measure nurse performance and efficiency. Rankin and Campbell also create maps of the work that goes on within each unit in the connected organizations. The maps show how ministries and other agencies outside the local setting of nursing organize the categories and push for standardization. As Rankin and Campbell argue, it is only possible to explore the surveillance and categorization evident in these processes through qualitative explorations based on interviews and observations in the local site. To do feminist surveillance studies following IE, one needs to be committed to ethnographic research, not only following surveillance texts to where they are used, but also showing how classification and categorization are integral to the regulation of people subject to surveillance. In this way, IE can contribute to methodological refinement in surveillance studies.

Conclusion

There remains a need for conceptual and methodological enhancement in the field of surveillance studies (Fuchs 2011; Marx 2007). Surveillance studies must develop a unique set of conceptual and methodological tools. Our purpose in raising these questions about surveillance studies is to invite attention to the development of a rationale and justification for surveillance studies, and to suggest ways of integrating a critical feminist voice to these lively discussions.

Feminist scholarship's critique of power relations and its vision of politics is a useful position from which to understand the work and the consequences of surveillance. Many feminists have provided remarkable analyses along these lines, most notably Smith, with her material focus on texts and ruling relations. Our purpose has been to provide a specific methodological approach for feminist surveillance studies in the social sciences. Drawing from the work of Smith provides one way of enhancing methodological clarity in surveillance studies. IE invites critical attention to the material practices involved in organizing surveillance. The work people do with texts when conducting surveillance is a point of entry for understanding how the material relations of surveillance are organized, and it is these relations that institutional ethnographers explore. Smith's sociological focus on how texts are made up of categorizations and classifications and how these texts move information from the site of local experience to extralocal organizations provides a Marxist materialist feminist perspective that can enrich feminist surveillance studies. The promise of drawing from feminism and IE in doing surveillance studies is to show how ruling relations are enabled by the texts and classifications that make up surveillance.

Notes

1. See Ball 2005; Eubanks 2006; Magnet and Rodgers 2012; Monahan 2009.
2. See Fuchs 2011; Marx 2007; Walby 2005b.
3. For research in policing studies, see Corsianos 2009; Ericson 1981; Ericson and Haggerty 1997; Manning 1977.
4. See Bigo 2002; Collier and Lakoff 2008; Daase 2008; Kessler and Hudson 2005.
5. See Gill 2004; Rempel 2004; Rudner 2007.
6. See Marcus 2005; O'Driscoll 1996; Rosenberg and Howard 2005.

BLAMING, SHAMING, AND
THE FEMINIZATION OF SOCIAL MEDIA

LISA NAKAMURA

We are creating a world that all may enter without privilege or prejudice according to race, economic power, military force, or station of birth. . . . Your legal concepts of property, expression, identity, movement, and context do not apply to us. They are based on matter, there is no matter here. Our identities have no bodies, so, unlike you, we cannot obtain order by physical coercion.

—John Perry Barlow, "A Declaration of the Independence of Cyberspace"

As the essays in this excellent volume show, surveillance does more than simply watch or observe bodies. It *remakes* the body as a social actor, classifying some bodies as normative and legal, and some as illegal and out of bounds. There is no form of surveillance that is innocent. Technologies such as body scanners, ultrasounds, networked genomics, and other increasingly compulsory forms of biometric monitoring serve two functions: to regulate, define, and control populations; and to create new gendered, racialized, and abled or disabled bodies through digital means. As Laura Hyun Yi Kang, Kelli D. Moore, Lisa Jean Moore and Paisley Currah, and Andrea Smith's works in this volume show, this has been true since well before the Internet appeared, with lock hospitals and homeless shelters functioning as surveillant state institutions that confined and monitored poor women, women of color, and migrant women. This volume describes how both predigital and digital technologies have enabled new and more comprehensive forms of "dataveillance" that disproportionately target women and minorities. This volume is a vital new contribution to digital media and feminist studies.

The essays in this collection illustrate how badly mistaken both the Internet's critics and its digital utopians were in the 1990s, when both cohorts asserted that the Internet would make surveillance impossible. As John Perry Barlow wrote in "A Declaration of Independence of Cyberspace" (1996), the Internet was a place where users left their bodies behind, and the lack of physical bodies prevented not only identification, but also the possibility of "physical coercion" of members by other Internet users and also by the state. The ability to participate anonymously or, as was and remains far more common, pseudonymously was an integral part of why Barlow and other Net utopians saw the Internet as valuable.

Before 2004, when Facebook and other social-media services began to require "real names" authentication—via what danah boyd describes as "terms of service [agreements that] explicitly require [their] users to provide their 'real names and information'" (2012, 29)—many online social spaces permitted users to construct their own bodies, bodies which supposedly did not definitively establish their users as female or male, as white or black or brown. Though, as boyd notes, not all Facebook users complied with the real-names requirements, and "late teen adopters [of Facebook] were far less likely to use their given name" (ibid., 29–30), it is now the norm for social-network-service (SNS) users to provide real names. This is a significant shift from the pre-SNS period, when the remaking or refashioning of one's body on the Internet was celebrated by digital utopians such as Barlow. Barlow, Mark Hansen, and others from this period envisioned the Internet as a race- and gender-neutral space where virtual bodies replaced real ones. They envisioned users' "electronic bodies" as a directly oppositional practice to states or other sociopolitical institutions that might define users in oppressive ways or seek to control their behavior.[1]

Yet the remarkable case of Natalie Blanchard, a depressed woman who lost her Canadian disability benefits because, according to the insurance company who accessed her Facebook pages, her profile pictures showed her in a bikini on vacation looking "too happy" to be depressed, reminds us that the real-names Internet has the potential to coerce us all (see Sawchuck 2010). For women on social-networking sites, there is a constant negotiation between the desire to connect and the need to self-regulate.

Our identities are inextricably attached to the cultural contingencies of our gendered bodies.

For instance, as Rachel E. Dubrofsky and Megan M. Wood discuss in this volume, female celebrities who post to Twitter are viewed as responsible for the displays that place them under surveillance, implicating them in their own objectification. At the same time, women on these sites generate a significant amount of the user traffic and profit for social-networking companies, and in fact, endure significant pressure to behave in ways that actively invite a sexualized gaze. Women perform much of the "free labor" of social media: they are more likely to use Facebook than men; they use picture-sharing services like Instagram and Pinterest more frequently (Duggan and Brenner 2013); they populate and generate original and unique content for fan bulletin boards; and they produce and share fan fiction. As Mark Andrejevic (2009) and others have shown, this subjects them to new and invisible forms of surveillance and enclosure as every click, every post, and every log-on is measured and often sold to advertisers.

In response to this troubling state of affairs, Geert Lovink and Korinna Patelis's Unlike Us project has brought together "a research network of artists, designers, scholars, activists, and programmers who work on 'alternatives in social media'" with the goal of propagating the "further development and proliferation of alternative, decentralized social media software" (Lovink and Patelis n.d.). This network proposes to produce an anti-Facebook form of social networking and encourages, as a first step, boycotting for-profit centralized social-media platforms. While it is hard for many in our current social-media age to envision a new system of free and publicly owned social media, it is difficult to imagine how, without this shift, users can be protected from having their personal data harvested and potentially sold.

While the development of alternative platforms for digital interaction is a promising goal given the huge amounts of time, data, and personal information we willingly give to for-profit corporations to keep, sell, or simply save, this approach has some problems. It is exactly those vulnerable populations — children, poor women, migrants, older women — who are the least able to "quit Facebook." Users who lack digital literacies as well as cultural ones are less likely to be aware of alternatives to services like Facebook, or indeed, to be aware of the risks associated with their use in the first place. As the essays in this volume show, women and people of color are still overwhelmingly the objects of the biometric and surveillance gaze, as they have always been. Lack of access to digital tools and techniques, the industry practice of shipping smartphones and other mobile devices preloaded with applications like Facebook, YouTube, and Twitter (Washington 2011), and, most important, a lack of awareness of options and training in how to seek out and install alternative platforms makes it unlikely that the most-surveilled populations in Canada and North America can escape from the "walled garden" of social media.[2]

In the introduction to this volume, Dubrofsky and Shoshana A. Magnet ask a timely question: "How do questions of empowerment and responsibility become articulated when individuals operate the technologies that functionally surveil them and are used to obstruct their right to the privileges of citizenship, including assistance from the state?" (00). Social media have become a space of intense surveillance and punishment of feminist activism and activity, most recently in the shared spaces of digital gaming.[3] Anita Sarkeesian, a Canadian American blogger and media critic whose video blog *Feminist Frequency* focuses on the profound sexism in commercial video games, discovered this the hard way when she put up a Kickstarter campaign in 2012 inviting readers to finance a video series on sexist tropes in games. Sarkeesian received personal messages that, as Mia Consalvo (2012) writes, established just how "toxic" the culture of digital gaming is, as male gamers flooded the Internet with death threats and user-generated video games that invited users to punch and bruise Sarkeesian's face.

Early Internet utopians claimed the Internet would give everyone the power to surveil, to see and not be seen, to become a bodiless and thus unseeable user. Instead, we have become more visible and trackable than ever. Social-media companies are now, for all intents and purposes, communication utilities that we depend on for access to friends and community. Female users and other users from marginalized and stigmatized groups are differentially targeted as objects of surveillance and victimization in social media. For example, Blanchard (the woman accused of looking too happy in her Facebook pictures, thus losing her disability insurance) and Sarkeesian lost their rights to safety, support, and state-recognized protection from harm by engaging in public activities that threatened patriarchal norms. While Blanchard's beach photos were the result of one of the most common and everyday uses of social networks — sharing pictures with friends — they exposed her to comparison with the normative "depressed body," a comparison in which she was found lacking. Sarkeesian was surveilled by a community of journalists and gamers who subjected her to forms of intensely gendered and racialized violence and oppression. She received numerous death threats and was mocked on many gaming forums for being "ugly," and Jewish, though in fact Sarkeesian is Armenian.

There is a key difference between these two cases. Sarkeesian was a blogger who sought readers and visibility when she posted her work and requests for project crowdfunding on the Internet. Blanchard was not. Whether women use the Internet to produce feminist work overtly critiquing sexist digital industries like gaming, as Sarkeesian did, or merely venture onto private networks such as Facebook to share pictures, they are exposed to both symbolic and legal violence.[4] Troublingly, the state is unlikely to provide solutions; online harassment is robustly resistant to policing partly because of anonymity and pseudonymity, and online threats often are not taken seriously, but rather are tolerated as part of Internet culture.

I am inspired by Dubrofsky and Magnet's call for an alternative to traditional forms of regulation like the surveillant policing and criminalization of offenders, a system that has been amply proven not to work well in the case of video game sexism and racism (Nakamura 2011). As Dubrofsky and Magnet ask, "How might we think about how to build coalitions across difference? A feminist approach to surveillance studies also argues for a reimagining of collective responses to the violence of state scrutiny, one that seeks to uproot and defy oppressive structural systems, envisioning collective forms of resistance to violence that do not involve state surveillance of those living either inside or outside its borders, and asks how we might make our communities safer while continuing to refuse surveillance practices" (this volume, 16).

One place to look for these possibilities is the world of feminist digital-gaming activism where there is a small but vital group of feminist, anti-ableist, and antiracist blogs, Tumblr sites, and Twitter hashtags (see #1reasonwhy and #YesAllWomen) that exemplify the community-driven options that the Internet makes available to women. These blogs successfully appropriate the social-media tools that we already have to exercise forms of countersurveillance that are noncoercive in nature. The blogs *Fat, Ugly or Slutty, Not in the Kitchen Anymore, The Border House, The Hathor Legacy,* and *Racialicious* collect racist, sexist, and homophobic hate speech that female and queer gamers have received while playing networked video games and publicize them for all to see (Nakamura 2012).[5] These sites do not solely rely on the state or on corporations such as Microsoft and Sony to "police" offenders (though readers are encouraged to submit report tickets to these companies if they deem that an appropriate response); instead, they produce feminist countersurveillant media that present an alternative to either criminalizing offenders, boycotting, or trying to shut down gaming networks, or breaking them for others.

When women create their own networks for posting content about video-game racism and sexism, they can have unexpectedly wide reaching and powerful effects. In a post entitled "Perspectives and Retrospectives: Vol 3," the author "gtz," a cofounder of *Fat, Ugly or Slutty*, tells a fascinating tale of her and her collaborators' work building a coalition of antiracist, antisexist gamers. As she writes, "We've received letters from parents expressing gratitude for the 'work' that we do and their thoughts on how it affects their childrens' lives. . . . We get 'thought this might interest you' emails from people linking us to various gaming, gender, and harassment-related issues that have popped up online. All over forums and blogs and Twitter people are expressing relief at *not feeling alone* in harassment" (gtz 2012). This post appeared in the "Staff Blog" section of the site on 1 February 2012, and it directly addresses Dubrofsky and Magnet's call for a community-driven option as a response to gamer violence. For as gtz reports,

> A couple of weeks ago, *FUoS* [*Fat, Ugly or Slutty*] had another first—a request from someone to have their harassing messages taken off the site. This person had googled their own username, and lo and behold, all the results came up with FAT UGLY OR SLUTTY DOT COM. We've had folks "featured" on the site show up in comments and defend their actions, or deliberately try and incite some flamewars . . . but this was new . . . this was the first time someone actually had expressed a modicum of regret after seeing it on *FUoS*.

gtz goes on to describe how she decided to handle the request to take down the poster's abusive message. The poster described how when he googled his username and saw his original post; he wrote to *FUoS*, "Can you remove that its dumb and immature im only 16 when I made that to sum chick cause I was bored and id like to not be reped in that way could you please take it down? I learned my lesson don't be a jackass on internet things." As gtz writes, "There's something, *something* in the email that says he gets it, even just a little bit, and I believe it." In the end, the site moderator decided keep the original post onsite, but remove all references to his username, thus protecting his privacy and reputation.

This decision to "police without policing," exemplified by gtz's actions in this case, embodies a feminist ethics of pedagogy and care. It responds to the harrasser's assertion to have "learned his lesson" by hailing an affective register; as gtz writes, "A lot of this is gut feeling and that's partly why I wanted to do this series." She identifies her decision to anonymize the young man's post to protect him from publicity and ridicule as emanating from her "gut," but there is clearly far more at play. As she writes, the site originated as a way to help women publicize gamic harassment, but had unexpected consequences.

Parents as well as bloggers, Twitter users, and gamers came together to form a feminist community based on media activism on *Fat, Ugly or Slutty*. Though their actions were the result of frustration and disenchantment with the game industry's ability or desire to address the toxic environment of many of its products, they advocated a two-pronged approach that included both "official" regulation and community-based documentation and activism. *Fat, Ugly or Slutty* models an alternative ethics of regulation that stands in sharp contrast to Sony and Microsoft's official complaint-handling policies in regard to their gaming platforms, a policy based on irregular enforcement of a terms-of-service agreement that is rarely read by players and is written in legal, rather than affective, discourse. As more of our lives continue to become mediated by social media and gamic worlds, we would do well to look out for such models. This is not a utopian story: there's no way to verify that the young man was telling the truth or that his experience will deter him from hate speech the next time he plays online games with women. It is, however, ultimately a hopeful one.

Notes

1. For an eloquent argument, see González 2009.
2. According to Jesse Washington (2011), people of color are far more likely to access the Internet from a mobile device, effectively creating "two Internets," one for privileged broadband users, and another for mobile users who must deal with the limitations of small keyboards, impoverished interfaces, and less interactivity: "Fifty-one percent of Hispanics and 46 percent of blacks use their phones to access the Internet, compared with 33 percent of whites, according to a July 2010 Pew poll. Forty-seven percent of Latinos and 41 percent of blacks use their phones for email, compared with 30 percent of whites. The figures for using social media like Facebook via phone were 36 percent for Latinos, 33 percent for blacks and 19 percent for whites."

3. For an excellent analysis of the pervasively antifeminist climate of computing culture generally, see Marwick 2013.

4. For an excellent account of the intermingling of these labor and leisure issues engendered by digital mobile media, see Gregg 2011.

5. See, respectively, http://www.fatuglyorslutty.com/, http://www.notinthe kitchenanymore.com/, http://www.theborderhouse.com/, http://www.thehathor legacy.com/, and http://www.racialicious.com/.

REFERENCES

Abu-Lughod, L. 2002. "Do Muslim Women Really Need Saving?: Anthropological Reflections on Cultural Relativism and Its Others." *American Anthropologist* 104 (3): 783–90.

Acland, R. 2009. "Social Network Services as Data Sources and Platforms for E-Researching Social Networks." *Social Science Computer Review* 27 (4): 481–92.

Ahmad, A. N. 2010. "Is Twitter a Useful Tool for Journalists?" *Journal of Media Practice* 11 (2): 145–55.

Ahmed, L. 1992. *Women and Gender in Islam: Historical Roots of a Modern Debate.* New Haven: Yale University Press.

Ahmed, S. 2000. *Strange Encounters: Embodied Others in Post-Coloniality.* London: Routledge.

Akçam, T. 2012. *The Young Turks' Crime against Humanity: The Armenian Genocide and Ethnic Cleansing in the Ottoman Empire.* Princeton, NJ: Princeton University Press.

Alexander, M. 2010. *The New Jim Crow: Mass Incarceration in the Age of Colorblindness.* New York: New Press.

———. 2012. *The New Jim Crow.* New York: New Press.

Alexander, M. J. 2005. *Pedagogies of Crossing: Meditations on Feminism, Sexual Politics, Memory, and the Sacred.* Durham, NC: Duke University Press.

Allen, P. G. 1986. *The Sacred Hoop.* Boston: Beacon.

Alloula, M. 1986. *The Colonial Harem.* Minneapolis: University of Minnesota Press.

Amani. 2010. "Introducing . . . Our Front Bump!" *Amani and Bob's Indian Surro-*

gacy (blog), 1 April. http://amaniandbobsurrogacy.blogspot.com/2010/04/introducing-our-front-bump.html.

Ammar, N. H. 2007. "Wife Battery in Islam: A Comprehensive Understanding of Interpretations." *Violence Against Women* 13 (5): 516–26.

Amnesty International. 2007. *Maze of Injustice*. New York: Amnesty International.

Anderson, K. 1991. *Chain Her by One Foot*. New York: Routledge.

Andrejevic, M. 2004. *Reality TV: The Work of Being Watched*. Lanham, MD: Rowman and Littlefield.

———. 2006a. "The Discipline of Watching: Detection, Risk, and Lateral Surveillance." *Critical Studies in Media Communication* 23 (5): 392–407.

———. 2006b. "Interactive (In)Security: The Participatory Promise of Ready.gov." *Cultural Studies* 20 (4–5): 441–58.

———. 2007. *iSpy: Surveillance and Power in the Interactive Era*. Lawrence: University Press of Kansas.

———. 2009. "Privacy, Exploitation, and the Digital Enclosure." *Amsterdam Law Forum* 1 (4). http://amsterdamlawforum.org/article/view/94/168.

Andrejevic, M., and K. Gates. 2014. "Big Data Surveillance: Introduction." *Surveillance and Society* 12 (2): 185–96.

Andrews, L. B. 1999. *The Clone Age: Adventures in the New World of Reproductive Technology*. New York: Holt.

Anonymous v. Weiner. 1966. 270 N.Y.S. 2d 319.

Anthias, F., and N. Yuval-Davis. 1992. *Racialized Boundaries, Race, Nation, Gender, Colour and Class and the Anti-Racist Struggle*. London: Routledge.

Antonelli, Paola. 2005. *Safe: Design Takes on Risk*. New York: Museum of Modern Art.

Appleby, T. 2011a. "Father Said Victims 'Betrayed Islam.'" *Globe and Mail*, 15 November, A5.

———. 2011b. "Polygamy Put Family at Risk of Deportation, Court Told." *Globe and Mail*, 30 November, A10.

———. 2012. "How Arrogance and Mistakes Led to a Murder Conviction." *Globe and Mail*, 30 January, A6.

Arons, J. 2007. *Future Choices: Assisted Reproductive Technologies and the Law*. Washington: Center for American Progress.

Attwood, F. 2011. "Through the Looking Glass?: Sexual Agency and Subjectification in Cyberspace." In *New Femininities: Postfeminism, Neoliberalism and Subjectivity*, edited by R. Gilland and C. Scharff, 203–14. Basingstoke, UK: Palgrave Macmillan.

Atwood, M. 1985. *The Handmaid's Tale*. Toronto: McClelland and Stewart.

Baily, M. A. 2007. "Why I Had Amniocentesis." In *Prenatal Testing and Disability Rights*, edited by E. Parens and A. Asch, 64–71. Washington: Georgetown University Press.

Balakrishnan, R. 1994. "The Social Context of Sex Selection and the Politics of Abortion in India." In *Power and Decision: The Social Control of Reproduction*, edited by G. Sen and R. C. Snow, 267–86. Cambridge: Harvard University Press.

Ball, K. 2005. "Organization, Surveillance and the Body: Towards a Politics of Resistance." *Organization* 12 (1): 89–108.

Ball, K., et al. 2009. "Surveillance Studies Needs Gender and Sexuality." *Surveillance and Society* 6 (4): 352–55.

Ballinger, A., and D. Graydon. 2007. *The Rough Guide to Film Noir*. London: Rough Guides.

Banet-Weiser, S. 2012. *Authentic TM: The Politics of Ambivalence in a Brand Culture*. New York: New York University Press.

Barbar, J. 2001. "History's Lessons." *Globe and Mail*, 22 September, F4.

Barlow, J. P. 1996. "A Declaration of the Independence of Cyberspace." Electronic Frontier Foundation, 8 February. https://projects.eff.org/~barlow/Declaration -Final.html.

Barthes, R. 1973. *Mythologies*. Translated by A. Lavers. Reprint, London: Paladin, 1957.

Bascaramurty, D., and C. Freeze. 2012. "Four Died for His 'Twisted' Honor." *Globe and Mail*, 30 January, A1.

Beck, U. 2002. "The Silence of Words and Political Dynamics in the World Risk Society." *Logos* 1 (4): 1–18.

Benedict, H. 1992. *Virgin or Vamp: How the Press Covers Sex Crimes*. New York: Oxford University Press.

Berger, J. 1972. *Ways of Seeing*. London: Penguin.

Bernstein, E. 2010. "Militarized Humanitarianism Meets Carceral Feminism: The Politics of Sex, Rights, and Freedom in Contemporary Antitrafficking Campaigns." *Signs* 36 (1): 45–71.

Best, J. 2008. *Stat-Spotting: A Field Guide to Identifying Dubious Data*. Berkeley: University of California Press.

———. 2012. *Damned Lies and Statistics: Untangling Numbers from the Media, Politicians, and Activists*. Berkeley: University of California Press.

Bhabha, H. 1994. "Of Mimicry and Men." In *Tensions of Empire*, edited by F. Cooper and A. L. Stoler, 152–60. Berkeley: University of California Press.

Bhattacharjee, A. 2000. "Plenary Address." Paper presented at the Color of Violence: Violence Against Women of Color conference, University of California, Santa Cruz.

———. 2001a. *In Whose Safety?: Women of Color and the Violence of Law Enforcement*. Philadelphia: American Friends Service Committee.

———. 2001b. "Private Fists and Public Force." In *Policing the National Body, The Color of Violence: Violence against Women of Color*, edited by A. Bhattacharjee and J. Silliman, 1–54. Boston: South End Press.

Bigo, D. 2002. "Security and Immigration: Toward a Governmentality of Unease." *Alternatives* 27 (1): 63–92.

Blatchford, C. 2009. "It's No Accident That Victims Were All Females." *Globe and Mail*, 24 July.

Bloche, M. G. 2004. "Race-Based Therapeutics." *New England Journal of Medicine* 351 (20): 2035–37.

Boeckel, F. B. 1929. "Women in International Affairs." *Annals of the American Academy of Political and Social Science* 143: 230–48.

Bonham, V. L., E. Warshauer-Baker, and F. S. Collins. 2005. "Race and Ethnicity in the Genome Era: The Complexity of the Constructs." *American Psychologist* 60 (1): 9–15.

Boseley, S. 2006. "10 Million Girl Fetuses Aborted in India." *Guardian*, 8 January. http://www.guardian.co.uk/world/2006/jan/09/india.sarahboseley/.

Bourdieu, P. 2004. *Science of Science and Reflexivity*. Chicago: University of Chicago Press.

Bowker, G. C., and S. L. Star. 1999. *Sorting Things Out: Classification and Its Consequences*. Cambridge: Massachusetts Institute of Technology Press.

boyd, d. m. 2007. "Why Youth (Heart) Social Network Sites: The Role of Networked Publics in Teenage Social Life." In *Youth, Identity, and Digital Media*, edited by D. Buckingham, 53–58. Cambridge: Massachusetts Institute of Technology Press.

———. 2008. "Facebook's Privacy Trainwreck: Exposure, Invasion, and Social Convergence." *Convergence* 14: 13–20.

———. 2012a. "The Politics of 'Real Names': Power, Context, and Control in Networked Publics." *Communications of the ACM* 55 (8): 29–31.

———. 2012b. "White Flight in Networked Publics?: How Race and Class Shaped American Teen Engagement with MySpace and Facebook." In *Race after the Internet*, edited by L. Nakamura and P. Chow-White, 203–22. New York: Routledge.

Brandt, A. M. 1987. *No Magic Bullet: A Social History of Venereal Disease in the United States since 1880*. London: Oxford University Press.

Brewer, D. D., S. Q. Muth, and J. J. Potterat. 2008. "Demographic, Biometric, and Geographic Comparison of Clients of Prostitutes and Men in the U.S. General Population." *Electronic Journal of Human Sexuality* 11 (9). http://www.ejhs.org/volume11/brewer.htm.

Bristow, E. J. 1977. *Vice and Vigilance: Purity Movements in Britain since 1700*. Dublin: Gill and Macmillan.

Brodwin, P. P. 2000. "Introduction." In *Biotechnology and Culture: Bodies, Anxieties, Ethics (Theories of Contemporary Culture)*, edited by P. P. Brodwin, 1–23. Bloomington: Indiana University Press.

Brown, J. 2008. *Babylon Girls: Black Women Performers and the Shaping of the Modern*. Durham, NC: Duke University Press.

Browne, S. 2009. "Getting Carded: Border Control and the Politics of Canada's Permanent Resident Card." In *The New Media of Surveillance*, edited by S. Magnet and K. Gates, 87–108. London: Routledge.

Bruckman, A. S. 1992. Identity Workshop. Retrieved May 24, 2012, from Identity Workshop. ftp://ftp.lambda.moo.mud.org/pub/MOO/papers.

Bruyneel, K. 2004. "Challenging American Boundaries: Indigenous People and the 'Gift' of U.S. Citizenship." *Studies in American Political Development* 18 (1): 30–43.

Bumgarner, A. 2007. "A Right to Choose?: Sex Selection in the International Context." *Duke Journal of Gender Law and Policy* 14: 1289–309.

Bumiller, E., and T. Shanker. 2012. "Panetta Warns of Dire Threat of Cyberattack on

U.S." *New York Times*, 11 October. http://www.nytimes.com/2012/10/12/world/panetta-warns-of-dire-threat-of-cyberattack.html.

Bumiller, K. 2009. "The Geneticization of Autism: From New Reproductive Technologies to the Conception of Genetic Normalcy." *Signs* 34 (4): 875–99.

Burchard, E. G., et al. 2003. "The Importance of Race and Ethnic Background in Biomedical Research and Clinical Practice." *New England Journal of Medicine* 348 (12): 1170–75.

Burris, B., and A. Hoplight. 1996. "Race in Cyberspace: The Culture of Costless Communities." Paper presented at the annual meeting of the Pacific Sociological Association, Seattle, 22 March.

Burton, A. 1994. *Burdens of History: British Feminists, Indian Women, and Imperial Culture, 1865–1915*. Chapel Hill: University of North Carolina Press.

Butler, J. 1990. *Gender Trouble: Feminism and the Subversion of Identity*. New York: Routledge.

———. 1993. *Bodies That Matter*. New York: Routledge.

———. 2004. *Precarious Life: The Powers of Mourning and Violence*. London: Verso.

———. 2007. "Torture and the Ethics of Photography." *Environment and Planning D* 25: 951–66.

Butterfield, Fox. 2000. "Study Shows a Racial Divide in Domestic Violence Cases." *New York Times*, 18 May. http://www.nytimes.com/2000/05/18/us/study-shows-a-racial-divide-in-domestic-violence-cases.html.

Byrd, J. 2011. *Transit of Empire*. Minneapolis: University of Minnesota Press.

Byron, G. 2002. *Symbolic Blackness and Ethnic Difference in Early Christian Literature*. New York: Routledge.

California v. Brown. 2009. BA353571.

Caplan, J. 2001. "'This or That Particular Person': Protocols of Identification in Nineteenth-Century Europe. In *Documenting Individual Identity: The Development of State Practices in the Modern World*, edited by J. Caplan and J. Torpey, 49–66. Princeton, NJ: Princeton University Press.

Carney, S. 2010. "Inside India's Rent-a-Womb Business." *Mother Jones* (March–April). http://motherjones.com/politics/2010/02/surrogacy-tourism-india-nayna-patel.

Cartwright, L. 1995. *Screening the Body: Tracing Medicine's Visual Culture*. Minneapolis: University of Minnesota Press.

———. 2008. *Moral Spectatorship: Technologies of Voice and Affect in Postwar Representations of the Child*. Durham, NC: Duke University Press.

Casper, M., and L. J. Moore. 2009. *Missing Bodies: The Politics of Visibility*. New York: New York University Press.

Cave, D. 2006. "New York Plans to Make Gender a Personal Choice." *New York Times*, 7 November, A1.

Charliecat and John. 2010. "Our Surrogate, Our Babies." *Chai Baby* (blog), 19 October. http://havingababyinindia.blogspot.com/2010/10/our-surrogate-our-babies.html.

———. 2014. "Happy Conception Day, 3 July." *Chai Baby* (blog), 4 July. http://

havingababyinindia.blogspot.com/search?updated-max=2011%E2%80%9302
%E2%80%9324T17%3A06%3A00%2B10%3A30&max-results=10.

Chen, C., J. Dulani, and L. Pipezna-Samara, eds. 2011. *The Revolution Starts at Home: Confronting Intimate Violence within Activist Communities.* Cambridge: South End Press.

———, eds. 2011. *The Revolution Starts at Home: Confronting Intimate Violence within Activist Communities.* Cambridge: South End Press.

Chopra, R., and R. Gajjala, eds. 2011. *Global Media, Culture, and Identity: Theories, Cases, and Approaches.* New York: Routledge.

Chow-White, P. A. 2012. "Genomic Databases and an Emerging Digital Divide in Biotechnology." In *Race after the Internet*, edited by L. Nakamura and P. A. Chow-White, 291–309. New York: Routledge.

Christie, N. 1994. *Crime Control as Industry: Toward Gulags, Western Style.* London: Routledge.

Chu, Henry. 2006. "Wombs for Rent, Cheap." *Los Angeles Times*, 19 April. http://articles.latimes.com/2006/apr/19/world/fg-surrogate19.

Chun, W. 2006. *Control and Freedom: Power and Paranoia in the Age of Fiber Optics.* Cambridge: Massachusetts Institute of Technology Press.

Clarke, R. 1994. "The Digital Persona and Its Application to Digital Surveillance." *Information Society* 10 (2): 77–92.

CNN.com. 2003. "Saddam 'Caught like a Rat' in a Hole." CNN.com, 15 December. http://www.cnn.com/2003/WORLD/meast/12/14/sprj.irq.saddam.operation/.

Cohen, N. S., and L. R. Shade. 2008. "Gendering Facebook: Privacy and Commodification." *Feminist Media Studies.* 8 (2): 210–14.

Cohen, S. 2011. *Folk Devils and Moral Panics: The Creation of the Mods and Rockers.* Abingdon, UK: Routledge.

Collier, S., and A. Lakoff. 2008. "Distributed Preparedness: The Spatial Logic of Domestic Security in the United States." *Environment and Planning D* 26 (1): 7–28.

Collins, P. H. 1990. "The Social Construction of Black Feminist Thought." In *Black Women in America: Social Science Perspectives*, edited by M. Malson et al., 745–54. Chicago: University of Chicago Press.

———. 2004. "Black Feminist Thought in the Matrix of Domination." In *Social Theory: The Multicultural and Classic Readings*, edited by C. Lemert, 535–46. Boulder: Westview.

Conan, N. 2010. "'Google Baby' Follows Birth Outsourced to India." *Talk of the Nation*, 15 June. National Public Radio. http://www.npr.org/templates/story/story.php?storyId=127860111.

Consalvo, M. 2012. "Confronting Toxic Gamer Culture: A Challenge for Feminist Game Studies Scholars." *Ada* 1 (1). http://adanewmedia.org/2012/11/issue1-consalvo/.

Consumers Union. 1990. "The Telltale Gene." *Consumer Reports* 55 (7): 483–88.

Converse, J. M. 2009. *Survey Research in the United States: Roots and Emergence 1890–1960.* New Brunswick, NJ: Transaction.

Cooper, R. S., J. S. Kaufman, and R. Ward. 2003. "Race and Genomics." *New England Journal of Medicine* 348 (12): 1166–70.

Corea, G. 1985. *The Mother Machine: Reproductive Technologies from Artificial Insemination to Artificial Wombs*. New York: Harper and Row.

Corneau, A. 2012a. "Britney Spears Shows Off Sexy Stomach in Purple Bikini." *Us Weekly*, 6 July. http://www.usmagazine.com/celebrity-body/news/britney-spears-shows-off-sexy-stomach-in-purple-bikini-201267.

———. 2012b. "Charlie Sheen Quits Twitter." *Us Weekly*, 14 July. http://www.usmagazine.com/entertainment/news/charlie-sheen-quits-twitter-2012147.

———. 2012c. "Louis C.K. Explains Daniel Tosh Tweet, Addresses Rape Joke Controversy." *Us Weekly*, 17 July. http://www.usmagazine.com/celebrity-news/news/louis-ck-explains-daniel-tosh-tweet-addresses-rape-joke-controversy-2012177.

———. 2012d. "Whoa!: Heidi Klum Shows Off Cleavage in Skimpy Bikini." *Us Weekly*, 5 July. http://www.usmagazine.com/celebrity-body/news/whoa-heidi-klum-shows-off-cleavage-in-skimpy-bikini-201257.

Corsianos, M. 2009. *Policing and Gendered Justice: Examining the Possibilities*. Toronto: University of Toronto Press.

Couldry, N. 2002. "Playing for Celebrity: *Big Brother* as Ritual Event." *Television and New Media* 3: 284–91.

Council, C. R. 1965. Letter to Carl L. Erhardt, Director of the Bureau of Records and Statistics, 11 June. City of New York Health Department. Archive from the New York Academy of Medicine.

Cover, R. 1986. "Violence and the World." *Yale Law Journal* 95: 1601–29.

Crenshaw, K. 1989. "Mapping the Margins: Intersectionality, Identity Politics, and Violence Against Women of Color." *Stanford Law Review* 143: 1241–99.

Crowdy, R. 1927. "The Humanitarian Activities of the League of Nations." *Journal of the Royal Institute of International Affairs* 6 (3): 153–69.

———. 1928. "The League of Nations: Its Social and Humanitarian Work." *American Journal of Nursing* 28: 350–52.

Currah, P. Forthcoming. *States of Sex: Regulating Transgender Identities*. New York: New York University Press.

Currah, P. and D. Spade. 2003. Transgender Law and Policy Institute and Sylvia Rivera Law Project. "Birth Certificate Sex Designation: An Overview of the Issues." February 6. http://archive.srlp.org/birth-certificate-sex-designation-overview-issues. Memo in possession of the authors.

Currah, P., and L. J. Moore. 2009. "'We Don't Know Who You Are': Contesting Sex Designations in New York City Birth Certificates." *Hypatia* 24 (3): 113–35.

Currah, P., and T. Mulqueen. 2011. "Securitizing Gender: Identity, Biometrics, and Gender Non-Conforming Bodies at the Airport." *Social Research* 78 (2): 557–82.

Daniels, J. 2009. *Cyber Racism: White Supremacy Online and the New Attack on Civil Rights*. Lanham, MD: Rowman and Littlefield.

Darling, M. J. T. 2004. "Eugenics Unbound: Race, Gender, and Genetics." Paper delivered at "Gender and Justice in the Gene Age," New York, 6–7 May. http://www.gjga.org/conference.asp?action=item&source=documents&id=62.

Darnovsky, M. 2004. "Revisiting Sex Selection: The Growing Popularity of New Sex Selection Methods Revives an Old Debate." *Gene Watch* 17 (1): 3–6.

DasGupta, S. 2010. "Gynecology as Corporeal Colonization: Violence, Veiling, and the Pelvic Exam in Narrative Cinema." Paper presented at the Health Embodiment and Visual Culture: Engaging Publics and Pedagogies conference, McMaster's University, Hamilton, Ontario, 18–20 November.

DasGupta, S., and S. Dasgupta. 2010. "Motherhood Jeopardized: Reproductive Technologies in Indian Communities." In *The Globalization of Motherhood: Deconstructions and Reconstructions of Biology and Care*, edited by J. Maher and W. Chavkin, 131–53. New York: Routledge.

———. 2011. "Transnational Surrogacy, E-Motherhood and Nation Building." In *Motherhood Online*, edited by M. Moravec, 283–313. Newcastle upon Tyne, UK: Cambridge Scholars Press.

Davis, A. 1981. *Women, Race, and Class*. New York: Vintage.

———. 1989. *Women, Culture, and Politics*. New York: Random House.

———. 2003. *Are Prisons Obsolete?* New York: Seven Stories Press.

Davis, A., and D. Rodriguez. 2000. "The Challenge of Prison Abolition: A Conversation." *Social Justice* 27 (3): 212–19.

Dean, M. 2009. *Governmentality: Power and Rule in Modern Society*. 2d edn. London: Sage.

Deer, S. 2009. "Decolonizing Rape Law: A Native Feminist Synthesis of Safety and Sovereignty." *Wicazo Sa Review* 24: 149–67.

Deleuze, G., and F. Guattari. 1987. *A Thousand Plateaus*. Minneapolis: University of Minnesota Press.

DelVecchio, M. 2011. "The Media's Contribution to Violence against Women." New Agenda blog, 10 April. http://www.thenewagenda.net/2011/04/10/how-media-contributes-to-violence-against-women/.

Demleitner, N. V. 1994. "Forced Prostitution: Naming an International Offense." *Fordham International Law Journal* 18 (1): 163–97. http://ir.lawnet.fordham.edu/ilj/vol18/iss1/5.

Denny, D. 2006. "Transgender Communities of the United States in the Late Twentieth Century." In *Transgender Rights*, edited by P. Currah, R. Juang, and S. P. Minter, 171–91. Minneapolis: Minnesota University Press.

Devault, M., and L. McCoy. 2002. "Institutional Ethnography: Using Interviews to Investigate Ruling Relations." In *Handbook of Interviewing: Context and Method*, edited by J. F. Gubrium and J. A. Holstein, 751–76. Thousand Oaks, CA: Sage.

Dhariwal, N. 2006. "The Curse of Having a Girl." *BBC News*, 29 June. http://news.bbc.co.uk/go/pr/fr/-/2/hi/programmes/5125810.stm.

Dickel, M. H. 1995. "Bent Gender: Virtual Disruptions of Gender and Sexual Identity." *Electronic Journal of Communication* 5: 95–117.

Dixon, T. L., and D. Linz. 2000. "Race and the Misrepresentation of Victimization on Local Television News." *Communication Quarterly* 27 (5): 547–73.

Dobuzinskis, A. 2011. "Celebrities May Temper Twitter Comments after 2011 Blun-

ders." Reuters.com, 31 December. http://www.reuters.com/article/2011/12/31
/us-twitter-misfires-idUSTRE7BUOGH20111231.

Dow, B. 1996. *Prime-Time Feminism: Television, Media Culture, and the Women's Move-ment since 1970*. Philadelphia: University of Pennsylvania Press.

Dowler, K., T. Fleming, and S. L. Muzzatti. 2006. "Constructing Crime: Media, Crime, and Popular Culture." *Canadian Journal of Criminology and Criminal Justice* 48 (6): 837–50.

Drexler, M. 2005. "Reproductive Health in the Twenty-First Century." *Radcliffe Quarterly* (winter). http://radcliffe.edu/print/about/quarterly/w05_health.htm.

Driskill, Q., C. Finley, B. J. Gilley, and S. L. Morgensen. 2011. "Introduction." In *Queer Indigenous Studies: Interventions in Theory, Politics and Literature*, edited by Q. Driskill, C. Finley, B. J. Gilley, and S. L. Morgensen, 1–28. Tucson: University of Arizona Press.

Du Bois, W. E. B. 1965/1999. "The Souls of Black Folk." New York: Avon Books. http://www.gutenberg.org/files/408/408-h/408-h.htm.

Dubrofsky, R. E. 2011a. *The Surveillance of Women on Reality TV: Watching "The Bachelor" and "The Bachelorette."* New York: Lexington.

———. 2011b. "Surveillance on Reality Television and Facebook: From Authenticity to Flowing Data." *Communication Theory* 21 (2): 111–29.

Duggan, M., and J. Brenner. 2013. *The Demographics of Social Media Users—2012.* Pew Research Center, 14 February. http://www.pewinternet.org/2013/02/14/the-demographics-of-social-media-users-2012/.

Dumenco, S. 2011. "Metrics Mess: Five Sad Truths about Measurement Right Now." *Advertising Age* 82 (9): 8–9.

Durham, A. 2012. "'Check On It': Beyoncé, Southern Booty and Black Femininities in Music Video." *Feminist Media Studies* 12 (1): 35–49.

Duster, T. 2005. "Race and Reification in Science." *Science* 307 (5712): 1050–51.

———. 2012. "The Combustible Intersection: Genomics, Forensics, and Race." In *Race after the Internet*, edited by L. Nakamura and P. A. Chow-White, 310–27. New York: Routledge.

Dworkin, Andrea. 1993. *Prostitution and Male Supremacy*. http://www.nostatusquo.com/ACLU/dworkin/MichLawJourl.html.

Dyer, R. 1997. *White: Essays on Race and Culture*. London: Routledge.

———. 2004. *Heavenly Bodies*. London: Routledge.

Eckholm, E. 2007. "In Turnabout, Infant Deaths Climb in South." *New York Times*, 22 April. http://www.nytimes.com/2007/04/22/health/22infant.html?pagewanted=all&_r=0.

Editorial Board of the Jewish Press. 2006. "Transgender Folly." *Jewish Press*, 15 November. http://genderology.com/component/content/article/11-gender-related-news/1775-newseditorial-nyusa-transgender-folly.

Eggenberger, N. 2012a. "Engaged Miley Cyrus Pushes Up Cleavage in Tight Corset." *Us Weekly*, 11 June. http://www.usmagazine.com/celebrity-style/news/pic-engaged-miley-cyrus-pushes-up-cleavage-in-tight-corset-2012116.

————. 2012b. "Kanye West Rants about Men's Fashion Trends He Hates on Twitter." *Us Weekly*, 7 May. http://www.usmagazine.com/celebrity-news/news/kanye-west-rants-about-mens-fashion-trends-he-hates-on-twitter-201275.

————. 2012c. "Pauly D Proves He Has Rock-Hard, Chiseled Bod." *Us Weekly*, 30 April. http://www.usmagazine.com/celebrity-body/news/pic-pauly-d-proves-he-has-rock-hard-chiseled-bod-in-new-shirtless-photo-2012304.

Ehrenreich, B. 2004. "Owning Up to Abortion." *New York Times*, 22 July, A21.

Elliot, D., and F. Endt. 1995. "Twins—with Two Fathers: The Netherlands; A Fertility Clinic's Startling Error." *Newsweek*, 3 July, 38.

Elmer, G. 2004. *Profiling Machines: Mapping the Personal Information Economy*. Cambridge: Massachusetts Institute of Technology Press.

Elster, N. R. 2005. "ART for the Masses?: Racial and Ethnic Inequality in Assisted Reproductive Technologies." *DePaul Journal of Health Care Law* 9 (1): 719–33.

Epstein, S. 2007. *Inclusion: The Politics of Difference in Medical Research*. Chicago: University of Chicago Press.

Ericson, R. 1981. *Making Crime: A Study of Detective Work*. Toronto: Butterworths.

Ericson, R. V., and K. D. Haggerty. 1997. *Policing the Risk Society*. Toronto: University of Toronto Press.

————. 2006. *The New Politics of Surveillance and Visibility*. Toronto: University of Toronto Press.

Esposito, R., and B. Ross. 2009. "Exclusive: Photos of the Northwest Airlines Flight 253 Bomb." ABCNews.com, 28 December. http://abcnews.go.com/blotter/northwest-airlines-flight-253-bomb-photos-exclusive/story?id=9436297.

Etengoff, A. 2002. "Digital Photography Helps Bolster Domestic Violence and Abuse Cases." *TG Daily*, 5 September. http://www.tgdaily.com/hardware-brief/13907-digital-photography-helps-bolster-domestic-violence-and-abuse-cases.

Eubanks, V. 2006. "Technologies of Citizenship: Surveillance and Political Learning in the Welfare System." In *Surveillance and Security: Technological Politics and Power in Everyday Life*, edited by T. Monahan, 89–107. London: Routledge.

Everett, A., ed. 2009. *Learning, Race, and Ethnicity: Youth and Digital Media, Digital Media and Learning*. Cambridge: MacArthur Foundation/Massachusetts Institute of Technology Press.

Ewen, E., and S. Ewen. 2006. *Typecasting: On the Arts and Sciences of Human Inequality*. New York: Seven Stories.

Fanon, F. 1965. *The Wretched of the Earth*. New York: Grove.

Farhi, P. 2009. "The Twitter Explosion." *American Journalism Review* (April–May). http://ajrarchive.org/Article.asp?id=4756.

Farley, M., et al. 2011. *Comparing Sex Buyers with Men Who Don't Buy Sex*. Report prepared for the Social Responsibility Annual Conference, Boston, 15 July. http://prostitutionresearch.com/topic/sex-buyers-the-demand/.

Farley, M., J. Bindel, and J. M. Golding. 2009. *Men Who Buy Sex: Who They Buy and What They Know*. London: Eaves. http://prostitutionresearch.com/topic/sex-buyers-the-demand/.

Farley, M., and E. Butler. 2012. "Prostitution and Trafficking—Quick Facts." *Prosti-*

tution Research & Education. http://www.prostitutionresearch.com/Prostitution %20Quick%20Facts%2012-21-12.pdf.

Farley, M., W. Freed, K. S. Phal, and J. Golding. 2012. "A Thorn in the Heart: Cambodian Men Who Buy Sex." Report prepared for the conference "Focus on Men Who Buy Sex: Discourage Men's Demand for Prostitution, Stop Sex Trafficking," co-hosted by the Cambodian Women's Crisis Center and Prostitution Research and Education, Phnom Penh, Cambodia, 17 July. http://prostitutionresearch .com/topic/sex-buyers-the-demand/.

Feigenson, N., and C. Spiesel. 2009. *Law on Display: The Digital Transformation of Legal Persuasion and Judgment.* New York: New York University Press.

Feldman, A. 2005. "On the Actuarial Gaze: From 9/11 to Abu Ghraib." *Cultural Studies* 19 (2): 203–26.

Ferguson, K. E. 1984. *The Feminist Case against Bureaucracy.* Philadelphia: Temple University Press.

Ferguson, P. M., A. Gartner, and D. K. Lipsky. 2007. "The Experience of Disability in Families: A Synthesis of Research and Parent Narratives." In *Prenatal Testing and Disability Rights*, edited by E. Parens and A. Asch, 72–94. Washington: Georgetown University Press.

Ferran, L. 2012. "Stink Bomb: Underwear Bomber Wore Explosive Undies for Weeks, FBI Says." ABCNews.com blog, 28 September. http://abcnews.go.com/blogs /headlines/2012/09/stink-bomb-underwear-bomber-wore-explosive-undies -for-weeks-fbi-says/.

Ferran, L., and L. Sher. 2009. "Exclusive: On 'Good Morning America,' Rihanna Says Going Back to Brown 'Not Right.'" ABCNews.com, 5 November. http://abcnews .go.com/GMA/rihanna-speaks-chris-brown-assault/story?id=8999410.

Ferreira da Silva, D. 2001. "Toward a Critique of the Socio-Logos of Justice: The Analytics of Raciality and the Production of Universality." *Social Identities* 7 (3): 421–54.

———. 2007. *Toward a Global Idea of Race.* Minneapolis: University of Minnesota Press.

Finlayson, A. 2012a. "Lingerie-Clad Miley Cyrus Shows Off Legs in Self-Portrait." *Us Weekly*, 24 April. http://www.usmagazine.com/celebrity-body/news/lingerie -clad-miley-cyrus-shows-off-legs-in-self-portrait-2012244.

———. 2012b. "Rihanna Goes Topless on Twitter." *Us Weekly*, 11 June. http:// www.usmagazine.com/celebrity-news/news/pic-rihanna-goes-topless-on -twitter-201283.

Finn, J. 2009. *Capturing the Criminal Image: From Mug Shot to Surveillance Society.* Minneapolis: University of Minnesota Press.

Finn, R. L. 2011. "Surveillant Staring: Race and the Everyday Surveillance of South Asian Women after 9/11." *Surveillance and Society* 8 (4): 413–26.

Fisher, J., and T. Monahan. 2011. "The 'Biosecuritization' of Healthcare Delivery: Examples of Post-9/11 Technological Imperatives." *Social Science and Medicine* 72: 545–52.

Flexner, A. 1914. *Prostitution in Europe.* New York: Century.

Fontanella-Khan, A. 2010. "India, the Rent-a-Womb Capital of the World." *Slate*, 23 August. http://www.slate.com/id/2263136/.

Foucault, M. 1976. *"Society Must Be Defended": Lectures at the College de France, 1975–1976.* Translated by D. Macey. New York: Picador.

———. 1978. *The History of Sexuality: An Introduction.* New York: Random House.

———. 1980. *The History of Sexuality.* Vol. 1. New York: Vintage.

———. 1994. *The Order of Things: An Archaeology of the Human Sciences.* New York: Vintage.

———. 1995. *Discipline and Punish: The Birth of the Prison.* New York: Vintage.

———. 1997. *Society Must Be Defended: Lectures at the College De France, 1975–1976.* New York: Picador.

Fraden, R. 2001. *Imagining Medea: Rhodessa Jones and Theater for Incarcerated Women.* Chapel Hill: University of North Carolina Press.

Franklin, S., and C. Roberts. 2006. *Born and Made: Ethnography of Preimplantation Genetic Diagnosis.* Princeton, NJ: Princeton University Press.

Friedberg, A. 2006. *The Virtual Window: From Alberti to Microsoft.* Cambridge: Massachusetts Institute of Technology Press.

Fuchs, C. 2010. "How Can Surveillance Be Defined? Remarks on Theoretical Foundations of Surveillance Studies. Research Paper No. 1." The Internet and Surveillance Research Paper Series. Edited by the Unified Theory of Information Research Group.

———. 2011. "How Can Surveillance Be Defined?" *Matrizes* 5 (1): 110–33.

———. 2013. "Political Economy and Surveillance Theory." *Critical Sociology* 39 (5): 671–87.

Fuller, G. 2008. "Welcome to Windows 2.1: Motion Aesthetics at the Airport." In *Politics at the Airport*, edited by M. B. Salter, 161–73. Minneapolis: University of Minnesota Press.

Fusco, C., and B. Wallis, eds. 2003, *Only Skin Deep: Changing Visions of the American Self.* New York: International Center of Photography.

Gabriel, J. 1998. *Whitewash: Racialized Politics and the Media.* London: Routledge.

Gabriel, T. 1996. "High-Tech Pregnancies Test Hope's Limit." *New York Times*, 7 January, A1, A18.

Garcia, C. A., and S. Suess Kennedy. 2003. "Picturing Powerlessness: Digital Photography, Domestic Violence, and the Fight over Victim Autonomy." *Hamline Journal of Public Law and Policy* 1 (1): 1.

Garland, D. 2001. *Mass Imprisonment: Social Causes and Consequences.* Thousand Oaks, CA: Sage.

Gates, K. 2011. *Our Biometric Future: Facial Recognition Technology and the Culture of Surveillance.* New York: New York University Press.

Gehi, P., and G. Arkles. 2007. "Unraveling Injustice: Race and Class Impact of Medicaid Exclusions of Transition-Related Health Care for Transgender People." *Sexuality Research and Social Policy* 14 (4): 7–35.

Gentleman, A. 2008. "India Nurtures Business of Surrogate Motherhood." *New*

York Times. 10 March. http://www.nytimes.com/2008/03/10/world/asia/10 surrogate.html?_r=2.

Ghosh, R. A., ed. 2005. *Code: Collaborative Ownership and the Digital Economy.* Cambridge: Massachusetts Institute of Technology Press.

Gilchrist, K. 2010. "Exploring Differences in Canadian Local Press Coverage of Missing/Murdered Aboriginal and White Women." *Feminist Media Studies* 10 (4): 373–90.

Gill, P. 2004. "Securing the Globe: Intelligence and the Post-9/11 Shift from 'Liddism' to 'Drainism.'" *Intelligence and National Security* 19 (3): 467–89.

Gillespie, T. 2000. "Narrative Control and Visual Polysemy: Fox Surveillance Specials and the Limits of Legitimation." *Velvet Light Trap* 45: 36–49.

Gilliom, J. 2001. *Overseers of the Poor: Surveillance, Resistance, and the Limits of Privacy.* Chicago: University of Chicago Press.

Gilmore, R. W. 2007. *Golden Gulag.* Berkeley: University of California Press.

Glynn, K. 2000. *Tabloid Culture: Trash Taste, Popular Power, and the Transformation of American Television.* Durham, NC: Duke University Press.

Goffman, E. 1959. *The Presentation of Self in Everyday Life.* New York: Anchor.

González, J. 2009. "The Face and the Public: Race, Secrecy, and Digital Art Practice." *Camera Obscura* 24 (1): 37–65.

Goodhand, A. 2012. "Flesh-Flaunting Miley Cyrus Is Sending 'a Terribly Sick Message' to Young Women, Says Therapist." Radar Online, 6 August. Retrieved from http://radaronline.com/exclusives/2012/08/miley-cyrus-weight-photos -eating-disorder-questions/.

Goodwin, C. 1994. "Professional Vision." *American Anthropologist* 96 (3): 606–33.

Gorman, D. 2008. "Empire, Internationalism, and the Campaign against the Traffic in Women and Children in the 1920s." *Twentieth Century British History* 19 (2): 186–216.

Goulding, W. 2001. *Just Another Indian: A Serial Killer and Canada's Indifference.* Calgary: Fifth House Press.

Government of India. 2010. The Assisted Reproductive Technologies (Regulation) Bill–2010. Ministry of Health and Family Welfare, New Delhi. http://www.scribd .com/doc/33533932/Art-Regulation-Draft-Bill1-india.

Grant, M. G. 2012. "DNA Database of Men Who Pay for Sex?: The Strange Push to Make Cops Collect DNA from Suspected Johns." AlterNet, 27 January. http:// www.alternet.org/story/153918/dna_database_of_men_who_pay_for_sex_the _strange_push_to_make_cops_collect_dna_from_suspected_johns.

Graves, J. L., Jr. 2001. *The Emperor's New Clothes: Biological Theories of Race at the Millennium.* New Brunswick, NJ: Rutgers University Press.

Green, A. 2009. "More States Embrace GPS Monitoring in Abuse Cases." *New York Times,* 8 May. http://www.nytimes.com/2009/05/09/us/09gps.html.

Greenberg, J. 1999. "Defining Male and Female: Intersexuality and the Collision between Law and Biology." *Arizona Law Review* 41: 265–91.

Greer, C. F., and D. A. Ferguson. 2011. "Using Twitter for Promotion and Branding:

A Content Analysis of Local Television Twitter Sites." *Journal of Broadcasting and Electronic Media* 55 (2): 198–214.

Gregg, M. 2011. *Work's Intimacy*. New York: Polity.

Grewal, I. 2003. "Transnational America: Race, Gender and Citizenship after 9/11." *Social Identities* 9 (4): 535–61.

Griffith, A. I. 1995. "Connecting Mothering and Schooling: The Discursive Organisation of Children's Development." In *Knowledge, Experience, and Ruling Relations: Studies in the Social Organization of Knowledge*, edited by A. Manicom and M. Campbell, 108–22. Toronto: University of Toronto Press.

Griffith, A. I., and D. E. Smith. 2005. *Mothering for Schooling*. New York: Routledge/Taylor Francis.

gtz. 2012. "Perspectives and Retrospectives: Vol. 3." *Fat, Ugly or Slutty* (blog), 1 February. http://fatuglyorslutty.com/2012/02/01/perspectives-and-retrospectives-vol-3/.

Gunn, J. 1999. "A Few Good Men: The Rockefeller Approach to Population, 1911–1936." In *The Development of the Social Sciences in the United States and Canada: The Role of Philanthropy*, edited by T. Richardson and D. Fisher, 97–114. New York: Ablex Publishing.

Guzik, K. 2009. "Governing Intimate Partner Abuse: The Effects of Pro-Arrest and No-Drop Prosecution for Domestic Batterers." Paper presented at the annual meeting of the Law and Society, J. W. Marriot Resort, Las Vegas, Nevada, 25 May. All Academic. http://www.allacademic.com/meta/p17700_index.html.

Haggerty, K. D. 2002. "The Politics of Statistics: Variations on a Theme." *Canadian Journal of Sociology/Cahiers Canadiens De Sociologie* 27 (1): 89–105.

———. 2006. "Tear Down the Walls: On Demolishing the Panopticon." In *Theorizing Surveillance: The Panopticon and Beyond*, edited by D. Lyon, 23–45. Cullompton, Devon: Willan.

———. 2009a. "Foreword: Surveillance and Political Problems." In *Surveillance: Power, Problems, and Politics*, edited by S. P. Hier and J. Greenberg, ix–xviii. Vancouver: University of British Columbia Press.

———. 2009b. "'Ten Thousand Times Larger . . .': Anticipating the Expansion of Surveillance." In *New Directions in Surveillance and Privacy*, edited by B. Goold and D. Neyland, 159–77. Cullompton, Devon: Willan.

Haggerty, K. D., and R. V. Ericson. 2000. "The Surveillant Assemblage." *British Journal of Sociology* 51 (4): 605–22.

Haimowitz, R., and V. Sinha, dirs. 2008. *Made in India*. DVD. http://www.madeinindiamovie.com/.

Hall, R. 2007. "Of Ziplock Bags and Black Holes: The Aesthetics of Transparency in the War on Terror." *Communication Review* 10 (4): 319–46.

Hall, S. 1980. "Encoding/Decoding." In *Culture, Media, Language: Working Papers in Cultural Studies, 1972–79*, edited by S. Hall et al., 128–38. London: Hutchinson.

Halley, J., P. Kotiswaran, H. Shamir, and C. Thomas. 2006. "From the International to the Local in Feminist Legal Responses to Rape, Prostitution/Sex Work, and

Sex Trafficking: Four Studies in Contemporary Governance Feminism." *Harvard Journal of Law and Gender* 29: 335–509.

Halsey, A. 2011. "TSA Debuts Less-Revealing Software for Airport Scanners." *Washington Post*, 2 February. http://www.washingtonpost.com/national/tsa-debuts -system-for-more-modest-scans/2011/02/01/ABI2FBE_story.html.

———. 2013. "TSA to Pull Revealing Scanners from Airports." *Washington Post*, 18 January. http://www.washingtonpost.com/local/trafficandcommuting/tsa-to -pull-revealing-scanners-from-airports/2013/01/18/1b7d5d22-6198-11e2-9940 -6fc488f3fecd_story.html.

Haltiwanger, J. 2010. "Cover Story: Citizen Journalism, Structural Discrimination, and the 'Post-racial' Internet." Masters of Media, 4 May. http://mastersofmedia .hum.uva.nl/wp-content/uploads/2010/08/cover_story-haltiwanger.pdf.

Han, S. 2011. "Strict Scrutiny: The Tragedy of Constitutional Law." In *Beyond Biopolitics: Essays on the Governance of Life and Death*, edited by P. Clough and C. Willse, 119–31. Durham, NC: Duke University Press.

Hansen, M. 2006. *Bodies in Code: Interfaces with Digital Media*. New York: Routledge.

Haraway, D. J. 1989. *Primate Visions: Gender, Race, and Nature in the World of Modern Science*. New York: Routledge.

Harmon, A. 2007. "Genetic Testing + Abortion." *New York Times*, 13 May. http:// www.nytimes.com/2007/05/13/weekinreview/13harm.html?adxnnl=1&adxnn lx=1410116408-kx8U/giZoN3u7mvernYvoQ.

Hartman, S. 1997. *Scenes of Subjection*. Oxford: Oxford University Press.

Hasinoff, A. A. 2008. "Fashioning Race for the Free Market on *America's Next Top Model*." *Critical Studies in Media Communication* 25 (3): 324–43.

Hathaway, H., dir. 1953. *Niagara*. United States: Twentieth Century Fox.

Haworth, A. 2007. "Surrogate Mothers: Womb for Rent." *Marie Claire*, 27 August. http://www.marieclaire.com/world-reports/news/surrogate-mothers-india.

Heinemann, K., dir. 2011. *Our Family, Made in India*. Made for "The Global Baby," special issue of *The Collection* (iPad magazine). http://www.katjaheinemann .com/#/multimedia-productions/our-family--made-in-india/SurrogacyIndia.

Helm, D. T., S. Miranda, and N. A. Chedd. 1998. "Prenatal Diagnosis of Down Syndrome: Mothers' Reflections on Supports Needed from Diagnosis to Birth." *Mental Retardation* 36 (1): 55–61.

Helmerhorst, F. M., et al. 2004. "Perinatal Outcome of Singletons and Twins after Assisted Conception: A Systematic Review of Controlled Studies." *British Medical Journal* 328 (7434): 261–64.

Herman Lewis, J. L. 1992. *Trauma and Recovery*. New York: Basic.

Hershatter, G. 1997. *Dangerous Pleasures: Prostitution and Modernity in Twentieth-Century Shanghai*. Berkeley: University of California Press.

Hershey, L. 1994. "Choosing Disability." *Ms*, July–August, 26–32.

Hesse-Biber, S. N., ed. 2012. *Handbook of Feminist Research: Theory and Praxis*. 2d edn. Thousand Oaks, CA: Sage.

Hier, S. P., and J. Greenberg. 2009. *Surveillance: Power, Problems, and Politics*. Vancouver: University of British Columbia Press.

HM Staff. "Courtney Love Goes Twitter Mental Once More, Maybe for the Last Time." 2012. Holy Moly, 5 May. http://www.holymoly.com/celebrity-news /courtney-love-goes-twitter-mental-once-more-maybe-last-time52053.

hooks, b. 1984. *Feminist Theory: From Margin to Center*. Boston: South End Press.

———. 1992. *Black Looks: Race and Representation*. Boston: South End Press.

———. 1997. *Cultural Criticism and Transformation*. Media Education Foundation. 66 min.

———. 2004. *The Will to Change: Men, Masculinity and Love*. New York: Washington Square Press.

Hookway, N. 2008. "'Entering the Blogosphere': Some Strategies for Using Blogs in Social Research. *Qualitative Research* 8: 91–113.

Hudson, H. 2005. "Doing Security as though Humans Matter: A Feminist Perspective on Gender and the Politics of Human Security." *Security Dialogue* 36 (2): 155–74.

Hunter, N. D., C. G. Joslin, and S. McGowan. 2004. *The Rights of Lesbians, Gay Men, Bisexuals, and Transgender People*. New York: American Civil Liberties Union.

Ibrahim, S. 2009. *Disturbia* (digital image tracing on canvas). Visual Therapy. http:// www.visualtherapyonline.com/?p=604.

INCITE! Women of Color Against Violence, ed. 2006. *Color of Violence: The INCITE! Anthology*. Cambridge: South End Press.

International Bill of Gender Rights. 1990. Reprinted in *Transgender Rights*, edited by P. Currah, R. Juang, and S. P. Minter, 327–31. Minneapolis: University of Minnesota Press, 2006.

In Touch Weekly Staff. 2011. "LeAnn Rimes: Starving for Attention?" *In Touch Weekly*, 13 April. http://www.intouchweekly.com/entertainment/news/leann-rimes -starving-attention.

Irvine, C. 2005. "On the Other Side of Silence: Levinas, Medicine, and Literature." *Literature and Medicine* 24: 8–18.

Ishaq, S. 2010. "Killing in the Name of 'Honor': The South Asian Community in the Canadian Context." Master's thesis, Concordia University, Montreal.

Jacobson, D. 1999. "Doing Research in Cyberspace." *Field Methods* 11: 127–45.

James, G. 1965. Letter from George James, Commissioner of Health, to Dr. Henry Kraus, Executive Secretary to the New York Academy of Medicine Committee of Public Health, 2 April. Archive from the New York Academy of Medicine.

Jeffrey, L. A., and G. M. MacDonald. 2006. *Sex Workers in the Maritimes Talk Back*. Vancouver: University of British Columbia Press.

Jeffreys, Sheila. 1997. *The Idea of Prostitution*. North Melbourne, Victoria: Spinifex.

Jiwani, Y. 2009. "Symbolic and Discursive Violence in Media Representations of Aboriginal Missing and Murdered Women." In *Violence in Hostile Contexts E-Book*, edited by D. Weird and M. Guggisberg, 63–74. Oxford: Inter-Disciplinary Press. http://www.inter-disciplinary.net/publishing/id-press/ebooks/understanding -violence-contexts-and-portrayals/.

———. 2011. "Trapped in the Carceral Net: Race, Gender and the 'War on Terror.'" *Journal of Global Media Studies (Canadian Edition)* 4 (2): 13–31.

————. 2014. "Posthumous Rescue: The Shafia Young Women as Worthy Victims." *Girlhood Studies* 7 (1): 27–45.

Jiwani, Y., and M. L. Young. 2006. "Missing and Murdered Women: Reproducing Marginality in News Discourse." *Canadian Journal of Communication* 31 (4): 895–917.

Johnson, R. H. 1919. "Adequate Reproduction." *Journal of Social Hygiene* 5: 223–26.

Johnson, Z. 2012. "Sexy!: Fergie Shows Off Major Cleavage, Rock Hard Abs in Skimpy Bikini." *Us Weekly*, 29 May. http://www.usmagazine.com/celebrity -body/news/sexy-fergie-shows-off-major-cleavage-rock-hard-abs-in-skimpy -bikini-2012295.

Johnson v. McIntosh. 1823. 21 U.S. 543, 567, 5 L. Ed. 681.

Kahn, J. 2004. "How a Drug Becomes 'Ethnic': Law, Commerce, and the Production of Racial Categories in Medicine." *Yale Journal of Health Policy, Law, and Ethics* 4 (1): 1–46.

————. 2006. "Patenting Race." *Nature Biotechnology* 24 (11): 1349–51.

————. 2007. "Race in a Bottle." *Scientific American* 297 (2): 40–45.

Kang, L. H. Y. 2002. *Compositional Subjects: Enfiguring Asian/American Women*. Durham, NC: Duke University Press.

Kantrowitz, B., and D. A. Kaplan. 1990. "Not the Right Father." *Newsweek*, 19 March, 50.

Kaplan, A. 2005. "Where Is Guantanamo?" *American Quarterly* 57: 831–58.

Kaplan, E. A. 1983. *Women and Film: Both Sides of the Camera*. New York: Routledge.

Kazanjian, D. 2003. *The Colonizing Trick*. Minneapolis: University of Minnesota Press.

Kennedy, A. C. 2008. "Eugenics, 'Degenerate Girls,' and Social Workers during the Progressive Era." *Affilia* 27: 22–37.

Kerr, D. 2013. "Microsoft Forges Ahead with Its Anti-Google Scroogle Campaign. C/Net, 4 March. http://www.cnet.com/news/microsoft-forges-ahead-with-its -anti-google-scroogle-campaign/.

Kerr, I., et al. 2009. *Lessons from the Identity Trail: Anonymity, Privacy, and Identity in a Networked Society*. Oxford: Oxford University Press.

Kershaw, S. 2002. "Digital Photos Give the Police a New Edge in Abuse Cases." *New York Times*, 3 September. http://www.nytimes.com/2002/09/03/nyregion /digital-photos-give-the-police-a-new-edge-in-abuse-cases.html.

Kessler, O., and C. Daase. 2008. "From Insecurity to Uncertainty: Risk and the Paradox of Security Politics." *Alternatives*. 33 (1): 211–32.

Kevles, D. J. 1985. *In the Name of Eugenics: Genetics and the Uses of Human Heredity*. New York: Knopf.

Kilbourne, J. 2000. *Can't Buy My Love: How Advertising Changes the Way We Think and Feel*. Glencoe, IL: Free Press.

Kimelman, D. 1990. "Poverty and Norplant: Can Contraception Reduce the Underclass?" *Philadelphia Inquirer*, 12 December, 18.

King, A. 2009. "Islam, Women and Violence." *Feminist Theology* 17 (3): 292–328.

Kinsman, G. W., and P. Gentile. 2010. *The Canadian War on Queers: National Security as Sexual Regulation*. Vancouver: University of British Columbia Press.

Kittay, E. F. 2007. *On the Expressivity and Ethics of Selective Abortion for Disability: Conversations with My Son: With Leo Kittay*. In *Prenatal Testing and Disability Rights*, edited by E. Parens and A. Asch, 165–95. Washington: Georgetown University Press.

Kleinfeld, J. 2005. "Tort Law and In Vitro Fertilization: The Need for Legal Recognition of 'Procreative Injury.'" *Yale Law Journal* 115 (1): 237–45.

Kneeland, G. J. 1913. *Commercialized Prostitution in New York City*. New York: Century.

Knepper, P. 2011. *International Crime in the Twentieth Century: The League of Nations Era, 1919–1939*. New York: Palgrave Macmillan.

———. 2012. "Measuring the Threat of Global Crime: Insights from Research by the League of Nations into the Traffic in Women." *Criminology* 50 (3): 777–809. doi: 10.1111/j.1745-9125.2012.00277.

Koch, K. 2010. "Are You Sharing Too Much about Baby Online?" The Bump, 18 October. http://pregnant.thebump.com/new-mom-new-dad/your-life/articles/oversharing-online.aspx.

Kohl, B. 2007. "On Indian Surrogates." *Huffington Post* blog, 30 October. http://www.huffingtonpost.com/beth-kohl/on-indian-surrogates_b_70425.html.

Kornblut, A. E. and P. Bacon. 2010. "Airport Security Uproar Frustrates White House Advisers." *Washington Post*, 22 November. http://www.washingtonpost.com/wp-dyn/content/article/2010/11/22/AR2010112207050.html.

Koyama, E. 2006. Disloyal to Feminism: Abuse of Survivors within the Domestic Violence Shelter System. In *Color of Violence: The INCITE! Anthology*, edited by INCITE! Women of Color Against Violence, 208–22. Cambridge: South End Press.

Kraszewski, J. 2004. "Country Hicks and Urban Cliques: Mediating Race, Reality, and Liberalism on MTV's *The Real World*." In *Reality TV: Remaking Television Culture*, edited by S. Murray and L. Ouellette, 179–96. New York: New York University Press.

Kruse, H. D., Executive Secretary, Committee on Public Health, New York Academy of Medicine: To: Subcommittee on Change of Sex on Birth Certificates for Transsexuals.

Kung, M. 2010. "'Google Baby' Documentary Sheds Light on Outsourcing Surrogacy." *Speakeasy (Wall Street Journal* blog), 16 June. http://blogs.wsj.com/speakeasy/2010/06/16/google-baby-documentary-sheds-light-on-outsourcing-surrogacy/.

Laughlin, H. H. 1920. "Eugenical Sterilization in the United States." *Journal of Social Hygiene* 6: 499–531.

League of Nations. 1921a. "Questionnaire Addressed to All Governments by the Secretary-General of the League with Reference to the Measures Already Taken or Proposed to be Taken to Combat the Traffic in Women and Children." *League of Nations Official Journal* (March–April 1921): 230–32.

League of Nations. 1921b. "International Conference on Traffic in Women and Children, Final Act." *League of Nations Official Journal* (July–August 1921): 596–605.

League of Nations. 1927. Report of the Special Body of Experts on Traffic in Women and Children, League of Nation Docs. C.52.M.52.1927.IV and C.52(2).M.52(1). 1927.IV.

League of Nations. 1932. Report to the Council of the Commission of Inquiry into Traffic in Women and Children in the East, League of Nations Doc. C.849.M.393.1932.IV.

Lenhart, A., and M. Madden. 2007. "Teens, Privacy and Online Social Networks." Pew Research Internet Project, 18 April. http://www.pewinternet.org/2007/04/18/teens-privacy-and-online-social-networks/.

Leppanen, K. 2007. "Movement of Women: Trafficking in the Interwar Era." *Women's Studies International Forum* 30 (6): 523–33.

Levine, P. 1994. "'Walking the Streets in a Way No Decent Woman Should': Women Police in World War I." *Journal of Modern History* 66 (1): 34–78.

———. 2003. *Prostitution, Race, and Politics: Policing Venereal Disease in the British Empire.* New York: Routledge.

Levy, A. 2005. *Female Chauvinist Pigs: Women and the Rise of Raunch Culture.* New York: Free Press.

Lewkowics, S. N. 2013. "Photographer as Witness: A Portrait of Domestic Violence." *LightBox (Time* blog), 27 February. http://lightbox.time.com/2013/02/27/photographer-as-witness-a-portrait-of-domestic-violence/.

Lewontin, R. 1995. *Human Diversity.* Boston: Freeman.

Limoncelli, S. A. 2006. "International Voluntary Associations, Local Social Movements, and State Paths to the Abolition of Regulated Prostitution in Europe, 1875–1950." *International Sociology* 21 (1): 31–59.

———. 2010. *The Politics of Trafficking: The First International Movement to Combat the Sexual Exploitation of Women.* Stanford: Stanford University Press.

Lippman, A. 1991. "Prenatal Genetic Testing and Screening: Constructing Needs and Reinforcing Inequities." *American Journal of Law and Medicine* 17 (1–2): 15–50.

Lorber, J. 1993. "Believing Is Seeing: Biology as Ideology." *Gender and Society* 7: 568–81.

Lovink, G., and K. Patelis. n.d. "About." Institute of Network Cultures, Unlike Us #3: Social Media: Design or Decline. http://networkcultures.org/unlikeus/about/.

Lowery, C. 2009. "An Explosion Prompts Rethinking of Twitter and Facebook." *Nieman Reports* (fall). http://www.nieman.harvard.edu/reportsitem.aspx?id=101894.

Lowman, J. 2000. "Violence and the Outlaw Status of (Street) Prostitution in Canada." *Violence Against Women* 6 (9): 987–1011.

Lowman, J., and C. Atchison. 2006. "Men Who Buy Sex: A Survey in the Greater Vancouver Regional District." *Canadian Review of Sociology / Revue Canadienne De Sociologie* 43 (3): 281–96.

Lowry, D. W. 2004. "Understanding Reproductive Technologies as Surveillant Assemblage: Revisions of Power and Technoscience." *Sociological Perspectives* 47 (4): 357–70.

Lubove, R. 1962. "The Progressives and the Prostitute." *Historian* 24: 308–30.

Lucal, B. 1999. "What It Means to Be Gendered Me: Life on the Boundaries of a Dichotomous Gender System." *Gender and Society* 13: 781–97.

Lunde, A. 1975. "The Birth Number Concept and Record Linkage." *American Journal of Public Health* 65: 1165–69.

Lunden, Ingrid. 2013. "73% of U.S. Adults Use Social Networks, Pinterest Passes Twitter in Popularity, Facebook Stays on Top." TechCrunch, 30 December. http://techcrunch.com/2013/12/30/pew-social-networking/.

Lyon, D. 1994. *The Electronic Eye: The Rise of the Surveillance Society*. Minneapolis: University of Minnesota Press.

———. 2001a. *Surveillance Society: Monitoring Everyday Life*. Buckingham: Open University Press.

———. 2001b. "Under My Skin: From Surveillance Papers to Body Surveillance." In *Documenting Individual Identity: The Development of State Practices in the Modern World*, edited by J. Caplan and J. Torpey, 291–310. Princeton, NJ: Princeton University Press.

———. 2003. *Surveillance as Social Sorting: Privacy, Risk and Digital Discrimination*. New York: Routledge.

———. 2006. "The Search for Surveillance Theories." In *Theorizing Surveillance: The Panopticon and Beyond*, edited by D. Lyon, 46–68. Cullompton, Devon: Willan.

———. 2007. *Surveillance Studies: An Overview*. Cambridge: Polity.

Mack, R. L. 2001. *The Digital Divide: Standing at the Intersection of Race and Technology*. Durham, NC: Carolina Academic Press.

MacKenzie, D. A. 1981. *Statistics in Britain, 1865–1930: The Social Construction of Scientific Knowledge*. Edinburgh: Edinburgh University Press.

Macleod, J., M. Farley, L. Anderson, and J. Golding. 2008. *Challenging Men's Demand for Prostitution in Scotland*. Glasgow: Women's Support Project. http://www.prostitutionresearch.com/ChallengingDemandScotland.pdf.

Maeve, D., and J. Brenner. 2013. *The Demographics of Social Media Users—2012*. Pew Research Internet Project, 14 February. http://pewinternet.org/Reports/2013/Social-media-users.aspx.

Magnet, S. A. 2007. "Feminist Sexualities, Race and the Internet: An Investigation of Suicidegirls.com." *New Media and Society* 9 (4): 577–602.

———. 2011. *When Biometrics Fail: Gender, Race, and the Technology of Identity*. Durham, NC: Duke University Press.

———. 2013. "Identity and the New Eugenics in the Newborn Screening Saves Lives Act." *Media, Culture and Society* 35 (1): 71–77.

Magnet, S., and T. Rodgers. 2012. "Stripping for the State: Whole Body Imaging Technologies and the Surveillance of Othered Bodies." *Feminist Media Studies* 12 (1): 101–18.

Mahraj, K. 2010. "Dis/locating the Margins: Gloria Anzaldúa and Dynamics in Feminist Learning." *Feminist Teacher* 1 (21): 1–20.

Manne, R. 2004. "Aboriginal Child Removal and the Question of Genocide, 1900–1940." In *Genocide and Settler Society: Frontier Violence and Stolen Indigenous Children in Australian History*, edited by A. D. Moses, 217–43. New York: Berghahn.

Manning, P. 1977. *Police Work: The Social Organization of Policing*. Long Grove, IL: Waveland.

Marcus, S. 2005. "Queer Theory for Everyone." *Signs* 31 (1): 191–218.

Marshall, J. 2010. "Bear Any Burden . . . (Don't Touch My Junk Edition)." *TPM Editor's Blog*, 22 November. http://talkingpointsmemo.com/edblog/bear-any-burden-don-t-touch-my-junk-edition.

Marshall, P. D. 1997. *Celebrity and Power: Fame in Contemporary Culture*. Minneapolis: University of Minnesota Press.

Martin, E. 1992. *The Woman in the Body: A Cultural Analysis of Reproduction*. Boston: Beacon.

Marwick, A. 1977. *Women at War, 1914–1918*. London: Croom Helm.

———. 2013. "Donglegate: Why the Tech Community Hates Feminists." Wired.com, 29 March. http://www.wired.com/2013/03/richards-affair-and-misogyny-in-tech/.

Marwick, A., and d. m. boyd. 2011. "To See and Be Seen: Celebrity Practice on Twitter." *Convergence* 17 (2): 139–58.

Marx, G. 1979. "External Efforts to Damage or Facilitate Social Movements: Some Patterns, Explanations, Outcomes, and Complications." In *The Dynamics of Social Movements*, edited by M. Zald and J. McCarthy, 94–125. Minneapolis: Winthrop.

———. 2007. "Desperately Seeking Surveillance Studies: Players in Search of a Field." *Contemporary Sociology* 35 (2): 125–30.

Mathews, T. J., and M. F. MacDorman. 2007. "Infant Mortality Statistics from the 2004 Period Linked Birth/Infant Death Data Set." *National Vital Statistics Reports* 55 (14): 1–32.

Mathiesen, T. 1997. "The Viewer Society: Michel Foucault's 'Panopticon' Revisited." *Theoretical Criminology* 1 (2): 215–34.

Mattelart, A. 1996. *The Invention of Communication*. Minneapolis: University of Minnesota Press.

Maxjulian. 2011. "Drapetomania . . . Catch It If You Can!" Afrospear Think Tank Blog. n.p., 21 January. http://afrospear.com/2011/01/21/drapetomania-catch-it-if-you-can/.

Mazer, J. P., R. E. Murphy, and C. J. Simonds. 2007. "I'll See You on 'Facebook': The Effects of Computer-Mediated Teacher Self-disclosure on Student Motivation, Affective Learning, and Classroom Climate." *Communication Education* 56: 1–17.

Mbembe, A. 2003. "Necropolitics." *Public Culture* 15 (1): 11–40.

McCaughey, B. 2005. "Why Are Infants at Risk in America?" Letter to the editor. *New York Times*, 14 January, A22.

McClintock, A. 1993. "Gonad the Barbarian and the Venus Flytrap: Portraying the Female and Male Orgasm." In *Sex Exposed: Sexuality and the Pornography Debate*, edited by L. Segal and M. McIntosh, 111–31. New Brunswick, NJ: Rutgers University Press.

McGrath, J. 2004. *Loving Big Brother: Performance, Privacy and Surveillance Space.* New York: Routledge.

McKittrick, K. 2006. *Demonic Grounds: Black Women and the Cartographies of Struggle.* Minneapolis: University of Minnesota Press.

McNeil, L. 2003. "Teaching an Old Genre New Tricks: The Diary on the Internet." *Biography* 26: 24–47.

McRobbie, A. 2008. "Young Women and Consumer Culture." *Cultural Studies* 22 (5): 255–65.

McRuer, R. 2006. *Crip Theory: Cultural Signs of Queerness and Disability.* New York: New York University Press.

Meiners, E. R. 2009. "Never Innocent: Feminist Trouble with Sex Offender Registries and Protection in a Prison Nation." *Meridians* 9 (2): 31–62.

Merry, S. E. 2001. "Spatial Governmentality and the New Urban Social Order: Controlling Gender Violence through Law." *American Anthropologist* 103: 16–29.

———. 2002. "Governmentality and Gender Violence in Hawai'i in Historical Perspective." *Social and Legal Studies* 11: 81–111.

Metz, C. 2009. "Google Chief: Only Miscreants Worry About Net Privacy." *The Register*, 7 December. http://www.theregister.co.uk/2009/12/07/schmidt_on_privacy/.

Metzger, B. 2007. "Toward an International Human Rights Regime during the Inter-War Years: The League of Nations' Combat of the Traffic in Women and Children." In *Beyond Sovereignty: Britain, Empire and Transnationalism, c. 1880–1950*, edited by K. Grant, P. Levine, and F. Trentmann, 54–79. New York: Palgrave Macmillan.

Meyerowitz, J. 2002. *How Sex Changed: A History of Transsexuality in the United States.* Cambridge, MA: Harvard University Press.

Meyers, M. 1997. *News Coverage of Violence against Women: Engendering Blame.* Thousand Oaks, CA: Sage.

Million, D. 2014. *Therapeutic Nations: Healing in an Age of Indigenous Human Rights.* Phoenix: University of Arizona Press.

Mink, G. 2002. *Welfare's End.* Ithaca, NY: Cornell University Press.

Mnookin, J. 1998. "The Image of Truth: Photographic Evidence and the Power of Analogy." *Yale Journal of Law and the Humanities* 10: 1–74.

Monahan, T. 2009. "Dreams of Control at a Distance: Gender, Surveillance and Social Control." *Cultural Studies ↔ Critical Methodologies* 9 (2): 286–305.

———. 2010. *Surveillance in the Time of Insecurity.* New Brunswick, NJ: Rutgers University Press.

Morgensen, S. 2011. *Spaces between Us: Queer Settler Colonialism and Indigenous Decolonization.* Minneapolis: University of Minnesota Press.

Mosco, V. 2004. *The Digital Sublime: Myth, Power, and Cyberspace.* Cambridge: Massachusetts Institute of Technology Press.

Mulvey, L. 1975. "Visual Pleasure and Narrative Cinema." *Screen* 16 (3): 6–18.

Mundy, L. 2007. *Everything Conceivable: How Assisted Reproduction Is Changing Men, Women, and the World.* New York: Knopf.

Murkoff, H., and S. Mazell. 2008. *What to Expect When You're Expecting*. 4th edn. New York: Workman.

Murphy, M. 2012. "Dark Side of Twitter: Stars Blame Tweets on Rehab, Low Self Esteem . . . Even Attempted Suicide." Fox News, 6 September. Retrieved from http://www.foxnews.com/entertainment/2012/09/06/dark-side-twitter-stars -blame-tweets-on-rehab-low-self-esteem-even-attempted/#ixzz2JW8gFIKW.

Murray, H. 2009. "Monstrous Play in Negative Spaces: Illegible Bodies and the Cultural Construction of Biometric Technology." In *The New Media of Surveillance*, edited by S. Magnet and K. Gates. London: Routledge.

Mykitiuk, R. 2000. "The New Genetics in the Post-Keynesian State." Social Science Research Network. http://papers.ssrn.com/sol3/papers.cfm?abstract_id =1745124.

Nakamura, L. 2002. *Cybertypes: Race, Ethnicity, and Identity on the Internet*. New York: Routledge.

———. 2011. "Race and Identity in Digital Media." In *Media and Society*, 5th edn., edited by J. Curran, 442–53. New York: Bloomsbury.

———. 2012. "'It's a Nigger in Here! Kill the Nigger!': User-Generated Media Campaigns against Racism, Sexism, and Homophobia in Digital Games." In *The International Encyclopedia of Media Studies: Media History and the Foundations of Media Studies*, edited by A. N. Valdivia and K. Gates, 508–9. Malden, MA: Wiley-Blackwell.

Nakamura, L., and P. Chow-White, eds. 2012. *Race after the Internet*. New York: Routledge.

Namias, J. 1993. *White Captives*. Chapel Hill: University of North Carolina Press.

National Center for Transgender Equality. 2004. "Air Travel Tips for Transgender People." http://transequality.org/Issues/travel.html.

National Vital Statistics Report. 2010. Vol. 59, no. 1. December 8, 2010, www.cdc .gov/nchs/data/nvsr/nvsr59/nvsr59_01.pdf.

Natisse, K. 2010. "Can African Americans Claim Kim Kardashian?" TheGrio.com, 28 December. http://thegrio.com/2010/12/28/can-african-americans-claim-kim -kardashian/.

Nelson, A., and J. W. Hwang. 2012. "Roots and Revelation: Genetic Ancestry Testing and the YouTube Generation." In *Race after the Internet*, edited by L. Nakamura and P. A. Chow-White, 271–90. New York: Routledge.

Neubeck, K. J. 2001. *Welfare Racism: Playing the Race Card against America's Poor*. New York: Routledge.

New York Academy of Medicine Committee on Public Health. 1966. "Change of Sex on Birth Certificates for Transsexuals." *Bulletin of the New York Academy of Medicine* 42: 721–24.

New York Academy of Medicine Subcommittee on Birth Certificate. 1965. "Birth Certificates, Change of Sex." Committee on Public Health, Public Health Archives. New York: New York Academy of Medicine.

New York City Board of Health. 2006. Resolution Comments: New York City Birth Certificate for Transgender People. Public document, copy on file with author.

New York City Department of Health and Mental Hygiene. 2005. *Executive Summary of the Advisory Committee to the New York City Department of Health and Mental Hygiene for the Amendment of Birth Certificates for Transgender Persons.* New York: New York City Department of Health and Mental Hygiene.

—————. 2006a. Notice of Intention to Amend Article 207 of the New York City Health Code: Notice of Public Hearing, 12 September.

—————. 2006b. Response to Public Comments and Additional Recommendations Regarding Proposal to Amend Section 207.05 of the New York City Health Code, 5 December.

New York City Health Code. 1971. Correction of Records: Filing of New Birth Certificates. Section 207.05 (a) (5).

Nielsen Company. 2010. "Led by Facebook, Twitter, Global Time Spent on Social Media Sites up 82% Year over Year." Nielsen NewsWire, 22 January. http://www.nielsen.com/us/en/insights/news/2010/led-by-facebook-twitter-global-time-spent-on-social-media-sites-up-82-year-over-year.html.

Nolan, R. 2012. "Behind the Cover Story: How Much Does Target Know?" *The 6th Floor* (*New York Times* blog), 21 February. http://6thfloor.blogs.nytimes.com/2012/02/21/behind-the-cover-story-how-much-does-target-know/.

Noriel, G. "The Identification of the Citizen: The Birth of Republican Civil Status in France." In *Documenting Individual Identity: The Development of State Practices in the Modern World*, edited by J. Caplan and J. Torpey, 28–48. Princeton, NJ: Princeton University Press.

Obasogie, O. K. 2006. "Slippery When Wet." *Biopolitical Times* blog, 15 December. http://www.geneticsandsociety.org/article.php?id=2049.

O'Driscoll, S. 1996. "Outlaw Readings: Beyond Queer Theory." *Signs* 22 (1): 30–51.

Offit, K., M. Sagi, and K. Hurley. 2006. "Preimplantation Genetic Diagnosis for Cancer Syndrome." *Journal of the American Medical Association* 296 (22): 2727–30.

Olwan, D. M. 2013. "Gendered Violence, Cultural Otherness, and Honor Crimes in Canadian National Logics." *Canadian Journal of Sociology* 38 (4): 533–55.

O'Neil, D. 2001. "Analysis of Internet Users' Level of Online Privacy Concerns." *Social Science Computer Review* 19: 17–31.

Oprah.com. 2007. "Journey to Parenthood." *Oprah Winfrey Show*, 1 January. http://www.oprah.com/world/Wombs-for-Rent/1.

Orbe, M. P., ed. 2008. "Special Issue of Race in Reality TV." *Critical Studies in Media Communication* 25 (4).

Ornstein, L. 2012. "Celebrity Twitter Pics of the Week!" Radar Online, 12 July. http://radaronline.com/exclusives/2012/07/celebrity-twitter-photos-teen-mom-espys-rihanna/.

Ossorio, P. 2007. "Prenatal Genetic Testing and the Courts." In *Prenatal Testing and Disability Rights*, edited by E. Parens and A. Asch, 308–33. Washington: Georgetown University Press.

Ott, J. 2010. "TSA Chief Endorses Body Imagers, Defines Role of Intelligence." *Aviation Daily*, 12 August, 1–2. http://awin.aviationweek.com/portals/awin/cmsfiles/media/pdf/ad_pdf/2010/08/12/avd_08_12_2010.pdf.

Oudshoorn, N. 1994. *Beyond the Natural Body: An Archeology of Sex Hormones.* London: Routledge.

"Outsourcing Life Itself: What India Teaches Us." 2007. *Maclean's,* 2 July, 4.

Packer, J. 2006. "Becoming Bombs: Mobilizing Mobility in the 'War on Terror.'" *Cultural Studies* 20 (4–5): 378–99.

Palmer, G. 2002. "Big Brother: An Experiment in Governance." *Television and New Media* 3: 295–310.

Pande, A. 2009a. "Not an 'Angel,' Not a 'Whore': Surrogates as 'Dirty' Workers in India." *Indian Journal of Gender Studies* 16: 141–73.

———. 2009b. "'It May Have Her Eggs but It's My Blood': Surrogates and Everyday Forms of Kinship in India." *Qualitative Sociology* 32: 379–97.

———. 2010. "Commercial Surrogacy in India: Manufacturing a Perfect Mother-Worker." *Signs* 35 (4): 969–99.

Papacharissi, Z. 2009. "The Virtual Geographies of Social Networks: A Comparative Analysis of Facebook, LinkedIn and ASmallWorld. *New Media and Society* 11 (1–2): 199–220.

———. 2010. *A Private Sphere: Democracy in a Digital Age.* Cambridge, MA: Polity.

Parens, E., and A. Asch. 2007. *Prenatal Testing and Disability Rights.* Washington: Georgetown University Press.

Parens, E., and L. P. Knowles. 2007. "Reprogenetics and Public Policy: Reflections and Recommendations." In *Reprogenetics: Law, Policy, and Ethical Issues,* edited by L. P. Knowles and G. E. Kaebnick, 253–94. Baltimore: Johns Hopkins University Press.

Parenti, C. 2003. *The Soft Cage: Surveillance in America: From Slavery to the War on Terror.* New York: Basic.

Parks, L. 2007. "Points of Departure: The Culture of U.S. Airport Screening." *Journal of Visual Culture* 6 (2): 183–200.

Parmelee, J. H., and S. L. Bichard. 2013. *Politics and the Twitter Revolution.* Lanham, MD: Lexington.

Pascoe, P. 2009. *What Comes Naturally: Miscegenation Law and the Making of Race in America.* Oxford: Oxford University Press.

Patel, T. 2006. *Sex-Selective Abortion in India.* New Delhi: Sage.

Pecora, V. P. 2002. "The Culture of Surveillance." *Qualitative Sociology* 25: 345–58.

Pence, E. 2001. "Safety for Battered Women in a Textually Mediated Legal System." *Cultures, Organizations, and Societies* 7 (2): 199–229.

Petchesky, R. P. 1987. "Fetal Images: The Power of Visual Culture in the Politics of Reproduction." *Feminist Studies* 13 (2): 263–92.

Pex, J. O. 2000. "Domestic Violence Photography." Crime Scene Investigator Network. http://www.crime-scene investigator.net/dv-photo.html.

Peterson, L. 2010. "*Essence* Magazine Accidentally Steps into an Intra/interracial Dating Minefield." *Racialicious* (blog), 12 January. http://www.racialicious.com/2010/01/12/essence-magazine-accidentally-steps-into-an-intrainterracial-dating-minefield/.

Pheterson, G. 1990. "The Category 'Prostitute' in Scientific Inquiry." *Journal of Sex Research* 27 (3): 397–407.

———. 1993. "The Whore Stigma: Female Dishonor and Male Unworthiness." *Social Text* 37: 39–64.

Pliley, J. R. 2010. "Claims to Protection: The Rise and Fall of Feminist Abolitionism in the League of Nations' Committee on the Traffic in Women and Children, 1919–1936." *Journal of Women's History* 22 (4): 90–113.

Pollack, S., V. Green, and A. Allspach. 2005. *Women Charged with Domestic Violence in Toronto: The Unintended Consequences of Mandatory Charge Policies*. March. http://www.womanabuse.ca.

Poster, M. 1995. *The Second Media Age*. Cambridge: Polity.

Povinelli, E. A. 2011. *Economies of Abandonment: Social Belonging and Endurance in Late Liberalism*. Durham, NC: Duke University Press.

Powell, C. M. 2007. "The Current State of Prenatal Genetic Testing in the United States." In *Prenatal Testing and Disability Rights*, edited by E. Parens and A. Asch, 44–53. Washington: Georgetown University Press.

Projansky, S. 2001. *Watching Rape: Film and Television in Postfeminist Culture*. New York: New York University Press.

Puar, J. K. 2007. *Terrorist Assemblages: Homonationalism in Queer Times*. Durham, NC: Duke University Press.

Puckrein, G. 2006. "BiDil: From Another Vantage Point." *Health Affairs* 25 (5): 368–74.

Pugliese, J. 2009. "Compulsory Visibility and the Infralegality of Racial Phantasmata." *Social Semiotics* 19 (1): 9–30.

Radar Staff. 2012a. "Holy Hannah!: Miley Cyrus Chops Off Her Hair." Radar Online, 13 August. http://radaronline.com/exclusives/2012/08/miley-cyrus-haircut -photos-twitter/.

———. 2012b. "Pals Urging 'Out of Control' Rihanna to Enter Rehab." Radar Online, 12 June. http://radaronline.com/exclusives/2012/06/rihanna-rehab -drinking-out-control/.

———. 2012c. "Too Sexy for Twitter?: Kim Kardashian Shares Really Racy Photos." Radar Online, 31 May. http://radaronline.com/exclusives/2012/05/kim -kardashian-bra-photos-twitter/.

Radio Canada. 2012. "Aide aux victimes des crimes d'honneur." 17 March. http://www .radio-canada.ca/nouvelles/societe/2012/03/17/001-harper-aide-organisme -sensibilisation-crime-honneur.shtml.

Ramazanoglu, C., and J. Holland. 2002. *Feminist Methodology: Challenges and Choices*. London: Sage.

Rankin, J., and M. Campbell. 2009. "Institutional Ethnography (IE), Nursing Work and Hospital Reform: IE's Cautionary Analysis." *Qualitative Social Research* 10 (2). http://www.qualitative-research.net/index.php/fqs/article/view/1258.

Raphael, J., and D. L. Shapiro. 2005. "Reply to Weitzer." *Violence Against Women* 11 (7): 965–70.

Rapp, R. 1999. *Testing Women, Testing the Fetus: The Social Impact of Amniocentesis in America*. New York: Routledge.

Razack, S. 1998. *Looking White People in the Eye: Gender, Race, and Culture in Courtrooms and Classrooms*. Toronto: University of Toronto Press.

———. 2004. "Imperilled Muslim Women, Dangerous Muslim Men and Civilised Europeans: Legal and Social Responses to Forced Marriages." *Feminist Legal Studies* 12 (2): 129–74.

———. 2008. *Casting Out: The Eviction of Muslims from Western Law and Politics*. Toronto: University of Toronto Press.

Reardon, J. 2005. *Race to the Finish: Identity and Governance in an Age of Genomics*. Princeton, NJ: Princeton University Press.

Reay, Diane. 2012. "Future Directions in Difference Research: Recognizing and Responding to Difference in the Research Process." In *Handbook of Feminist Research: Theory and Praxis*, 2nd edn., edited by S. N. Hesse-Biber, 627–40. Thousand Oaks, CA: Sage.

Reddy, U. M., et al. 2007. "Infertility, Assisted Reproductive Technology, and Adverse Pregnancy Outcomes: Executive Summary of a National Institute of Child Health and Human Development Workshop." *Obstetrics and Gynecology* 109 (4): 967–77.

Rempel, R. 2004. "Canada's Parliamentary Oversight of Security and Intelligence." *International Journal of Intelligence and Counterintelligence* 17 (4): 634–54.

Report of the Secretary of the Interior. 1887. 50th Congress, 1st Session, House of Representatives, Ex. Doc. 1, part 5, p. 7. Washington: Government Printing Office.

Richie, B. 1996. *Compelled to Crime: The Gender Entrapment of Black Battered Women*. New York: Routledge.

———. 2000. Plenary Presentation. Paper presented at the Color of Violence: Violence Against Women of Color conference, University of California, Santa Cruz.

Rifkin, M. 2011. *When Did Indians Become Straight? Kinship, the History of Sexuality, and Native Sovereignty*. Oxford: Oxford University Press.

Ringrose, J. 2011. "Are You Sexy, Flirty, or a Slut?: Exploring 'Sexualisation' and How Teen Girls Perform/Negotiate Digital Sexual Identity on Social Networking Sites." In *New Femininities: Postfeminism, Neoliberalism and Identity*, edited by R. Gill and C. Scharff, 99–116. London: Palgrave.

Ringrose, J., and K. Barajas. 2011. "Gendered Risks and Opportunities?: Exploring Teen Girls' Digital Sexual Identity in Postfeminist Media Contexts." *International Journal of Media and Cultural Politics* 7 (2): 121–38.

Ritchie, A. 2006. "Law Enforcement Violence against Women of Color." In *Color of Violence: The INCITE! Anthology*, edited by INCITE! Women of Color Against Violence, 138–56. Cambridge: South End Press.

Roberts, D. 1991. "Punishing Drug Addicts Who Have Babies: Women of Color, Equality, and the Right of Privacy." *Harvard Law Review* 104 (7): 1419–82.

———. 1998. *Killing the Black Body: Race, Reproduction, and the Meaning of Liberty*. New York: Vintage.

———. 2002. *Shattered Bonds: The Color of Child Welfare*. New York: Basic.

———. 2005. "Privatization and Punishment in the New Age of Reprogenetics." *Emory Law Journal* 54 (3): 1343–60.

———. 2008. "Is Race-Based Medicine Good for Us?: African-American Approaches to Race, Biotechnology, and Equality." *Journal of Law, Medicine, and Ethics* 36 (3): 537–45.

Robertson, C. 2010. *The Passport in America: The History of a Document*. Oxford: Oxford University Press.

Robertson, J. A. 2003. "Ethical Issues in New Uses of Preimplantation Genetic Diagnosis." *Human Reproduction* 18 (3): 465–71.

Robertson, K. 2012. "Un-Settling Questions: The Construction of Indigeneity and Violence against Women." PhD diss., University of California, Los Angeles.

Romero, Frances. 2011. "Did Airport Scanners Give Boston TSA Agents Cancer?" *Time*, 30 June. http://healthland.time.com/2011/06/30/did-airport-scanners -give-boston-tsa-agents-cancer/.

Rosario, V. 2002. "Intersexes: The Molecular Deconstruction of Sex." Paper presented at the Feminist Research Seminar, Center for the Study of Women, University of California. Los Angeles, 15 October.

Rose, N. 1999. *Powers of Freedom: Reframing Political Thought*. Cambridge: Cambridge University Press.

———. 2007. *The Politics of Life Itself: Biomedicine, Power, and Subjectivity in the Twenty-First Century*. Princeton, NJ: Princeton University Press.

Rosenberg, K., and J. Howard. 2005. "Finding Feminist Sociology: A Review Essay." *Signs* 33 (3): 675–96.

Rothman, B. K. 1989. *Recreating Motherhood: Ideology and Technology in a Patriarchal Society*. New York: Norton.

———. 2000. *Recreating Motherhood*. New Brunswick, NJ: Rutgers University Press.

———. 2001. *The Book of Life: A Personal and Ethical Guide to Race, Normality, and the Implications of the Human Genome Project*. Boston: Beacon.

———. 2004. "Motherhood under Capitalism." In *Consuming Motherhood*, edited by J. Taylor, L. L. Layne, and D. F. Wozniak, 19–30. New Brunswick, NJ: Rutgers University Press.

Rudner, M. 2007. "Canada's Communications Security Establishment, Signals Intelligence, and Counter-Terrorism." *Intelligence and National Security* 22 (4): 473–90.

Rule, J. 1973. *Private Lives and Public Surveillance: Social Control in the Computer Age*. London: Allen-Lane.

Rule, J. B., et al. 1983. "Documentary Identification and Mass Surveillance in the United States." *Social Problems* 31: 222–34.

Russo, M. 1994. *The Female Grotesque: Risk, Excess, and Modernity*. New York: Routledge.

Ryan, H., and J. Rubin. 2012. "LAPD Tries to Fire Cops Thought to Have Leaked Rihanna Photo to TMZ." *Los Angeles Times* blog, 29 June. http://latimesblogs

.latimes.com/lanow/2012/06/lapd-tries-to-fire-cops-that-allegedly-tipped
-tmz-sold-rihanna-pics.html.

Sachs, A. 2010. "A Reporter Faces the Naked Truth about Full-Body Airport
Scanners." *Washington Post*, 7 February, http://www.washingtonpost.com/wp
-dyn/content/article/2010/02/04/AR2010020402882.html.

Said, E. W. 1978. *Orientalism*. New York: Vintage.

Saldaña-Portillo, M. J. 2003. *The Revolutionary Imagination in the Americas and the
Age of Development*. Durham, NC: Duke University Press.

Salter, M. B. 2006. "The Global Visa Regime and the Political Technologies of the
International Self: Borders, Bodies, Biopolitics." *Alternatives* 31 (2): 167–89.

Sanders, Teela. 2008. *Paying for Pleasure: Men Who Buy Sex*. Cullompton, Devon:
Willan.

Sankar, P., and J. Kahn. 2005. "BiDil: Race Medicine or Race Marketing?" Supple-
mental Web exclusive, *Health Affairs* (11 October): W455–W463. http://content
.healthaffairs.org/content/early/2005/10/11/hlthaff.w5.455.full.pdf+html.

Saul, S. 2005. "F.D.A. Approves a Heart Drug for African-Americans." *New York
Times*, 24 June, C2.

Sawchuk, K. 2010. "Trial by Facebook: Contextual Privacy, Surveillance and the Case
of Natalie Blanchard." Keynote address for the Café Féministe Speaker Series,
Department of Women's Studies, University of Ottowa, Ontario, 17 September.

Saxton, M. 2007. "Why Members of the Disability Community Oppose Prenatal
Diagnosis and Selective Abortion." In *Prenatal Testing and Disability Rights*,
edited by E. Parens and A. Asch, 147–64. Washington: Georgetown University
Press.

Schatz, R. 1990. "Sperm Bank Mix-Up Claim: Woman Sues Doctor, Bank; Says
Wrong Deposit Used." *Newsday*, 9 March, 5.

Schoen, J. 2005. *Choice and Coercion: Birth Control, Sterilization, and Abortion in Public Health and Welfare*. Chapel Hill: University of North Carolina Press.

Schroeder, L. O. 1973. "Renaissance for the Transsexual: A New Birth Certificate."
Journal of Forensic Sciences 18 (3): 237–45.

Scott, J. C. 1998. *Seeing Like a State*. New Haven: Yale University Press.

Scott, J. W. 2007. *The Politics of the Veil*. Princeton, NJ: Princeton University Press.

Scott, R. M. 2009. "A Contextual Approach to Women's Rights in the Qur'an: Readings of 4:34." *Muslim World* 99: 60–85.

Scully, E. 2001. "Pre-Cold War Traffic in Sexual Labor and Its Foes: Some Contemporary Lessons." In *Global Human Smuggling: Comparative Perspectives*, edited by
D. Kyle and R. Koslowski, 74–106. Baltimore: Johns Hopkins University Press.

See, S. 2009. *The Decolonized Eye*. Minneapolis: University of Minnesota Press.

The Sentencing Project. 2005. "New Incarceration Figures: Growth in Population
Continues." The Sentencing Project. http://www.sentencingproject.org/pdfs
/1044.pdf.

Severa, J. 1995. *Dressed for the Photographer: Ordinary Americans and Fashion*. Kent,
OH: Kent State University Press.

Shapiro, S. 1950. "Development of Birth Registration and Birth Statistics in the United States." *Population Studies* 4: 86–111.

Shearer-Cremean, C., and C. L. Winkelmann, eds. 2004. *Survivor Rhetoric: Negotiations and Narrativity in Abused Women's Language.* Toronto: University of Toronto Press.

Sherwin, R., N. Feigenson, and C. Spiesel. 2006. "Law in the Digital Age." *Boston University Journal of Science and Technology Law* 12 (2): 231–55.

Shirinian, N. 2012. "Recognizing the 'Others': Adding a New Ethnicity Checkbox to the Application Would Recognize the Cultures of Some of Those Currently Classified as 'Caucasian.'" *Daily Californian*, 29 April. http://www.dailycal.org/2012/04/29/recognizing-the-others/.

Shohat, E., and R. Stam. 1994. *Unthinking Eurocentrism: Multiculturalism and the Media.* New York: Routledge.

Silva, D. F. 2001. "Toward a Critique of the Socio-Logos of Justice: The *Analytics of Race* and the Production of Universality." *Social Identities* 7 (3): 421–54.

———. 2007. *Toward a Global Idea of Race.* Minneapolis: University of Minnesota Press.

Singer, E. 2007. "Choosing Babies." MIT *Technology Review* (March–April). http://www.technologyreview.com/Biotech/18303/.

Skotko, B. 2005. "Mothers of Children with Down Syndrome Reflect on Their Postnatal Support." *Pediatrics* 115 (1): 64–77.

Smith, A. 2005a. *Conquest: Sexual Violence and American Indian Genocide.* Cambridge, MA: South End Press.

———. 2005b. "Domestic Violence, the State, and Social Change." In *Domestic Violence at the Margins: Readings on Race, Class, Gender, and Culture*, edited by N. J. Sokoloff and C. Pratt, 146–54. New Brunswick, NJ: Rutgers University Press.

———. 2006. "Conquest: Sexual Violence and American Indian Genocide." *Color of Violence: The INCITE! Anthology*, edited by INCITE! Women of Color Against Violence, 66–73. Cambridge: South End Press.

———. 2008. *Native Americans and the Christian Right: The Gendered Politics of Unlikely Alliances.* Durham, NC: Duke University Press.

Smith, A. M. 2007. *Welfare Reform and Sexual Regulation.* New York: Cambridge University Press.

———. 2010. "Neo-Eugenics: A Feminist Critique of Agamben." *Occasion* 2 (20 December). http://arcade.stanford.edu/sites/default/files/article_pdfs/Occasion_v02_Smith_122010_0.pdf.

Smith, D. E. 1987. *The Everyday World as Problematic: A Feminist Sociology.* Toronto: University of Toronto Press.

———. 1988. *The Everyday World as Problematic: A Feminist Sociology.* Boston: Northeastern University Press.

———. 1990. *Texts, Facts, and Femininity: Exploring the Relations of Ruling.* New York: Routledge.

———. 1999. *Writing the Social: Critique, Theory, and Investigations.* Toronto: University of Toronto Press.

———. 2006. "Incorporating Texts into Ethnographic Practice." In *Institutional Ethnography as Practice*, edited by D. E. Smith, 65–88. Oxford: Rowman and Littlefield.

Smith, D. M. 1994. "A Theoretical and Legal Challenge to Homeless Criminalization as Public Policy." *Yale Law and Policy Review* 12 (2): 487–517.

Smith, S. M. 1999. *American Archives: Gender, Race, in Visual Culture*. Princeton, NJ: Princeton University Press.

Sokoloff, N. 2005. *Domestic Violence at the Margins*. New Brunswick, NJ: Rutgers University Press.

Spar, D. L. 2006. *The Baby Business: How Money, Science, and Politics Drive the Commerce of Conception*. Boston: Harvard Business School Press.

Spivak, G. C. 1999. "Can the Subaltern Speak?" In *A Critique of Postcolonial Reason: Toward a History of the Vanishing Present*, by G. C. Spivak, 175–87. Cambridge, MA: Harvard University Press.

Stabile, C. 1998. "Shooting the Mother: Fetal Photography and the Politics of Disappearance." In *The Visible Woman: Imaging Technologies, Gender, and Science*, edited by P. A. Treichler, L. Cartwright, and C. Penley, 171–97. New York: New York University Press.

Stabile, C. A. 2006. *White Victims, Black Villains: Gender, Race, and Crime News in U.S. Culture*. New York: Routledge.

Stannard, D. E. 1992. *American Holocaust*. Oxford: Oxford University Press.

Statistic Brain. 2014. "Social Networking Statistics." Statistic Brain, 1 January. http://www.statisticbrain.com/social-networking-statistics/.

Statistics Canada. 2011. *Family Violence in Canada: A Statistical Portrait*. Ottawa: Ministry of Industry.

Steinbock, B. 2007. "Disability, Prenatal Testing, and Selective Abortion." In *Prenatal Testing and Disability Rights*, edited by E. Parens and A. Asch, 108–23. Washington: Georgetown University Press.

Stern, L. A., and K. Taylor. 2007. "Social Networking on Facebook." *Journal of the Communication, Speech and Theatre Association of North Dakota* 20: 9–20.

Stevens, J. 1999. *Reproducing the State*. Princeton, NJ: Princeton University Press.

Sturken, M., and L. Cartwright. 2001. *Practices of Looking: An Introduction to Visual Culture*. Oxford: Oxford University Press.

Subramanian, S. 2007. "Wombs for Rent." *Maclean's* 120 (2 July): 40–47.

Sullivan, R. 1990. "Mother Accuses Sperm Bank of a Mix-up." *New York Times*, 9 March, B1.

Sulmers, C. 2009. "Get the Look: Rihanna on 20/20 in Fendi's Fur-Trim Turtleneck Sweater Dress." *Fashion Bomb Daily*, 9 November. http://fashionbombdaily.com/2009/11/09/get-the-look-rihanna-on-20-20-in-fendi-fur-trim-turtleneck-sweater-dress/.

Sundén, J. 2003. *Material Virtualities: Approaching Online Textual Embodiment*. New York: Peter Lang.

Surabhi, Sharma, dir. 2012. *Can We See the Bump Please?* DVD. Produced by Sama, Resource Group for Women and Health.

Surrogacy India Online Support Group. 2009. "A Typical Indian Daily Diet for a Surrogate?" (discussion thread). http://surrogacyindia.forum5.com/viewtopic.php?t=419&mforum=surrogacyindia.

Tagg, J. 1993. *The Burden of Representation: Essays on Photographies and Histories.* Minneapolis: University of Minnesota Press.

Tapscott, D., and A. D. Williams. 2007. *Wikinomics: How Mass Collaboration Changes Everything.* New York: Penguin.

Taslitz, Andrew E. 1999. *Rape and the Culture of the Courtroom.* New York: New York University Press.

Taylor, J. S. 2000. "An All-Consuming Experience: Obstetrical Ultrasound and the Commodification of Pregnancy." In *Biotechnology and Culture: Bodies, Anxieties, Ethics,* edited by P. E. Brodwin, 147–70. Bloomington: Indiana University Press.

———. 2008. *The Public Life of the Fetal Sonogram.* New Brunswick, NJ: Rutgers University Press.

Taylor, J. S., L. L. Layne, and D. E. Wozniak, eds. 2004. *Consuming Motherhood.* New Brunswick, NJ: Rutgers University Press.

Thompson, R. G. 1996. *Freakery: Cultural Spectacles of the Extraordinary Body.* New York: New York University Press.

Times of India. 2009. "Experts Chew Over Surrogacy at Meet." 5 March. http://timesofindia.indiatimes.com/articleshow/4225555.cms.

Timson, J. 2011. "Let's Call 'Honor Killing' What It Is." *Globe and Mail,* 2 December, L3.

TMZ Staff. 2012a. "Charlie Sheen Flip-Flops: I'm Re-joining Twitter." TMZ.com, 14 August. http://www.tmz.com/2012/08/14/charlie-sheen-rejoins-twitter/.

———. 2012b. "Charlie Sheen: Twitter SUCKS!!! I'm Signing Out Forever." TMZ.com, 12 July. http://www.tmz.com/2012/07/12/charlie-sheen-quits-twitter/.

Tobin, H. J. 2006–2007. "Against the Surgical Requirement for Change of Legal Sex." *Case Western Reserve Journal of International Law* 38: 393–435.

Tong, S. T., et al. 2008. "Too Much of a Good Thing?: The Relationship between Number of Friends and Interpersonal Impressions on Facebook." *Journal of Computer-Mediated Communication* 13 (3): 531–49.

Torrey, M. 1991. "'When Will We Be Believed?' Rape Myths and the Idea of a Fair Trial in Rape Prosecutions." *University of California, Davis, Law Review* 24 (4): 1013–71.

Transgender Law and Policy Institute. 2007. "Non-Discrimination Laws that Include Gender Identity and Expression." http://www.transgenderlaw.org/ndlaws/index.htm.

Treichler, P., L. Cartwright, and C. Penley, eds. 1998. *The Visible Woman: Imaging Technologies, Gender and Science.* New York: New York University Press.

Turkle, S. 1995. *Live on the Screen: Identity in the Age of the Internet.* New York: Simon and Schuster.

Tyler, I. 2011. "Pregnant Beauty: Maternal Femininities under Neoliberalism." In *New Femininities: Postfeminism, Neoliberalism and Identity,* edited by R. Gill and C. Scharff, 17–34. New York: Palgrave Macmillan.

Tyma, A. 2007. "Rules of Interchange: Privacy in Online Social Communities: A Rhetorical Critique of MySpace.com." *Journal of the Communication, Speech and Theatre Association of North Dakota* 20: 31–39.

Us Weekly Staff. 2012. "Kanye West Returns to Twitter to Remember Steve Jobs." *Us Weekly*, 6 October. http://www.usmagazine.com/celebrity-news/news/kanye-west-returns-to-twitter-to-remember-steve-jobs-2012610.

Vade, D. 2005. "Expanding Gender and Expanding the Law: Toward a Social and Legal Conceptualization of Gender that Is More Inclusive of Transgender People." *Michigan Journal of Gender and the Law* 11: 253–316.

van den Daele, W. 2006. "The Spectre of Coercion: Is Public Health Genetics the Route to Policies of Enforced Disease Prevention?" *Community Genetics* 9 (1): 40–49.

van der Meulen, E. 2011. "Sex Work and Canadian Policy: Recommendations for Labor Legitimacy and Social Change." *Sexuality Research and Social Policy* 8 (4): 348–58.

van der Meulen, E., E. M. Durisin, and V. Love, eds. 2013. *Selling Sex: Experience, Advocacy, and Research on Sex Work in Canada*. Vancouver: University of British Columbia Press.

Van Dijk, J. 2005. *The Transparent Body: A Cultural Analysis of Medical Imaging*. Seattle: University of Washington Press.

Viner, Katherine. 2002. "Feminism as Imperialism: George Bush Is Not the First Empire-Builder to Wage War in the Name of Women." *Guardian*, 21 September, http://www.theguardian.com/world/2002/sep/21/gender.usa.

Volpp, L. 2006. "Disappearing Acts: On Gendered Violence, Pathological Cultures, and Civil Society." Conference paper included in "The Humanities in Human Rights: Critique, Language, Politics." *PMLA* (October): 1631–36.

Wacquant, L. 2002. "From Slavery to Mass Incarceration: Rethinking the 'Race Question' in the U.S." *New Left Review* 13 (January–February): 41–60. Reprinted in *Why Punish? How Much?: A Reader on Punishment*, ed M. Tonry, 387–402. Oxford: Oxford University Press, 2011.

Wade, M. 2009a. "Cheap Wombs for Rent . . . Nine-Month Contracts Only and No Bond." *Sydney Morning Herald*, 31 January. http://www.smh.com.au/news/world/cheap-wombs-for-rent-x2026-ninemonth-contracts-only-and-no-bond/2009/01/30/1232818725688.html.

———. 2009b. "The Takeaway Baby Boom." *Sydney Morning Herald*, 31 January. http://www.smh.com.au/news/world/the-takeawaybabyboom/2009/01/30/1232818725697.html?page=fullpage#contentSwap1.

Walby, K. 2005a. "How Closed-Circuit Television Surveillance Organizes the Social: An Institutional Ethnography." *Canadian Journal of Sociology* 30 (2): 189–215.

———. 2005b. "Institutional Ethnography and Surveillance Studies: An Outline for Inquiry." *Surveillance and Society* 3 (2–3): 158–72.

Walby, K., and A. Smith. 2012. "Surveillance, Sex, and Sexuality: Lenses and Binary Frames." In *Policing Sex*, edited by P. Johnson and D. Dalton, 54–66. London: Routledge.

Walker, L. 1979. *The Battered Woman*. New York: Harper and Row.

———. 1984. *The Battered Woman Syndrome*. New York: Harper and Row.

Walters, S. D. 1995. *Material Girls: Making Sense of Feminist Cultural Theory*. Berkeley: University of California Press.

Walther, J. B., et al. 2008. "The Role of Friends' Appearance and Behavior on Evaluations of Individuals on Facebook: Are We Known by the Company We Keep?" *Human Communication Research* 34 (1): 28–49.

Ward, L. M. 2002. "Whose Right to Choose?: The 'New' Genetics, Prenatal Testing, and People with Learning Difficulties." *Critical Public Health* 12 (2): 187–200.

Warhol, A. 1962. *Marilyn Diptych* (acrylic paint on canvas). The Andy Warhol Foundation for the Visual Arts. Artists Rights Society, NY and Design and Artists Copyright Society, and Tate Collection, London.

Warren, J. F. 1993. *Ah Ku and Karayuki-san: Prostitution in Singapore, 1870–1940*. Singapore: Oxford University Press.

Washington, J. 2011. "For Minorities, New 'Digital Divide' Seen." *USA Today*, 10 January. http://usatoday30.usatoday.com/tech/news/2011-01-10-minorities -online_N.htm.

Watkins, C. 2009. *The Young and the Digital: What the Migration to Social Networking Sites, Games, and Anytime, Anywhere Media Means for Our Future*. Boston: Beacon.

Webb, M. 2007. *Illusions of Security: Global Surveillance and Democracy in the Post-9/11 World*. San Francisco: City Lights.

Weheliye, A. G. 2014. *Habeas Viscus: Racializing Assemblages, Biopolitics, and Black Feminist Theories of the Human*. Durham, NC: Duke University Press.

Weil, E. 2006. "A Wrongful Birth?" *New York Times Magazine*, 12 March, 48–53.

Weitzer, R. 2005a. "Flawed Theory and Method in Studies of Prostitution." *Violence Against Women* 11 (7): 934–49.

———. 2005b. "New Directions in Research on Prostitution." *Crime, Law and Social Change* 43 (4–5): 211–35.

———. 2005c. "Rehashing Tired Claims about Prostitution: A Response to Farley and Raphael and Shapiro." *Violence Against Women* 11 (7): 971–77.

Wendell, S. 1996. *The Rejected Body: Feminist Philosophical Reflections on Disability*. New York: Routledge.

Wente, M. 2001. "U.S. Will Never Be the Same." *Globe and Mail*, 12 September, A1.

Werbner, P. 2007. "Veiled Interventions in Pure Space: Honor, Shame and Embodied Struggles among Muslims in Britain and France." *Theory, Culture and Society* (2): 161–86.

West, C., and D. H. Zimmerman. 1987. "Doing Gender." *Gender and Society* 1: 125–51.

Wexler, L. 2000. *Tender Violence: Domestic Visions in an Age of U.S. Imperialism*. Chapel Hill: University of North Carolina Press.

White, D., and J. Du Mont. 2009. "Visualizing Sexual Assault: An Exploration of the Use of Optical Technologies in the Medico-Legal Context." *Social Science and Medicine* 68: 1–8.

Wilderson, F. B., III. 2010. *Red, White and Black: Cinema and the Structure of U.S. Antagonisms*. Durham, NC: Duke University Press.

Williams, L. 1989. *Hard Core: Power, Pleasure and the "Frenzy of the Visible."* Berkeley: University of California Press.

Williams, R. 2005. *Like a Loaded Weapon*. Minneapolis: University of Minnesota Press.

Wilson, S. 1990. *Tate Gallery: An Illustrated Companion*. Rev. edn. London: Tate Publishing.

Winfrey, O., and L. Ling. 2007. "Lisa Ling Investigates: Wombs for Rent." Oprah .com, 11 October. http://www.oprah.com/oprahshow/Lisa-Ling-Investigates -Wombs-for-Rent.

Wolfe, P. 1999. *Settler Colonialism and the Transformation of Anthropology*. London: Cassell.

Wong, M. 2009. "Is It Over-Sharing to Post Fetal Ultrasounds on Facebook?" *The Juggle (Wall Street Journal* blog), 27 July. http://blogs.wsj.com/juggle/2009/07 /22/is-it-over-sharing-to-post-fetal-ultrasounds-on-facebook/.

Wood, M. M. 2013. "When Celebrity Women Tweet: Examining Authenticity, Empowerment, and Responsibility in the Surveillance of Celebrity Twitter." Master's thesis, Communication, University of South Florida, Tampa.

Woolston, H. B. 1921. *Prostitution in the United States*. New York: Century.

World Vision. 2009. *Surrogates for Hire* (podcast). http://www.worldvision.org /worldvision/radio.nsf/stable/ED1E72059D09300888257179005D0FBF?Open Document.

Wortley, S. 2002. "Misrepresentation or Reality?: The Depiction of Race and Crime in the Toronto Print Media." In *Marginality and Condemnation: An Introduction to Critical Criminology*, edited by B. Schissel and C. Brooks, 501–11. Halifax, Nova Scotia: Fernwood.

Wortley, S., B. Fischer, and C. Webster. 2002. "Vice Lessons: A Survey of Prostitution Offenders Enrolled in the Toronto John School Diversion Program." *Canadian Journal of Criminology* 44: 369–402.

Wynter, S. 1997. "Columbus, the Ocean Blue, and Fables that Stir the Mind: To Reinvent the Study of Letters." In *Poetics of the Americas*, edited by B. Cowan and J. Humphries, 22–29. Baton Rouge: Louisiana State University Press.

The Yogyakarta Principles: Principles on the Application of International Human Rights Law in Relation to Sexual Orientation and Gender Identity. 2007. http:// www.yogyakartaprinciples.org/principles_en.htm.

Yoshino, K. 2006. "Sex and the City: New York City Bungles Transgender Equality." *Slate*, 11 December. http://www.slate.com/id/2155278/.

Young, H. 2010. *Embodying Black Experience: Stillness, Critical Memory and the Black Body*. Ann Arbor: University of Michigan Press.

Zak, L., dir. 2009. "Exclusive: Rihanna Speaks Out." *20/20*, 9 November. http:// abcnews.go.com/2020/video?id=9020947.

Zakaria, R. 2010. "The Cheapest Wombs: India's Surrogate Mothers." *Ms. Magazine*

blog, 25 June. http://msmagazine.com/blog/blog/2010/06/25/the-cheapest
-womb-indias-surrogate-mothers/.

Zennie, M. 2013. "Doctors, Lawyers, Teachers and Students among 104 Men Pictured in 'Wall of Shame' after They Were Arrested for Soliciting Prostitutes in
Operation 'Flush the Johns.'" *Mail Online*, 3 June. http://www.dailymail.co.uk
/news/article-2335372/Operation-Flush-Johns-Nassau-County-DA-posts
-pictures-104-arrested-prostitution-sting.html.

Zerai, A., and Rae Banks. 2002. *Dehumanizing Discourse, Anti-drug Law, and Policy in
America: A Crack Mother's Nightmare*. Aldershot: Ashgate.

Zhao, D., and M. B. Rosson. 2009. "How and Why People Twitter: The Role that
Micro-blogging Plays in Informal Communication at Work." *Proceedings of the
Thirteenth ACM International Conference on Supporting Group Work*, 243–52. New
York: Association for Computing Machinery. ACM Digital Library. http://dl.acm
.org/citation.cfm?id=1531710.

Zine, J. 2009. "Unsettling the Nation: Gender, Race, and Muslim Cultural Politics in
Canada." *Studies in Ethnicity and Nationalism* 9 (1): 146–93.

Zureik, E., and M. B. Salter. 2005. *Global Surveillance and Policing: Borders, Security,
Identity*. Cullompton, Devon: Willan.

CONTRIBUTORS

SEANTEL ANAÏS is assistant professor in the Department of Sociology at the University of Winnipeg. Her research program focuses on critical security studies and critical sociolegal studies. Her two ongoing projects examine the materialities of Cold War sites of security, one with regard to their recent transformations, and the other about mass litigation in war material contamination cases. Her articles have appeared in the *Canadian Journal of Law and Society*, the *Canadian Journal of Sociology*, *Critical Discourse Studies*, *Cultural Politics*, *Security Dialogue*, and *Deviant Behavior*.

MARK ANDREJEVIC is associate professor of media studies at Pomona College. He examines popular culture and new media from the perspectives of critical theory and cultural studies. He is interested in the ways in which forms of surveillance and monitoring enabled by the development of new media technologies impact the realms of economics, politics, and culture. He has written numerous articles and book chapters on topics including interactive media, surveillance, digital art, and reality TV. He is the author of *Infoglut: How Too Much Information Is Changing the Way We Think and Know* (2013), *iSpy: Surveillance and Power in the Interactive Era* (2007), and *Reality TV: The Work of Being Watched* (2003).

PAISLEY CURRAH is professor of political science and women's and gender studies at Brooklyn College and the Graduate Center of the City University of New York. Currah is a founding editor, with Susan Stryker, of *TSQ: Transgender Studies Quarterly*. He is coeditor of *Corpus: An Interdisciplinary Reader on Bodies and Knowledge*

(2011) and *Transgender Rights* (2006). Among the articles he has published are "Homonationalism, State Rationalities, and Sex Contradictions" (*Theory and Event*, 2013) and "Securitizing Gender: Identity, Biometrics, and Gender Non-conforming Bodies at the Airport" (*Social Research*, 2011). His book *States of Sex: Regulating Transgender Identities* (forthcoming) looks at contradictions in state definitions of sex.

SAYANTANI DASGUPTA is assistant professor of clinical pediatrics at Columbia University and teaches in both the Columbia University graduate program in narrative medicine and the graduate program in health advocacy at Sarah Lawrence College. She is the co-chair of the Columbia University Seminar on Narrative, Health and Social Justice and a faculty fellow in the Columbia Center for the Study of Social Difference. She is the author of many book chapters and scholarly articles on medical education, reproduction, race, and surrogacy, and is the coeditor of an award-winning collection of women's illness narratives, *Stories of Illness and Healing: Women Write Their Bodies* (2007). She is also coeditor, with Shamita Das Dasgupta, of *Globalization and Transnational Surrogacy in India: Outsourcing Life* (2014).

SHAMITA DAS DASGUPTA is a cofounder of Manavi, an organization in the United States that focuses on violence against women in the South Asian community. She has taught at Rutgers University and in the clinical law program at the New York University School of Law. In addition to publishing multiple articles in her areas of specialization—ethnicity, gender, immigration, and violence against women—she has written several books: *The Demon Slayers and Other Stories: Bengali Folktales* (1995), *A Patchwork Shawl: Chronicles of South Asian Women in America* (1998), *Body Evidence: Intimate Violence against South Asian Women in America* (2007), and *Mothers for Sale: Women in Kolkata's Sex Trade* (2009). Her most recent book, which she co-edited with Sayantani DasGupta, is *Globalization and Transnational Surrogacy in India: Outsourcing Life* (2014).

RACHEL E. DUBROFSKY is associate professor in the Department of Communication at the University of South Florida. Her work is rooted in a critical/cultural studies tradition, with a focus on digital culture (television, social media), and an emphasis on the role of surveillance and issues of race and gender. Her book *The Surveillance of Women on Reality Television: Watching* The Bachelor *and* The Bachelorette, explores how the surveillance context of a TV program impacts gendered and racialized bodies. Her work has appeared in such journals as *Critical Studies in Media Communication; Communication Theory; Communication, Culture and Critique;* and *Feminist Media Studies*. She is currently working on a book, *Under Surveillance: Mediating Race and Gender*, examining the cultural shift from older digital media (TV, film) to newer digital media (social networking sites) with an emphasis on surveillance, race, and gender.

RACHEL HALL is associate professor of communication studies at Louisiana State University. Her book *Wanted: The Outlaw in American Visual Culture* (2009) provides a history and cultural critique of practices surrounding "wanted" posters for outlaws and of the everyday performances of vigilante viewership elicited by the posters. She is currently completing *The Transparent Traveler: The Performance and Culture of Airport Security* (2015). She has also begun work on a cultural history of child safety in North America. Her essays have appeared in *Performance Research*, *Women's Studies Quarterly*, *The Communication Review*, *Camera Obscura: Feminism, Culture and Media Studies*, and *Hypatia: Journal of Feminist Philosophy*.

YASMIN JIWANI is professor in the Department of Communication Studies at Concordia University, Montreal. Her doctoral research, in communication studies, from Simon Fraser University, examined issues of race and representation in Canadian television news. Her research interests include mediations of race, gender, and violence in the context of war stories, femicide reporting in the press, and representations of women of color in popular and mainstream media. Her recent publications include "Discourses of Denial: Mediations of Race, Gender, and Violence" (*Canadian Journal of Political Science*, 2007), as well as the collection *Girlhood: Redefining the Limits* (2005, coedited with Candis Steenbergen and Claudia Mitchell). Her work has appeared in *Social Justice*, *Violence Against Women*, *Canadian Journal of Communication*, the *Journal of Popular Film and Television*, *Topia*, *International Journal of Media and Cultural Politics*, and the *University of Toronto Quarterly*, as well as in numerous anthologies.

LAURA HYUN YI KANG is associate professor of Women's Studies, English and Comparative Literature at the University of California, Irvine. She is the author of *Compositional Subjects: Enfiguring Asian/American Women* (2002) and *The Traffic in Asian Women* (forthcoming). She recently served as the editor of the theme unit on "Sex," in *A Companion to Contemporary Documentary Film* (2014, edited by Alex Juhasz and Alisa Lebow). Kang has published essays in *American Quarterly*, *Feminist Studies*, *Journal of Asian American Studies*, *Vectors*, *Positions*, and *Visual Anthropology Review*.

UMMNI KHAN is associate professor in the Department of Law and Legal Studies at Carleton University. Her research looks at the construction and regulation of stigmatized sexual practices, with a particular focus on BDSM and sex work. Her book *Vicarious Kinks: Sadomasochism in the Socio-Legal Imaginary* (2014) examines the ways criminal regulation of consensual sadomasochism rests on problematic ideological claims that engage psychiatry, antipornography feminism, and pop culture. On the topic of sex work, she has written a number of articles, including "Prostituted Girls and the Grownup Gaze" (*Global Studies of Childhood*, 2011), "Running in (to) the Family: Eight Short Stories about Sex Workers, Clients, Husbands, and Wives" (*Journal of Gender, Social Policy and the Law*, 2011) and "'Johns' in the Spotlight: Anti-prostitution Efforts and the Surveillance of Clients" (forthcoming).

SHOSHANA AMIELLE MAGNET is associate professor in the Institute of Women's Studies and the Department of Criminology at the University of Ottawa. Her work is on security, technologies, surveillance, and inequality. Some of the technologies she studies are biometrics, radio frequency identification, backscatter X-rays, as well as robotics, including robots used in the military. Her book *When Biometrics Fail: Race, Gender and the Technology of Identity* (2011) examines the security state, surveillance, identity, technology, and human rights.

KELLI MOORE is currently the University of California President's Postdoctoral Fellow in Rhetoric at Berkeley. She earned her doctorate in communication at the University of California, San Diego. Her research examines photographic and digital media in the production of visibility and speech in battered women, and situates these practices and customs within ongoing debates about trauma theory, facilitated communication, visual literacy, and embodiment.

LISA JEAN MOORE is a medical sociologist and professor of sociology and gender studies at Purchase College, State University of New York. Her books include *Buzz: Urban Beekeeping and the Power of the Bee* (2013, with Mary Kosut), *Gendered Bodies: Feminist Perspectives* (2010, with Judith Lorber), *Missing Bodies: The Politics of Visibility* (2009, with Monica Casper), *Sperm Counts: Understanding Man's Most Precious Fluid* (2008), and *The Body Reader: Essential Social and Cultural Readings* (2010, coedited with Mary Kosut). Her newest collaboration, with Monica Casper, is *The Body: Social and Cultural Dissections* (forthcoming). Her most recent scholarship investigates the intraspecies relationships between humans and *Limuli* (Atlantic horseshoe crabs).

LISA NAKAMURA is Gwendolyn Calvert Baker Collegiate Professor of the Department of American Cultures and the Department of Screen Arts and Cultures at the University of Michigan, Ann Arbor. She is the author of *Digitizing Race: Visual Cultures of the Internet* (2010), which won the Asian American Studies Association 2010 book award in cultural studies, and *Cybertypes: Race, Ethnicity and Identity on the Internet* (2002). She is coeditor of *Race in Cyberspace* (2000, with Beth Kolko and Gilbert Rodman) and *Race After the Internet* (2011, with Peter Chow-White). She is writing a monograph on social inequality in digital media culture, titled *Workers without Bodies: Towards a Theory of Race and Digital Labor*.

DOROTHY E. ROBERTS is the fourteenth Penn Integrates Knowledge Professor, George A. Weiss University Professor, and the inaugural Raymond Pace and Sadie Tanner Mossell Alexander Professor of Civil Rights at the University of Pennsylvania, where she holds appointments in the Law School, the Department of Africana Studies, and the Department of Sociology. An internationally recognized scholar, public intellectual, and social-justice advocate, she has written and lectured extensively on the interplay of gender, race, and class in legal issues and has been a leader in transforming public thinking and policy on reproductive health, child welfare, and bioethics. She is the author of the award-winning books *Killing the Black Body: Race, Reproduction, and the Meaning of Liberty* (1997) and *Shattered Bonds: The Color of Child Welfare* (2002), as well as coeditor of six books on constitutional law and gender. She has also published more than eighty articles and essays in books and scholarly journals, including the *Harvard Law Review, Yale Law Journal,* and *Stanford*

Law Review. Her latest book is *Fatal Invention: How Science, Politics, and Big Business Re-create Race in the Twenty-First Century* (2011).

ANDREA SMITH is associate professor of media and cultural studies at the University of California, Riverside. Her publications include *Native Americans and the Christian Right: The Gendered Politics of Unlikely Alliances* (2008) and *Conquest: Sexual Violence and American Indian Genocide* (2005). She is coeditor, with Audra Simpson, of *Theorizing Native Studies* (2014). She is also the editor of *The Revolution Will Not Be Funded: Beyond the Nonprofit Industrial Complex* (2009), and coeditor of *The Color of Violence: The Incite! Anthology.* Smith is a cofounder of Incite! Women of Color Against Violence and of the Critical Ethnic Studies Association.

KEVIN WALBY is assistant professor of criminal justice at the University of Winnipeg. His recent articles appear in the *British Journal of Criminology, Policing and Society, Law and Social Inquiry, Law, Culture and the Humanities, Urban Studies, Qualitative Inquiry, Sociology, Current Sociology,* and *International Sociology.* He is the author of *Touching Encounters: Sex, Work, and Male-for-Male Internet Escorting* (2012). He is co-editor of *Emotions Matter: A Relational Approach to Emotions* (2012, with Alan Hunt and Dale Spencer), *Brokering Access: Power, Politics, and Freedom of Information Process in Canada* (2012, with Mike Larsen), and *Policing Cities: Urban Securitization and Regulation in the Twenty-first Century* (2013, with Randy K. Lippert). He is coauthor of *Municipal Corporate Security in International Context* (2014, with Randy K. Lippert).

MEGAN M. WOOD is a doctoral student in the Department of Communication at the University of North Carolina, Chapel Hill. Her research interests include digital media, television, feminism, race, and popular and consumer culture. Her work focuses on social media, attending to how posts, interactions, and discussions in these spaces articulate race, gender, sexuality, and class, and concomitant issues of inequality. She has published articles in journals including *Communication Studies, Review of Communication, and Sexuality and Culture.*

INDEX

antiprostitution feminism, 6, 189–90, 204, 207

antitrafficking: history, 39–40; League of Nations efforts, 41–43, 55–56; organizations, 45–46; racial grouping and, 53–55; White Slave Traffic Agreements, 46–47

antiviolence movements, 31–36, 89

Asch, Adrienne, 179

Asian women, 44, 53–55

assimilation, 29

Atkins, J. D. C., 28–29

Atwood, Margaret, 165, 169

authenticity, call to, 98–99, 101

backscatter x-rays, 5, 17n1, 134, 163–64; discontinued use of, 147, 149n11; privacy concerns of, 147; safety tests, 149n10

Barlow, John Perry, 221, 222

Bernstein, Elizabeth, 6, 191, 202, 204

Best, Joel, 193, 194, 196

Bhabha, Homi, 29

Bhattacharjee, Anannya, 32, 38n5

BiDil, 175

biometric technologies, 13, 221, 223; binary codes, 15; racial and gender preconceptions of, xv, 15; testing on prisoners, 9

biopolitics, 128; Foucault on, 22–23; racial dimension of, 131; Rose's analysis of, 180, 182; settler colonialism and, 23

biopower, 23, 24, 62, 110

biotechnologies, 14, 165; in prison system, 204, 205; race-based, 171–72, 176, 184–85

birth certificates: dual function of, 63; fraud and, 65–66; "no gender" designation on, 66–67, 68; the state and, 61–62; surveillance of, 8; of transgender people, 68–74; of transsexual people, 58–59, 64–67

birth control, 181, 182

birthers, 62

black women. *See* women of color

Blanchard, Natalie, 13, 222, 224–25

blogs: activism on, 225–27; *AfroSpear*, 205; *Feminist Frequency*, 224–25; fetal images posted on, 154, 159–60, 162; images of surrogate belly bumps on, 160–62, 163; of intended parents (IPs), 150, 152–53, 157–58, 166nn4–5

bodies: as borders, 89–90, 128; celebrity, 93–94; digital, 96; identity, 8, 9; Muslim, 11, 84, 90; of native peoples, 27; "normal," 23, 90, 133; power and, 86, 90; precarious, 86, 89; terrorist, 139, 141; virtual, 222; vulnerability of, 5, 9, 91, 206. *See also* veiled bodies

borders: bodies as, 89–90, 128; outsourcing, 90–91, 133; surveillance at, 8, 40–41, 44, 53

boyd, danah, 222

Brodwin, Paul P., 158

brothels, 14, 45, 46, 169

Brown, Jayna, 122

Browne, Simone, 13

Bruyneel, Kevin, 29

Bureau of Social Hygiene (BSH), 50–51

Bush, George W., 37

Bushnell, Katharine, 45–46

Butler, Josephine, 45

Butler, Judith, 37, 86

Campbell, Marie, 219

Can We See the Baby Bump Please? (Surabhi), 162

carceral feminism, 6, 191, 202–3

Cartwright, Lisa, 96, 108, 115, 120

categories: biological, 175, 176, 184–85; biometric, 15; and classifications in text, 218–19, 220; crime, 200–201; of discrimination, xiii–xiv, 5; gender, 8, 61, 63–67, 75, 213–14; of human hierarchy, 110; for native

169–70, 177, 183, 186n19; prenatal testing, 176–77, 179, 186n17; privatization of, 179; race-based, 174–76; reasons for doing, 179–80; screening for disease, 183

Gilchrist, Kristen, 81

Gilmore, Ruth Wilson, 22

Globe and Mail, 81, 92nn2–3

Glynn, Kevin, 115

Goffman, Erving, 66

Goodwin, Charles, 114–15

Google, xvi, xviii; reaction to "Scroogled" campaign, xii

Google Glass, xv

Goulding, Warren, 81

governance: indigenous systems of, 27; neoliberal, 176, 179–80, 181, 183; reflexive, 129, 136, 138

Grant, Melissa G., 203

Griffith, Alison I., 215

Haggerty, Kevin D., 156, 165; definition of surveillance, 191, 211; on surveillant assemblages, 153, 157; on surveys and statistical analyses, 192, 199

Hall, Rachel, 4, 11, 13, 99, 101; aesthetics of transparency, xviii, 14, 153–54, 156; on the normalized body, 90

Halsey, Ashley, 147

Handmaid's Tale, The (Atwood), 165, 169

Hansen, Mark, 222

Hartman, Saidiya, 32

Health Insurance Portability and Accountability Act of 1996 (HIPAA), 144–45

Hershatter, Gail, 48

Hershey, Laura, 182

heteronormativity, 24, 91, 147, 151, 204

heteropatriarchy: the state and, 25, 38; white supremacy and, 7, 23–24

heterosexuality, 14, 133

hierarchies, 110, 169, 170–71, 213

Holland, Janet, 193, 194

Homeland Security, Department of (DHS), 149n10

honor killings, 81, 85–86, 90–91, 92n1; antiviolence organizations and, 89. *See also* Shafia murders

hooks, bell, 7, 10

Houston IVF, 174

human difference, 109–11, 122

Human Genome Project, 175

Hussein, Saddam, 129–30

Hymans, Paul, 41

hypervisibility, 7, 11, 25, 128; femicide and, 80

Ibrahim, Sham, 133; *Disturbia*, 108, 116–19, 123

immigration: of prostitutes, 44, 46; racial purity and, 45, 51–52

Indian women. *See* surrogates, Indian

indigenous peoples. *See* native peoples

infant mortality rates, 170–71

informational profile, 9

information gathering, 210–12, 216

information society, 210

institutional ethnography (IE), 209–10, 214–19

intelligence studies, 209, 211–13

interiority and exteriority, 127; of surrogates, 154, 156, 157, 162

International Bureau (IB), 46, 48

Internet, 222, 224–25, 227n2

invisibility. *See* visibility and invisibility

Ishaq, Shaima, 91

Islam, 80, 84–86, 92n1

James, George, 64

Jeffries, Sheila, 194

Jiwani, Yasmin, 7, 11, 128

Johnson, Bascom, 51, 52–53, 57n4

Johnson v. Calvert, 173

Jorgensen, Christine, 64

Kang, Laura Hyun Yi, 8, 10

Kaplan, Amy, 37

Kaplan, Anne, 97
Karande and Associates, 174
Kardashian, Kim: body and sexuality, 94, 102–3; racialization of, 101–2
Kazanjian, David, 35
Khan, Ummni, xi, 6, 40
Kinsie, Paul, 53
Kipling, Rudyard, 88, 92n3
Klum, Heidi, 101
Knepper, Paul, 42–43, 53
knowledge practices, 213–14
Koyama, Emi, 33–34

Laarhuis, Gerard, 85
Ladies National Association (LNA), 45
land expropriation, 26, 28
Laughlin, Harry, 186n23
League of Nations: Advisory Committee on the Traffic in Women and Children, 42, 48, 56; *Commission of Enquiry into Traffic in Women and Children in the East* (1932), 42–43, 53–54; International Conference on the Traffic in Women and Children, 41; International Convention for the Suppression of the Traffic in Women and Children, 42, 47; *Report of the Special Body of Experts on Traffic in Women and Children* (1927), 42–43, 45, 52–53; trafficking questionnaire, 47
Leppanen, Karina, 56
Levine, Philippa, 44, 56n1
Limoncelli, Stephanie, 56
Loomis, George, 124n6
Lowman, J., 206
Lowry, Deborah Wilson, 152, 153–54
Lyon, David, 38n3, 59, 156, 213; definition of surveillance, 2, 22, 24, 211; on surveillance studies, 25, 31

MacKenzie, Donald A., 181
Magnet, Shoshana Amielle, xv, 97, 131, 208, 224–26; on body scanners, 142, 163; on outsourcing the border, 90–91, 133; surveillant scopophilia concept, 12, 137
male gaze: agency and, 98–99; airport security and, 136, 148; invitation of, 10, 11, 98, 101, 104; Mulvey's concept, 10, 96–98; race and, 11, 99–103, 136; studies on, 151
Mammy image, 107, 111
Maranger, Robert, 85
Marie Claire, 150–51
Marilyn Diptych (Warhol), 116, 118–19
marital status, 62, 76n3
Marx, Gary, 209, 210–11
masculinity, 25, 115, 139; deviance and, 191
Mathiesen, Thomas, 82, 202–3
Mattelart, Armand, 8
Mbembe, Achille, 23
McKittrick, Katherine, 103
McNeil, Laurie, 153
McRuer, Robert, 133
media: consumers, 141; coverage of terrorism, 128, 129–30; coverage of transgender people, 67, 73; digital, 94, 118; femicide stories, 81; fertility clinic stories, 172–74; newer vs. older, 13; panopticism of, 82, 85, 91; promotion of genetic technologies, 172; race and, 81; reporting on Muslims, 79–80, 84–85, 87; studies, 10, 16, 209. *See also* social media
medical examinations: of prostitutes for venereal diseases, 39, 44–45, 51, 56n1; of Saddam Hussein, 129–30
Meiners, Erica, 202
men of color, 6, 205
Merry, Sally Engle, 107–11, 114
Metzger, Barbara, 57n5
Meyerowitz, Joanne, 64
Microsoft, 227; "Scroogled" campaign, xii

millimeter-wave machines, 134–35, 147, 149n11

Million, Dian, 30

miscegenation, 62

Mnookin, Jennifer, 108

monitoring practices: of nurses, 219; in organizations, 210, 213–14, 216; of transnational movements of women, 46–47

monitoring technologies: power and, xi, xvii; uses and abuses of, xiii

Monroe, Marilyn, 116, 118, 124n6

Moore, Kelli D., 8, 12, 129

Moore, Lisa Jean, 8

Morgensen, Scott, 22, 24

Mother Machine, The (Corea), 169

Mulvey, Laura, 10, 96–98

Muslim immigrants, 80, 90, 92

Muslim women: agency of, 168n17; media portrayal of, 84–85; "outing" of, 163; screening technologies and, 5; surveillance of, 80; as threats and victims, 91–92

Mykitiuk, Roxanne, 179

National Institute of Standards and Technology (NIST), 149n10

National Security Agency (NSA), x

National Vigilance Association (NVA), 46

native peoples: civilizing strategies of, 27–29; gender/sexual violence among, 30–31, 35; heteropatriarchy/patriarchy and, 26–27; lack of media attention, 81; as "rapeable," 7, 16, 24; sexual surveillance of, 21–22; women's organizations, 89

Nazi Germany, 23

neoliberalism: privatization and governance and, 129, 171, 176, 179, 180–81, 183; racial inequality and, 184–85

neutrality: in data collection, xii–xiii; transparency and, 133

Newborn Screening Saves Lives Act, 13

New York City Department of Health (DOH), 64

New York City Department of Health and Mental Hygiene (DOHMH): Board of Health, 72–73; Health Code, 67; no-surgery proposal for transgender people, 72–74; Transgender Advisory Committee, 68–72, 75n2

New Yorker, 137, 138, 141–42, 143

New York Times, 35, 73, 134, 178; "The Fertility Market" article, 173; report on digital photography, 118, 124n9

New York Times Magazine, 174

Noriel, Gerard, 63

normalizing logics, 22–23, 28, 31

not-seeing practices: in photographing skin color, 122–23; of settler colonialism, 22, 25–26

Obama, Barack, 62

Olwan, Dana M., 81, 89

opacity effects, 127–28, 129, 141

Oprah Winfrey Show, 166n1

orientalism, 87, 139, 151, 166n2

Ott, James, 146

Our Family, Made in India (Heinemann), 161–62

Pacific Fertility Center, 174

Packer, Jeremy, 141

Pande, Amrita, 155, 156–57, 159, 167n7

panopticons, 2, 82, 86, 153

Parens, Erik, 179

Parks, Lisa, 132

Pascoe, Peggy, 62

Patel, Nayna, 158

patriarchy: native communities and, 26–27; in perception of Muslim men, 80, 84; power, 90

penal abolition, 1, 6, 17n2

Philadelphia Inquirer, 181

photography: Abdulmutallab underwear exhibit, 139–41; of battered
women of color, 8, 12, 114–15, 122–
23; of black nursemaids, 111; digital
vs. Polaroid, 114, 124n9; fetal, 158–
60; pregnant belly images, 160–62;
of Rihanna's injuries, 108–9, 111–14;
technology, 110

Pistole, John, 146

Pliley, Jessica, 48, 57n6

policing: bodies, 154; colonial, 25; of
Muslim communities, 80; online,
225, 226, 227; sex industry, 46, 190;
studies, 209, 211–13; surrogate mobility, 159; by women, 8; in women's
shelters, 33–34

population control, 170–71, 180–82

postfeminism, 99, 101, 104; voluntary
transparency and, 136, 138

poverty: agency and, 167n8; criminalization and, 6, 200; of women of
color, 181–82

power: bodies and, 86, 90; in classification and categorization practices,
208, 210; information collection
and, xii; media, 82; patriarchal, 90;
race and, 110, 118, 129, 181; relations in organizations, 213–14;
state, 8, 69, 84, 89, 110; surveillance
and, x–xi, 220, 224

prison: biometric technology testing
in, 9, 204; racial disparity in, 181,
206; surveillance practices in, 2;
women of color in, 5

privacy: airport screening process and,
144–46; bodily, 15; inequality, 32;
loss of, 37; online, 226–27; rights, 4,
149n12; surveillance studies on, 31

privatization, 171, 176, 179, 183

professional vision, 114–15

prostitution. See sex industry clients;
sex work

Prostitution Research and Education
(PRE): carceral strategies, 202–5,

207; founding and goals, 190, 194;
overview of reports, 190, 192–93;
statistical claims, 199–202; surveys
and research methods, 195–98, 206;
webpage, 193–94

"prosumer" concept, 13

Puar, Jasbir, 9, 131, 139

publicity, 118

public protection, 65–66

public-shaming strategies, 202–3

Pugliese, Joseph, 86, 88–89

race: agency and, 11, 99–100, 103, 104,
136; as a biological category, 175,
176, 184–85; biometric technologies and, 15; fertility clinics and,
170, 173–76, 179; in/visibility of, 92;
media reporting of, 81; pharmaceuticals based on, xiv, 175–76; as
a technology strategy, 123, 124n8;
violence and, 7

raciality, analytics of, 107–10, 120, 122

racialization: black women performers
and, 122; boundaries, 89–90; of
Kim Kardashian, 101–3; of native
peoples, 24; police photographs
and, 108–9; stereotypes, 163

racial purity, 45, 52, 62, 172

racism: biopolitical, 23; of carceral politics, 204–5; scientific apparatus of,
108, 110; video game, 225, 226. See
also racialization

Radar Online, 100, 102

Ramazanoglu, Caroline, 193, 194

Rankin, Janet, 219

Raphael, Jody, 196–97

Rapp, Rayna, 169–70

Razack, Sharlene, 3, 85–87

reality TV, 12–13, 98

reproductive choice, 171, 176–78, 182,
183

Reproductive Genetics Institute, 174

Reproductive Health Specialists, 174

reproductive technologies: assisted

Smith, Andrea, 5, 7; not-seeing practices, 6, 122–23
Smith, Dorothy, 6, 210; on texts in organizations, 209, 213, 214–15, 220
Snow, William F., 51
Snowden, Edward, x
social control, 192, 202, 204, 212
social media: alternative platforms, 223–24; fertility clinic websites, 173–74; harassment on, 224–27; qualitative studies on, 106n1; real-name requirements for, 222; surveillance function of, 224; synopticons of, 82, 91; women's agency and, 93. See also blogs; Facebook; Twitter
social-purity reformers, 46, 50
somatechnics, 86–88
Spears, Britney, 101
Stabile, Carol A., 81, 158
Stam, Robert, 130
Stannard, David, 21
state: birth certificates and, 61–63, 74; carceral, 205, 206; colonial and postcolonial, 21–22, 25–27; domestic abuse and, 109, 113; eugenics and, 180, 181–82; gender standards, 59–60, 63–64, 74–75; modern, 22–23; police, 72; power, 8, 69, 84, 89, 110; reproductive choices and, 182–83; response to violence, 5–6, 7, 31–36; security, 127–29, 133–34, 137, 142, 146–47; surveillance practices/strategies, 7, 9, 14, 30–31, 34–38
state-building process, 48
stereotypes: of black women, 171; of disabled people, 180; of femininity, 99; of veiled bodies, 163
stigmatization: of Muslim women, 80; of prostitution, 206; of sex clients, 190, 198, 203; of surrogates, 151
Sturken, Marita, 96, 148n3
suicidegirls.com, 97
Sulmers, Claire, 122
Sundquist, Alma, 52

Superman, 137
surrogates, Indian: advertising for, 150–51; blogs by intended parents (IPs), 150, 152–53, 159–62, 166nn4–5; costs and earnings, 155, 167nn7–8; headless or veiled images of, 154, 156, 160–62, 164–66; online communications with, 155–56; process, 151, 156–57, 166n3; surveillance of, 14, 157–58
surveillance: abusers, 1; as an active social process, 89; definitions, x, 2, 22, 131, 210–11; of disability, 13–14; foundational structures of, 7; managerial practices and, 214; material relations of, 217–19, 220; old and new forms of, 191–92; in organizations, 213–19; outsourcing of, 91, 92; of pregnant women, 176; society, 156, 192, 210
surveillance studies: colonialism and, 14, 21–23, 25–26; conceptual and methodological clarity in, 209–10, 210–13, 219–20; feminist approach to, 3–4, 6, 7, 9, 15–16, 36, 225; power relations and, xi–xii, 210; scholarship, 2, 4; "seeing" and, 25–26; use of surveys in, 191–92. See also feminist surveillance studies
surveillant assemblages: concept, 153, 157, 162; Puar on, 9; reproductive technologies as, 152, 153–54
surveillant scopophilia, 12, 137
surveys, 191–92, 195
synopticons, 82, 86, 91, 203

Taylor, Janelle, 167n11
terrorism: prevention, 128–29, 131–32, 148; threats of, 127–28, 164
terrorists: Abdulmutallab's failed attack, 138–41; bodies, 14; the look of, 9, 89; protection from, 136
text, surveillance, 209, 213, 214–19, 220
Thompson, Rosmarie Garland, 133